The Harpsichord Concerto

from

Musicalische Neu-Jahrs-Gedichte von der Musicgesellschaft auf der Teutschen Schul in Zürich
(1776), no. 92, plate xciii.

The German Concerto

Five Eighteenth-Century Studies

PIPPA DRUMMOND

Clarendon Press · Oxford

1980

Oxford University Press, Walton Street, Oxford OX2 6DP
OXFORD LONDON GLASGOW
NEW YORK TORONTO MELBOURNE WELLINGTON
KUALA LUMPUR SINGAPORE JAKARTA HONG KONG TOKYO
DELHI BOMBAY CALCUTTA MADRAS KARACHI

Published in the United States by
Oxford University Press, New York

© *Pippa Drummond* 1980

British Library Cataloguing Publication Data
Drummond, Pippa
　　The German concerto.—(Oxford monographs on music).
　　1. Concerto—History and criticism 2. Music—
　　Germany—History and criticism—18th century
　　I. Title　　II. Series
　　785.6'0943　　ML1263　　78–41150

ISBN 0–19–816122–0

Text set in 14 on 15 pt VIP Bembo, printed by photolithography,
and bound in Great Britain at The Pitman Press, Bath

Preface

In the early eighteenth century the term "concerto" was most commonly applied to an instrumental work for one or more soloists and orchestra. Originally an Italian art form, the concerto developed at Bologna and Rome during the closing years of the seventeenth century. Although it was essentially a creation of the late baroque period the distinctive features of the concerto had existed earlier: the idea of contrasting different sonorities, for instance, had been used not only in the concertato church music of Gabrieli at Venice but also in the English verse anthem and in the trio episodes of Lully's theatre music. The concerto proper was formed when the principle of tutti/solo contrast was applied to the instrumental sonata. The ripieno parts were then doubled to ensure greater contrast between tutti and solo groups and a new, orchestral form came into being.

The earliest exponents of this genre were almost all members of, or associated with, the Bolognese school. That they approached the concerto by way of the instrumental sonata is evident from the close stylistic relationship between the two forms. Torelli's trumpet sonatas differ little in style from his solo concertos and the correspondence between Corelli's trio sonatas and his op. 6 set of concertos is even more pronounced. Indeed, these last works may be distinguished from Corelli's sonatas only by virtue of their instrumentation whereby the concertino (trio sonata) group is contrasted with the richer tones of a string orchestra.

The "Bolognese" concerto spread to the southern Germanic states in the last decade or so of the seventeenth century. Although both Torelli and dall'Abaco were active in Germany for a period, it was, paradoxically, the concertos of Corelli that proved most influential. Corelli's chief disciple in South Germany was Georg Muffat. He had heard

concertante works by Corelli in Rome in 1682 and on his
return he began to apply tutti/solo principles to the ever
popular French suite, producing the earliest examples of the
German "concertized suite". Around him gathered a
number of lesser composers such as Aufschnaiter and Pez,
both of whom published sets of concertos during the late
seventeenth and early eighteenth centuries.

Despite this South German/Austrian school the influence
of the Corellian type of concerto did not spread immediately to other parts of Germany. In the northern and central
states only the chamber music of Corelli was known and it
was not until the second decade of the eighteenth century
that his concertos reached these parts. By this time, however, the new Venetian concerto was on the scene, proving
immensely popular with composers and performers alike.
The Corellian concerto was almost completely over-
shadowed by the more brilliant works of Albinoni, Vivaldi,
and the two Marcellos and never became a serious rival to
the Venetian type.

The leading exponents of the Venetian concerto had all
been trained in the field of opera. They introduced into their
concertos several operatic devices, the most important
being the ritornello principle and the aria-like slow movement. The three-movement form of the Italian opera sinfonia (fast–slow–fast) was preferred to the more traditional
designs of the 'sonata da camera' and 'da chiesa' and their
concertos were less dependent on the structure and style of
the instrumental sonata than were Bolognese works. There
was a general trend towards the solo concerto (as opposed
to the concerto grosso) and, although the violin still
remained a favourite solo instrument, woodwinds were also
used as soloists. Finally, the distinction between solo and
ripieno groups was underlined by the use of figurative
material for solo sections.

German composers adapted the Italian art form to their
own culture in a number of ways. Although the majority
took the Venetian concerto as their point of departure
individual composers differed widely in their application of

the same basic principles. Some used concerto elements within the context of the French suite; others became completely immersed in the Italian style; others again combined various features of the Italian concerto with the traditional Germanic qualities of elaborate counterpoint and rich polyphony.

For this reason the ensuing study of the German concerto is approached through the works of individuals. Out of the hundreds of concertists active in Germany during this period I have decided to concentrate on five: J. S. Bach, Handel, Telemann, Hasse, and Emanuel Bach. The inclusion of the first two needs little justification, given their pre-eminence. Some might quarrel with the inclusion of Handel since the majority of his concertos were written in England. However, they remain the work of a German composer and one whose catholic taste gives us an insight into a rich variety of national styles. Telemann again is an obvious choice, being one of the most popular and important composers of his day. As for Hasse and Emanuel Bach, their works reflect two important trends in the development of the mid-eighteenth-century concerto: Hasse's works are representative of the operatic type of concerto written by some advanced Italianate composers of the 1720s and the compositions of Emanuel Bach exemplify the change from an elegant rococo style to the more expressive idiom of the *Empfindsamkeit*.

The manuscript of this book was completed at the end of 1975 and it has not been possible to take account of subsequent research.

Abbreviations

RISM abbreviations are used for library locations.

Acknowledgements

I should like to thank the following for their help: Dr. F. W.

Sternfeld of the University of Oxford; Dr. Keiser of the Hessische Landes- und Hochschulbibliothek, Darmstadt; Professor A. J. B. Hutchings; Dr. R. Bullivant of the University of Sheffield; and the staff of the following libraries: The Music Faculty, The Bodleian Library, Oriel College, Oxford; The British Library, London; the Rowe Music Library, Cambridge; Santa Cecilia, Rome; and the Music Department Library, University of Sheffield. Finally thanks are due to my husband for his encouragement and forbearance.

Contents

Johann Sebastian Bach

1. Introduction

Bach's output as a concertist was, in contemporary terms, relatively small. Six concerti grossi, two concertos for solo violin, one double concerto, a triple concerto for flute, violin, and clavier, and thirteen works for one or more claviers and orchestra—this represents the sum total of his contribution.[1] Yet the possibilities of concertante writing and ritornello form obviously fascinated him for he applied the basic elements of concerto design to a wide range of works, from large-scale choral compositions to smaller suite-movements and chorale preludes. The opening 'Kyrie' from the Mass in B Minor, for instance, bears all the marks of a concerto fugue, while the G minor Prelude to the third English suite (BWV 808)[2] provides a classic example of ritornello form. These well-known movements give some indication of the extent to which Bach relied on concerto principles even when writing for voices and orchestra or for the keyboard alone. A study of the concertos, therefore, sheds light not only on Bach's handling of one specific genre but on an important area of his compositional technique as a whole.

The concertos themselves span a wide period of Bach's creative life. They fall naturally into three groups according to their place and date of composition: those written (or

---

[1] Disregarding the concerto arrangements of the Weimar period; fragmentary works such as BWV 1059 and 1045; spurious compositions such as Anh. 155; BWV 1065 which is based on a Vivaldi concerto; and the curious reference to a violin concerto with accompaniment for '3.VV. A. viol°. Obl: et B.' discovered recently in the archives at Ulm (see K. Häfner, 'Ein bisher nicht beachteter Nachweis zweier Konzerte J. S. Bachs', *Bach-Jahrbuch*, lx (1974), 123–5).

[2] BWV = W. Schmieder, *Thematisch-Systematisches Verzeichnis der musikalischen Werke von Johann Sebastian Bach (Bach-Werke-Verzeichnis)* (*Leipzig*, 1950).

rather, arranged) at Weimar within the years 1708–17; those composed at Cöthen where Bach was kapellmeister from 1717 to 1723; and those stemming from his Leipzig period (1723–50). In the first category come the transcriptions for clavier and for organ, BWV 972–87 and 592–6; the second group includes the concertos for solo and double violin and, traditionally, the Brandenburg concertos (some of which may, however, have originated during the Weimar period despite their 1721 dedication date),[3] with the clavier concertos forming a third and final group. There is, then, a distinct difference between the type of concerto cultivated by Bach at various stages of his career, for which, as we shall see, external circumstances must be held responsible.

From his youth Bach had been trained as a violinist and it was probably in this capacity that he first encountered the Italian concerto. Unfortunately, the exact date of this encounter has not been recorded. It is possible, as Friedrich Blume suggests, that Bach performed some Italian concertos as early as 1703 during his initial term of service at Weimar.[4] Albinoni's first concertos were certainly in print by that date, as were comparable works by Torelli;[5] and although Vivaldi's earliest concerto publication—L'Estro Armonico, op. 3—should probably be dated somewhat later,[6] individual works from the set were circulating in manuscript copies which are believed to antedate the printed edition. There is, however, one problem in accepting so

---

[3] See pp. 20–4.

[4] F. Blume, 'J. S. Bach's Youth', The Musical Quarterly, liv (1968), 15.

[5] Albinoni's op. 2, the Sinfonie e Concerti a Cinque, was published in both Italy and the Netherlands. Sala's edition came out in Venice in 1700; the Amsterdam edition could be even earlier, though it cannot date from before 1696 when Roger began his publishing activities. Torelli's op. 5 set, the Sinfonie a tre e Concerti a quattro, was published in Bologna in 1692.

[6] There is some controversy surrounding the precise publication date of Vivaldi's op. 3 set. The Italian scholar Rinaldi dated the first edition 'around 1702' but he may have been misled by the low publisher's number. (Old numbers were sometimes reallocated if the earlier stock had sold out.) Ryom's date of 1711 is more realistic; certainly copies of the set were advertised in London during that year (cf. M. Tilmouth, 'A Calendar of References to Music in Newspapers published in London and the Provinces (1660–1719)', The Royal Musical Association Research Chronicle, i (Cambridge, 1961), p. 80).

early a date: Bach's own compositions of the period show no trace of Venetian influence; it is only around 1714 that radical style-changes suggest a sudden awareness of the Vivaldian manner.[7] In the event, this later date accords well with other information concerning the dissemination of the Venetian concerto in Germany, for the main impact of the new form was felt in the second decade of the century. It is at this stage that references to Vivaldi's concertos begin to appear in German literature and correspondence;[8] at this stage, too, that a whole generation of young composers (Stölzel, Heinichen, and Pisendel, to name but a few) sought tuition from Italy's leading concertists.

By all accounts, Weimar was an early stronghold of the new orchestral music. That concertos were known and performed there in 1713 is evident from a letter written by one of Bach's pupils, Philipp David Kräuter, begging permission of the Protestant School Board Augsburg for leave to continue his studies at Weimar where 'much fine Italian and French music can be heard, particularly profitable to me in composing Concertos and Ouvertures'.[9] What part Bach himself played in promoting the new music is unclear. But he was not the only Weimar musician to show an interest in the concerto. His friend (and relative on the Lämmerhirt side) J. G. Walther made a number of concerto transcriptions for the organ[10] and there was encouragement too from the aristocracy in the shape of Prince Johann Ernst,

---

[7] M. Geck, 'Gattungstraditionen und Altersschichten in den Brandenburgischen Konzerter, *Die Musikforschung*, xxiii (1970), 150.

[8] Among the earliest references are those by von Uffenbach, 1712 (W. Kolneder, 'Das Früschaffen Antonio Vivaldis', *Internationale Gesellschaft für Musikwissenschaft, Fünfter Kongress Utrecht 3–7 July 1952, Kongressbericht* (Amsterdam, 1953), p. 260) and Quantz, 1714 (J. J. Quantz, autobiography in F. W. Marpurg, *Historisch-Kritische Beyträge zur Aufnähme der Musik*, 5 vols. (Berlin, 1754–60; facsimile edition Hildesheim, 1970), i. 205).

[9] Cited by H-J. Schulze, 'J. S. Bach's Concerto-arrangements for organ—studies or commissioned works?', *The Organ Yearbook*, iii (1972), 7.

[10] Fourteen keyboard transcriptions by Walther are available in vol. xxvi-xxvii of *Denkmäler deutscher Tonkunst*, ed. M. Seiffert (Leipzig, 1906; revised H. J. Moser (Wiesbaden, 1958)). The concertos are based on works by Albinoni, Blamr, Corelli, Gentili, Manzia, Meck (or Megck), Taglietti, Telemann, and Torelli.

the young nephew of the reigning Duke, whose travels brought him into close contact with the latest musical developments.

2. The Weimar Transcriptions

The earliest examples of Bach's interest in the concerto are the sixteen concertos for solo clavier (BWV 972–87) and the five concertos for organ (BWV 592–6) which Bach arranged while at Weimar. (There is a seventeenth clavier concerto (BWV 592a) but this is another version of the organ transcription BWV 592; as for the 'sixth' organ concerto, listed by Schmieder as BWV 597 and published in Peters's *Orgelwerke* book ix, p. 30, it is not known for certain whether Bach made the arrangement; nor has the concerto on which it was, presumably, modelled been traced.) In the *Bach-Gesellschaft* edition of 1894 the clavier transcriptions were published under the title *XVI Concerte nach A. Vivaldi*.[11] This was a misnomer as only six works can be shown to derive from Vivaldi. Of the remainder, three are based on concertos by Prince Johann Ernst, one is modelled on a concerto by Telemann, and one derives from Alessandro Marcello;[12] five others are unidentified at present. For his

[11] These works were first published by Peters of Leipzig in 1851 under a very similar title: *XVI/Concertos/d'après des Concertos pour le Violon/de/Antonio Vivaldi/arrangés/pour le piano seul/par/Jean Sébastien Bach/publiés pour la première fois/par S. W. Dehn et F. A. Roitzsch* which in turn goes back to a MS. copy of nos. 1–9, 11, and 12 headed *XII Concerti di Vivaldi, elaborati di J. S. Bach*. This MS., once in the possession of Johann Ernst Bach, is now preserved at D-Bds, Mus. ms. Bach P. 280. (The tenth concerto of the J. E. Bach MS. did not appear in the 1851 edition since it was designed for organ rather than clavier.)

[12] For the identification and study of the original sources see the following publications: J. Rühlmann, 'Antonio Vivaldi und sein Einfluss auf Johann Sebastian Bach', *Neue Zeitschrift für Musik*, 1, 8, 15 Nov. 1867, lxiii, 393–7, 401–5, 413–16; P. Spitta, *Johann Sebastian Bach: his Work and Influence on the Music of Germany, 1685–1750*, tr. C. Bell and J. A. Fuller-Maitland, 3 vols. (London, 1884, 1889), i. 412–16; P. G. Waldersee, 'Antonio Vivaldi's Violinconcerte unter besonderer Berücksichtigung der von Johann Sebastian Bach bearbeiteten', *Vierteljahrsschrift für Musikwissenschaft*, i (1885), 356–80; A. Schering, 'Zur Bach-Forschung', *Sammelbände der Internationalen Musik-Gesellschaft*, iv (1902–3), 234–43 and v (1903–4), 565–70; E. Praetorius, 'Neues zur Bach-Forschung', *Sammelbände der Internationalen Musik-Gesellschaft*, viii (1906–7), 95–101; M. Schneider, 'Das Sogenannte " Orgelkonzert d=moll von Wilhelm Friedemann Bach" ', *Bach-Jahrbuch*, viii (1911), 23–36; R. Eller, 'Zur Frage Bach-Vivaldi', *Bericht über den internationalen musikwissenschaftlichen*

organ concertos, Bach used similar models, selecting two works by Johann Ernst and three by Vivaldi. Full details are given in Table I (see pp. 6–8).

The transcription of vocal and instrumental music for the keyboard was widely practised in Germany and Bach's arrangements are part of a continuing tradition which can be traced right back to medieval times.[13] Yet to acknowledge this is not to explain the motivation behind the Weimar arrangements or, indeed, the purpose which they served. Was Bach writing for his own personal satisfaction or did he make the arrangements in response to some external commission? This problem has intrigued Bach scholars from the nineteenth century on. One theory can be discarded at the outset however: although, as Forkel implied,[14] the transcriptions may have proved useful to Bach in his study of the new concerto genre, they were not designed for such purposes in the first place. For if Bach's principal objective was to obtain a study-score (the original manuscripts were usually in parts) why did he alter certain passages to create a more idiomatic keyboard texture? Again, he would scarcely have chosen as models the works of a young Prince whose concertos, though warmly praised by so discerning a critic as Mattheson,[15] were not those of an established master.

It is possible, of course, that Bach made the transcriptions

Kongress Hamburg 1956, eds. W. Gerstenberg, H. Husmann, H. Heckmann (Kassel, 1957), 80–5; W. Kolneder, *Antonio Vivaldi: his Life and Work*, tr. B. Hopkins (London, 1970), pp. 103–15. A useful summary is provided by J. T. Igoe, 'Bachs Bearbeitungen für Cembalo solo. Eine Zusammenfassung', *Bach-Jahrbuch*, lvii (1971), 91–7.

[13] cf. T. Göllner, 'J. S. Bach and the tradition of keyboard transcriptions', *Studies in Eighteenth-Century Music: a Tribute to Karl Geiringer on his Seventieth Birthday*, ed. H. C. Robbins Landon in collaboration with R. E. Chapman (London, 1970), pp. 253–60.

[14] 'Opportunely Vivaldi's Concertos for the Violin, then recently published, gave him the guidance he needed. He had often heard them praised as admirable works of art, and conceived the happy idea of arranging them for the clavier. Hence he was led to study their structure, the musical ideas on which they are built, the variety of their modulations, and other characteristics' (J. N. Forkel, *Johann Sebastian Bach: his Life, Art and Work*, tr. and ed. C. S. Terry (London, 1920), p. 71).

[15] J. Mattheson, *Exemplarische Organisten-Probe* (Hamburg, 1719), p. 203.

Table 1

The clavier arrangements BWV 972–87 (*Bach-Gesellschaft xlii.* 59–170); also BWV 592a (*Bach-Gesellschaft, xlii.* 282–8)

BWV no.	Key of Bach's transcription	Original source
972	D	Vivaldi, op. 3, no. 9, a violin concerto in D major, RV(= Ryom Verzeichnis) 230
973	G	Vivaldi, op. 7, no. 8 (Book II, no. 2), a violin concerto in G major, RV 299
974	D minor	Alessandro Marcello, no. 2 of *Concerti à Cinque* (Amsterdam, 1716[1]), an oboe concerto in C minor or D minor[2]
975	G minor	Vivaldi, op. 4, no. 6, a violin concerto in G minor, RV 362[3]
976	C	Vivaldi, op. 3, no. 12, a violin concerto in E major, RV 265
977	C	Unidentified
978	F	Vivaldi, op. 3, no. 3, a violin concerto in G major, RV 310
979	B minor	Unidentified
980	G	Vivaldi, op. 4, Book I, no. 1, a violin concerto in B♭ major, RV $\begin{cases} 383^4 \\ 381 \end{cases}$
981	C minor	Unidentified
982	B♭	Prince Johann Ernst of Saxe-Weimar, op. 1, no. 1, a violin concerto in B♭ major[5]
983	G minor	Unidentified
984	C	Prince Johann Ernst of Saxe-Weimar—the original is lost
985	G minor	Telemann, violin concerto in G minor[6]
986	G	Unidentified
987	D minor	Prince Johann Ernst of Saxe-Weimar, op. 1, no. 4, a violin concerto in D minor[7]
592a (a clavier version of BWV 592)	G	Prince Johann Ernst of Saxe-Weimar, op. [?]2, no. 1 (see also BWV 592)

The organ transcriptions BWV 592–6 (*Bach-Gesellschaft xxxviii.* 149–202; for BWV 596 see the Augener edition, no. 5863)

BWV no.	Key of Bach's transcription	Original source
592	G	Prince Johann Ernst of Saxe-Weimar, op. [?]2, no. 1, a violin concerto in G major[8]

593	A minor	Vivaldi, op. 3, no. 8, a double violin concerto in A minor, RV 522
594	C	Vivaldi, op. 7, Book II, no. 5, a violin concerto in D major, RV 208[9]
595 (a single movement work)	C	Prince Johann Ernst of Saxe-Weimar; this movement is based on the same (lost) original as BWV 984[10]
596	D minor	Vivaldi, op. 3, no. 11, a double violin concerto in D minor, RV 565[11]

---

[1] For the dating of this publication see B. Paumgartner, 'Nochmals "Zur Frage J. S. Bach-Marcello"', *Die Musikforschung*, xi (1958), 342.

[2] There has been much controversy as to whether the original concerto was written by Benedetto Marcello or by his brother, Alessandro. Eitner ('Benedetto Marcello'. *Monatshefte für Musikgeschichte*, xxiii (1891), 193) believed it to be by Benedetto since he had seen a manuscript of the transcription at Darmstadt (in what is now the Hessische Landes- und Hochschulbibliothek) entitled '*Concerto de B. Marcello accomodé au Clavecin de J. S. Bach*'. His view was supported half a century later by P. Aldrich ('Bach's Technique of Transcription and Improvised Ornamentation', *The Musical Quarterly*, xxxv (1949), 33–4) who claimed to have seen, at the Liceo Musicale, Bologna, a copy of the Benedetto Marcello original. The matter was complicated when Frank Walker pointed out in 1950 that the oboe concerto in question had been published by Roger of Amsterdam under Alessandro's name (see F. Walker, 'A Little Bach Discovery', *Music and Letters*, xxxi (1950), 184). All in all, it seems likely that Alessandro was the author. This is not simply a case of accepting the authority of print over manuscript—a dangerous exercise when dealing with eighteenth-century editions in particular—but rather that the evidence on the other side is extremely thin. In the first place there is some doubt as to the authenticity of the Darmstadt title (A. van der Linden, 'Zur Frage J. B. Bach-Marcello', *Die Musikforschung*, xi (1958), 82–3)—another manuscript of the same work at Schwerin is attributed merely to Marcello, no Christian name being specified; in the second place, no trace of Aldrich's manuscript can now be found at Bologna (E. T. Ferand, 'Marcello: A. oder B.?', *Die Musikforschung*, xii (1959), 86). A further controversy surrounds the key of Bach's model. All the manuscript versions of the Marcello concerto (including Aldrich's) are said to have been in C minor; yet Roger (who often transposed concertos before publication) gives D minor as the tonality. Which source did Bach use? It would be convenient to assume that he based his transcription on a D minor version (either Roger's edition or another copy in the same key) since no transposition would then be involved. (If Bach's model was in C minor one has the task of explaining why, on this occasion, he made the transposition up a tone (i.e. from C minor to D minor) when his other arrangements were either left in the original key or else transposed downwards (H. Shanet, 'Why did J. S. Bach Transpose his Arrangements?', *The Musical Quarterly*, xxxvi (1950), 199).) Against this, however, must be set the fact that Bach normally worked from manuscript sources and not from printed editions (R. Eller, op. cit., pp. 80–5). The question must, therefore, remain unresolved.

[3] Waldersee showed in 1885 that the 3rd movement of the transcription corres-

ponds, not to the printed source, but to a manuscript version of the work at Darmstadt (Waldersee, op. cit. 358, 368). Unfortunately this manuscript is now no longer in existence.

[4] The 2nd and 3rd movements do not correspond with the printed edition of op. 4, Book I, no. 1. However, all three movements agree with a manuscript version of the concerto at Uppsala (Caps 61:7). That this manuscript could not have been Bach's direct source though, is shown by R. Eller, op. cit., p. 82.

[5] This concerto was among those engraved by Telemann in 1718. The title of the set ran as follows: *Six CONCERTS à un Violon concertant, deux Violons, une Taille; et Clavecin où Basse de Viole, de feu S.A.S. Monseigneur le Prince JEAN ERNESTE, Duc de Saxe-Weimar, Opera Ima . . .*

[6] MSS. at Dresden (D-Dl(b), Musikabteilung 2392/0/17 and 17(a)); Darmstadt (D-DS, 1033/91).

[7] From the above-mentioned set—see note 5 for details.

[8] The 1st movement is based on the same original as BWV 592a; the concerto may therefore be attributed to Johann Ernst (see J. T. Igoe, op. cit. 92).

[9] Bach's transcription corresponds, not to the printed edition, but to a manuscript version of the concerto at Schwerin (the Wissenschaftliche Allgemeinbibliothek, formerly the Landesbibliothek), MS. 5565; however, as Eller has shown (op. cit., p. 82) this manuscript was not Bach's ultimate source either; presumably the transcription was made from another copy which has now disappeared.

[10] Although Spitta knew there was a manuscript copy of the transcription bearing the title: *Concerto dell' illustrissimo Principe Giovanni Ernesto, Duca di Sassonia, appropriato all' Organo a 2 Clav. e Pedale da Giovanni Sebastiano Bach*, he continued to question Johann Ernst's authorship on the grounds that the work was too Vivaldian in manner! Doubtless he was misled also by the fact that Bach had made a clavier version of the same concerto (BWV 984) which was at that stage (along with the other clavier arrangements) believed to be by Vivaldi (see P. Spitta, op. cit. i. 630).

[11] BWV 596 was for a long time attributed to W. F. Bach on the grounds that the manuscript, though in his father's writing, bore the inscription 'di W. F. Bach./manu mei Patris descript'. It was only in 1911 that Max Schneider identified the concerto as J. S. Bach's arrangement of Vivaldi's op. 3, no. 11 (see M. Schneider, op. cit. 23–36).

for his own use[16] and that he was influenced in this by the organ arrangements of his friend Johann Gottfried Walther, organist of SS. Peter and Paul, Weimar, and music tutor to Prince Johann Ernst. But this is speculative, since we do not know whether Walther's transcriptions antedate those of

[16] A theory is held in some quarters that organ transcriptions of the type made by Walther and Bach were intended for performance during the Communion. This view has its origins in a more general remark of Forkel's that in Bach's time 'it was usual to play a Concerto or instrumental Solo during the Communion office. Bach composed many of these pieces himself . . .' (J. N. Forkel, op. cit., p. 137).

Bach. Besides, it is conceivable that both composers were reacting jointly to a third stimulus.

For some time now the idea that Prince Johann Ernst was behind the transcriptions has been in circulation. Spitta observed that the musicians surrounding the Prince would be obliged to show interest in the Italian concerto 'if only out of respect for him'[17] and C. S. Terry went even further, suggesting that it was largely due to Johann Ernst's influence that Bach started work on the project.[18] Recently this theory has been given added weight by the resurrection of some forgotten evidence concerning similar concerto arrangements in Amsterdam. The passage in question (which contains a rare reference to the practice of transcription) occurs during a discourse on orchestral music in Mattheson's *Das beschützte Orchestre*:

That this species of music also allows itself to be performed *zur Curiosité* on an instrument with full harmony (such as organ or clavier) is shown by, amongst others, the famous blind organist of the Nieuwe Kerk, Amsterdam, Msr. de Graue [i.e. de Graaf] who knows by heart all the most recent Italian concertos, sonatas, etc. with three to four parts and played them in my presence on his wonderful instrument with uncommon neatness of finger.[19]

First cited in Geck's article for *Die Musikforschung* 1970, the implications of this passage were followed up swiftly by Hans-Joachim Schulze who saw a possible connection between the Amsterdam keyboard arrangements and Weimar.[20] Prince Johann Ernst of Weimar travelled exten-

---

[17] P. Spitta, op. cit. i. 411.

[18] C. S. Terry, *Bach: a Biography* (London, 1928), p. 57.

[19] "Dass auch eben diese Species sich auf einem einzigen vollstimmigen Instrumente/Z.E. auf der Orgel oder dem Clavier/zur Curiosité tractiren lasse/bewiess unter andern vor einigen Jahren der berühmte/aber blinde Organiste an der Neuen Kirchen auf dem Damm zu Amsterdam/Msr. de Graue: welcher alle die neuesten Italiänischen Concerten, Sonaten &c. mit 3. à 4. Stimmen aus wendig wuste/und mit ungemeiner Sauberkeit auf seiner wunderschönen Orgel in meiner Gegenwart heraus brachte" (J. Mattheson, *Das Beschützte Orchestre* (Hamburg, 1717), pp. 129f.). The translation in the text is from H-J. Schulze, op. cit. 6. As Schulze points out, the precise date of Mattheson's visit is not known. According to his autobiography Mattheson was in the Netherlands in 1704; however, the context of the passage quoted above suggests a date shortly after 1710.

[20] See H-J. Schulze, op. cit. 4–10.

sively throughout his short life and Schulze, working from archival evidence, was able to build up a fascinating picture of his contacts with the Low Countries. We learn, for example, that the Prince was based at Utrecht from February 1711 to 8 July 1713 and that, after a journey to Dusseldorf in February 1713, the royal party stopped at Amsterdam. (Unfortunately we do not know whether the Prince actually heard de Graaf play, though it is possible as the latter was organist of the Nieuwe Kerk from 1702–38.) Amsterdam was one of the leading centres for music printing in the early eighteenth century and Johann Ernst would, therefore, have had ample opportunity to purchase copies of the most recent orchestral music. That he did so is suggested by certain entries in the Weimar account books for the summer and autumn of 1713. One item, dated 15 July 1713 (i.e. immediately after his return to court), mentions expenses incurred in 'binding the books of music'; another, dated 23 September 1713, records payment to a cabinet maker 'for a cupboard for the music'. Although the precise contents of the Weimar music library have not been recorded, one imagines that Johann Ernst stocked it with the most fashionable (which meant the latest) works. He himself took a lively interest in contemporary artistic developments as is evident from the six violin concertos (published posthumously in 1718) which he wrote under Walther's direction and which follow Vivaldian models very closely. His interest in the new Italian concerto must have influenced the type of music cultivated at Weimar. Moreover, there may have been an even more direct link between his enthusiasm for the new style and the keyboard transcriptions of Bach and Walther: if we accept that the Prince heard some of de Graaf's concerto arrangements while in Amsterdam (as is possible), he may well have commissioned similar works on his return home.

Acceptance of this theory has profound implications for dating, as Schulze realized, for if Bach's transcriptions were made at the instigation of Johann Ernst, they must surely have been written between July 1713 (the date of his return from Holland) and July 1714 when the eighteen-year-old Prince left Weimar for what was to be the last time. (He died in 1715 before returning to court.) This date fits well with evidence from other sources: according to the eminent Bach scholar Georg von Dadelsen, watermarks in the autograph manuscript of BWV 596—the only one of the arrangements to be preserved in Bach's hand—suggest a date of around 1714–16.[21] Although it is dangerous to argue on the basis of one example alone, this fact, together with the circumstantial evidence presented by Schulze, makes 1713–14 the most plausible date yet suggested for Bach's keyboard arrangements.

The problems facing Bach as a transcriber of orchestral concertos for the keyboard were comparable to those of a translator. How far should the original be preserved and how far should it be modified to suit the new medium? Bach steered a middle course: while he did not hesitate to alter certain details here and there (sometimes even rewriting whole episodes in a more idiomatic keyboard style), he seldom altered the substance of the original.[22] True, a comparison of some of the Vivaldi arrangements with their printed counterparts reveals considerable discrepancies. But many of these may be attributed to Bach's use of deviant manuscript sources rather than his methods of transcription. If BWV 980, for example, is compared with the normal printed version of Vivaldi's op. 4, Book I, no. 1, it will be

---

[21] G. von Dadelsen, *Beiträge zur Chronologie der Werke Johann Sebastian Bachs*, Tübinger Bach-Studien, ed. W. Gerstenberg, iv/5 (Trossingen, 1958), p. 79.

[22] An interesting exception occurs in Bach's transcription of one of Johann Ernst's concertos. Both the 1st movement of BWV 984 (for clavier) and the single-movement work for organ, BWV 595, derive from the same original; however, the clavier version has 66 bars, the organ transcription, 81. This expansion in BWV 595 is spread fairly evenly over the movement as may be seen by comparing the two versions:

BWV 984		*BWV 595*
Bars 1–9	correspond to	1–15 (+6)
Bars 10–18	correspond to	16–24
Bars 19–29	correspond to	25–43 (+8)
Bars 30–66	correspond to	44–81 (+1)

seen that only the first movements are related. However, all three movements of the keyboard arrangement agree with a different version of the Vivaldi concerto preserved in manuscript at Uppsala. Similarly with BWV 594: the Bach transcription contains virtuoso cadenzas in the outer movements which do not appear in the printed edition of Vivaldi's op. 7. Moreover, the second movements are completely unrelated. But a manuscript at Schwerin (D-Swl 5565) gives the cadenza to the 1st movement and also contains the substituted 2nd movement.

Although Bach did not normally make radical changes to the length or substance of his models certain alterations were, of course, necessitated by the change of medium. It will be noticed that in a number of cases the arrangements are set in a lower key than the originals—mostly a tone down. This transposition was not to accommodate local variations in pitch, but simply to bring the highest notes of the original solo part within the rather restricted compass of contemporary keyboard instruments.[23] Bach's organ at Weimar possessed no top D (d''') even after its reconstruction in 1714 and there are places in BWV 596 where the high passages of Vivaldi's concerto have had to be altered.[24] Similarly with the clavier transcriptions: although the upper limit of the clavier was continually being extended throughout the eighteenth century, the instrument for which the Weimar transcriptions were written could only reach c'''. Contemporary violin and oboe concertos were not, however, particularly adventurous in their exploitation of upper registers and in most cases transposition down a tone was sufficient to bring the highest notes of the original within range. Occasionally, though, when e''' figured prominently in the solo part, transposition down a third became necessary (as in BWV 976).

Bach's technique of transcription was simple yet effective. In fast movements the solo part was assigned to the right

[23] For a detailed exposition of this see H. Shanet, op. cit. 180–203.
[24] See H. Keller, *The Organ Works of Bach*, tr. H. Hewitt (New York, 1967), p. 88.

hand of the clavier player, while the left hand was given a more spirited version of the original figured bass line, often realizing the implied harmony with broken chords:

EXAMPLE I
(a) Vivaldi, op. 3, no. 3 (Malipiero ed. no. 408), 1st movement, bars 7–9 (outer parts only); (b) Bach, clavier arrangement no. 7 (BWV 978), 1st movement, bars 7–9[25]

Slow movements were transcribed fairly literally too, especially when the original material was decorative in style. The simple Largo, however, which contained no written-out ornamentation, presented a greater challenge in that the harpsichord, having a somewhat dry tone, was incapable of sustaining notes for any length of time and could not hope to reproduce the sonorous effect of legato string writing. Bach surmounted this particular difficulty by decorating the original melodic line—adding the type of ornamentation that was so important in contemporary performance:

[25] The Bach examples are taken, whenever possible, from the *Neue Bach-Ausgabe*. This series is, however, still in progress so that it is sometimes necessary to refer to the old *Bach-Gesellschaft* edition. References to other sources are given in footnotes.

EXAMPLE 2

(a) Vivaldi, op. 7, Book II, no. 2 (Malipiero ed. no. 449), Largo,
cantabile, bars 1–4; (b) Bach, clavier arrangement no. 2 (BWV 973),
Largo, bars 1–4

Although many of Bach's revisions stem from his desire to
create a truly idiomatic keyboard work, not all the alterations may be placed in this category. Occasionally he
imposes his own ideas on the original—enriching the harmony with suspensions, fitting in snippets of imitation,
extending contrary motion scale passages, and adding figuration to static bass lines. In the following passage, for
instance, there was no necessity for him to add the 7–6
suspensions of bar 29 but they do enliven the harmonic
scheme and make the texture more varied:

EXAMPLE 3

(a) Vivaldi, op. 3, no. 8 (Malipiero ed. no. 413), 1st movement, bars
27–30; (b) Bach, organ transcription no. 2 (BWV 593), 1st movement,
bars 27–30

Three further examples are given below, all from the 1st movement of the seventh clavier arrangement. In each case, Bach's additions make the original more complex:

EXAMPLE 4
Addition of imitation
(*a*) Vivaldi, op. 3, no. 3, (Malipiero ed. no. 408), 1st movement, bars 1–2 (short score); (*b*) Bach, clavier arrangement no. 7 (BWV 978), 1st movement, bars 1–2

EXAMPLE 5
Extension of contrary motion scale passages
(*a*) Vivaldi, op. 3, no. 3 (Malipiero ed., no. 408), 1st movement, bars 28–9 (short score); (*b*) Bach, clavier arrangement no. 7 (BWV 978), 1st movement, bars 28–9

EXAMPLE 6
Addition of figuration to a static bass line
(*a*) Vivaldi, op. 3, no. 3, (Malipiero ed. 408), 1st movement, bars 41–2 (short score); (*b*) Bach, clavier arrangement no. 7 (BWV 978), 1st movement, bars 41–2

In so far as a similar predilection for imitation, contrary motion passages, and figurative bass lines is evident in Bach's own compositions, it may be said that he imposed something of his personal style on the transcriptions. Certainly the arrangements sound utterly unlike the originals; nor is the change of medium wholly responsible. In the course of transcription, Bach has created orderly, 'artificial' works which have more in common with the solid traditions of German keyboard music than with the colourful vivacity of the orchestral concerto.

3. The Brandenburg Set; the Violin Concertos

Important though the Weimar period was, Bach's real achievements in the field of instrumental music belong to the years 1717–23, during his appointment as kapellmeister to Prince Leopold of Anhalt-Cöthen. It was here that he wrote out the fair copy of the Brandenburg concertos; here, too, that the concertos for violin and orchestra came into being.

The Brandenburg Concertos

The autograph score of the *Six Concerts Avec plusiers Instruments*, to use the original title, is dated 24 March 1721. It contains an elaborate Preface in French explaining the circumstances of composition and extolling the virtues of Christian Ludwig, Margrave of Brandenburg, to whom the set was dedicated. From the Preface one gathers that Bach had met the Margrave a few years earlier[26] and received what was effectively a commission from him. Unfortunately, details of the meeting are not given, but it has been suggested that the two met in Berlin towards the end of 1718 or early the following year. This is certainly possible as

---

[26] The phrase used is 'une couple d'années', cf. the facsimile edition of the Brandenburg concertos (Leipzig, 1950), with notes by P. Wackernagel. For a detailed description of the autograph manuscript see Wackernagel's 'Beobachtungen am Autograph von Bachs Brandenburgischen Konzerten', *Festschrift Max Schneider zum achtigsten Geburtstag*, ed. W. Vetter (Leipzig, 1955), pp. 129–38.

Bach was sent to Berlin sometime that winter to purchase a new harpsichord for Cöthen.[27]

Although the concertos were dedicated to Christian Ludwig, they were not written with his requirements in mind. The instrumentation gives this away, for the first and second concertos in particular are very richly scored. Indeed, given the meagre resources of the Margrave's establishment—in 1734 only six musicians were on the pay roll[28] and there is no indication that the kapelle was any larger in 1721—nos. 5 and 6 were probably the only concertos of the set which could have been performed without outside assistance.[29]

The resources of Prince Leopold's court at Cöthen were much better suited to performances of the Brandenburgs, as has often been remarked. Fortunately the composition of this kapelle is well documented[30] and we know that in Bach's time the orchestra boasted a number of distinguished musicians, many of whom had come from Berlin when Frederick Wilhelm I disbanded his Hofkapelle in 1713. The concertos of the Brandenburg set, with their varied instrumentation, gave ample opportunity for these distinguished performers to display their skills: the virtuoso violin part of no. 4 would, presumably, have been played by Josephus Spiess and the solo part of the second concerto by the brilliant trumpet player, Schreiber. Prince Leopold was himself a skilled gambist and could therefore have partici-

[27] On 1 March 1719 Bach received 130 Thaler for the harpischord built in Berlin ('das in Berlin gefertigte') and for travelling expenses (cf. H. Wäschke, 'Die Hofkapelle in Cöthen unter Joh. Seb. Bach', *Zerbster Jahrbuch*, iii (1907), 33).

[28] Cf. H. Besseler, ed., *Sechs Brandenburgischen Konzerte: Kritischer Bericht*, Neue Bach-Ausgabe, vii/2 (Kassel, 1956), p. 18; and, id., 'Markgraf Christian Ludwig von Brandenburg', *Bach-Jahrbuch*, xliii (1956), 18–35.

[29] The dedicatory score shows no trace of wear and some scholars have used this as evidence that the concertos were not performed at the Margrave's court. The state of this particular manuscript, however, proves little, since scores (as opposed to parts) were seldom used in performance.

[30] See the following publications: R. Bunge, 'Johann Sebastian Bachs Kapelle zu Cöthen und deren nachgelassene Instrumente', *Bach-Jahrbuch*, ii (1905), 14–47; H. Wäschke, op. cit. 31–40; C. S. Terry, op. cit., pp. 119–23 and *Bach's Orchestra* (London, 1932, reprinted 1958), pp. 5–7; F. Smend, *Bach in Köthen* (Berlin, 1951), pp. 16–26; H. Besseler, *Sechs Brandenburgischen Konzerte*, p. 20.

pated in performances of the sixth concerto which calls for
two viola da gamba players. As for Bach, he directed the
orchestra from one of the string desks,[31] except in the fifth
concerto where he must surely have taken over the harpsichord part.[32]

The only concerto whose instrumentation does not correspond exactly to the resources available at Cöthen is no. 1.
However, this discrepancy is more apparent than real, for
although there were no resident horn players in Leopold's
establishment (and the first concerto includes two corni da
caccia parts), players could be brought in from neighbour-
ing courts when required. Indeed, according to records
preserved in the Cöthen archives, two 'Waldhornisten' were
summoned to Cöthen on 6 September 1721 and again on 6
June 1722 and 10 May 1724.[33] These visits obviously marked
some special occasion and it is entirely possible that they

[31] There has been some confusion over which instrument Bach played in the
Cöthen orchestra. Besseler assumes that he played the viola, partly because the
records make no mention of any other viola players. Forkel also tells us that on
informal occasions 'Bach liked to play the Viola, an instrument which put him, as it
were, in the middle of the harmony in a position from which he could hear and
enjoy it on both sides' (J. N. Forkel, op cit., p. 108). This information probably
derives from a letter which Forkel received from C. P. E. Bach around 1774. The
original is, however, much more explicit: 'As the greatest expert and judge of
harmony, he liked best to the play the viola, with appropriate loudness and softness.
In his youth, and until the approach of old age, he played the violin cleanly and
penetratingly, and thus kept the orchestra in better order than he could have done
with the harpsichord' (the English translation of Emanuel's letter is from *The Bach
Reader*, eds. H. T. David and A. Mendel (London, 1945; revised with supplement
1966), p. 277). It is probable, therefore, that Bach directed the orchestra from one of
the violin desks, though he may have played the viola in certain works (e.g.
Brandenburg no. 6). The fact that no viola players are listed on the Cöthen pay roll is
not a problem since four unnamed ripienists were also attached to the kapelle and
these players could well have supplied the inner parts.

[32] According to Besseler, the theory that Bach played the harpsichord part of no. 5
himself is supported by the fact that this particular concerto lacks a second violin
part. Besseler takes this to mean that one of the violinists transferred to the viola
when Bach vacated the desk. Unfortunately his argument falls down when it is
realized that the third concerto has parts for no fewer than three violas. He himself
supposed that these three parts would be taken by the unnamed ripieno players (cf.
note 31) without seeing that the same players could have participated in no. 5.

[33] F. Smend, *Bach in Köthen* (Berlin, 1951), pp. 153–4. In the final entry, for May
1724, the names of the two horn players are given: Hans Leopold and Wenzel Franz
Seydler. The use of the term 'Waldhornisten' in these records lends support to the
view that Bach's corni da caccia parts were intended, not for the Jagdhorn as Terry

indicate a performance, or performances, of the first Brandenburg concerto.

The fact that the Brandenburg concertos fit Leopold's kapelle so well has led scholars to believe that they were originally designed for Cöthen. However, this implies that all six works were composed within the period 1717 (when Bach took up his appointment at court) and 1721 (the date of dedication)—a line taken by Besseler but subject to criticism in more recent publications. It is obvious from stylistic evidence that the concertos were written at varying stages. There is, for example, a great difference between the early version of no. 1 (BWV 1046a) and the more modern writing of the fifth concerto. Considerations of this nature prompted Besseler[34] to divide the concertos into three groups as follows:

c. 1718   no. 6; the early version of no. 1; no. 3 (i.e. all those concertos without tutti/solo contrast)

c. 1719   no. 2; the 3rd movement of no. 1 (not in the early version); no. 4

c. 1720   no. 5

No one has seriously challenged the validity of Besseler's actual groups; however, it has recently been suggested that the early concertos should be backdated to the Weimar period, thus widening the time span between early and late works.

One of the first to advocate this with respect to Brandenburg no. 1, was Johannes Krey. In an article for the *Besseler Festschrift* (1961)[35] he investigated the relationship between the two different versions of the concerto and made some important suggestions regarding their chronology and early

---

maintained (C. S. Terry, *Bach's Orchestra*, p. 45), nor for the octave transposing Jagdhorn, as Dart suggested (see 'Bach's "Fiauti d'Echo" ', *Music and Letters*, xli (1960), 340–1), but for the Waldhorn itself. A persuasive argument that Bach intended these horn parts to be played on the Waldhorn is constructed by H. Fitzpatrick, 'The Austro-Bohemian School of Horn-Playing, 1680–1830; its Players, Composers, Instruments, and Makers: the Evolution of a Style' (D.Phil. thesis, University of Oxford, 1965), pp. 64–74.

[34] H. Besseler, 'Zur Chronologie der Konzerte Joh. Seb. Bachs', *Festschrift Max Schneider*, pp. 115–28.

[35] 'Zur Entstehungsgeschichte des ersten Brandenburgischen Konzerts', *Festschrift Heinrich Besseler zum sechzigsten Geburtstag* (Leipzig, 1961), pp. 337–42.

history. Before considering his ideas, however, it will be necessary to say a few words about the less familiar version: BWV 1046a.

The principle source for this is a copy, made in 1760, by C. F. Penzel, a Prefect of St. Thomas's, Leipzig. Despite the relatively late date of the manuscript most scholars believe this version to be earlier than that which appears in the dedicatory score.[36] Some idea of the relationship between the two versions can be gained from the following outline which sets out, in general terms, the movement-structure and instrumentation of each:

Sinfonia (BWV 1046a)		*Brandenburg concerto no. 1 (BWV 1046)*
1st movement (no tempo indication); wind and strings	=	1st movement (similar); wind and strings + solo violino piccolo[37]
Adagio, sempre piano; wind and strings	=	Adagio; wind and strings + solo violino piccolo
——		Allegro; wind and strings + solo violino piccolo
Menuet; wind and strings	=	Menuet; wind and strings (+ violino piccolo)
Trio a 2 Hautbois et Basson	=	Trio; oboe I, oboe II and bassoon
Menuet; wind and strings	=	Menuet; wind and strings (+ violino piccolo)
——		Polonaise; strings only
——		Menuet; wind and strings (+ violino piccolo)
Trio pour les Cors de chasse; horn I, horn II, violins I and II in unison	=	Trio; horn I, horn II, oboes in unison
Menuet; wind and strings	=	Menuet; wind and strings (+ violino piccolo)

It will be noticed that the 3rd movement and the Polonaise

[36] Cf. the arguments adduced by H. Besseler, *Sechs Brandenburgischen Konzerte* pp. 43f. Prominent among the dissenters is Gerber (*Bachs Brandenburgischen Konzerte* (Kassel, 1951), p. 57) who believes the Sinfonia to be the later version (with leanings towards the modern symphony in its three-movement structure and Minuet and Trios). The weight of scholarly opinion is, however, behind Besseler whose arguments are based on textual rather than stylistic observations.

[37] As its name implies, the violino piccolo was a smaller version of the violin, tuned a minor third higher.

do not appear in the Sinfonia: they were later additions. Some changes of instrumentation were also made in the revised version. A part for violino piccolo was added and the scoring of the second Trio altered so that the bottom line was provided by unison oboes rather than violins. (Presumably this change was thought necessary because of the insertion of the Polonaise with its concentrated string tone.) There was also a notational change: the bassoon part was moved from its original position above the continuo and placed underneath the wind group—a seemingly insignificant alteration, but one which symbolized the new role of that instrument in progressive instrumental music.

Many of Krey's theories about Brandenburg no. 1 stem indirectly from Besseler. The latter had, for example, already pointed out the similarity between certain elements of the first Brandenburg concerto and the 'Hunting' Cantata no. 208, 'Was mir behagt, ist nur die muntre Jagd', which was performed at the birthday celebrations of the Prince of Weissenfels and which Spitta dated as 1716.[38] Krey developed the idea, suggesting that the early version of no. 1 actually served as the Overture to this work. There is much to commend his view. First, the cantata begins, not with an instrumental introduction as was usual in festive works of this kind, but with a soprano recitative. Furthermore, the autograph score of the cantata lacks a title page, which could mean that the title appeared at the head of a 'missing' instrumental piece. Looking at the concerto, one is struck by the fact that both its tonality and instrumentation[39] correspond to that of the cantata. Stylistically, too, the works are very similar, as is seen by comparing the opening movement of the concerto with the cantata's first aria: both have exuberant flourishes for the horns.[40] Finally, it will be

[38] H. Besseler, *Sechs Brandenburgischen Konzerte*, pp. 21f.

[39] The only real difference being that the early version of Brandenburg no. 1 calls for three oboes, whereas the cantata specifies two only.

[40] That Bach intended the 1st movement of Brandenburg no. 1 as a royal salute is evident from the nature of these hunting calls, see H. Fitzpatrick, *The Horn and Horn-Playing and the Austro-Bohemian tradition from 1680–1830* (London, 1970), pp. 60–2.

remembered that the early version of Brandenburg no. 1 was headed 'Sinfonia'—the standard title for instrumental overtures to vocal works.

Why, then, did Bach revise the work at some later date? Krey suggests that the new version was made for the court orchestra at Dresden. Bach certainly visited the court in the late summer of 1717 and it is quite possible that some of his own works were performed on that occasion. Many of the changes in the later version are explicable in these terms. The violino piccolo part was, presumably, added for the benefit of Volumier, the French-born konzertmeister; moreover, the incorporation of tutti/solo contrast would bring the work into line with the modern Italian concertos which were proving so fashionable at court. (The 3rd movement may have been added for similar reasons—to give Volumier another solo movement and to create a standard fast–slow–fast complex of movements at the beginning of the work.) As for the addition of a Polonaise, this may be interpreted as a concession to local taste, for Augustus I, Elector of Saxony, was also King of Poland and Polish music was frequently performed at his court.

According to Krey therefore, the early version of Brandenburg no. 1 probably served as a three-movement overture to Cantata no. 208, being performed with the cantata at Weissenfels in 1716; the later version of the concerto was most likely written for Dresden and performed there in 1717; this work then received its first Cöthen performance—probably on 6 September 1721.[41]

Through its association with Cantata no. 208, Krey assigns the early version of Brandenburg no. 1 to the year 1716. But another eminent Bach scholar, Martin Geck, is of a different opinion.[42] While accepting Krey's suggestions regarding the early performances of the concerto (as outlined above), he backdates the Sinfonia even further—to 1713. This is done partly on the basis of Dürr's suggestion that Cantata no. 208 could have been performed in that

---

[41] See pp. 19–20.
[42] M. Geck, op. cit. 139–52.

year,[43] partly because he believes the work originated in a period before Bach came into contact with the Vivaldian concerto (i.e. before 1714). However, neither argument is particularly convincing and on the whole Krey's dating is preferable.

Brandenburg no. 3 is also backdated by Geck. Here the argument turns on a particular notational device which Bach stopped using around 1715. Prior to that date the note B♭ was sometimes raised a semitone by means of a # sign rather than a ♮. This old-fashioned notation is not found in the dedicatory score of the Brandenburgs but does occur in Cantata no. 174 (1729) which is an arrangement (in part) of material from the third Brandenburg concerto. Presumably Bach made the cantata arrangement from a manuscript copy which pre-dates the dedicatory score. And since he stopped using the old notation around 1715 it follows that the third concerto must have been composed before this.[44]

To complete the picture, Geck places the sixth concerto (the remaining member of the 'early group') in the Weimar period, suggesting that it may have originated as a trio sonata that was subsequently rewritten when Bach prepared the dedicatory score. We are, therefore, presented with a number of alternative datings for some members of the set. And, although we shall probably never know beyond all doubt which of the alternatives is correct, the following dates seem the most plausible: no. 1 early version, 1716, later version, 1717; no. 2, c. 1719; no. 3, before 1715; no. 4, c. 1719; no. 5, c. 1720; no. 6, c. 1718 or earlier.

To return to a point made in the previous paragraph, it is quite possible that several of the concertos were rewritten

[43] A. Dürr, *Festmusiken für die Fürstenhäuser von Weimar, Weissenfels und Köthen: Kritischer Bericht*, Neue Bach-Ausgabe i/35 (Kassel, 1964), pp. 39f.

[44] Geck believes that the third concerto, like the first, was originally designed as an overture; he adduces stylistic evidence for this and points out that when Bach re-used material from the concertos in later cantatas the opening movements of both works served as introductions, the 1st movement of no. 1 becoming the Overture to Cantata no. 52 (1726), and the 1st movement of no. 3 becoming the Overture to Cantata no. 174 (1729). By contrast, the more Vivaldian concertos of the set were never used in this manner.

before they attained their final form. Brandenburg no. 1 provides evidence for this of course, and so, too, does no. 5. Another version (BWV 1050a) of this concerto has been published in a modern edition by Alfred Dürr (see the *Neue Bach–Ausgabe* vii/2 (Kassel, 1975)). The source for this is a manuscript copy made by Bach's son-in-law, Altnikol (1719–59), and all the evidence suggests that it is an early draft of the concerto. There are many places, for instance, where Bach has filled out the plain lines of the original with ornamentation—one example being given below:

EXAMPLE 7
Bach, Brandenburg concerto no. 5, 1st movement, bar 9 (cembalo part only); (*a*) from the Altnikol copy; (*b*) standard version

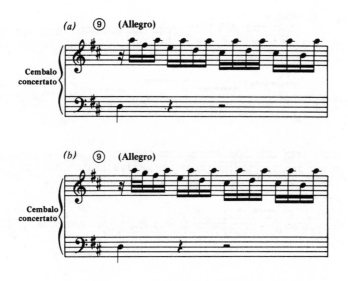

Of even greater interest is the following passage in which Bach transforms a neutral bass line into a dramatic rising scale:

EXAMPLE 8

Bach, Brandenburg concerto no. 5, 1st movement, bars 95–101
(cembalo part only); (a) from the Altnikol copy; (b) standard version

Here the second version is infinitely superior, lending a
sense of urgency to the whole. Other alterations were made
to the rhythmic structure of the 1st movement. In the early
draft there are some static moments, especially where the
semiquaver movement stops abruptly. In the later version,
however, these gaps are filled in by the solo harpsichord:

EXAMPLE 9

Bach, Brandenburg concerto no. 5, 1st movement, bar 130 (full score—ripieno violins and violas are resting); (a) from the Altnikol copy; (b) standard version

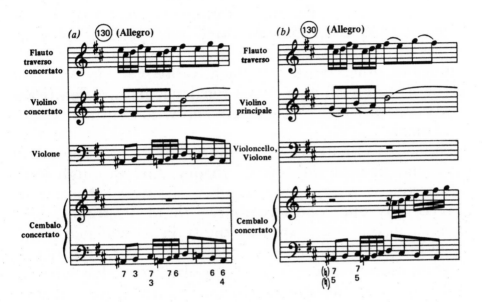

Significant though these changes are, the greatest discrepancy between the two versions of the 1st movement occurs in the cadenza. The draft cadenza is much shorter, being only 18 bars long (as opposed to 65). In the early version the cadenza opens rhapsodically, without reference to the principal solo theme. Its ending too is more conventional than that of the later version: there is no swerve to B minor—indeed, Bach clings to the notes A and D (dominant and tonic) despite the ancillary chromaticism.

The slow movements are virtually identical, except that less ornamentation is used in the early version and the rhythm here is more relaxed. (It is only in the later version that the dotted figure becomes so pervasive.) As for the Finale, the two versions correspond very closely, though the early one is four bars shorter than its successor.

The existence of early versions such as that discussed above is one argument against the theory that the Brandenburgs were composed as a cycle. Advocates of this theory[45] point to motivic similarities between certain concertos—e.g. the prominence of auxiliary-note patterns at the beginning of nos. 1, 3, and 6—and stress the fact that nos. 2, 4, and 5 all end with a fugue. Yet these arguments are fragile in the extreme. It is true that auxiliary-note patterns play an important role in concertos 1, 3, and 6, but so they do in a number of other works by Bach; moreover, the fact that nos. 2, 4, and 5 all have fugal Finales is hardly significant since many of Vivaldi's concertos end with a similar type of movement.

The sources themselves provide one of the most powerful arguments against the 'cyclic' theory, for, although individual concertos exist in a number of single manuscripts, there is only one collective source: the dedicatory score.[46] Then again one must consider the stylistic evidence which suggests very strongly that the works were written at different dates. Finally, it has been observed[47] that whereas Bach's series are usually scored for the same instrument or instruments throughout—compare the six solos for violin alone (BWV 1001–6) or the six sonatas for violin and cembalo concertato (BWV 1014–19)—the Brandenburg concertos are characterized by great variety of instrumentation.

It was once customary to pay tribute to the 'unique' instrumentation of the Brandenburgs and certainly there is a wealth of colour within the set as a whole. Yet the instrumentation of the separate concertos is, with one outstanding exception, not all that original. Similar combinations may be found in the concerti grossi of Telemann and Graupner; indeed, the colourful grouping of wind instruments within the concertino, far from being an

---

[45] The theory has recently been developed by R. Eller, 'Serie und Zyklus in Bachs Instrumentalsammlungen', *Bach-Interpretationen. Walter Blankenburg zum 65. Geburtstag* [Blankenburg Festschrift], ed. M. Geck (Göttingen, 1969), pp. 126–43.

[46] H. Besseler, *Sechs Brandenburgischen Konzerte*, p. 14. One source contains nos. 4 and 6; another, nos. 1, 2, 5, and 6, but the autograph score remains the only known source to contain all six works.

[47] Ibid. 22.

unusual feature, was a predominently German trait, stemming, perhaps, from the old Stadtpfeiffer traditions.
Although the choice of a solo violino piccolo for the first
concerto could be described as irregular, other instances of
its use are not unknown.[48] As for the enigmatic fiauti d'echo
of the fourth Brandenburg, Bach might have intended these
parts for the fashionable bird-flageolet, as Dart suggested,[49]
but it is far more likely that he was writing for the normal
flûtes-à-bec and that the exotic name derives from the echo
passages of the slow movement.[50]

Quite exceptional, on the other hand, was the use of a
harpsichord soloist in Brandenburg no. 5. Composed
around 1720, this work provides us with the first known
example of a new genre: the keyboard concerto.

Until the beginning of the eighteenth century the role of
the harpsichord in orchestral and chamber music had been
severely restricted. As a solo instrument, of course, it
possessed an extensive repertoire, but in ensemble music of
the early and middle baroque the clavier merely strengthened the bass line and filled out the harmony in accor-
dance with the figures. Bach was one of the first composers
to free the harpsichord from its conventional role. Three of
his sonatas for flute (BWV 1030–2) and several of those for
violin (BWV 1014–20, 1022) boast a concertante harpsichord part. These works are clearly duos, not solo sonatas,
for the two instruments are given the same type of material
and are treated as equal partners throughout. Significantly,
the sonatas with obbligato cembalo were written at about
the same time as the fifth Brandenburg concerto and it has
been suggested that the fine new harpsichord which Bach
purchased from Berlin in 1719 stimulated his activities in

---

[48] The Breitkopf thematic catalogue for 1762 lists a set of six concertos, and six
sonatas for the instrument (*The Breitkopf Thematic Catalogue: the Six Parts and Sixteen
Supplements 1762–1787*, ed. B. S. Brook (New York, 1966), p. 71). Bach himself
owned a violino piccolo though he made infrequent use of the instrument in his own
compositions (C. S. Terry, *Bach's Orchestra*, pp. 20, 126).

[49] T. Dart, 'Bach's "Fiauti d'Echo" ', 331–41.

[50] D. Higbee, 'Bach's "Fiauti d'Echo" ', *Music and Letters*, xliii (1962), 192–3.

this field.[51]

Technically, Brandenburg no. 5 is a concerto grosso with three soloists: flute, violin, and harpsichord. It is obvious, however, from Bach's treatment of the respective solo instruments that he was thinking in terms of the keyboard concerto. Not only is there a brilliant cadenza for harpsichord towards the end of the 1st movement, but throughout this Allegro and in the Finale too, the harpsichord emerges as the most prominent of the three soloists.

The technique of singling out one member of the concertino group for special treatment is not confined to the fifth concerto. In no. 4, for instance, the solo violin is the protagonist while the two fiauti d'echo are treated variously—usually as solo instruments in their own right, but sometimes as accompanists to the flamboyant violin line. Similarly with Brandenburg no. 2: trumpet tone completely dominates the outer movements of this concerto; it is only in the slow movement that the remaining members of the concertino (recorder, oboe, and violin) come to the fore. Examples such as these prompted Geiringer to observe that Bach often divided his orchestra into three, rather than two, main groups: the principal soloist, the rest of the concertino, and the rank and file.[52]

Significantly, the two orchestral concertos of the set (nos. 3 and 6) also show Bach's preoccupation with different grouping techniques. Here the strings are divided—not into tutti/solo groups—but according to their range. A concertante effect is then obtained by passing material from one group to another, as in the following passage:

EXAMPLE 10
Bach, Brandenburg concerto no. 3, 1st movement, bars 8–10 (full score)

---

[51] K. Geiringer, in collaboration with I. Geiringer, *Johann Sebastian Bach: the Culmination of an Era* (London, 1967), p. 320.
[52] Ibid. 319.

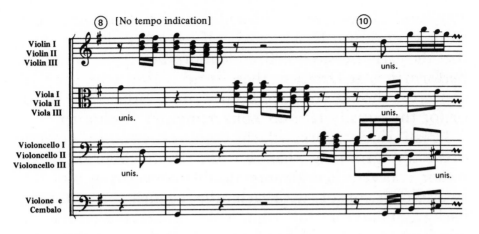

The Violin Concertos

It is generally accepted now that Bach's violin concertos—the double concerto in D minor (BWV 1043) and the
two concertos for solo violin and orchestra
(BWV 1041–2)[53]— originated during the Cöthen period.
Stylistically, the double concerto has affinities with the sixth
Brandenburg concerto and for this reason Besseler dated it
to the same year as the latter (*c.* 1718).[54] The two solo
concertos he dated around 1720 making them contemporary
with the fifth of the Brandenburg set.

These violin concertos were probably written for
Josephus Spiess and the Cöthen orchestra. This is the
simplest (and most likely) explanation. But other possibilities should not be discounted. It is conceivable, as C. S.
Terry remarked, that Bach intended the works for the
Dresden kapellmeister, Pisendel.[55] Certainly the two men
were acquainted for Pisendel had met Bach at Weimar in

---

[53] There is also a fragment of a 'concerto' in D major (BWV 1045) for solo violin,
oboes, trumpets, strings and timpani. This work, which is printed in vol. xxi of the
Bach-Gesellschaft edition, was probably intended as an instrumental introduction
(Sinfonia) to one of Bach's church cantatas (now presumed lost). The fragment is
preserved in Bach's hand and has the following heading: 'J. J. Concerto à 4 Voci, 3
Trombe, Tamburi, 2 Hautb, Violino conc: 2 Violini, Viola e Cont.'.

[54] H. Besseler, 'Zur Chronologie der Konzerte Joh. Seb. Bachs', p. 118.

[55] C. S. Terry, 'Bach's Dresden Appointment', *The Musical Times*, lxxiii (1932),
316.

1709 and Bach himself visited Dresden fairly frequently from 1717 onwards. Moreover, if we accept Krey's theory that the early version of Brandenburg no. 1 was revised for performance at Dresden, there is no reason why the violin concertos should not have been written either for Pisendel, or for the equally famous konzertmeister, Volumier.[56]

In all three works Bach employs a more orthodox orchestral grouping than for the Brandenburgs. The D minor concerto is a genuine double concerto in which the two soloists consort with each other against a rich orchestral background. As for the solo concertos, these are unashamedly Vivaldian. Here the rich counterpoint of Bach's concerto grosso writing gives way to a lyrical style of composition with emphasis on one melodic line. The solo episodes are far more dependent on sequential figuration than corresponding sections of the Brandenburg concertos, and the whole texture of the music is lighter.

4. The Leipzig Concertos

Although the Cöthen period proved the most creative for Bach in terms of the instrumental concerto, the years at Leipzig opened up new opportunities in one special field: the keyboard concerto. A list of the keyboard concertos composed by Bach during these years shows their immense variety: it includes seven concertos for solo clavier and orchestra (BWV 1052–8), the 'Italian' concerto for clavier alone (BWV 971), three concertos for two claviers and orchestra (BWV 1060–2), two concertos for three claviers and orchestra (BWV 1063–4), and a concerto for four claviers and orchestra—this last being an arrangement of Vivaldi's concerto for four violins, op. 3, no. 10. Traditionally also, the triple concerto in A minor for flute, violin, harpsichord, and strings (BWV 1044) is placed in the

---

[56] Terry (ibid.) does not consider the possibility that Bach's violin concertos were written for Volumier since he dated the works after 1733 and Volumier died in 1728. However, if we accept a date of 1718 or earlier for the violin concertos, then Volumier's name must come under consideration too.

Leipzig period, though there is some controversy over its date.[57]

In fact the dating of all these keyboard concertos poses problems. Schmieder[58] placed them within a relatively narrow band—1730–6—but the autograph score of the seven solo concertos is now thought to stem from the period 1735–44[59] so that the end-date is obviously fairly elastic. Indeed, it seems reasonable to suppose that the concertos are contemporaneous with Bach's directorship of the Leipzig Collegium Musicum. Bach had succeeded G. B. Schott as director of this student music society in 1729 and continued in this capacity, with one or two intermissions, until 1741 or even later.[60] There is little doubt that the concertos were first performed at the weekly concerts of the society. We may assume also that Bach was assisted by other members of his family. According to Forkel, who derived much of his information from C. P. E. Bach, the 'proficiency of his elder sons and pupils, and his wife's talent as a singer, were a further source of strength to the Society, whose direction undoubtedly made these years the happiest in Bach's life'.[61] Although Wilhelm Friedemann moved to Dresden in 1733 and Emanuel left Leipzig for Frankfurt-on-the-Oder in 1735, they would surely have participated in the Collegium concerts during the early years of Bach's directorship: the tradition that Bach wrote the concertos for three harpsichords to play with his eldest sons supports this view.[62]

In these Leipzig concertos Bach relies to a considerable extent on material from his own earlier works. Some of the concertos are arranged from cantata movements; others are

---

[57] H. Eppstein ('Zur Vor-und Entstehungsgeschichte von J. S. Bachs Tripelkonzert a moll (BWV 1044)', *Jahrbuch Staatlichen Institut Musikforschung*, 1970 (1971), 34–44) believes that the work was probably written at Cöthen *c.* 1720. For further details see p. 36.

[58] W. Schmieder, op. cit.

[59] W. Fischer, 'Wiedergewonnene Solokonzerte Johann Sebastian Bachs: Bemerkungen zum Supplement der Neuen Bach-Ausgabe', *Musica*, xxv/2 (1972), 133.

[60] W. Neumann, 'Das „Bachische Collegium Musicum" ', *Bach-Jahrbuch*, xlvii (1960), 5–27.

[61] J. N. Forkel, op. cit., p. 42.

[62] P. Spitta, op. cit. iii. 144.

transcriptions of his violin concertos. As will be seen from Table 2, the relationship between arrangement and model is often rather complex and it is sometimes difficult to establish the priority of the different versions. Nevertheless, some

Table 2. Bach's clavier concertos

BWV no.	Key	Other versions of the same material	Additional information
Seven concertos for clavier and orchestra, BWV 1052–8 (*Bach-Gesellschaft xvii.* 3–220 and 314–15) Written *c.* 1730–3 (Schmieder); [1730–6 (Besseler)][1]			
1052 and 1052a[2]	D minor	Allegro = Introduction to Cantata no. 188, 'Ich habe meine Zuversicht', *c.* 1728; Allegro and Adagio = Introduction and first chorus (no. 2) of Cantata no. 146, 'Wir müssen durch viel Trübsal', *c.* 1740 (Spitta)	Probably preserves a lost violin concerto in the same key, *c.* 1720; reconstructed as such by R. Reitz (see Schmieder, p. 590) and, more recently, by W. Fischer in vol. vii/2 (Supplement) of the *Neue Bach-Ausgabe* (Kassel, 1970). Bach's authorship has been disputed[3]
1053	E	1st movement and Siciliano[4] = Sinfonia and alto aria (no. 5) of Cantata no. 169, 'Gott soll allein mein Herze haben', *c.* 1726; 3rd movement = Sinfonia to Cantata no. 49, 'Ich geh' und suche mit Verlangen', *c.* 1726	May possibly preserve a lost violin concerto in D or an oboe concerto,[5] although both Spitta (iii. 137) and Schweitzer (*J. S. Bach*, i. 411 note) think that it was originally conceived for the clavier. *Not* reconstructed by Fischer
1054	D[6]	Arranged from Bach's violin concerto in E major, BWV 1042, dated *c.* 1720[7]	
1055[8]	A		May preserve a lost violin concerto[9] or a concerto for oboe d'amore.[10] Fischer's reconstruction for oboe d'amore in

			NBA vii/2 (Supplement) has been challenged by W. Mohr who believes the original to be for a string instrument— probably viola.[11] Spitta (iii. 137–8) implies that the clavier version is the original
1056	F minor	Largo = Sinfonia to Cantata no. 156, 'Ich steh' mit einem Fuss im Grabe', *c.* 1729	Probably preserves a lost violin concerto in G minor, *c.* 1719; reconstructed as such by G. Schreck (see Schmieder, p. 590) and, more recently, by W. Fischer in *NBA* vii/2 (Supplement)
1057	F	Arranged from Bach's Brandenburg no. 4, BWV 1049, *c.* 1719	
1058	G minor	Arranged from Bach's violin concerto in A minor, BWV 1041, *c.* 1720	

Fragment (first nine bars) of a concerto for clavier and orchestra, BWV 1059 (*Bach-Gesellschaft xvii*, Foreword, p. xx)
Written *c.* 1730 (Schmieder)

1059	D minor	= part of the Sinfonia to Cantata no. 35, 'Geist und Seele wird verwirret', *c.* 1726	May preserve a lost violin concerto in D minor, *c.* 1719[12]

The 'Italian' concerto for solo keyboard, BWV 971 (*Bach-Gesellschaft iii.* 139–53)
Written 1734, published Nuremberg 1735, in part II of the *Clavier-Übung*[13]

971	F		The opening theme of the 1st movement is borrowed from the finale of a 'Symphonie' in Muffat's *Florilegium Primum* of 1695[14]

Concerto for flute, violin, harpsichord, and strings, BWV 1044
(*Bach-Gesellschaft xvii.* 223–72)
Written after 1730 (Schmieder) but see Additional Information column

1044	A minor	1st and 3rd movements are a lengthier version of the Prelude and Fugue in A Minor for solo clavier, BWV 894, *c.* 1717; Adagio = 2nd movement of the third of six sonatas for organ, BWV 527, after 1727 or possibly, after 1723[15]	The traditional view is that the concerto was developed from these works. However, in a recent article by Hans Eppstein, it is suggested that the Prelude and Fugue was itself based on a lost keyboard concerto and that the organ sonata BWV 527 may also be an arrangement of an earlier instrumental trio—now lost. Eppstein believes that stylistic elements in the A minor concerto point to a composition date around that of Brandenburg no. 5 (*c.* 1720)[16]

Concertos for two claviers and orchestra, BWV 1060–2 (*Bach-Gesellschaft xxi*[2]. 3–118)

1060	C minor		May preserve a lost concerto for two violins[17] or a concerto for violin and oboe;[18] reconstructed as a concerto for violin and oboe in C minor by W. Fischer in *NBA* vii/2 (Supplement)
Written *c.* 1730 (Schmieder)			
1061	C		Probably written originally for the keyboard (see A. Schweitzer, *J. S. Bach*, i. 413)
Written between 1727 and 1730 (Schmieder)			
1062	C minor	Arranged from Bach's concerto for two violins in D minor, BWV 1043, *c.* 1720 (Schmieder); [*c.* 1718 (Besseler)]	
Written 1736 (Schmieder)			

Concertos for three claviers and orchestra, BWV 1063–4 (*Neue Bach-Ausgabe vii/6*. 3–114; also *Bach-Gesellschaft xxxi*[3]. 3–102)
Written between 1730 and 1733 (Schmieder)

1063	D minor	May preserve a lost concerto for flute, violin, and oboe; *not* reconstructed by Fischer. Bach's authorship of the original has been disputed[19]
1064	C[20]	May preserve a lost concerto for three violins; reconstructed as such (in D major) by W. Fischer, *NBA vii/2* (Supplement). Bach's authorship of the original has been questioned.[21]

Concerto for four claviers and orchestra, BWV 1065 (*Neue Bach-Ausgabe vii/6*. 117–75; also *Bach-Gesellschaft xliii*. 71–98)
Written between 1730 and 1733 (Schmieder)

1065	A minor	Arranged from Vivaldi's concerto in B minor for four violins and orchestra, op. 3, no. 10, RV 580

---

[1] Dates of the concerto originals are from Schmieder (op. cit.) while dates in square brackets are those suggested by H. Besseler ('Zur Chronologie der Konzerte Joh. Seb. Bachs', pp. 115–28). Unless otherwise stated, cantata dates are those given by A. Dürr, 'Zur Chronologie der Leipziger Vokalwerke J. S. Bachs', *Bach-Jahrbuch*, xliv (1957), 5–162.

[2] BWV 1052a, an earlier version of BWV 1052, is printed in the *Bach-Gesellschaft*, xvii. 275–313.

[3] It has been suggested (1) that the original concerto was by a member of Vivaldi's school (P. Hirsch, 'Uber die Vorlage zum Klavierkonzert in d=moll', *Bach-Jahrbuch*, xxvi (1929), 153–74 and 'Nachtrag zu dem Beitrag "Über die Vorlage zum Klavierkonzert in d=moll', *Bach-Jahrbuch*, xxvii (1930), 143–4), and (2) that Emanuel Bach was responsible for the arrangement (A. Aber, 'Studien zu J. S. Bachs Klavierkonzerten', *Bach-Jahrbuch*, x (1913), 5–30).

[4] The clavier part of the Siciliano also exists in an earlier, slightly simpler version, cf. *Bach-Gesellschaft*, xvii. 314–15.

[5] See K. Geiringer, op. cit., p. 171 note 3.

[6] Presumably these clavier arrangements were transposed downwards for the same reason as the Weimar transcriptions: to bring the highest notes of the violin part within range for the keyboard.

[7] Fragments of an earlier arrangement of the E major violin concerto are printed in the *Bach-Gesellschaft*, xvii. 316–17.

[8] An earlier version of the Larghetto's clavier part is printed in the *Bach-Gesellschaft*, xvii. 318–19.

[9] See A. Schweitzer, *J. S. Bach*, tr. E. Newman, 2 vols. (London, 1911), i. 411 note; also F. Spiro, 'Ein verlorenes Werk Johann Sebastian Bach's', *Zeitschrift der Internationalen Musik-Gesellschaft*, vi (1904), 100–4.

[10] D. F. Tovey, *Essays in Musical Analysis* (London, 1936, first published 1935), ii. 196–8.

[11] W. Mohr, 'Hat Bach ein Oboe-d'amore-Konzert geschrieben?', *Neue Zeitschrift für Musik*, cxxxiii (1972), 507–8. His argument turns on the spiccato arpeggios of the opening which could not be played on the oboe d'amore and which Tovey suggested had been written specially for the clavier version. Mohr maintains that the arpeggios are an integral part of the theme and that without them the opening bars would be devoid of character. He suggests that the original version was for a string instrument—probably viola since the range is too low for the violin.

[12] This work was restored to the violin by Frotscher and published in Halle, 1951. The editor derived the concerto's three movements from nos. 1, 2, and 5 of the cantata.

[13] For details of the first edition see G. Kinsky, *Die Originalausgaben der Werke Johann Sebastian Bachs* (Vienna, 1937), pp. 29ff.

[14] A. Schering, 'Zur Bach-Forschung', 243.

[15] For a comparison of this concerto with the original material see H. Boettcher, 'Bach's Kunst der Bearbeitung, dargestellt am Triple-konzert a-moll', *Von deutscher Tonkunst. Festschrift zu Peter Raabes 70. Geburtstag* (Leipzig, 1942, pp. 95–113).

[16] H. Eppstein, op. cit. 33–44.

[17] See A. Schweitzer, op. cit. i. 415–6 note.

[18] W. Voigt, 'Über die Originalgestalt von J. S. Bach's Konzert für zwei Klaviere in C moll (Nr. 1)', *Vierteljahrsschrift für Musikwissenschaft*, ii (1886), 482–7.

[19] W. Schmieder, op. cit., p. 593.

[20] A number of early copies of the concerto are in D, as is the incipit given by Breitkopf (*The Breitkopf Thematic Catalogue: the Six Parts and Sixteen Supplements 1762–1787*, ed. B. S. Brook (New York, 1966), p. 553); Spitta (op. cit. iii. 147 note) presented a strong case for D being the original key of the clavier version, but the concerto was printed in C in the *Bach-Gesellschaft* edition and has thus become known in the lower key.

[21] Schmieder, op. cit., p. 593.

attempt to pull together existing information is necessary here.[63]

In those works which are based on existing concertos (i.e. BWV 1054, 1057, 1058, 1062, and 1065) it is possible to

[63] An earlier summary may be found in N. Carrell, *Bach the Borrower* (London, 1967), but information concerning the concertos is scattered throughout the book; moreover, since 1967 there have been considerable developments in this field, including the publication of vol. vii/2 (Supplement) of the *Neue Bach-Ausgabe* which offers 'reconstructions' for five of the concertos.

study further Bach's art of transcription. He still relies on methods evolved at Weimar in that the solo part is given to the right hand of the clavier player and the basso continuo line placed on the lower stave, but at the same time hints of a more advanced keyboard style appear. In the following passage, for instance, the left hand is given an ornamental version of the basso continuo line which complements, rhythmically, the brilliant semiquavers of the top part:[64]

EXAMPLE 11

Bach, clavier concerto no. 7 in G minor (BWV 1058), 1st movement, bars 89–96 (clavier and basso continuo part)

[64] See H. Hering, 'Bachs Klavierübertragungen', Bach-Jahrbuch, xlv (1958), 94–113. A similar development in keyboard style may be observed in the two versions of the D minor clavier concerto. In the early version (BWV 1052a) the left hand of the clavier is treated as a continuo part, often having a succession of repeated notes; in corresponding passages from the later version (BWV 1052), however, it is given soloistic figuration to match that of the right hand (compare 1st movement, bars 7–11, printed in the Bach-Gesellschaft, xvii. 275 and 3).

Occasionally, too, the clavier part affords some insight into Bach's ornamentation technique. If the violin part of the fourth Brandenburg concerto is compared with the upper stave of the clavier part in BWV 1057 it will be noticed that Bach has added one or two ornaments of the type which might have occurred spontaneously during performance:

EXAMPLE 12

Bach, (a) Brandenburg concerto no. 4, 1st movement, bars 92–4 (solo violin part only); (b) clavier concerto no. 6 in F major (BWV 1057), 1st movement, bars 92–4 (clavier part only)

It was the existence of these clavier arrangements which first led scholars to suspect that many of the remaining clavier concertos were transcriptions of earlier works which have, presumably, disappeared. W. Rust, who edited the solo clavier concertos for volume xvii of the *Bach-Gesellschaft* edition, paid much attention to the presence of violinistic idioms in the keyboard parts; passages of bariolage in the solo harpsichord part of the D minor concerto, for example, convinced him that the original was for violin (see Rust's Preface, pp. xiv, xv). This type of evidence is not in itself conclusive, for the transference of idioms from one medium to another was an important part of Bach's compositional technique. But there are other factors which point in the same direction. All seven clavier concertos (together with a fragment of an eighth and the beginnings of a ninth) survive in the same autograph source, the handwriting of which seems to indicate that the concertos were transcribed at roughly the same time. It seems reasonable, therefore, to assume that all the works in the collection are transcriptions. Further evidence comes from the nature of the score itself. As Fischer observes,[65] traces of reworkings are found in the shape of various deletions, insertions, and variants. Of particular interest are the numerous crossings-out in the left hand of the cembalo which suggest that Bach was working from a pre-existing continuo part. Moreover, the whole lay-out of the score is significant: the bar lines were obviously ruled first (at fixed distances), then the ripieno parts were fitted in; finally Bach added the solo keyboard part but since this was rather ornate the notes sometimes spilled over to the right of the existing bar lines.

As indicated earlier, there have been several attempts to 'reconstruct' the lost models on which Bach's clavier concertos are thought to be based. Initially, however, this was not done on a scientific basis. It was only after Siegele's exhaustive study of Bach's transcription techniques[66] that Fischer was able to make a scientific reconstruction by applying Bach's methods in reverse.

Not only has there been speculation concerning the 'original' versions of some of these clavier concertos, Bach's authorship of certain works has also been disputed. The works in question are the concerto for clavier and orchestra in D minor (BWV 1052) and the two concertos for three harpsichords (BWV 1063 and 1064). In none of these cases, however, have decisive arguments been formulated to discredit their attribution to Bach. The superb D minor concerto is so utterly consistent with Bach's stylistic and formal procedures—see, for example, the characteristic pedal point of the 1st movement (bars 148–68), the cantilena slow movement with its quasi-ostinato bass, and the

---

[65] W. Fischer, *Verschollene Solokonzerte in Rekonstruktion: Kritischer Bericht*, Neue Bach-Ausgabe, vii/7 (Supplement) (Kassel, 1971); also, id., 'Wiedergewonnene Solokonzerte Johann Sebastian Bachs', 133–4.

[66] Ulrich Siegele, *Kompositionsweise und Bearbeitungstechnik in der Instrumentalmusik Joh. Seb. Bachs* (Dissertation, Tübinger, 1957).

anapaestic rhythms of the Finale (especially, bars
13 ff.)—that it is difficult to understand why some scholars
attribute it to a member of the Vivaldi school. As for the
concertos for three harpsichords, Schmieder may be correct
in his belief that the original versions were not by Bach at
all, but a close study of these works reveals little that is alien
to Bach and much that is typical. The formal scheme of
BWV 1063 is thoroughly characteristic—indeed the plan of
the 1st movement's final section is virtually identical with
the 3rd movement of the A major concerto (BWV 1055).[67]
Nor is there any pressing reason to doubt Bach's authorship
of this particular concerto on stylistic grounds. Although
the ritornello of the 1st movement has a slightly unfamiliar
ring, the whole movement is similar in spirit to the first
Allegro of Brandenburg no. 4; moreover, the extended
pedal point (bars 233–44) is a prominent feature of many
concertos by Bach. The C major triple concerto (BWV
1064) has one or two doubtful elements,[68] though Bach's
authorship may be supported by the style of the fugal
Finale—particularly by the presence of a striking rhythmic
figure found also (in slightly altered form) in the 1st
movement of the fourth Brandenburg concerto—compare
BWV 1064, 3rd movement, bars 97–8 (cembalos II and III)
with Brandenburg no. 4, 1st movement, bars 79–83.

Before leaving the clavier concertos two further points
must be mentioned, both of which concern the balance
between solo and ripieno instruments. When writing for
more than one harpsichord Bach tended to allow the soloists
to dominate the whole ensemble. This predominance of
harpsichord tone is especially noticeable in the C major
concerto for two claviers and orchestra, BWV 1061. In the
1st movement the soloists are completely dominant, there
being no genuine tutti ritornello at all. In the following slow
movement the two claviers are entirely unsupported and in
the fugal Finale the ripieno instruments do little more than

---

[67] See pp. 64–5.
[68] E.g. the particular variation form of the Siciliano (A A′ B B′) which does not
occur in any other concerto movement by Bach.

double the solo parts. Exceptional though this particular concerto is,[69] the same tendency may be observed in the two concertos for three claviers and (understandably) in the concerto for four claviers based on Vivaldi's op. 3, no. 10.

The second point concerns the role of the clavier in the opening tutti. Normally the keyboard soloist would have realized the figured bass line extempore or else played in unison with the tutti instruments. However, Bach occasionally gives the harpsichord an unusual measure of independence by permitting it to ornament, rather than duplicate tutti material:

EXAMPLE 13

Bach, clavier concerto in A major, BWV 1055, 1st movement, bars 1–2[70]

[69] It is thought that the string parts may not be by Bach at all for only the clavier parts are autograph. Forkel remarked that the concerto 'may be played without the String quartet and still sounds admirable' (J. N. Forkel, op. cit., p. 131). If the work were originally conceived for two harpsichords alone it would find a parallel in W. F. Bach's *Concerto à due cembali concertati* in F major.

[70] Compare also the opening of the 3rd movement of Bach's E major clavier concerto, BWV 1053.

In this example the ornamental harpsichord part is, to be sure, little more than a written-out realization of the figured bass, but the fact that Bach notated it explicitly is, in itself, significant.

5 · The Concertos: General Structure; Movement Types

It is obvious that Bach's intimate acquaintance with the Venetian concerto (as evidenced by the Weimar transcriptions) conditioned his whole approach to the form. Indeed, his adherence to the principles of the new solo concerto was, in some respects, more rigid than that of the Italians themselves. In his concertos the three-movement Sinfonia plan (fast–slow–fast) is completely dominant: the 'da chiesa' arrangement (slow–fast–slow–fast) does not occur and the 'da camera' form, with its succession of stylized dance movements, is extremely rare. (It is only in the first Brandenburg concerto that dance movements play a significant part and, as we have seen, there were probably special reasons for this.)[71] There is, moreover, a firm commitment to ritornello principles and a tendency to organize the form in a more methodical way than Vivaldi. As for the arrangement of movements, this bears a close relationship to the Venetian concerto: the opening movement is usually a concerto-style Allegro with strong rhythms and great vitality; the central movement, slow and intimate, frequently written in a chamber music idiom; the Finale, a lighthearted movement in which dance rhythms are often prominent. There is, however, a slight change in the relative importance of the movements. By about 1720 the proportions of the concerto had become standardized and it was generally accepted that the 1st movement was the weightiest of the three—both in length and content. Quantz, writing in or before 1752, assumed as a matter of course that the 1st movement of a concerto would be conceived on a

---

[71] Cf. p. 23.

broader and more majestic scale than the Finale,[72] and this is reflected in many contemporary works. Bach, however, seems to have attached more importance to the last two movements of his concertos than was customary. His first movements remained dominant but were balanced by weightier Finales (three of the Brandenburg concertos, it will be recalled, have fugal Finales of substantial proportions and there are similar examples in the clavier concertos); moreover, since Bach seldom if ever[73] reduced the slow movement to the status of a link passage, he struck a more equable balance between the three movements of the concerto than many of his contemporaries.

Movement Types

The majority of Bach's opening movements are written in the taut and exciting concerto style that was so often associated with fast ritornello movements. The preferred time signature is $\frac{4}{4}$, though exceptions do occur—notably in the fourth Brandenburg concerto whose 1st movement proceeds in a lilting triple metre. This particular movement is unusual in that it is written in dance, rather than concerto, style. More typical is the 1st movement of the second Brandenburg concerto which opens with the following ritornello:

EXAMPLE 14

Bach, Brandenburg concerto no. 2, 1st movement, bars 1–8 (first violin and basso continuo parts only).

[No tempo indication]

Violino I in ripieno

Violoncello e Cembalo all' unisono

[72] Compare his instructions for first and last movements in J. J. Quantz, *On Playing the Flute*, tr. E. Reilly (London, 1966), pp. 311–15.

[73] The chords which separate the 1st and 3rd movements of Brandenburg no. 3 might constitute such a link (see M. Geck, op cit. 144–5) but it is far more likely that they form the final cadence of an extempore movement which would have been inserted during performance.

This passage embraces all the most important features of concerto style: the steadily-moving, non-thematic bass; the energetic treble line with its rapid movement—often at double the pace of the lower part (i.e. semiquavers against quavers); the repetition within the melody (as in bars 1–2, 3–4, 5–6) which serves to increase momentum; the aggressive, mechanical rhythms and the breathless onrush to the main cadence point (at bar 8).

The central movements provide a sharp contrast to their neighbours in tempo, key, and style. The preferred key here is either the relative or the subdominant. Occasionally a slow movement will begin in one key and end in another[74] as in certain of Corelli's concertos, but this is exceptional. A particularly interesting feature of Bach's slow movements is that the majority fall into one of three categories according to their style of composition, and that the three categories themselves—trio sonata, Siciliano, and cantilena—seem to be associated in Bach's mind with the concerto grosso, clavier concerto, and violin concerto respectively.

The slow movement in trio sonata style figures in many of the concerti grossi (e.g. Brandenburg nos. 2, 5, 6 and the

[74] E.g. the slow movement of the sixth Brandenburg concerto which begins in Eb and ends in G minor; cf. also the slow movement of the C minor concerto for two claviers and orchestra (BWV 1060) where exactly the same scheme is used, though the final chord is major.

double violin concerto). In the Brandenburg set Bach
normally reduces his instrumental forces for the slow
movement,[75] sometimes leaving the solo instruments to
consort alone. It is natural that in these circumstances he
should turn to a chamber music style:

EXAMPLE 15
Bach, Brandenburg concerto no. 5, 2nd movement, bars 1–8

[75] This applies to all the slow movements of the set with the exception of no. 4
which is written in the Corellian manner: the concertino is treated as a unified group
and simply repeats tutti material at a lower dynamic level. (In this connection there is
evidence that Vivaldi sometimes used actual chamber music pieces as slow movements in some of his concertos, cf. M. Talbot, 'Some overlooked MSS in
Manchester', *The Musical Times*, cxv (1974), 944.)

Like Bach's trio sonatas, these slow movements exhibit a remarkable economy of material. The Affettuoso from the fifth Brandenburg concerto (see Ex. 15) is built up almost entirely from two motifs, the first of which (*a*) is presented by the solo violin in the opening bar, and the second (*b*) by the clavier in bar 7. Thereafter hardly a bar passes without reference to one of these motifs, either in original or inverted form.

If the trio sonata is associated with the concerto grosso, the Siciliano has equally strong links with the clavier concerto. Examples of this type of movement occur in BWV 1053, 1055, and 1063. In each case the simple lines of the traditional dance movement are heavily overlaid with ornamentation. Indeed, such is the sophistication and intricacy of the decoration that the pastoral qualities of the original almost disappear:

EXAMPLE 16

Bach, clavier concerto in E major, BWV 1053, 2nd movement, bars 7–10 (clavier part only)

The movements in cantilena style belong primarily to the violin concertos,[76] though additional examples occur in the 'Italian' concerto (BWV 971), and in BWV 1052—itself probably a revision of a lost violin concerto. In the slow movements of the E major and A minor violin concertos (which are among the loveliest that Bach ever wrote) the soloist has an expressive, ornate melody over a quasi-ostinato bass. The bass line is firmly anchored to one note—G sharp in the following passage—from which it continually strains away and to which it constantly returns:[77]

EXAMPLE 17

Bach, violin concerto in E major, BWV 1042, 2nd movement, bars 1–11 (full score)

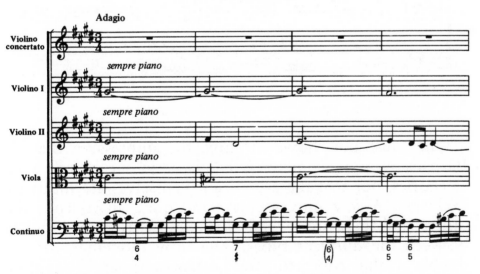

[76] And to Bach's violin music in general: compare the 'adagio ma non tanto' of the E major violin sonata, BWV 1016.

[77] Cf. also the bass part of BWV 1041, 2nd movement, bars 1–4 where the 'pedal' note is C.

One must not, however, give the impression that all
Bach's slow movements may be placed in one of the above
categories, nor that the categories themselves are mutually
exclusive. A few movements stand quite apart from the
others, and there are several examples of cross-fertilization
between the different types. The slow movement of the
double violin concerto, for instance, is in $\frac{12}{8}$—a time
signature often associated with the Siciliano—yet it is
written in trio sonata style; the slow movement of the fifth
clavier concerto (BWV 1056) is obviously a cantilena but

lacks the characteristic ostinato bass,[78] while the central movement of the fourth clavier concerto (BWV 1055) draws elements from both the Siciliano and cantilena categories.

For the Finale Bach employs three principal movement-types: the 'ritornello allegro' (see the Finale of BWV 1060 which is more like a first, than final, movement); the Venetian Finale with its lilting $\frac{3}{8}$ metre and periodic phrase structure (as in the last movement of the F minor clavier concerto); and the concerto fugue in which a fugal exposition replaces the opening ritornello section (as in the Finale of the A minor violin concerto). It will be noticed that although dance rhythms are prominent in some last movements, the genuine dance Finale (e.g. binary minuet or gigue) is extremely rare. The only real example occurs in Brandenburg no. 1, both versions of which end with a self-styled minuet; another instance of a binary (but untitled) Finale occurs in the third concerto of the same set.

By comparison with a composer such as Handel, Bach did not employ a particularly wide range of movement-types in his concertos. However, it goes without saying that the fertility of his musical invention offsets any lack of variety in this respect. To take one example: the fugal Finale was a type much favoured by Bach, yet this one category embraces a number of strikingly individual movements. The vivacious concerto-style Finale of Brandenburg no. 2, for example, bears little resemblance either to the austere fugal writing of the 3rd movement of BWV 1064, or to the gigue-like Finale of the fifth Brandenburg; each movement is totally different in mood and in its arrangement of material.[79] And a similar diversity marks almost all the

[78] The rhythm ♪♫ is, however, consistently employed in the bass part and may be regarded as a substitute ostinato.

[79] This brings to mind Forkel's assessment of Bach's fugues: '. . . each is endowed with peculiar excellencies of its own, has its own distinctive individuality, and displays a melodic and harmonic scheme in keeping with it. The man who can play one of Bach's Fugues is familiar with, and can play, one only; whereas knowing one, we can perform portfolios of Fugues by other composers of Bach's period' (J. N. Forkel, op cit., p. 87).

categories discussed above.

6. Ritornello Structures

The importance of ritornello form to Bach's concertos cannot be overestimated. It is a pre-requisite of the 1st movement and an important unifying device in many Finales too. Even where other formal methods (e.g. fugue, 'da capo' structure) are used, Bach seems reluctant to abandon ritornello principles. Moreover, although his central movements are seldom cast in full ritornello form, there are several examples of the 'framed' slow movement in which an extended solo section is enclosed by two tutti statements of the ritornello (see the slow movements of BWV 1042, 1052, 1053, and 1055).

The history of ritornello form can be traced back to the instrumental ritornellos of seventeenth-century Italian opera. The first composers to transfer this essentially operatic device to the concerto were, of course, the Venetians and, although there is a considerable difference in organization between the concertos of, say, Vivaldi and Albinoni, certain basic principles emerge in their ritornello movements which enable us to generalize about the form. Normally a Venetian ritornello movement has at least four statements of the ritornello, these tutti sections being separated from each other by episodes for the soloist or solo group (concertino) which are lighter and more brilliant in style. Although entries of the tutti are seldom confined to the presentation of the ritornello statements, the structure depends heavily on the opposition between ritornello (tutti) and solo sections. In its simplest form, therefore, the ground plan of a typical ritornello movement (in major mode) may be represented as follows:

Ritornello 1	tutti	tonic
Solo 1	solo	tonic, moving to dominant
Ritornello 2	tutti	dominant
Solo 2	solo	modulatory
Ritornello 3	tutti	various related keys, e.g. the relative or, very occasionally, the tonic

| Solo 3 | solo | various related keys, moving back to (or remaining in) the tonic |
| Ritornello 4 | tutti | tonic |

This, then, was the type of ritornello scheme which Bach inherited.

Although the scheme as represented above looks rather inflexible, in practice it admitted a great deal of variety. Vivaldi, for example, frequently developed the initial material in subsequent tutti sections so that the second and third ritornellos might differ considerably from the first. Bach's approach was more methodical in that he tended to concentrate on the ritornello motifs themselves rather than evolve new material from them. In his Allegro movements tutti interruptions are numerous and sometimes give the (usually misleading) impression that he is working within a six- or seven-ritornello framework.

The broadest definition of a ritornello is a passage which recurs at various points during a movement or complex of movements. In a concerto, the ritornello is that recurring tutti passage with which the movement begins and which lasts until the beginning of the first solo episode[80] (e.g. bars 1–8 of the 1st movement of Brandenburg no. 2). While there is no problem in identifying the first and last statements of the ritornello, the number and exact position of the middle statements is not always so sharply defined. This is especially true of Bach's concertos where one has to distinguish between structurally important ritornello statements and passing references to the opening tutti material. To take a specific example: in the 1st movement of the C minor concerto for two harpsichords and orchestra (BWV 1060) there are a number of references to the opening tutti material, yet only four of these are substantial enough to be called ritornello statements (ritornello 1 = bars 1–8, C minor; 2 = 43–50, G minor; 3 = 89–96, C minor; 4 = 103–10, C minor). The remainder (e.g. at bars 13–14,

---

[80] This definition is applicable to the orchestral concertos (e.g. Brandenburg nos. 3 and 6) in so far as it is possible to identify their 'tutti' and 'solo' sections from the texture used.

16–17, 19–20, 23–6, 33–6, 53–4, 61–4, 71–4, 99–102) must be
regarded as tutti interruptions since they do not affect, in
any radical sense, the structural design of the whole.

Bach normally worked within a four-ritornello
framework, though movements with three or five statements are also to be found.[81] The key structure follows that
of the Venetian concerto with first and last ritornellos in the
tonic and the second ritornello usually in the dominant key.
In a movement with four ritornellos the penultimate statement could theoretically be presented in any related key
though in practice Bach preferred the relative or, sometimes, the tonic. Curiously, in his five-ritornello movements Bach tended to avoid the dominant key for his second
ritornello statement,[82] concentrating instead on a closely-
related minor key or on the subdominant area. Typical in
this respect are the following movements:

Brandenburg no. 4, 1st movement			Brandenburg no. 6, 1st movement		
Bar	Key	Ritornello	Bar	Key	Ritornello
1–83	G	1	1–17	B♭	1
137–57	E minor	2	46–52	C minor	2
209–35	C	3	73–80	G minor	3
323–44	B minor	4	86–91	E♭	4
345–427	G	5	114–30	B♭	5

Internal Organization of the Ritornello

Up to this point the ritornello has been treated as a unit, but
its own internal structure is not without interest. The
opening ritornello is usually composed of at least three
sections, the most important being those at the beginning
and end: the head and tail. The head-motif must be particularly striking, of course, for it stamps character and indi-

[81] Cf. the 1st movement of the A minor violin concerto (BWV 1041) and the 1st
movement of Brandenburg no. 4 respectively.

[82] That this is only a tendency is shown by the gound plan of BWV 1052, 1st
movement, where the five ritornello statements are in the following keys: (1) bars
1–7, D minor; (2) bars 13–22, D minor/A minor; (3) bars 56–62, A minor; (4) bars
104–9, G minor; (5) bars 184–90, D minor.

viduality on the whole movement. It is also the motif most frequently associated with tutti interruptions to solo episodes. The tail-motif is slightly less important but must always be strongly cadential since it is with these bars that the movement ends. Example 18 shows the clearly defined head (*a*) and tail (*c*) sections within the ritornello of BWV 1060, 1st movement:

EXAMPLE 18
Bach, concerto for two claviers and orchestra, BWV 1060, 1st movement, bars 1–8 (first violin part only)

Although Bach's ritornelli may be divided into a number of sections the texture and style of the writing tends to remain constant throughout. There are few changes of dynamic, except where a direct echo effect is intended as in BWV 1056, 1st movement, bars 4, 8, and virtually no strong contrasts of material. In some cases Bach deliberately smooths over the divisions in a ritornello, relating the sections by means of common rhythmic formulas. This happens in the 1st movement of Brandenburg no. 3 where the anapaestic rhythms of the head–motif are subsequently used to accompany the unbroken semiquavers of the *Fortspinnung* section (second half of bar 2):

EXAMPLE 19

Bach, Brandenburg concerto no. 3, 1st movement, bars 1–3 (outer parts only)

Subsequent Statements of the Ritornello

Subsequent ritornello statements differ a great deal as to how faithfully they reproduce the material of the opening. Staying with Brandenburg no. 3, 1st movement, we find that both the second and final ritornello statements (bars 38f., 125f.) follow the first very closely (though the last ritornello is extended slightly to include three bars (132–5) of 'solo' writing). In other movements, however—particularly those with a longer-than-average opening tutti—the middle statements of the ritornello may be severely curtailed. The first Allegro of Brandenburg no. 4 provides a case in point. Here the opening ritornello is conceived on a broad scale (lasting 83 bars in all) and drastic cuts are made in the middle statements as the following analysis reveals:

Bach, Brandenburg concerto no. 4, 1st movement: internal organization of ritornello statements

Bar	Section	Material	Comments
1	Ritornello 1 basically in G major	A	
13		B	
23		A	
35		C	Combines with a 'falling thirds'
47		B	figure from B
57		A	
68		D	Uses transformed elements from A (i.e. ♩ ♫♪ of bar 4 becomes

♫♩♫ of bars 69f.) and the 'falling thirds' figure from B; the cadence bars are new

137	Ritornello 2 basically in E minor	A	Greatly curtailed
142		D	
209	Ritornello 3 basically in C major	A	Altered to include a suspended figure not unlike that appearing in section D
227		D	Last part only
323	Ritornello 4 basically in B minor	A	Curtailed and altered slightly
329		D	
345	Ritornello 5 basically in G major	A	As ritornello 1
357		B	
367		A	
379		C	
391		B	
401		A	
412		D	

Only at the end of the movement, therefore, is the opening ritornello repeated in full.

Exceptional Usages

In the foregoing movement each of the five ritornello statements ends in the same key as it began, so that, in spite of transient modulations, the first ritornello can be described as 'in G major', the fourth, 'in B minor' etc. On rare occasions, however, Bach uses a modulating ritornello which begins in one key, moves gradually to another, and then establishes that second key area with a firm cadence point. The 1st movement of the A minor violin concerto is quite exceptional in that two of its three ritornello statements are of this type—the first (bars 1–24) modulating from A minor to its dominant, E minor, and the second (bars 51–84) moving from C major to E minor again. (The final statement, which begins at bar 142, is altered to remain in the tonic throughout.)

Another device used occasionally by Bach is that of the 'split' ritornello. This is the exact reverse of a tutti interruption in that a brief solo passage is allowed to disrupt the normal progress of a tutti ritornello. An example occurs in the 1st movement of the same violin concerto (BWV 1041). Here the second ritornello (bars 51ff.) is interrupted by short solo passages in three places—bars 61–2, 65–6, and 74–8—and after each interruption the tutti continues the ritornello from the point at which it was previously broken off. Exactly the same device may be found in certain Vivaldi concertos. Indeed, one of the best examples occurs in the 1st movement of op. 3, no. 8,[83] a work which Bach transcribed.

Solo Episodes

Although the type of material presented by the soloist(s) at the beginning of the first solo episode is very varied, three broad categories may be distinguished: the solo section may open with a reference to ritornello material, with a new theme, or with brilliant solo figuration.

The first category is the largest—and affords a surprising flexibility of treatment. Normally the soloist will repeat a few bars only of the opening tutti before going its own way (see the E major violin concerto, 1st movement, bars 12–14). Occasionally, however, more substantial portions of the ritornello are repeated, as in the 3rd movement of the first Brandenburg concerto (bars 17–20). Another exceptional example is provided by the Finale of Brandenburg no. 6. At the beginning of the first solo section (bar 8) the two viola da braccio exchange a new and distinctive semiquaver motif. The prominence of this motif together with the abrupt change of rhythm disguises the fact that the whole passage is merely a variant of the original tutti material:

EXAMPLE 20

Bach, Brandenburg concerto no. 6, 3rd movement; (*a*) bars 1–4 (outer

---

[83] See bars 68–71 and 79–86.

parts only); (*b*) bars 8–12 (viola da braccio I and II, violoncello—other
instruments are resting)

Other movements also fall midway between the first and second categories in that their first solo episode *appears* to open with a new theme but is in fact related to previous material. The 3rd movement of the double violin concerto provides a characteristic example. Here the opening ritornello is in four sections—A (bars 1–4), B (4–8), A′ (8–10), C (11–21)—and it is from section B that Bach evolves a new solo theme:

EXAMPLE 21
Bach, double violin concerto, BWV 1043, 3rd movement (concertino violin I part only);
(*a*) bars 4–6 (=ritornello, section B); (*b*) bars 21–4 (=beginning of the first solo episode)

Into the second category come such movements as Brandenburg no. 2, 1st movement, and the first Allegro of the double violin concerto where there is no discernible relationship between the new solo theme and ritornello material. Obviously this results in a greater contrast between the concertino and ripieno groups and this contrast is heightened by the fact that the solo theme, once presented, remains the exclusive property of that group—it cannot be taken up by the ripieno instruments.

One might expect this type of thematic contrast to be prominent in the orchestral concertos, i.e. those in which there is no division into tutti and solo groups. It would, after all, provide a simple and effective substitute for the alternation of tutti and solo tone-colours on which ritornello form so greatly depends. Yet it is only in the 'Italian' concerto that Bach resorts to such methods.[84] In the third and sixth Brandenburg concertos the illusion of tutti/solo contrast is created more by changes of texture than by any thematic dualism.

The third category—use of figurative material at the head of the first solo section—is the smallest of the three. One of the rare examples occurs in the opening movement of the fourth Brandenburg concerto where, after an unusually lengthy ritornello, the solo episode starts with non-thematic figuration on the violin (bar 83). The exceptional nature of the first tutti may well be significant here since it is the concertino instruments, not the ripieno group, who dominate the opening bars and this automatically reduces the importance of the first solo entry when it arrives.

So far we have considered the first solo section in isolation. Subsequent solo episodes are less predictable because their content and arrangement of material depends so much on what has gone before. The only generalizations that can be made are that the writing is more figurative than in the first solo, that ritornello motifs are often prominent, both in solo parts and in the accompaniment, and that new themes are not normally introduced after the first solo section.

Both the first and subsequent solo episodes are distinguished from the ritornello by a certain lightening of texture. Even so, the contrast between tutti and solo sections is not as pronounced as in Vivaldi for Bach tends to avoid the three-part, repeated-quaver accompaniment of the Italians and seldom entrusts his bass line to the upper strings alone. Indeed, in his hands the ripieno instruments assume increased importance. During solo episodes they will often present fragments of the ritornello as a background to the brilliant roulades of the solo part (as in Brandenburg no. 5, 1st movement, bars 10, 13, etc.); occasionally also Bach lets the tutti gradually take over in the course of a concertino

[84] See the distinctive solo theme of the 1st movement which Bach introduces at bar 30.

passage so that the listener only really becomes aware of the tutti texture when the cadence at the end of the section arrives and there is another abrupt change in texture as the next solo episode begins. An extreme example of this may be found in the 1st movement of Brandenburg no. 2. The second solo episode begins at bar 28 with a concertino texture (plus bass); the tutti instruments then enter (bar 30) and 'accompany' the soloists with motifs from the first ritornello. It is not, however, until the cadence of bar 39 that we fully appreciate what has happened: the solo texture has first been thickened by the tutti instruments and this has been followed (at bar 36) by an unobtrusive statement of the ritornello itself. It is by such subtle methods as these that Bach avoids too rigid a contrast between tutti and solo sections.

Interrelationship of Solo Episodes

An important feature of Bach's ritornello movements is the close relationship which exists between successive solo episodes. This may be achieved through the consistent use of ritornello motifs or, more importantly, through the transference of complete passages from one episode to another. The 1st movement of the double violin concerto is typical in this last respect. Even within the first solo there is some repetition (bars 21–9 recur at 37–45); then during the second solo episode Bach recapitulates a more extensive solo passage to conclude the movement and make a well-rounded form:

Bach's double violin concerto, BWV 1043, 1st movement: outline analysis

Bar	Section	Key	Principal areas of repetition
1	Ritornello 1	D minor	
21	Solo 1	D minor to A minor	Bars 37–45 correspond to bars 21–9 but the material has been transposed from D minor to A minor
46	Ritornello 2	A minor to G minor	Bars 53–8 correspond to bars 8–13 transposed down a fifth

58	Solo 2	G minor, modulatory to D minor (tonic re-established at bar 77)	Bars 69 to the end correspond to bars 30–49, transposed so that the original modulation from D minor to A minor becomes a modulation from G minor to D minor
85	Ritornello 3	D minor	

The Final Section: Recapitulatory Designs

It will be noticed that in this same movement the tonic key is re-established some nine bars before the final ritornello statement. When this happens another section is, in effect, created; and when the return to the home key coincides with the repetition of important thematic material (as in bar 77 of the above where the solo theme suddenly reappears) it is obvious that Bach is moving towards a recapitulatory design. A very similar example occurs in the opening movement of Brandenburg no. 1. Here also the final section begins with a restatement of material from the beginning of the first solo episode:

Bach, Brandenburg concerto no. 1, 1st movement, outline analysis of final section

Bar	Key	Material	Comments
57	F to C	From the beginning of solo 1 (see bars 13–17)	Solo 1 begins at bar 13; in the repeat an additional bar is inserted (bar 57)
63	F to B♭ to F	From the beginning of solo 2 (see bars 34–42)	Solo 2 begins at bar 33; in the repeat the first bar of this solo section is omitted
72	F	Ritornello	

If the key structure of this final section is compared with that of corresponding passages earlier in the movement it will be noticed that Bach has transposed his second solo material up a fourth so that, instead of ending in C major (as at bars 42–3), the passage cadences in the tonic key of F (bars 71–2). Of course repetition of material in a dominant/tonic relationship had long been an important feature of binary form.[85] But despite this, it was some time before composers began to use the device freely in their ritornello movements, and here Bach led the way.[86]

Of particular interest also are those movements in which the repetition of solo material is preceded by references to ritornello material in the home key. These brief references to ritornello material are usually presented by the tutti, though the soloists may take over this role if their initial solo theme has been a restatement of ritornello material (see Brandenburg no. 1, 3rd movement, bars 84ff.).[87] Occasionally also, the tutti presents the ritornello material while the soloist adds its own embroidery, as in the 1st movement of the A minor violin concerto (BWV 1041), bars 122ff.

An extension of this idea may be observed in some of the later clavier concertos where, instead of alluding briefly to the opening tutti material, Bach sets the whole of the penultimate ritornello in the tonic key before proceeding with his now customary repetition of solo material. Taking the 3rd movement of the A major clavier concerto as our model, we find the following arrangement in the final section:

Bach, clavier concerto in A major (BWV 1055), 3rd movement, outline analysis of final section

Bar	Key	Material	Comments
138	A	Ritornello	Curtailed, but obviously a ritornello statement rather than a brief reference
146	A	From the beginning of solo 1 (see bars 24–31)	Originally in the tonic

---

[85] The binary Finale of Brandenburg no. 3 shows exactly the same type of key relationship. Here material from the latter part of the first section (bars 5–12), originally in the dominant key of D major, is repeated at the end of the second section (cf. bars 41–8) where it is transposed to the home key of G.

[86] Although Vivaldi made tentative experiments along the same lines, he tended to regard the subdominant/tonic relationship as equally important—see the 1st movement of his op. 3, no. 8 (Malipiero ed. no. 413), in which material originally heard in the subdominant key (at bars 48ff.) returns in the tonic for the final section (bars 87ff.).

[87] The theme is presented by the solo violino piccolo and the whole passage derives, not from the opening of the movement itself, but from the beginning of the first solo episode (see bars 17ff.).

154 A   From the beginning of solo 2   Extended; originally in E
          (see bars 60–74)   major
176 A   Ritornello

Here indeed is the recapitulation in rudimentary form and, although the analogy with classical sonata form should not be pressed too far,[88] the similarities are unmistakable: in both cases there is a return to the tonic key area coinciding with repetition of material from the beginning of the movement; this is followed—either immediately or at some later stage—by presentation in the tonic of material first heard in the dominant key during an earlier part of the movement.

The type of recapitulatory design outlined above is strikingly similar to that employed by Emanuel Bach in his own concertos and it may be that he took over the idea from his father. Emanuel was certainly familiar with these clavier concertos: in the catalogue of Sebastian's works which he compiled for Mizler's *Musikalische Bibliothek*[89] he listed them under a separate category (and not all Sebastian's instrumental music received such preferential treatment); moreover, it seems likely that BWV 1052 was performed in Berlin under his direction since all the parts survive in Emanuel's hand.[90] It is possible, of course, that the son influenced the father but the fact that some of J. S. Bach's earlier concertos have the same type of formal arrangement as his clavier concertos[91] makes this, on the whole, unlikely.

---

[88] It must be stressed that the similarities between Bach's recapitulatory designs and classical concerto form pertain to the final section alone, and here only in a rudimentary way. In Bach's concerto movements there is no second-subject group and no real development section so that the dualistic concept of sonata form as exemplified in many concertos of the later classical period was obviously foreign to him.

[89] L. Mizler, *Musikalische Bibliothek* (Leipzig, 1754; facsimile Hilversum, 1966), iv. 169.

[90] See G. von Dadelsen, *Bemerkungen zur Handschrift Johann Sebastian Bachs seiner Familie und seiner Kreises*, Tübinger Bach-Studien, ed. W. Gerstenberg, Heft i (Trossingen, 1957), p. 40.

[91] The penultimate ritornello of the fifth Brandenburg concerto, 1st movement, is in the tonic key (bars 121–39)—this is Krüger's 'Scheinreprise' (W. Krüger, 'Das "Concerto grosso" Joh. Seb. Bachs', *Bach-Jahrbuch*, xxix (1932), 24). The repetition

7. Composite Structures

Some of Bach's concerto movements, particularly the Finales, have complex structures which unite a number of different formal methods. Ritornello structure is combined with 'da capo' form; 'da capo' form is used in conjunction with fugal writing; other fugal movements are cast in ritornello form; and in one case—the Finale of Brandenburg no. 6—elements of ritornello, 'da capo', and rondo form are all combined within a single movement.

Most of Bach's 'da capo' movements may be classed as 'aria structures' for they display that combination of ritornello and 'da capo' form which was so popular in vocal music of the time. In this respect the plan of BWV 1042, 1st movement, is representative not only of a whole category of Bach's concerto movements but also of many cantata movements as well:[92]

Bach, violin concerto in E major (BWV 1042), 1st movement, outline analysis

Bar	Key	Material	Section
1	E	Ritornello 1	A
12	E to B	Solo 1	
25	C# minor to B	Ritornello 2	
35	E	Solo 2	
43	F# minor to E	Ritornello 3	
53	C# minor modulating to . . .	Solo 3	B

---

of material is heard within this ritornello as a solo interruption. An additional example is provided by the 1st movement of the A minor violin concerto. In this movement the final section begins at bar 122. A fragment of material from the first solo episode is then repeated (and extended) in a dominant/tonic relationship—compare bars 44ff. with bars 135–40—before the final statement of the ritornello at bar 142.

92 The aria 'Ätzet dieses Angedenken' from Cantata no. 207 ('Vereinigte Zwietracht') is cast in an almost identical form and this is one of many such cantata movements.

101	E	Ritornello 4		
106	G# minor	Solo 4		
123	E	Ritornello 5	A	Bars 123 to the end are an exact repeat of bars 1–52
134	E to B	Solo 5		
147	C# minor to B	Ritornello 6		
157	E	Solo 6		
165	F# minor to E	Ritornello 7		

Several points of general interest emerge from this movement. In the first place it will be noticed that the transition from the central section (B) to the 'da capo' is singularly abrupt. The middle section ends with an adagio cadence in G# minor and the third and final section then begins immediately in the key of E (bar 123). Tertiary key changes of this type occur at the same point in other 'da capo' movements (e.g. the E major clavier concerto, BWV 1053, 1st movement, bars 113–4 (C# minor to E) and 3rd movement, bars 258–9 (G# minor to E); also, Brandenburg no. 6, 3rd movement, bars 65–6 (G minor to B♭)) and in each case their effect is the same: to create a decisive tonal break between sections.

The other general point to emerge from the 1st movement of BWV 1042 concerns the thematic integration of the central section. Although contrasting in key and, to a certain extent, in texture, the middle section is related thematically to what has gone before. Indeed, in this particular movement, the central section assumes some of the qualities of a development. To be sure, the solo part consists merely of figuration in Vivaldi's manner, but underneath this the ripieno instruments make numerous references to the triadic motif with which the movement begins. Already in section (A) this head-motif has undergone some alteration (see bars 17–19, 35–7) and development is taken a stage further during the middle section (cf. bars 53–6, 95–7, 107–13).

In the category of 'da capo' movements one ought also to include the Finale of Brandenburg no. 5. This is a 'da

capo'/fugue,[93] not a 'da capo'/ritornello movement, yet it
has many of the characteristics discussed above. There is an
abrupt change of key (from B minor to D major) between
the central and 'da capo' sections (see bars 232–3) and the
middle section contains numerous references to the opening
material (in this case, the fugue subject) not only in the
shape of tutti interruptions but in solo parts as well, for the
principal theme of this B minor section is derived from the
opening statement as the following example reveals:

EXAMPLE 22

Bach, Brandenburg concerto no. 5, 3rd movement; (*a*) bars 1–3 (solo
violin) = the fugue subject; (*b*) bars 79–82 (solo flute part only) = the
theme on which the middle section is based

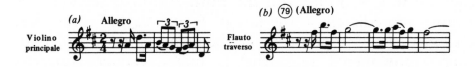

For his fugal movements Bach retains the division of the
orchestra into tutti and solo groups; all these movements
are, therefore, concerto fugues in which figurative solo
passages alternate with more contrapuntal tutti sections.
Frequently too, the fugal exposition acts as a ritornello. The
3rd movement of the A minor violin concerto provides a
typical example. Here it is the opening fugal exposition
(bars 1–25) which binds everything together, recurring at
two later points in the movement (bars 59–72 and 115–41).
The intervening solo episodes are based either on the solo
theme (first heard at bar 25f.) or on idiomatic figuration,
with the ripieno instruments interjecting fragments of ritornello material from time to time.

In the majority of these concerto fugues the exposition is
presented jointly by the concertino and ripieno groups. On
occasions, however, the opening bars are entrusted to the

---

[93] The Finale of Brandenburg no. 5 is the only 'da capo' movement in the
concertos which is completely independent of ritornello form.

soloists alone. This has far-reaching implications for the rest of the movement in that the exposition, being no longer associated with the tutti, cannot function as a ritornello in the conventional sense. In such cases Bach either dispenses with ritornello form altogether (as in the fifth Brandenburg concerto) or else introduces a tutti ritornello at some later point. In the 3rd movement of the second Brandenburg concerto, for example, the soloists present the fugal exposition but it is the tutti passage of bars 47–57 which recurs in the manner of a ritornello.[94]

As implied earlier, the Finale of the sixth Brandenburg concerto is something of a curiosity from the formal point of view. The opening tutti recurs at various stages of the movement (bars 38–45, 66–73, and 103–10), always in the tonic key and without modification of material or scoring. This suggests rondo form, but between these recurring statements there are brief tutti interruptions of the kind associated with ritornello movements (see bars 13–14, 52–3, 78–9). Moreover, all this takes place within the framework of a 'da capo' form which has the characteristic tonal hiatus between central and final sections (bar 65, G minor to B♭). The Finale is, therefore, a synthesis of rondo, ritornello, and 'da capo' forms and a fine example of how successful this type of cross-fertilization can be.

8. Rondo Structures

Pure rondo form is not often used by Bach in his concertos—he seems to have preferred the more flexible ritornello structures. But the Finale of his E major violin concerto provides one notable example. This movement is a rondeau in the strict French tradition: not only is the principal theme periodic, the intervening episodes (or couplets as the French called them) are also cast in regular phrase lengths of sixteen bars each (or a multiple thereof).[95] The resulting form is

---

[94] This tutti passage recurs at bars 79–85, 97–107, and 126–36; the movement ends as it began, however, with a solo statement of the fugue subject (bars 136–9).

[95] The form may be represented as follows: ABACADAEA in which each unit lasts sixteen bars except for section (E) which is 32 bars long.

much more sectional than was customary for Bach and there is little relationship between episodes or, for that matter, between the rondo and solo material.

The rondo principle is used also in Brandenburg no. 1, though on a much broader scale. Here the repetitions of the Menuet bind together a series of dance movements, the distinction between rondo (Menuet) and episodes (Trios, Polonaise) being underlined by colourful changes of instrumentation:

Bach, Brandenburg concerto no. 1(second version), arrangement of dance movements and their instrumentation

Analogy with rondo structure	Type of dance	Instrumentation
A	Menuet	Tutti
B	Trio 1	Two oboes and bassoon
A	Menuet	Tutti
C	Polonaise	Strings only; violino piccolo tacet
A	Menuet	Tutti
D	Trio 2	Two horns, three oboes in unison
A	Menuet	Tutti

9. Style

Bach's work has often been described as the culmination of the baroque. Certainly his music is richly-woven, intricate, and ornate, containing few hints of the light rococo idiom which was already current in other parts of Europe. How far this may be attributed to temperament and how far to his early training in the Germanic style is a matter for debate; but it is clear that both factors were important.

According to Emanuel Bach, his father's 'serious temperament drew him by preference to music that was serious, elaborate, and profound . . .'.[96] As will be seen below, this seriousness comes out in every aspect of his composi-

---

[96] The passage occurs in the Obituary notice written by Emanuel Bach and Agricola and published in L. Mizler, *Neu eröffnete Musikalische Bibliothek* (Leipzig, 1754; facsimile Hilversum, 1966), vol. iv, part 1, pp. 170–1. The translation is from *The Bach Reader*, eds. H. T. David and A. Mendel, rev. edn. with supplement (London, 1966), p. 222.

tion—from the thorough working-out of figures, the dislike of histrionics and empty virtuosity, to the original treatment of conventional formulas, the intricacy of his melodic writing, the skilful combination of lines and patterns, and the exploitation of all available harmonic and contrapuntal techniques.

Although the elaboration of motifs was of fundamental importance to so much instrumental (and vocal) music of the baroque era, Bach showed particular enthusiasm for the technique. He sometimes constructed whole movements from one or two figures alone[97] and was well aware of the force generated by the repetition (at speed) of vital rhythmic motifs. This last point may be illustrated by reference to Brandenburg no. 3, 1st movement, where the constant reiteration of anapaestic rhythms creates mounting tension and excitement. The figure on which this movement is based (see Ex. 19) was a commonplace in Bach's time, but its use here is highly original: sometimes part of the theme, sometimes part of the accompaniment, it always supplies a strong, propulsive rhythm to the whole. (Contributing also to the rythmic vitality is the throbbing quaver accompaniment (see, for example, bars 47ff., viola part) and the energetic bass line which almost over-reaches itself in the headlong, downward rush of bars 87–91.) This movement is typical in that there are very few breaks in continuity. Apart from the caesura at bars 77–8 where a new countersubject is introduced which provides material for a short fughetta, the semiquavers continue uninterrupted from beginning to end.

The principle of dramatic contrast did not, on the whole, commend itself to Bach who was more concerned with preserving the unity of a movement than with creating strong contrasts of mood or material. To this end he avoided the type of 'block' construction found in some Handelian movements. For similar reasons too, perhaps, he rejected such fashionable devices as the *pianoïdée* (a quiet

---

[97] See p. 48.

contrasting section within the ritornello)[98] and the rapid dynamic fluctuations beloved of Vivaldi and his compatriots.[99]

Unlike Handel or Vivaldi, Bach had no experience as a dramatic composer. Of course one should not minimize his debt to operatic methods—substantial evidence for this is found not only in the cantatas (with their operatic forms) but in some concerto movements too[100]—nor suggest that drama is absent from his music (consider, for example, the forceful unexpected cadence at bar 109 in the 1st movement of BWV 1052 or the sudden piano which underlines the harmonic surprises of Brandenburg no. 2, 1st movement (bars 50, 72, and 107)). Yet it must be said that Bach seldom includes a theatrical effect for its own sake or sacrifices the continuity of a movement by introducing strong contrasts of material or over-fussy dynamic changes.

Consistent with this attitude is Bach's avoidance of the programme concerto, a genre much cultivated by Vivaldi. It may also explain the restrained nature of his solo writing for, although his concertos often make considerable demands on the soloist from a technical standpoint (see, for example, the pyrotechnics of the solo violin part in the last movement of Brandenburg no. 4), they are never allowed to degenerate into displays of empty brilliance: in the final version of the long cadenza to Brandenburg no. 5, for instance, the harpsichord part, though essentially figurative, utilizes material from the first solo episode (compare bars 9–10 with bars 154ff.), and we have already seen how skilfully Bach's solo episodes are linked to their surrounding sections by the imaginative use of thematic accompaniment (p. 61).[101]

[98] For a more detailed explanation of this device see W. Krüger (*Das Concerto Grosso in Deutschland* (Reinbek, 1932), p. 26) who appears to have coined the term.

[99] Nevertheless, exceptions do occur, as in the E major violin concerto (BWV 1042), 3rd movement, bars 121–3, where the dynamic marking of the solo violin part is altered every half bar.

[100] E.g. the use of 'da capo'/ritornello structures, see p. 66.

[101] In the Finale of the fourth Brandenburg concerto itself the brilliant violin solo which forms the apex of the movement (bars 87–127) is integrated with the other sections by tutti references to the fugue subject (bars 105ff.).

Like all eighteenth-century composers Bach relied heavily on a common stock of patterns and phrases that had been built up over the years. Paradoxically, it is in the treatment of these conventional formulas that the full extent of his originality may be seen. In his hands jaded progressions are suddenly brought to life: in sequences, for example, the judicious alteration of one note can transform an uninteresting cycle of fifths[102] into a passage of immense subtlety. Particularly characteristic is the following progression (Ex. 23) in which one note of a sequence is flattened, causing a transient modulation to the dark-hued subdominant key (within the general context of C major):

EXAMPLE 23

Bach, Brandenburg concerto no. 3, 1st movement, bars 29–31 (outer parts only)

Bach's melodic style was well suited to forms of abstract instrumental music such as the concerto. To claim that he was primarily an instrumental composer would be dangerous in the extreme, for the cantatas and passions contain some of his finest music. Yet the fact remains that many of his vocal lines are written in a thoroughly instrumental idiom.[103] Bach's predilection for transferring vocal, keyboard, and orchestral styles from one medium to another is well known and, by analogy, one might expect the concertos to contain some imitation of vocal idioms. But

[102] i.e. a progression of chords based on roots a fifth apart.

[103] The extent to which Bach's early vocal music in particular was influenced by instrumental idioms may be seen in the opening chorus of Cantata no. 131, 'Aus der Tiefe'.

this is not the case. Allegro themes are written, for the most part, in energetic concerto style and simple periodic melodies appear only in Finales of dance-like character.[104] Even the slow-movement themes are instrumental in style. Indeed, the intricacy of the melodic writing in some of these movements surpasses anything in Vivaldi or Handel: it was only equalled by a few exceptional composers of the next generation such as Tartini (1692–1770) and his pupil J. G. Graun (1703–71). One of Bach's most elaborate slow movements is the Andante of his A minor violin concerto. Here there is a wealth of ornamentation; expressive leaps are beautifully counterbalanced by stepwise movement and the line twists and turns in an often unexpected, but always satisfying, manner:

EXAMPLE 24

Bach, violin concerto in A minor, BWV 1041, 2nd movement, bars 9–14 (ripieno parts in short score)

[104] As, for example, the Finale of the E major violin concerto, BWV 1042.

J. A. Scheibe, writing around 1745, was one of the first to recognize that Bach frequently wrote out his ornamentation in full: 'Every ornament, every little grace, and everything that one thinks of as belonging to the method of playing, he expresses completely in notes; and this not only takes away from his pieces the beauty of harmony but completely covers the melody throughout.'[105] His bias is irrelevant here. What is significant is the possibility that the elaborate melodic style which we regard as peculiarly characteristic of Bach could be a rationalization of contemporary performance techniques. Or, to cite a more recent author who carries the idea a stage further: 'Bach, like other composers of the time, conceived his musical ideas in the form of simpler basic melodies, but . . . he, contrary to customary procedure, worked out the ornamentation on paper instead of leaving it to the inspiration and taste of the individual performer . . . Bach's music did not actually sound so different from that of his contemporaries: it merely *looked* different.'[106]

[105] J. A. Scheibe, *Der critischer Musikus*, 2nd edn. (Leipzig, 1754, facsimile Hildesheim, 1970), pp. 62–3 (tr. *The Bach Reader*, op. cit., p. 238).

[106] P. Aldrich, 'Bach's Technique of Transcription and Improvised Ornamentation', *The Musical Quarterly*, xxxv (1949), 29, 30.

Interesting though this last view is, it should be regarded with due caution. To be sure, there are some examples which suggest that Bach added ornamentation to a basically simple line: in the 2nd movement of Brandenburg no. 1, for instance, the melody can be divested of its ornamentation and, as shown below, we are then left with a plain descending scale:

EXAMPLE 25

Bach, Brandenburg concerto no. 1, 2nd movement, bars 1–4; (*a*) original version (oboe and string parts only); (*b*) melodic line with ornamentation removed

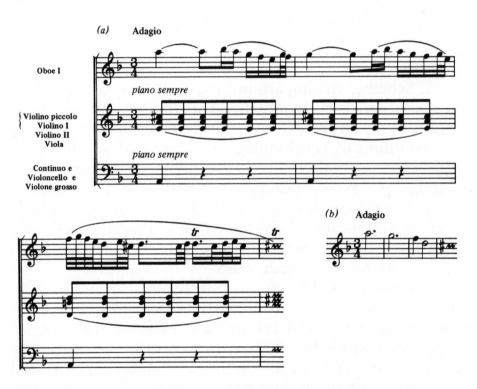

But not all Bach's florid melodies are of this type. In the well-known cantilena from the F minor clavier concerto (BWV 1056) the ornaments form an integral part of the melodic line and it is not possible to separate the embellishments from the melodic kernel. Examples such as this are considerably more numerous than the first type. In fact, it could be argued that the essence of Bach's melodic style lies in the paradoxical concept of 'the ornament as essential';[107] in this respect it is unlikely that his slow movements sounded at all similar to those of, say, Handel or Vivaldi, however lavishly decorated the latter were in performance.

Much of the complexity of Bach's music stems from his habit of presenting simultaneously, in different parts, a number of distinctive, and often totally independent, lines. Two instances of this are shown below. In the first (Ex. 26) there are four parts and three principal strands. The solo violin has a semiquaver motif which descends in thirds; the recorders have a contrasting pattern which moves in the opposite direction (i.e. upwards), is characterized by step-wise motion and introduces another rhythm (♫♩♪); the third strand is purely supportive yet even this simple bass part has its own distinctive rhythm:

EXAMPLE 26

Bach, Brandenburg concerto no. 4, 1st movement, bars 69–72 (solo violin, recorder, and bass parts only; the ripieno instruments fill out the harmony in the same rhythm as the bass)

The second passage (Ex. 27) is, if anything, more complex for, although there are only two thematic strands (the second recorder part is a free imitation of the first at a half-bar's distance and the continuo embroiders the cello line), rhythmically none of the parts coincides:

[107] There is a problem of terminology here, for the word ornamental usually conveys the ancillary meaning 'inessential'. But when, as in Bach's music, ornamentation becomes an integral part of the melody, the term loses part of its meaning.

EXAMPLE 27

Bach, Brandenburg concerto no. 4, 3rd movement, bars 160–3
(recorders I and II, cello, and continuo parts only; other instruments
are resting)

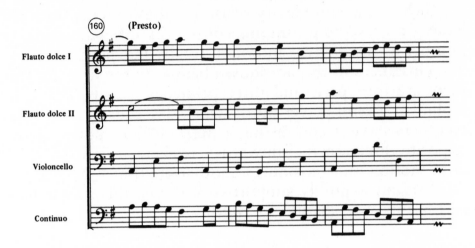

It will be noticed that in both the preceding examples the free movement of individual parts produces some harsh dissonances: false relations are created at bars 70 (C/C#) and 71 (D/D#) of Example 26, and in Example 27 the interweaving of the recorder parts produces repeated seconds in the last half of bar 162. In each case, however, the strident effect of these discords is softened not only by the fast tempo but also by the fact that the underlying harmony is clear and consonant.

To achieve this freedom of movement for the individual parts Bach uses a wide range of passing notes. As Forkel appreciated:

. . . every one of the . . . parts must flow melodically and freely. But to secure that result it will be necessary to introduce between the notes which begin a phrase and establish its general atmosphere other notes which often are not consonant with those employed in the other parts and whose incidence is governed by the accent. This is what we call a *transitus regularis et irregularis* [i.e. an unaccented and accented passing note]. Each part starts from a fixed point, and returns to it, but travels freely between them. No one has made more use of such progressions than Bach in order to colour his parts and give them a characteristic melodic line.[108]

It is the frequency with which passing notes are used which gives such smoothness to Bach's lines. Stepwise movement is common, for angular leaps tend to be filled in with a succession of faster-moving notes—part of the old 'division' technique. Particularly characteristic are passages of stepwise contrary motion such as the following. Here there are two principal motifs, one (*a*) being an upward series of four quavers, the other (*b*), a semiquaver motif whose general direction is downwards. Here again the free movement of parts produces passing dissonance, as at the end of bar 6 where the simultaneous use of both melodic and harmonic forms of the minor scale results in false relations between the first oboe and bassoon parts:

EXAMPLE 28
Bach, Brandenburg concerto no. 1, 1st movement, bars 6–7 (oboe and bassoon parts only)

These passages of contrary motion are a recurrent feature of Bach's style. An extended example occurs in the 1st movement of the A minor violin concerto (BWV 1041), where the two outer parts, starting from the interval of a third (at bar 127), diverge steadily until they are over three octaves apart (bar 133).

---

[108] J. N. Forkel, op. cit., p. 75.

More formal contrapuntal devices such as double counterpoint, canon, and fugue also play a significant part in the
concertos though their presence is seldom ostentatious.
Double counterpoint is confined mainly to solo episodes
and the inversion of parts usually takes place immediately
after the original presentation of the passage:

EXAMPLE 29
Bach, 'Italian' concerto for solo keyboard, BWV 971, 3rd movement,
bars 25–33[109]

Canon, on the other hand, may occur at any point—often in
the most unexpected places. It appears as part of the
ritornello in the 3rd movement of the double violin concerto and in the 1st movement of Brandenburg no. 6. But its
most surprising usage is, perhaps, in the slow movement of
the first Brandenburg concerto where the florid opening
theme is presented in canon by first oboe and violino
piccolo at bars 12–14 and 23–5. In all these cases the canon is
extremely close[110] yet the flow of invention is unimpaired.
As Forkel observed, Bach uses 'canon at all intervals and in

[109] Compare also the 1st movement of the double violin concerto (BWV 1043),
bars 21–9.

[110] Passages of close imitation are also frequent: e.g. Brandenburg no. 4, 1st
movement, bars 235–7, and the C minor concerto for two claviers and orchestra
(BWV 1060), 1st movement, bars 50–2.

movements of all kinds so easily and naturally that the workmanship is not perceptible and the composition sounds as smoothly as though it were in the free style'.[111]

As for Bach's fugal technique, some aspects of this have already been discussed but one should stress the extent to which Bach restrained his technical virtuosity in these concerto movements. There is not the same interest in contrapuntal devices—inverted subjects, augmentation, diminution, and so on—which characterizes the fugues of *The Well Tempered Clavier* or *The Art of Fugue*; nor, indeed, would these devices have been particularly appropriate to the freer concerto fugue. While stretto plays an important part in many of the concertos' fugal movements it is seldom treated strictly: in fact the original outlines of the theme are often altered quite substantially. Sometimes statements of the fugue subject are themselves subject to variation during the course of a movement. This technique, which springs from the old fantasia tradition, is employed in the Finale of the fourth Brandenburg concerto where three different versions of the subject appear:

EXAMPLE 30

Bach, Brandenburg concerto no. 4, 3rd movement; (*a*) original form of the subject, bars 1–5(viola); (*b*) first variant, bars 67–71 (bass); (*c*) second variant, bars 159–63 (first recorder)

It must be admitted that Bach's preoccupation with contrapuntal techniques sometimes led him to ignore the

[111] J. N. Forkel, op. cit., p. 88.

tone-quality and capabilities of individual instruments. In
the 1st movement of the second Brandenburg concerto the
countersubject to the solo theme is announced by the solo
violin (bars 12–14). Subsequently the same phrase appears in
the oboe and recorder parts (bars 16–18 and 20–2 respectively). Although admirably suited to the violin—the countersubject relies for its effect on the rapid crossing of
strings—the passage sounds out of place on the wind
instruments and is ungrateful to play. This example is not
atypical; it seems that Bach always attached more importance to the demands of good counterpoint than to any
niceties of instrumentation.

To consider harmony and counterpoint as separate elements has obvious practical advantages, yet it can be
dangerous too. The dangers become particularly acute when
discussing a composer such as Bach for the interaction of
harmonic and contrapuntal elements is fundamental to his
style. In contrapuntal passages the harmonic structure is
always clearly defined; conversely, the free movement of
parts sometimes results in the formation of rich and unusual
chords.[112] In his music vertical and horizontal threads are as
interdependent as the warp and weft of a closely-woven
fabric and in this respect it is obviously a distortion to
separate the two for analysis. However, certain aspects of
his harmonic practice (e.g. the type of chords employed) can
be dealt with separately and it is these matters which are
considered below.

Harmonically, the concertos have as broad a range as any
of Bach's works. Triads on every degree of the scale are
used freely, as are their inversions.[113] Moreover, Bach's
liking for chords of the seventh (both diatonic and chromatic) and for dominant-based chords (e.g. dominant sevenths,
ninths, elevenths) is much in evidence. Some idea of the

[112] An example of the logical movement of independent parts creating an
augmented chord occurs in Brandenburg no. 1, 3rd movement, bar 59.
[113] The use of the term 'inversion' does not imply that Bach himself thought of
the chords in this way. In fact Emanuel told Kirnberger that neither he nor his father
agreed with the theories of Rameau, see J. P. Kirnberger, *Die Kunst des reinen Satzes
in der Musik*, part 2 (Berlin, 1779), p. 188 (tr. *The Bach Reader*, p. 450).

richness of his harmonic style may be gained from the following passage in which diminished and dominant sevenths play an important part:

EXAMPLE 31
Bach, concerto for three claviers in D minor (BWV 1063), 2nd movement, bars 1–8 (solo clavier parts only)

In quick movements, of course, the harmony is more straight-forward. Nevertheless, Bach seldom resorts to the simple alternation of tonic and dominant chords on which even an artist of Handel's calibre relied so heavily.

After dominant and diminished sevenths the chromatic chord most favoured by Bach is the tonic with flattened seventh—C, E, G, B♭ in the key of C major. Being the dominant seventh of F major this chord has a strong subdominant flavour and its use at the beginning of a movement creates a dark colouring that is peculiarly characteristic of Bach. One of the most striking examples occurs in the Menuet of the first Brandenburg concerto. Despite the prominent tonic pedal on the horns the presence of the flattened seventh (E♭) in bars 1 and 3 introduces a hint of subdominant tonality; only at bar 5 is the listener made fully aware of the true key:

EXAMPLE 32

Bach, Brandenburg concerto no. 1, Menuet, bars 1–5 (wind parts only)

The chord which balances this on the sharp (i.e. dominant) side of the key is the major triad (or seventh) on the supertonic—D, F#, A, (C) in C major. This chord was also in Bach's vocabulary but is not used so frequently as its counterpart. In the following example, which shows a typical usage, the fourth degree of the scale is raised to create a feeling of dominant tonality:

EXAMPLE 33

Bach, double violin concerto, 3rd movement, bars 18–20 (the chromatic supertonic seventh is marked with an asterisk)

The chromatic element in this supertonic chord, the sharpened fourth, is also, of course, the leading note of the dominant. In this capacity it is frequently used to prepare the listener for a dominant pedal—as in the 1st movement of the D minor clavier concerto (BWV 1052) at bars 162–7 where the bass pivots all round the dominant note (G#, A, B♭, A, G#) before settling on to it.

So far Bach's original treatment of pedals has not been mentioned but it is an important feature of his style. Although pedal points are often found in other concerto movements of the time, they tend to be short and harmonically rather repetitious. (In most cases the bass supports a simple alternation of $\frac{5}{3}$ $\frac{6}{4}$ chords.) Bach's pedals are of a completely different order. First, they can be extremely lengthy—lasting anything up to 21 bars. Secondly, the harmonic superstructure is far more adventurous than the simple alternation of chords described above: indeed, Bach sometimes introduces harmonies that are strongly dissonant with the pedal note, as in the 3rd movement of the A minor violin concerto, BWV 1041, bars 105–17. In his hands these pedals assume a structural significance. Positioned at the end of the last solo section,[114] they serve to increase tension and prepare the listener for the return of the home key. And where, as in the 1st movement of the D minor concerto (BWV 1052), a dominant pedal leads straight into the final ritornello statement, the whole passage acquires the character of a classical 'Ruckführung'.[115]

10. **Bach and His Contemporaries**

Any assessment of Bach's position *vis-à-vis* his contemporaries must take account of his artistic relation to Vivaldi

---

[114] Very occasionally one comes across a pedal point earlier in the movement, cf. Brandenburg concerto no. 5, 1st movement, bars 93–100. Its use at this point marks the end of the F# minor episode and prepares the new key of A major. Later in the movement (bars 201–13) Bach introduces another pedal point in the regular position, i.e. just before the final ritornello.

[115] Literally 'leading back'. In music this term is normally applied to the link section between development and recapitulation.

and, although passing references to Vivaldi's concertos have already been made, the importance of the subject makes further discussion imperative.

Formal similarities between the concertos of Bach and Vivaldi go far beyond the conventional use of three-movement from and the ritornello principle.[116] There are Vivaldian precedents for Bach's 'framed' slow movement, the decorative cantilena, use of ostinato figures in slow movements, brilliant solo cadenzas in Allegro movements, the concerto fugue and the application of ritornello form to orchestral concertos.[117] Moreover, it is possible to discover isolated examples in Vivaldi of some of Bach's more idiosyncratic formal devices. The 'split' ritornello, for example, is sometimes found in Vivaldi,[118] though on the whole he preferred to use the 'modified' ritornello (some-thing which Bach avoided). Vivaldi also experimented with the repetition of solo material: in the 1st movement of op. 3, no. 8 (Malipiero ed. no. 413), for example, he brings back earlier solo material (originally heard in the subdominant key at bars 48ff.) in the tonic during the final section (at bars 87ff.), and we have already noticed this type of repetition in some of Bach's concerto movements (though in his case the repeated material usually stands in a tonic/dominant rela-tionship to the original). But there is a vital distinction to be drawn: in Vivaldi's works these devices take the form of isolated experiments, whereas Bach made them a more regular part of his concerto technique. As a further illustra-tion of this one could cite the use of thematic accompani-ment in solo episodes. Sporadic instances do occur in

---

[116] For a full discussion see H-G. Klein, *Der Einfluss der vivaldischen Konzertform im Instrumentalwerk Johann Sebastian Bachs* (Ph.D. thesis, Hamburg, 1969), Sammlung musikwissenschaftlicher Abhandlungen liv (Strasbourg, 1970).

[117] The 'larghetto e spiritoso' of Vivaldi's op. 3, no. 8, provides an example of a 'framed' slow movement which is written in cantilena style and based on a rhythmic ostinato. For an example of the brilliant unsupported cadenza see the Finale of Vivaldi's concerto RV 212a (Malipiero ed. no. 312). For a discussion of Vivaldi's use of the concerto fugue and ritornello form in orchestral concertos see W. Kolneder, *Antonio Vivaldi*, pp. 56–7 and 150 respectively.

[118] See p. 58.

Vivaldi[119] but it was Bach who first appreciated the enorm-
ous potential of this device for thematic integration.

Stylistically too, Bach owes much to the Italian master;
the forceful 'unison' ritornello derives from Vivaldi and his
fellow concertists, as does the energetic concerto style itself.
Moreover, there are thematic resemblances which confirm
Bach's close acquaintance with the Venetian concerto. At
the beginning of this century Arnold Schering[120] drew
attention to the thematic relationship between one of Vivaldi's sonatas (preserved in manuscript at Dresden) and the
opening of Bach's double violin concerto:

EXAMPLE 34
(a) Vivaldi, sonata, incipit (Dresden, Sächsische Landesbibliothek, Cx
1095 (RV 26, 4th movement)); (b) Bach, double violin concerto, 1st
movement, incipit

Equally striking is the resemblance between the following
incipits:

EXAMPLE 35
(a) Vivaldi, concerto for two flutes in C major RV 533 (Malipiero ed.
no. 101), 1st movement, incipit; (b) Bach, Brandenburg concerto no.
2, 1st movement, bars 5–6 (first violin part only)

[119] Cf. the Finale of Vivaldi's op. 3, no. 12. The example is discussed in W.
Kolneder, op. cit., p. 58; Kolneder draws attention to the fact that this particular
concerto was one of those which Bach transcribed (as BWV 976).

[120] A. Schering, *Geschichte des Instrumentalkonzerts bis auf die Gegenwart* (Leipzig,
1905), p. 83 note.

and

EXAMPLE 36

(a) Vivaldi violin concerto in D major RV 213 (Malipiero ed. no. 347),
1st movement, incipit; (b) Bach, Brandenburg concerto no. 5, 1st
movement, bars 1–2, incipit

These examples do not imply direct plagiarism for the themes are not identical—the resemblance is one of spirit rather than letter. There is a sense also in which these ideas should be regarded as common property. Vivaldi's concertos, being more accessible than those of Albinoni or lesser-known Italians, naturally invite comparison with Bach's; but there are similar resemblances between Bach's themes and those of other Italians such as Torelli.[121] In one case, also, Bach seems to have looked nearer home for inspiration—to the work of an aristocratic Vivaldi-follower, Prince Johann Ernst. In the following example the second part of each theme is remarkably similar:

EXAMPLE 37

(a) Prince Johann Ernst, fifth concerto, incipit;[122] (b) Bach, violin
concerto in E major (BWV 1042), 1st movement, incipit

[121] A. Schering (ibid. 83) draws attention to the similarity between the solo theme of Bach's double violin concerto, 1st movement, bars 21ff., and a passage from a Torelli concerto that J. G. Walther arranged for the organ—compare Walther's fourteenth organ concerto arrangement, 2nd movement, bars 17–19.

[122] The example is taken from A. Pirro, *L'Esthétique de Jean-Sébastien Bach* (Paris, 1907), pp. 408–9.

Important though these parallels are, there is another side to the picture. Few people would mistake a concerto by Bach for one by Vivaldi and this is because they recognize, either consciously or subconsciously, the fundamental differences in style which separate them. Bach's concertos have a richer texture, a more adventurous harmonic idiom than Vivaldi's; care is lavished on detail—on the free movement of inner parts and on the logical working-out of patterns in each separate strand of the music. (All this stems directly, of course, from the German musical tradition in which Bach had been brought up.[123]) Vivaldi's concertos, on the other hand, are far simpler in texture; there is a clarity of writing here (even in fugal movements) which springs from the subordination of contrapuntal to harmonic techniques; moreover, he has an acute awareness of instrumental colour[124] and, although his concertos lack polish and rely over-much on stereotyped formulas, they have a glowing

[123] Emanuel Bach stressed that the continued study of German masters was of great importance to his father: 'Besides Froberger, Kerl, and Pachelbel, he heard and studied the works of Frescobaldi, the Baden Capellmeister Fischer, Strunck, some old and good Frenchmen, Buxtehude, Reincken, Bruhns, and the Luneberg organist Böhm'. (This passage occurs in a letter from C. P. E. Bach to Forkel which has been printed by M. Schneider in *Bach-Urkunden*, Veröffentlichungen der Neuen Bachgesellschaft, xvii, no. 3, tr. *The Bach Reader*, p. 278.)

[124] More acute than Bach's. One wonders how Bach could ever have contemplated transcribing the slow movement in particular of Vivaldi's op. 3, no. 10, for four claviers. Bach's arrangement is a highly skilled exercise in transcription but the harpsichord parts, however complex, cannot hope to reproduce the sonorous effect of the original string lines which interweave with one another in a fascinating way.

spontaneity and panache which was never equalled by Bach. In general terms, the stylistic contrast between the concertos of these two men reflects the perennial conflict between the colour (and brashness) of Mediterranean culture and the more serious, measured approach of North European composers.

As a concertist Bach's influence was rather limited. Three reasons may be advanced for this: first, only one of his concertos (BWV 971 for solo harpsichord) was published during his lifetime so that, despite the existence of manuscript copies, they were not widely disseminated; secondly, his style of writing was rapidly falling out of favour; and thirdly, with the exception of his own sons, none of his pupils appears to have had much interest in the concerto.[125] It was, therefore, left to the next generation of Bachs to continue the tradition of the keyboard concerto, and this they did with conspicuous success. Bach's youngest son, Johann Christian, spent much of his life in London writing attractive concertos in the lucid, pre-classical style which delighted the public and enthralled the young Mozart on his visit to England. Emanuel and Friedemann Bach were of a more serious disposition and, despite Friedemann's eccentricity and Emanuel's preoccupation with the expressive style, both remained to some extent under the shadow of their father.

[125] Forkel, on the authority of C. P. E. Bach, mentions the following as distinguished pupils of Bach: Vogler, Homilius, Transchel, Goldberg, Krebs, Altnikol, Agricola, Müthel, Kirnberger, Kittel, Voigt, Schubart (see J. N. Forkel, op. cit., pp. 101–3).

II

George Frideric Handel

1. Introduction

Of the five composers discussed in this study, Handel was the only one who spent the greater part of his working career outside his native country. As is well known, he made a brief visit to London in 1710 and returned two years later to settle permanently in England. While it is absurdly chauvinistic to claim him as an 'English' composer, as some have done, he was naturally affected by the different cultural environment of his host country. Of course his own resourcefulness played a large part in this, for he was quick to assess and to exploit (in the best sense of that word) the local situation. As far as the concertos were concerned, this sometimes meant altering his style to suit the requirements of a specialized market, as in the op. 6 concertos with their strong Corellian flavour; it also meant exploring further, in the shape of the organ concerto, the important role which that instrument had traditionally held in English ensemble music. Handel's adaptability is reflected too in the varied nature of his concertos which include concerti grossi (for oboes and strings), solo concertos (for organ, oboe, and violin), and some large-scale pieces 'a due cori', designed, possibly, for outdoor performance. Such versatility was unusual: indeed, looking at the eighteenth century as a whole, it must be said that few other composers made so comprehensive a contribution to the history of the concerto.

2. The Concertos: Sources, Chronology, Instrumentation, and Historical Background

Recently the primary sources for Handel's concertos have been re-examined in great detail. This work has been undertaken mainly in connection with the new collected edition of his work, the *Hallische Händel-Ausgabe* which will, when completed,[1] supersede Chrysander's monumental *Händel-Gesellschaft* edition. In their efforts to establish an authoritative text for the concertos the editors have encountered formidable problems. Apart from all the commonplace difficulties of assessing the reliability of sources and deciding between alternative readings, they have had to contend with the composer's own capriciousness. It seems that the idea of producing a 'definitive' version was completely foreign to Handel. If the occasion demanded he would re-use material, reverse the order of movements, or re-score existing music for entirely different forces—all of which has created textual difficulties of the first order.

Chronological problems also abound. For although publication dates are readily available, it is often impossible to assign precise dates of composition to individual works. Once again the situation is complicated by Handel's propensity for re-working old material. Sometimes there is no way of establishing the priority of different versions without recourse to the contentious methods of stylistic analysis. In the discussion which follows, therefore, the concertos are not arranged in strict order of publication nor according to any other putative chronological grouping. They are divided by genre and discussed under four subject headings: concerti grossi, organ concertos, miscellaneous works for soloist and orchestra, and the concertos 'for double chorus'.

The Concerti Grossi—opus 3

As it happens the six concerti grossi of op. 3 were the first concertos by Handel to be published in England;[2] they were

---

[1] The first volume of the *Hallische Händel-Ausgabe* was issued in 1955, under the general editorship of M. Schneider and R. Steglich. Since then, progress has been slow but sure; at the time of writing four volumes of concertos are available: op. 4 (iv/2) ed. Matthaei, op. 3 (iv/11) ed. Hudson, eight concertos (iv/12) ed. Hudson, and op. 6 (iv/14) ed. Hoffmann and Redlich.

[2] For a description of the printed editions see W. C Smith (assisted by C. Humphries), *Handel: A Descriptive Catalogue of the Early Editions*, 2nd edn. (Oxford, 1970). The principal manuscript sources for Handel's concertos are listed (by Smith) as an appendix to G. Abraham, ed., *Handel: a Symposium* (London, 1954). More

brought out by the London music publisher, John Walsh, in 1734. The circumstances surrounding their publication are rather unusual in that two different printings occurred within a very short space of time. The earliest bore a postscript connecting the works with a royal wedding:

Concerti Grossi Con Due Violini e Violoncello di Concertino Obligati e Due Altri Violini Viola e Basso di Concerto Grosso Ad Arbitrio Da G. F. Handel. Opera Terza. NB. Several of these Concertos were perform'd on the Marriage of the Prince of Orange with the Princess Royal of Great Britain in the Royal Chappel of St. James's . . . London. Printed for and Sold by I: Walsh . . . No. 507.[3]

Since the wedding in question took place on 14 March 1734 the set was obviously published some time after this, though we do not know the exact date of issue nor the number of copies involved. What is certain, however, is that the early edition was soon superseded by another from the same publishing house. Advertised in the *Country Journal: or, The Craftsman* for 7 December 1734 this new printing differed from the original in several important respects. For one thing the postscript linking the concertos with the royal wedding was erased; this was a relatively minor alteration made, presumably, because the event no longer aroused general interest. But there were other more significant changes which affected the composition of the set as a whole. The fifth concerto was extended by the addition of three further movements to make a five-movement work, while the fourth concerto was omitted entirely and replaced by another. This second printing, which appears to have circulated far more widely than the first, formed the basis of all subsequent editions. The alterations outlined above, therefore, found their way into the *Händel-Gesellschaft* edition and so achieved canonical status.

It was not until the 1950s that interest in the original printing of op. 3 was rekindled. At this stage a copy of the

---

detailed information regarding source material is, of course, available in the foreword to vol. iv/11 of the *Hallische Händel-Ausgabe*, ed. F. Hudson (Kassel, 1959) and in the accompanying *Kritischer Bericht* (Kassel, 1963).

[3] Cf. W. C. Smith, op cit., p. 218.

rare first edition was found among the Balfour collection of
early Handel editions and first prints at the National Library
of Scotland[4] and the strange history of the original fourth
concerto (which we shall refer to as op. 3 no. 4b) was
unravelled. It appears that Walsh issued the concerto in two
different collections: as part of the first op. 3 printing, and,
subsequently, as the fifth of six concertos by 'Geminiani and
other Eminent Italian Authors', *Select Harmony Third Collection*. Although the title of this last publication is so uninfor-
mative, the names of individual composers are given in the
orchestral parts. Curiously though, the 'Handel' work bears
no indication of authorship; it is completely anonymous.
This raises a number of questions. Why, for example, did
Handel allow Walsh to publish one of his concertos
anonymously? Was he even responsible for the concerto in
the first place? No unequivocal reply can be given to this
last, and central, question. As Frederick Hudson points out
in his Foreword to volume iv/11 of the *Hallische Händel-
Ausgabe*, the style of writing is not uncharacteristic of
Handel. This work opens with a Largo in the composer's
favourite French manner (see Ex. 1) and the Allegro movements have all the drive and vitality one would expect.

EXAMPLE 1[5]
Handel, op. 3 no. 4b, 1st movement, bars 1–4

[4] For details see H. F. Redlich, 'A New "Oboe Concerto" by Handel', *The Musical
Times*, xcvii (1956), 409–10.
[5] Examples are taken, wherever possible, from the *Hallische Händel-Ausgabe*.
Because this edition is still in progress, however, it is sometimes necessary to rely on
the old *Händel-Gesellschaft* edition. When examples stem from other sources a
footnote is appended.

On the other hand, it seems unlikely that Handel would have granted permission for Walsh to issue the work anonymously, especially after it had been included under his own name in the op. 3 set.

We have also to explain the substitution of no. 4a in the second printing. If no. 4b were unauthentic, this would, of course, provide a very satisfactory answer. Stanley Sadie suggests[6] that a simple error in Walsh's workshop may have been responsible. He points out that since the first printing of op. 3 and the third volume of Walsh's *Select Harmony* bear adjacent publishing numbers, concerto 4b (a work originally destined, he assumes, for the *Select Harmony* collection) could have slipped into the op. 3 set by mistake. The error was then rectified by Walsh in his second edition.

Although the approximate publication date for Handel's op. 3 set can be deduced from contemporary advertisements, there is little information as to when individual works were composed. Moreover, scholarly opinion has always been divided on the subject. Chrysander, the nineteenth-century biographer and editor of Handel's work, dated some of the set as early as 1711–12[7] and this line was pursued also by Max Seiffert in his edition of the concerti grossi. In both cases, the argument rested on stylistic analysis. Samuel Arnold, on the other hand, gave a very different date for the set. In his edition of *c.* 1796 we are told that the concertos were 'Chiefly Composed at Cannons, in the Year 1720.'[8] An even later date is assigned to the set by the eighteenth-century music historian, Sir John Hawkins, who maintained that the concertos were 'composed on occasion of the marriage of the prince of Orange with the Princess Royal' (that is, 1734). Unfortunately we do not know whether Hawkins was speaking from personal knowledge or whether he was simply reinterpreting the 'royal wedding' postscript which had appeared on the first edition.

---

[6] S. Sadie, *Handel Concertos*, BBC Music Guides (London, 1972), p. 16.

[7] F. Chrysander, *G. F. Händel*, vol. i (Leipzig, 1858), p. 359.

[8] Since Arnold gives an erroneous publication date one is reluctant to place too much faith in his composition date, though stylistically it is possible.

One suspects the latter for, although it seems likely that some of the concertos were performed at the wedding (possibly as interlude music between the acts of Handel's *Il Parnasso in Festa* which was performed on the eve of the wedding), certain movements were in existence long before that date. The 1st movement of op. 3, no. 6, for example, was originally written for the opera *Ottone* and had been performed in that context during the 1720s;[9] similarly with op. 3, no. 4a, whose opening movement served as the second overture to *Amadigi* in 1716.[10] Clearly then, individual concertos and, in some cases, separate movements, were composed at different stages of Handel's career and for several different occasions. One assumes it was only after the wedding festivities that Handel (or Walsh) decided to capitalize on public interest by collecting together a variety of suitable works and publishing them in the customary set of six.

Several other factors indicate that the compilation of the op. 3 set was a scissors-and-paste affair. In the first place, the concertos rely heavily on previously-composed material—more so than either the op. 6 set or the major collections of organ concertos. A detailed list of these and other borrowings may be found in Appendix A, but it is worth emphasizing here how frequently Handel plundered the Chandos anthems in particular.[11] The internal structure of some concertos also suggests that they were put together in a somewhat arbitrary fashion. The key scheme of the first concerto, for example, is curiously unbalanced, the opening movement being in B♭ major and the remaining two in G minor. This type of asymmetrical design is most unusual,

---

[9] Probably during the 1726 performance rather than the 1723 première, cf. F. Hudson's Foreword to vol. iv/11 of the *Hallische Händel-Ausgabe*, p. vii.

[10] The history of this last work was known to Charles Burney who explains that it was written for an operatic benefit performance with proceeds going to members of the orchestra—hence its popular title 'Orchestra Overture' (or orchestra concerto as it was sometimes called); C. Burney, *An Account of the Musical Performances in Westminster-Abbey, and the Pantheon, May 26th, 27th, 29th; and June the 3d, and 5th, 1784. In Commemoration of Handel* (London, 1785), p. 104 note.

[11] Perhaps it was this which led Arnold to associate the concertos with Cannons, the Duke of Chandos's palatial residence at Edgware.

for Handel was generally very careful to see that his concertos began and ended in the same key. Then we have the strange instrumentation of the sixth concerto. The work has only two movements, and while the first is scored conventionally enough (for strings and oboes), the Finale with its long solo passages for obbligato organ sounds totally out of place in a concerto grosso. (Indeed, the same movement reappears as the final movement of one of the later organ concertos (op. 7, no. 4) in which context it is far more effective.)

Variety of instrumentation is, in fact, an important feature of the set. The composition of the solo group varies widely in individual concertos and is even subject to alteration between movements. Although the works early acquired the title of 'Oboe Concertos' this was something of a misnomer since it is often the violins rather than the oboes which come to the fore. A concerto like op. 3, no. 2, has very little solo writing for the oboes in its quick movements, 'most of the divisions, and difficult passages, being assigned', as Burney reminds us, 'to the principal violin'.[12] Besides violins and oboes, other solo instruments also make an occasional appearance. Recorders are prominent in the slow movement of op. 3, no. 1, and the bassoon too is sometimes featured, either as the bass of a woodwind trio—see the French-style episodes of op. 3, no. 4, 3rd movement—or as a soloist in its own right. (We know, for instance, that the important bassoon melody in the Minuet of op. 3, no. 4, was generally performed as a solo, although at the large-scale concerts of the 1784 Handel Commemoration it was played by no fewer than twenty-four bassoonists![13]) The composition of the ripieno group is, of course,

[12] C. Burney, op. cit., p 48. (Burney's remark is slightly inaccurate in that the solo passages are given to *two* concertante violins, not one.).

[13] Ibid. 105: 'The *finale* is a very pleasing minuet, with a solo part for a bassoon. The late celebrated performer on that instrument, Miller, used to acquire great applause by his tone, and manner of playing this movement, at public places. It was now performed by twenty-four bassoons, of which the unity of effect was truly marvellous. The violoncellos were very judiciously ordered to play only the under part in this strain.'

far less flexible, yet Handel manages to achieve some variety even here by the judicious use of divided strings. Sometimes, indeed, he abandons the tutti/solo division altogether and treats the orchestra as a single unit, this approach being particularly effective in contrapuntal movements, where clarity of part-writing is more important than colour contrasts.

Opus 6

We come now to the other set of concerti grossi written by Handel: the twelve Grand Concertos, op. 6.[14] Most of these works seem to have been composed in the space of a month—between 29 September and 30 October 1739. The completion dates which Handel appended to every concerto except the ninth, are as follows: no. 1, 29 September; no. 2, 4 October; no. 3, 6 October; no. 4, 8 October; no. 5, 10 October; no. 6, 5 October; no. 7, 12 October; no. 8, 18 October; no. 9 (undated); no. 10, 22 October; no. 11, 30 October; no. 12, 20 October. Already, on 29 October, John Walsh, Handel's publishing agent, was advertising for subscribers.[15] Despite the high price asked (two guineas for each copy), the response was enthusiastic and the subscription list, when published as part of the set on 21 April 1740, bore one hundred names. Among the subscribers were members of the aristocracy, composers such as Defesch and Weidemann, concert promoters like Jonathan Tyers of Vauxhall Gardens, and numerous musical societies; we may reasonably assume, therefore, that these concertos were heard at private concerts given by the aristocracy, at music clubs, and in the pleasure gardens of London.

Originally, of course, the concertos served a very different function, designed as they were to provide interlude music for Handel's oratorios. Not that this diminished their stature as independent works of art: a glance at the advertisements for the 1739–40 season shows that the instrumen-

---

[14] The opus number did not appear on the first edition; it was added later, in 1741.

[15] The op. 6 set was the only collection of Handel's instrumental works to be published by subscription.

tal pieces were regarded as an attraction in their own right. Besides, unlike the organ concertos which were written for specific oratorio performances, these Grand Concertos were composed before the winter season was under way; clearly Handel was storing up material in anticipation of the busy months ahead.[16] We learn from contemporary advertisements that ten of the op. 6 set were performed during the winter of 1739–40; unfortunately, though, individual concertos are never identified so that it is seldom possible to associate them with particular oratorios.[17]

Apart from the numerous borrowings (notably from Muffat's *Componimenti Musicali* and from Handel's own works), the most important textual problem raised by the op. 6 set is that of instrumentation. According to the Walsh edition of 1740 the concertos were scored for 'Four Violins, a Tenor Violin, a Violoncello/ with a Thorough Bass for the Harpsichord'. It will be noticed that there is no mention of oboes,[18] nor were any parts printed for them. Yet in the (incomplete) autograph score (GB-Lbm, RM 20. g. 11) we find separate oboe parts supplied for four out of the twelve concertos: nos. 1, 2, 5 (only the middle movements are preserved in this source), and 6. Which then is the authorita-

[16] See R. Fiske, 'Handel's Organ Concertos—do they belong to particular Oratorios?', *The Organ Yearbook*, iii (1972), 18.

[17] Advertisements make it plain that various 'Concerto's for several Instruments, never perform'd before' were heard in connection with the following: a performance of the *Ode for St. Cecilia's Day* and *Alexander's Feast* (November 1739)—two concertos; a revival of *Acts and Galatea* (13 December 1739)—two concertos; a performance of *L'Allegro* (February 1740)—two concertos; a revival of *Saul* (March 1740)—one concerto; a revival of *Israel in Egypt* (April 1740)—one concerto; a revival of *L'Allegro* (April 1740)—two concertos. Unfortunately it is not possible to match the concertos and oratorios by key (see p. 109f. for a discussion of this method as applied to the organ concertos). Some do fit (op. 6, no. 5 in D major was probably heard as the Overture to the *Ode to St. Cecilia*, its first two movements being, of course, indentical with those of the Overture proper; op. 6, no. 8 in C minor would fit tonally between Acts 2 and 3 of *Saul*, while op. 6, nos. 3 and 7, could have been heard before Acts 2 and 3 of *L'Allegro* which begin in E minor and Bb major respectively) but several do not. This is hardly surprising since Handel wrote the op. 6 set *before* the 1739–40 oratorio season was fully under way.

[18] In connection with this it is worth noting that Walsh announced the set as being for strings (no mention of wind parts) from the preliminary advertisement of 29 October 1739 onwards.

tive version, the autograph or the print?

The fact that most editors of the op. 6 set, including Arnold and Chrysander, followed Walsh in suppressing these oboe parts is not particularly significant. But it is surprising, especially as there seems little justification for their action. One might conceivably argue that the oboe parts are irrelevant since they make no substantial contribution to the concertos in question; they merely reinforce the tutti sections either by doubling the melodic lines or, more rarely, by emphasizing important harmony notes. Again, one could maintain that the unusual position of the oboe parts—at the foot of the autograph score rather than at its head—suggests they were perhaps an afterthought, or an optional luxury, or both. But these arguments are not strong. The opposite viewpoint is put succinctly by Hans Redlich, co-editor of the concertos for the *Hallische Händel-Ausgabe*,[19] who believes that the oboes were an integral part of Handel's original conception since they appear both in the autograph score and in one of the most reliable secondary sources, Egerton 2944 (GB-Lbm, Granville Collection). His case was strengthened dramatically when another important source, known as the Aylesford copy, passed into the ownership of Manchester Public Libraries and at last became accessible to scholars.[20] This copy of the op. 6 set which is almost certainly in J. C. Smith's handwriting and which stems, therefore, from a source very close to Handel himself again gives oboe parts for the first, second, fifth, and sixth concertos. (Unfortunately, the copy became available for inspection just after the relevant volume of the *Hallische Händel-Ausgabe* had been published. As Redlich himself explains in *The Musical*

---

[19] See the Foreword to vol. iv/14 (*Zwölf Concerti Grossi Opus 6*) of the *Hallische Händel-Ausgabe* (Kassel, 1961), ed. A. Hoffmann and H. F. Redlich; also H. F. Redlich, *Kritischer Bericht* to *HHA*, iv/14 (Kassel, 1964).

[20] The Aylesford copy of the op. 6 set, formerly in the possession of the late Sir Newman Flower, was only accessible to a handful of scholars. In 1965, however, the copy was acquired by Manchester Public Libraries (catalogued as v. 85). Details of this source are given by A. D. Walker in *Georg Frideric Handel: The Newman Flower Collection in the Henry Watson Music Library* (Manchester, 1972), p. 17.

Times (1968),[21] it supplies the oboe parts for the first two movements of the fifth concerto (found neither in the defective autograph nor in Egerton 2944 which omits the oboes at that point), and the collected edition should be amended accordingly.) There is also a practical reason for believing that these four concertos were originally performed with oboes. We know that certain of the set—possibly these very works—served as interlude music to Handel's *Ode for St. Cecilia's Day* and to *L'Allegro*, both of which include oboes in their scoring. It would be natural, therefore, for Handel to use his resources to the full in the intervening instrumental pieces.

One question remains: why were the original oboe parts omitted from Walsh's edition? Several factors may have been involved. In the first place, it was obviously cheaper to publish the concertos without additional wind parts. Secondly, the omission of 'stray' oboe parts would give a tidier appearance to the whole collection. One must also consider the market at which this type of music was aimed. Some small music societies with predominantly string orchestras found it difficult to muster sufficient wind players for their concerts. Sales prospects would, therefore, improve if the relatively unimportant oboe parts could be omitted, and doubtless Walsh, as a shrewd businessman, gave due weight to such considerations.

Although these Grand Concertos are remarkably varied in form and style, the collection has a strong Corellian flavour. As in the twelve concertos of Corelli's op. 6, so here there are no strict rules governing the number of movements, although each work has its succession of alternating slow and quick movements. The composition of the concertino group remains constant throughout, except in the one orchestral concerto (op. 6, no. 7) and in certain isolated movements (e.g. the 3rd movement of op. 6, no. 4) where there is no division into solo and ripieno groups. Two violins, cello, and continuo form the solo group—that same

---

[21] H. F. Redlich, 'The oboes in Handel's Opus 6', *The Musical Times*, cix (1968), 530–1.

combination which Corelli employed in his own op. 6 and which provides a lingering testimony to the old relationship between the early concerto and the trio sonata—and, although individual members of the concertino sometimes emerge as soloists in their own right (see, for example, the first violin part in the 4th movement of no. 6), the solo group is treated, for the most part, as a collective unit. Like Corelli, Handel uses the two groups to provide contrasts of dynamics rather than material. Indeed, the concertino often functions as a miniature tutti, repeating phrases at a lower dynamic level.

At this point a digression is needed to explain the overwhelming influence which Corelli's music exerted in England at that time. The basis for this obsession with Italian music had been laid in the seventeenth century when there was an influx of foreign, mainly Italian, musicians to London. As the enclave of Italian musicians grew, so did the influence of the Southern style until, in the last two decades of the century, the mania for Italian music reached such extravagent proportions that English composers felt obliged to imitate the work of their foreign competitors. Even Purcell did obeisance, as the Preface to his twelve 'Sonata's of Three Parts' (1683), written in 'just imitation of the most fam'd Italian Masters', makes plain.[22] Nor did the movement end there. In 1695, the year of Purcell's death, the works of Italy's leading instrumental composer, Arcangelo Corelli, began to circulate in Britain, and this event turned what might have been a passing phase into a lasting cult. English composers now felt free to mention their models by name, knowing that the words 'Compos'd in Imitation of Arcangelo Corelli'[23] would act as a powerful sales recommendation.

The earliest references to Italian concertos in England concern the works of Venetian composers such as Albinoni

[22] The Preface is reproduced in vol. v of *The Works of Henry Purcell*, ed. J. A. Fuller-Maitland (London, 1893).

[23] William Topham's Six Sonatas op. 3 bore this recommendation when published by Walsh in 1709.

and Vivaldi;[24] Corelli's concertos were not published in London until 1715, some two years after his death. Yet it was the Corellian concerto which captivated the musical public—a curious anomaly, since in showing their preference for these rather austere works English audiences reversed all continental trends. There have been several attempts to explain this state of affairs. Perhaps a national conservatism was responsible: Hawkins thought Vivaldi's concertos 'wild and irregular'.[25] Furthermore, we know that the numerous musical societies active in London and the provinces preferred the less demanding works of Corelli to the more brilliant solo concertos of Vivaldi and his heirs. No music publisher could afford to discount the tastes of these societies for they were the principal subscribers to the innumerable sets of concertos and overtures then being issued. That ease of performance was an important factor in determining the popularity of such works is evident from the following lines—part of a letter written in 1741 by Mr. R. Price to Lord Haddington: 'I was at a concert at Lord Brooke's where Carbonelli played the first fiddle; Tate brought with him some concertos of Loccatelli [sic] without solo parts, which are extremely easy, but because there were some passages out of the common road, they looked upon them as the most extravagent things in the world and not to be played at sight.'[26] In this climate it is hardly surprising to find Handel reverting to the old Corellian manner for his op. 6 set of 1739.

The Concerto in Alexander's Feast

The magnificent C major concerto, first performed in

---

[24] Some of Albinoni's concertos were advertised as early as 1702 (see M. Tilmouth, 'A Calendar of References to Music in Newspapers published in London and the Provinces (1600–1719),' *The Royal Musical Association Research Chronicle*, i (Cambridge, 1961), p. 44). Vivaldi's op. 3 set was advertised in 1711—four years before the London edition of Corelli's op. 6 (ibid. 80).

[25] J. Hawkins, *A General History of the Science and Practice of Music*, 5 vols. (London, 1776), v. 214.

[26] This letter, dated 19 December 1741 and written from London, is printed in the *Historical Manuscripts Commission, 12th report, appendix, part ix: The Beaufort Manuscripts* (London, 1891), p. 205.

Alexander's Feast[27] is the only other one to employ a trio sonata solo group. Completed on 25 January 1736, this work was published by Walsh four years later as the first item in his *Select Harmony Fourth Collection* (advertised on 11 December 1740). Although doubts have been expressed as to the authenticity of the concerto,[28] it seems likely that Handel was the author. Sceptics bring forward two principal arguments against Handel's authorship, one based on Walsh's propensity for attributing works incorrectly, the other based on stylistic considerations. Both arguments will be reconsidered here.

To be sure, Walsh was sometimes careless in his attribution of works, but in this particular instance he seems to be above blame. Although some of the advertisements displayed on publications of later works by Handel imply that he was the sole author of *Select Harmony Fourth Collection*, the actual title page mentions three composers: Handel, Veracini, and Tartini.[29] Furthermore, on inspection of the parts, one finds that these three names appear (on the concertino first violin part) at the beginning of the first, fourth, and fifth concertos respectively. It is clear that Walsh intended them to cover more than one concerto. The first concerto (from *Alexander's Feast*) bears Handel's name, but the second and third, though seemingly anonymous, are also by him. (These are the two oboe concertos in B♭ major, see p. 122.) The fourth concerto is stylistically quite distinct from the first three and bears Veracini's name, while the fifth concerto is credited to Tartini. Since the sixth and last

---

[27] According to R. Fiske, this concerto could not have been performed at the beginning of the second act as formerly believed, since the keys do not correspond (the concerto is in C major and Act 2 of *Alexander's Feast* begins in B minor). Fiske suggests that the concerto was played in the middle of the last recitative where there is a C major cadence and where Handel wrote in the autograph 'segue il Concerto per Organo'. Presumably Handel changed his mind later about what type of concerto should be included here, see R. Fiske, 'Handel's Organ Concertos', 14–22.

[28] *Handel: a Symposium*, ed. G. Abraham, p. 212.

[29] The full title is as follows: 'SELECT HARMONY Fourth Collection. SIX CONCERTOS in Seven Parts For Violins and other Instruments Compos'd by Mr: HANDEL TARTINI and VERACINI London . . . I. Walsh . . . No. 682'.

concerto also proves to be by Tartini[30] it would appear that Walsh has, on this occasion, been meticulously careful in attributing the works to their correct authors.

The stylistic arguments against Handel's authorship do not rest on very secure foundations either. It is held that the tutti passage with which the 1st movement opens is too lengthy for Handel. However, other examples, though infrequent, may be found: a ritornello of similar length occurs, for instance, in the 4th movement of op. 6, no. 6. As for the notion that the concerto is too Vivaldian for Handel,[31] this statement could apply with equal force to the 3rd movement of Handel's violin concerto (the *Sonata a cinque*), about whose authenticity few doubts are entertained. Moreover, the Vivaldian energy which characterizes the 1st movement of the *Alexander's Feast* concerto has its counterpart elsewhere—see, for example, bars 18–24 of the 2nd movement of op. 6, no. 9. It is, of course, possible that the 1st movement of the C major concerto was based on a ritornello by an Italian composer and that Handel merely added his own solo episodes; after all, he used this technique on another occasion when re-working the opening movement of Telemann's *Musique de Table* concerto, Book 1, no. 5, for his organ concerto in D minor (see p. 116). But to accept this is to acknowledge Handel's decisive part in the final shaping of the work, and so the wheel comes full circle once more.

The Organ Concertos

In turning to the organ concertos we are dealing with a

[30] See J. A. Fuller-Maitland and A. H. Mann, *Catalogue of the Music in the Fitzwilliam Museum, Cambridge* (London, 1893), p. 33. The Tartini concertos in question are nos. 1 and 2 of a collection of seven concertos for strings, MS. no. 23, G. 2.

[31] This is implied in *Handel: a Symposium*, ed. G. Abraham, p. 212. See also A. Schering (*Geschichte des Instrumentalkonzerts, p.* 68) who sees a relationship between the opening theme of Handel's *Alexander's Feast* concerto and Vivaldi's op. 8, no. 6. The similarity is, however, no more striking than that between the Handel work and Telemann's A major concerto from the *Musique de Table*, Book 1—see M. Seiffert, *Beihefte zu den Denkmälern deutscher Tonkunst*, ii, *Georg Philipp Telemann Musique de Table* (Wiesbaden, 1960), p. 18.

completely different genre. These works fall into the category of solo concertos and, as such, maintain a very different balance between solo and tutti elements. A sharp distinction is made between the type of material given to the soloist and that given to the ripieno group; the solo writing becomes more figurative in style and more brilliant in effect, while the supporting instruments play a humbler role.

Altogether four sets of organ concertos by Handel were published during the eighteenth century. Not all, however, were of equal importance. The second set, which Walsh advertised on 8 November 1740, was originally published without orchestral parts (see p. 113), and consisted primarily of arrangements of some of the Grand Concertos.[32] For us, the only importance of this second set lies in the fact that it provides the sources for two of the miscellaneous organ concertos (nos. 13, 14) which will be discussed later on. The fourth set of organ concertos was published late in the eighteenth century by Samuel Arnold and is again relatively unimportant. It contains the organ concerto in D minor which relies so heavily on Telemann's *Musique de Table*, and also the strange organ concerto or 'Ouverture' as it is called, whose music reappears in the F major concerto 'a due cori'. These works will also be discussed at a later point, which leaves us with the two principal collections of organ concertos: the first and third sets.

The first of these (later known as op. 4)[33] was advertised by Walsh on 4 October 1738 in an edition said to have been authorized and corrected by Handel. The fact that this was an authoritative version is stressed on the title page which bears the following declaration: 'These Six Concertos were Publish'd by M[r]. Walsh from my own Copy Corrected by my Self, and to him only I have given my Right therein. George Frideric Handel.'[34] Elsewhere we learn that Walsh's anxiety to issue a definitive version stemmed from the

---

[32] Nos. 9, 11, 10, 1, 5, and 6. (The first concerto of the *Second Set* also contains material from the trio sonata op. 5, no. 6.)

[33] The set was not given an opus number until the edition of December 1738.

[34] W. C. Smith, *Handel: A Descriptive Catalogue*, p. 224.

circulation of what he termed a 'spurious and incorrect Edition . . . publish'd without the Knowledge, or Consent of the Author'.[35] No copy of this publication has been traced, so that we do not know whether it was, in fact, the work of a competitor or whether Handel had taken exception to an earlier and inaccurate printing by Walsh himself. The second concerto from the op. 4 set had certainly been issued before October 1738. It appeared complete in *The Lady's Entertainment* ('To which is Prefix'd the celebrated Organ Concerto Compos'd by Mr. Handel'), advertised by Walsh in September 1738, while the final Minuet from the same work found its way into a collection *circa* 1735 entitled *SOLOS For a GERMAN FLUTE . . .* Vol. II, part VII . . . *Walsh . . . No. 394.*

As so often with Handel's concertos it is impossible to assign precise composition dates to these six concertos (although, as will be seen later on, the dates of their first performance can be conjectured). Only one concerto (op. 4, no. 4) is dated in the autograph score—25 March 1735—and even here no firm conclusions can be drawn since the work appears in a different form from the printed one: the last movement has a choral ending, an 'Alleluja' chorus, which is based on the material of the Finale and which appears as a vocal movement in Handel's *Il Trionfo del Tempo* (1737).

Circumstantial evidence proves more helpful with respect to dating. We know that it was around 1732–5 that Handel began to introduce organ concertos into his oratorios. The first definite evidence for this comes in March 1735 when a notice appeared in the *London Daily Post* advertising a performance of *Esther* at the Theatre Royal with '. . . two new Concerto's on the Organ'.[36] But some of Handel's organ concertos may well have been heard before this. Unfortunately, neither Burney nor Hawkins, informative though they are, really clarify the matter. Both agree on the novelty of the organ concerto and on the fact that such

---

[35] Cf. *The London Daily Post, and General Advertiser*, 27 Sept. 1738.
[36] Cf. O. E. Deutsch, *Handel: A Documentary Biography* (London, 1955), p. 383.

works were first introduced into performances of *Esther*. However, they disagree as to the exact date of this event. Hawkins puts it definitely in 1732, while Burney is somewhat ambivalent. In one passage he implies a date of 1736,[37] and in another he discusses the concertos in the context of the 1732–3 performances of *Esther* and *Deborah:*

It was during these early performances of Oratorios, that HANDEL first gratified the public by the peformance of CONCERTOS ON THE ORGAN, a species of Music wholly of his own invention, in which he usually introduced an extempore fugue, a diapason-piece, or an adagio, manifesting not only the wonderful fertility and readiness of his invention, but the most perfect accuracy and neatness of execution.[38]

Fortunately, there is more specific information about the actual concertos performed. Op. 4, no. 2, was linked with *Esther* from very early days. Its Finale was published around 1735 under the title 'Concerto Minuet Esther'[39] and Burney confirms the association, informing us that 'The favourite movement at the end of his second organ-concerto was long called the *Minuet in the Oratorio of Esther*, from the circumstance of its having been first heard in the concerto which he played between the parts of that Oratorio.'[40] Op. 4, no. 3, was also linked with *Esther* while op. 4, no. 6, was first performed, along with the C major concerto grosso already discussed, in *Alexander's Feast*.

The other major set of organ concertos, op. 7, was published posthumously on 23 February 1761. Most of these concertos seem to have been written after 1740, all the dateable works falling within the period 1740 to 1751. (The

---

[37] 'Thus far' (1736 from the context) 'no organ concerto is mentioned; but April 7th and 14th, when the oratorio of *Esther* was performed, Handel played *two* concertos each night', C. Burney, *A General History of Music from the Earliest Ages to the Present Period*, 4 vols. (London, 1789), iv. 392.

[38] C. Burney, *In Commemoration of Handel*, p. 23 of the 'Sketch of the Life of Handel' section. (For what it is worth, the 1733 date is also supported by the author of the anonymous and highly-coloured *Anecdotes of George Frederick Handel and John Christopher Smith* (London, 1799), p. 24.)

[39] In *SOLOS For a GERMAN FLUTE,* Vol. II, Part VII, see p. 107.

[40] C. Burney, *In Commemoration of Handel*, p. 23 note of the 'Sketch of the Life of Handel' section.

earliest dated concerto is no. 1 (17 February 1740), and the latest is no. 3, whose first Minuet bears the words 'Fine G. F. Handel January 4. 1751 geendiget'.) In the case of this particular set Walsh's edition proves invaluable, since the autographs are in considerable disarray. It was in 1751 that Handel's eyesight began to fade which might have contributed something to the disorganization. This fact could also explain the incomplete nature of certain concertos. At times the performer is asked to extemporize whole movements, and, while the op. 4 concertos also offer some scope for improvisation, these later works leave much more to the soloist.

Apart from the examples given in the penultimate paragraph, there is no direct evidence which enables us to link individual concertos with their respective oratorios. However, as Roger Fiske has shown in a recent article for the *Organ Yearbook*, it is possible to suggest a relationship on grounds of key. Taking the four dated concertos of op. 4 and 7 as his starting point (op. 4, no. 4; op. 7, nos. 1, 2, and 3) and comparing their keys with those of oratorios advertised and performed a few days or weeks later, he discovered that whenever Handel 'dated the autograph of an organ concerto, it can be shown that Act 2 or Act 3 of an oratorio performed a week or two later began in the same key'.[41] On the basis of this Fiske proceeded to offer a first performance date for fourteen of the organ concertos. These are as follows:

Concerto	Probable date of first performance	Oratorio
Op. 4, no. 1 in G minor/ G major	1.4.35	Before Act 1 of *Athalia*—revival
Op. 4, no. 2 in B♮	1733— see also p. 108 above	

[41] R. Fiske, 'Handel's Organ Concertos', 14.

Op. 4, no. 3 in G minor	5.3.35	Before Act 2 of *Esther*—revival
Op. 4, no. 4 in F	26.3.35	Before Act 3 of *Deborah*—revival
Op. 4, no. 5 in F	5.3.35	Before Act 3 of *Esther*—revival
Op. 4, no. 6 in B♭	19.2.36	As a harp concerto in Act 1 of *Alexander's Feast*—première
Second Set, no. 1 in F (no. 13)	4.4.39	Before Act 1 of *Israel in Egypt* —première
Second Set, no. 2 in A (no. 14)	20.3.39	Before Act 2 of *Alexander's Feast*—revival. (Although Act 2 begins in B minor the previous act ends in the key of the concerto (A major))
Op. 7, no. 1 in B♭	27.2.40	Before Act 1 of *L'Allegro*—première
Op. 7, no. 2 in A	18.2.43	Before Act 2 of *Samson*—première
Op. 7, no. 3 in B♭	22.2.51	Before Act 2 of *Belshazzar*—première
Op. 7, no. 4 in D minor/ D major	16.3.50	Before Act 3 of *Theodora*—première
Op. 7, no. 5 in G minor	1.3.51	Before *The Choice of Hercules*—première
Op. 7, no. 6 in B♭	14.2.46	Before Act 2 of *The Occasional Oratorio*—première

Although Walsh issued op. 4 and op. 7 as suitable for the 'Harpsichord or Organ', this was standard publishers' practice in England. Most of the concertos (with the exception of op. 7, no. 1[42]) are written for manuals alone and could therefore be played on the harpsichord. Indeed, at this stage, when so few English organs were equipped with a pedal board, there was little technical difference between music for the different keyboard instruments. However, since all the contemporary references refer to Handel's performance of these works *at the organ* and since the autographs specify the organ as the solo instrument, we may be certain that they were written with that particular instrument in mind. Only in one case is there any real doubt as to what solo instrument was intended, and the harpsichord is not involved in the controversy.

[42] And the possible exception of op. 4, no. 3, where pencil marks added by Handel to the autograph indicate that the lowest line could, perhaps, have been intended for the pedal.

Op. 4, no. 6, is the one work which seems to have been written for another solo instrument. Although a solo organ is specified in Walsh's edition the work was almost certainly conceived as a harp concerto. The autograph score (GB-Lbm, RM. 20.g.12) is headed 'Concerto per la Harpa' and a similar direction occurs in the Newman Flower copy at Manchester; moreover, indications in the score of *Alexander's Feast* (after the recitative 'Timotheus plac'd on high') refer to a concerto for harp.[43] The designation 'per il Liuto e l'Harpa' found on a copy of the continuo part in the King's Music Library (GB-Lbm 19. a.1.) is a strange variant since no lute part has survived. The matter is further complicated by Hawkins who maintained that op. 4, no. 6, was originally a 'solo for the flute'. But since he also described the fifth concerto as a 'lesson for the harp, composed for the younger Powel'[44] he was probably muddling the two concertos. This view is supported by the fact that op. 4, no. 5, does indeed exist in the form of a recorder sonata, namely op. 1, no. 11.

As regards the composition of the ripieno group, the op. 4 set yields few surprises. Oboes are used to duplicate violin lines in the traditional baroque manner, and the string ensemble is laid out conventionally: for two violins, viola, and continuo. In this last respect the op. 7 set is far more adventurous. Several movements call for three violin parts; the first and second violins then play in unison while the third violins double the viola part. With the continuo instruments supplying the bass, a three-part texture is produced in which the inner line is given added weight. It is difficult to see why Handel adopted this extra violin part. However, there seems to have been a shortage of good viola players in England at that time which may account for it;[45] the two viola parts found in certain movements of the op. 3 set do not vitiate the argument since, as Chrysander sug-

[43] See Hans Dieter Clausen, *Händels Direktionspartituren 'Handexemplare'*, Hamburger Beiträge zur Musikwissenschaft, Band 7 (Hamburg, 1972), p. 103 note.

[44] J. Hawkins, op cit. v. 356–7 note.

[45] See A. Hutchings, 'The English Concerto With or For Organ', *The Musical Quarterly*, xlvii (1961), 202–3.

gested,[46] these movements may well have been written for a German orchestra whose resources were generally better than their English counterparts.

While on the subject of instrumentation, a word must be said concerning the opening movement of op. 7, no. 4. The first few bars of this dark-hued movement are entrusted to divided cellos and bassoons with the lower stave of the organ part (marked 'tasto solo e l'ottava bassa') providing the continuo. In the other version of this movement which Chrysander published separately (see the *Händel-Gesellschaft* edition, vol. xlviii, p. 51), an extra organ part is included; however, since the second organ functions as a continuo instrument throughout, the general effect is much the same. The principal difference between the two versions lies in their endings. The op. 7 movement was obviously designed to lead into the following Allegro since it closes with an inconclusive phrygian cadence on A. The 'double organ' piece, on the other hand, is seven bars longer and finishes in the tonic key of D minor.[47] It could, therefore, be played as a separate item although, being a single-movement work, it is seldom performed in this manner.

Miscellaneous Organ Concertos

Four other organ concertos remain for discussion. Of these, the first two (now known as nos. 13 and 14) were issued in 1740 as part of Walsh's *Second Set*. Although both works contain material familiar from the Grand Concertos they deserve full consideration since it is obvious that they were designed as genuine organ concertos and not simply as keyboard arrangements. In the first place, we have autographs for each concerto.[48] (No such manuscripts exist for nos. 3–6 of the *Second Set* which suggests that they were

---

[46] F. Chrysander, op cit. i. 359.

[47] For a discussion of the sources see the Foreword to vol. iv/12 of the *Hallische Händel-Ausgabe*, ed. F. Hudson. It appears that the two-organ version preceded op. 7, no. 4, since in one source (Fitzwilliam Museum, Cambridge, MS. 30. H. 14, pp. 37–44) Handel has pencilled in those alterations which appear in the op. 7 movement.

[48] GB—Lbm, RM. 20. g. 12 (nos. 1 and 2); also RM. 20. g. 14 (no. 1, fragment, dated 2 Apr. 1739).

arranged in the publisher's workshop.) In the second place, although Walsh never published orchestral parts for nos. 3–6, he did eventually supply the missing orchestral parts for nos. 1 and 2 (in January 1760). Finally, a comparison of these two concertos with corresponding movements from the op. 6 set shows that we are dealing for the most part not with straight-forward keyboard transcriptions but with separate versions of related material.

The first organ concerto of the *Second Set* (our no. 13) has long gone under the title of *The Cuckoo and the Nightingale* from the stylization of bird song found in its 2nd movement. The inclusion of these passages may represent an attempt to capture public interest. Descriptive concertos of this type were certainly popular with English audiences despite the fact that some critics viewed them with scorn.[49] A cuckoo concerto by Vivaldi had been printed in London around 1720,[50] and the English composer Lampe (himself a friend of Handel) produced a work in similar vein. The musical ideas behind the thirteenth concerto, however, can be traced to a much earlier work: Kerll's *Capriccio Kuku*.[51] The latter was written in 1679 and must have been known to Handel who re-used its opening theme without significant alteration in his own programme work:

EXAMPLE 2

(a) Kerll, *Capriccio Kuku*, version 'a',[52] bars 1–3; (b) Handel, organ concerto no. 13 in F major, *The Cuckoo and the Nightingale*, 2nd movement, bars 27–30

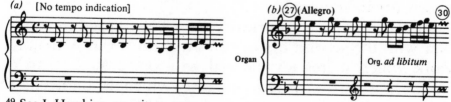

[49] See J. Hawkins, op. cit. v. 214.

[50] RV 335. The title of the London edition ran as follows: 'Two Celebrated Concertos the one Commonly called the Cuckow and the other Extravaganza'. Printed for I. Walsh and I. Hare (London ?1720).

[51] This point was made by O. A. Mansfield, 'The Cuckoo and the Nightingale in Music', *The Musical Quarterly*, vii (1921), 261–77.

[52] Three versions of this capriccio ('a', 'b', and 'c') are given in vol. ii/2 of *Denkmäler der Tonkunst in Bayern*, ed. A. Sandberger, pp. 38–46.

This particular movement of the thirteenth concerto is directly related to the 2nd movement of op. 6, no. 9. For some reason, though, the distinctive cuckoo calls are completely absent from the string version. This led Streatfield to conclude that they were an afterthought and that priority lay with the Grand Concertos.[53] However, Handel did not always expand his original ideas when rearranging material for later works; on the contrary, he often tightened up the structure, eliminating long-winded or inappropriate ideas in the second cast. So that this argument is open to criticism. External evidence also undermines Streatfield's position. The autograph of the organ concerto bears the words 'Fine G. F. H. London. April 2. 1739' in the composer's own script. We have, therefore, a definite completion date for the work. Unfortunately, the ninth concerto of op. 6 is undated (the only one of the whole set to lack a specific date), but since the remaining concertos were all written in September and October of 1739 it is usually assumed that no. 9 stems from the same period—which would, of course, give priority to the organ concerto. On the whole, the weight of modern scholarship supports this view. But the matter is still open for debate. There are added complications in that a few movements of the op. 6 set are now known to have been in existence by 1738, and, although this discovery does not pertain to the movements in question, it is possible that Handel mulled over the op. 6 set for a year or more,[54] in which case the organ version could have derived from op. 6 as Streatfield suggested.

Similar doubts as to priority have been raised in connection with the second organ concerto (no. 14 in A major), a work which shares its material with op. 6, no. 11. In this instance, it is the organ concerto which is undated; the

[53] R. A. Streatfield, *Handel*, 2nd edn. (London, 1910), p. 335.
[54] As Wilhelm Mohr suggests in 'Händel als bearbeiter eigener Werke: Dargestellt an fünf Orgelkonzerten', *Händel-Jahrbuch*, xiii–xiv (1967–8), 83–112. Mohr also discusses the three-fold relationship between op. 5, no. 6, op. 6, no. 9, and this thirteenth organ concerto in some detail.

concerto grosso, as we have seen, was completed on 30 October 1739. Traditionally, the organ concerto has been regarded as an arrangement of the string work. But since the autograph of the former contains several alterations (made, one assumes, in the process of creation) whereas the autograph score of op. 6, no. 11, is free from such blemishes, one must question the validity of this judgement.[55]

Although the two versions of this A major concerto are very closely related, the organ work is the simpler, as may be seen by comparing select passages (e.g. 1st movement, bars 5–6, or the Finale, bars 28ff.). Both concertos have the delightful 1st movement, complete with its bird-like tremolos and warblings (a movement thought by Burney to be 'uncommonly wild and capricious for the time when it was composed'[56]); however, the fugal Allegro is replaced in the organ version by the direction 'Organo ad libitum'. And there is a further discrepancy in lay-out: op. 6, no. 11, has a short 'largo, e staccato' movement between the fugal Allegro and the Andante; in the organ concerto the same slow movement, now marked Grave, is inserted between the Andante and the final Allegro, while the op. 6 concerto has no intervening movement at this point.

Handel's fifteenth organ concerto was not printed until 1797 when Arnold included it in his *First Collection*. As Max Seiffert has shown,[57] both movements are based on a recorder sonata from Telemann's *Musique de Table* set, a publication to which Handel subscribed in 1733. Although we do not know the exact date of composition there are indications—from watermarks in the autograph manuscript (GB-Lbm RM. 20. g. 14)—that the arrangement was made between 1740 and 1744.[58]

In reworking Telemann's material Handel shows all his customary resourcefulness. In the 1st movement, for exam-

---

[55] Cf. S. Sadie, *Handel Concertos*, pp. 34–5.
[56] C. Burney, *In Commemoration of Handel*, p. 66.
[57] M. Seiffert, *Georg Philipp Telemann Musique de Table*, p. 26.
[58] See F. Hudson in the Foreword to vol. iv/12 of the *Hallische Händel-Ausgabe* p. ix.

ple, he transforms the opening of Telemann's cantabile by ignoring the implied harmonic scheme and turning the original bass line into a unison ritornello:

EXAMPLE 3

(a) Telemann, *Musique de Table*, Book 1, no. 5, 1st movement, bars 1–3;[59] (b) Handel, organ concerto no. 15 in D minor, 1st movement, bars 1–6 (organ part only)

He also takes over unobtrusive portions of the solo recorder part (compare bars 13–14 of the Telemann movement with bars 63–4 of the Handel) so that the correspondence between the two movements is obviously not fortuitous. Yet despite the identity of material, Handel's version deserves to be treated as an independent work and not merely as an

[59] Example from *Georg Philipp Telemann: Musikalische Werke*, vol. xii, *Tafelmusik Teil 1*, ed. J. P. Hinnenthal (Kassel, 1959), p. 108.

arrangement, for he expands Telemann's ideas, giving them, at the same time, his own personal stamp. Particularly characteristic of Handel are the passages at bars 79–81 and 117–20 in which the Neapolitan chord is treated in a homorhythmic context, such usage being rare in Telemann.

After this, the remainder of the concerto is rather insubstantial. The 2nd and 3rd movements are not written out; instead we find the direction 'Organo adagio ad libitum et poi una Fuga allegro ad libitum poi Segue $\frac{9}{8}$'.[60] The Finale which follows is again based on Telemann's sonata (last movement), though here the borrowing is confined to the opening theme.

Arnold's edition of *Concertos &c. For the Organ In Score, now first Published 1797* also contains (pp. 46–80) the organ concerto in F major which was later issued under the title 'Ouverture' in Chrysander's *Händel-Gesellschaft* edition (see vol. xlviii, pp. 68–100). This seven-movement work is richly scored, with parts for two horns, two oboes, two bassoons, strings, and organ. It is more in the nature of a concerto grosso than a solo concerto, and it comes as no surprise to learn that the music also exists in a version for double orchestra.[61] The two versions correspond fairly closely, although the 'Ouverture' ends with a March[62] which is omitted from the double-orchestra concerto, while the latter has an extra section in the $\frac{12}{8}$ Allegro to make a 'da capo' form. As it stands, this F major organ concerto is unwieldy in the extreme. Yet Handel may not be responsible for its ungainliness. The solo organ part (which is the only surviving autograph source) contains just four move-

---

[60] Given in the *Hallische Händel-Ausgabe* but not in the *Händel-Gesellschaft* edition. This direction suggests that Handel did not intend using Telemann's central movements (a non-fugal Allegro and a Dolce) here. An acceptable slow movement for this fifteenth concerto would be the solitary Adagio for two organs discussed in connection with op. 7, no. 4, although the resultant key scheme—three movements in D minor—might prove monotonous.

[61] See the *Händel-Gesellschaft* edition, vol. xlvii, Supplement, pp. 203–41.

[62] From *Judas Maccabaeus* (*Händel-Gesellschaft* edn., vol. xxii, p. 189). The idea for both movements derives from Muffat's *Componimenti Musicali* (cf. *Händel-Gesellschaft* edn., Supplement no. 6, ed. F. Chrysander (Leipzig, 1894), p. 139).

ments: a French overture (1st movement); an *ad lib.* direction (in place of the 2nd movement); an Andante (5th movement); and the final March (7th movement). It seems likely, then, that Arnold inserted the remaining movements—all of which come from the third concerto 'a due cori' (see p. 125).[63]

History of the Organ Concerto

At this point, our survey must be interrupted to allow discussion of the origins and early history of the organ concerto.

It is clear that Handel's contact with English traditions was a vital element in his cultivation of this new genre 'of which he may be said to be the inventor'.[64] Since the beginning of the baroque period the chamber organ had occupied a position of peculiar importance in England, being used in both sacred and secular contexts. We learn from literary sources that English writers regarded the organ as a perfectly normal continuo instrument,[65] surpassing even the harpsichord in popularity. This preference is, perhaps, surprising given the fact that many German composers of the time preferred to write for plucked continuo instruments such as the lute and harpsichord, except when their chamber music was designed for church performance. Two explanations may be offered: the first lies in the intrinsic nature of the English organ and the second in the social and political upheavals of the Commonwealth period.

By the seventeenth century the church organs of northern Europe had reached an advanced stage of their develop-

---

[63] The question of priority is not absolutely settled. For the opposite viewpoint see W. Mohr, 'Händel's 16. Orgelkonzert', *Händel-Jahrbuch*, xii (1966), 77–91, who believes that the keyboard version preceded the double concerto. The crux of his argument rests on slight differences in handwriting—evidence that is not particularly convincing.

[64] J. Hawkins, op. cit. v. 355.

[65] Cf. C. Simpson in *The Division-Violist* (London, 1659), p. 21: 'A *Ground* . . . is prickt down in two *Severall Papers*: One, for him who is to Play the *Ground* (upon an *Organ, Harpsecord*, or what other *Instrument* may be apt for that purpose;) *the Other*, for him who playes upon the *Viol* . . .'

ment. The scale on which these magnificent instruments were built completely dwarfed the chamber organs of Italian and English churches. Moreover, the Germanic schools of organ composition stood unrivalled in their excellence. In these circumstances it is understandable that the small chamber organ gained little ground in Germany or the Netherlands. As for the large organ, this had no place in music performed outside the precincts of the church. Consequently there was little scope for the organ as a continuo instrument in secular ensemble music. The English organ, on the other hand, was at a rudimentary stage of its development, as yet without pedal board[66] and with far fewer stops than its German counterpart. These chamber organs were no more cumbersome than the modern upright piano and could therefore be used in a more intimate setting.

But size was not the only factor involved. The traditional role of the organ in English ensemble music was given fresh impetus by the political events of the Commonwealth period. During this time severe restrictions were placed on artistic activities for, although the Puritans were not opposed to music *per se*, they disapproved of public theatrical performances and of elaborate church music. The Parliamentary edicts which resulted in the closure of theatres and the desecration of churches are well known. Surprisingly, some of these measures, which appeared to strike at the very roots of artistic enterprise, produced unforeseen fringe benefits. The prohibitions actually stimulated private music-making, for example. Furthermore, many of the church organs offered for sale during this period were purchased by inn-keepers and their fellows at very reasonable rates.[67] Nor was there any lack of practitioners since

[66] One or two English organs were equipped with pedal boards in the early years of the eighteenth century. St. Paul's organ certainly possessed one by 1720 or 1721 (see W. Sumner, *The Organ* (London, 1952), p. 173) and according to Burney Handel used 'to play on that organ, for the exercise it afforded him, in the use of the pedals' (C. Burney, *In Commemoration of Handel*, p. 33 note of the 'Sketch of the Life of Handel' section).

[67] A. Hutchings, 'The English Concerto With or For Organ', *The Musical Quarterly*, xlvii (1961), 201.

redundant church musicians were forced to seek employment in whatever sphere of secular music was open to them.
In this way, the organ confirmed its place in English secular
music—a position it was to lose only in the last quarter of
the eighteenth century.

When Handel arrived in England, then, he encountered
this indigenous tradition of using the organ in secular
ensemble music. To explain his creation of the concerto for
organ, however, one must look more closely at another
aspect of the contemporary scene: the presentation of theatrical works. The custom of providing separate musical
entertainments between (or sometimes within) the acts of
plays or operas was as well established in eighteenth-
century England as on the Continent. These additional
items, which could be of vocal or instrumental music,
contributed greatly to the success of a production. Handel
himself was in the habit of playing harpsichord pieces in his
operas as the various contemporary editions of *Rinaldo*
reveal. In Walsh's original score, the improvised versions
are not written out, but for his 1711 edition of the airs from
Rinaldo Walsh commissioned William Babell (1690–1723) to
reconstruct Handel's popular extemporizations some of
which (judging by the pieces which Chrysander then
reprinted for the *Händel-Gesellschaft* edition[68]) demanded
great technical dexterity. It would seem but a short step
from these brilliant interludes to the creation of the organ
concerto proper.

One question remains: why did Handel chose the organ
rather than the harpsichord as his solo instrument when he
directed both opera and oratorio performances from the
harpsichordist's desk? The answer is, one suspects, two-
fold. In the first place there was, as we have seen, a
deep-rooted love of the organ in eighteenth-century
England. Secondly, although Handel was obviously a skilled harpsichordist, he excelled at the organ. It was his first
instrument and he had built up a considerable reputation in

---

[68] Vols. xlviii and lviii; see especially xlviii, pp. 240ff.

this field. While in Italy his skills had been pitted against those of Domenico Scarlatti and, as Mainwaring so graphically describes, Handel was judged the better organist of the two.[69] Already in Italy we find him introducing pieces for solo organ into his dramatic works—see, for example the famous organ solos in *Il Trionfo del Tempo* (first version, 1708). Presumably he made similar experiments in England and 'finding that his own performance on the organ never failed to command the attention of his hearers, he set himself to compose, or rather make up, concertos for that instrument and uniformly interposed one in the course of the evening's performance'.[70]

The practical aspect was obviously the crux of the matter for Handel had a great following as a performer. Even Hawkins, usually so ready with criticism, could find nothing to fault in his organ playing:

As to his performance on the organ, the powers of speech are so limited, that it is almost a vain attempt to describe it otherwise than by its effects. A fine and delicate touch, a volant finger, and a ready delivery of passages the most difficult, are the praise of inferior artists: they were not noticed in Handel, whose excellencies were of a far superior kind; and his amazing command of the instrument, the fullness of his harmony, the grandeur and dignity of his style, the copiousness of his imagination, and the fertility of his invention were qualities that absorbed every inferior attainment. When he gave a concerto, his method in general was to introduce it with a voluntary movement on the diapasons, which stole on the ear in a slow and solemn progression; the harmony close wrought, and as full as could possibly be expressed; the passages concatenated with stupendous art, the whole at the same time being perfectly intelligible, and carrying the appearance of great simplicity. This kind of prelude was succeeded by the concerto itself, which he executed with a degree of spirit and firmness that no one ever pretended to equal.[71]

Several other writers comment on Handel's remarkable

---

[69] J. Mainwaring, *Memoirs of the Life of the Late George Frederic Handel* (London, 1760), p. 60.
[70] J. Hawkins, op. cit. v. 356.
[71] Ibid. v. 413.

powers of improvisation[72] and doubtless his facility in this direction explains the occasional *ad lib.* markings in the solo part of op. 4. Towards the end of his life he began to rely on this technique to an even greater extent: in the 2nd movement of op. 7, no. 4, for example, the organist is called upon to improvise at no fewer than six different points! This skill (together with the benefits of an exceptional memory) stood Handel in good stead after his blindness. According to Burney he practised almost incessantly during the oratorio season

and, indeed, that must have been the case, or his memory uncommonly retentive; for after his blindness, he played several of his *old* organ-concertos, which must have been previously impressed on his memory by practice. At last, however, he rather chose to trust to his inventive powers, than those of reminiscence: for, giving the band only the skeleton, or ritornels of each movement, he played all the solo parts extempore, while the other instruments left him, *ad libitum*; waiting for the signal of a shake, before they played such fragments of symphony as they found in their books.[73]

Miscellaneous Solo Concertos

Under this heading come Handel's three oboe concertos and his 'sonata' for violin, all of which are grouped together in volume iv/12 of the *Hallische Händel-Ausgabe*.[74] The earliest printed source for two of the three oboe concertos was Walsh's *Select Harmony Fourth Collection* (1740). The first number of the set was, of course, the C major concerto in *Alexander's Feast*, and this was followed by two oboe concertos, both in B♭ major. Since no autograph for either

---

[72] It seems that Handel excelled in fugal improvisation, cf. J. Mattheson: 'He was a skilful organist: more skilful than *Kuhnau* in fugue and counterpoint, particularly *ex tempore*', *Grundlage einer Ehren-Pforte* (Hamburg, 1740); tr. O. E. Deutsch, ed., op. cit., p. 502.

[73] C. Burney, *In Commemoration of Handel*, p. 30 of the 'Sketch of the Life of Handel' section.

[74] The first two concertos published in vol. xlvii of the *Händel-Gesellschaft* edition (pp. 1–15, 71–9, and 80–98) are not considered in the course of this chapter since they appear to be early sketches for movements of Handel's *Water Music* and *Fireworks Music* respectively.

concerto has survived Walsh's edition is more than usually important.[75] Although no firm composition dates can be assigned to these two concertos, most scholars agree that they are early works, the first dating, perhaps, from Handel's Hamburg period.[76] An early date is suggested by the manner of writing: movements are short and the ideas are not subjected to the development that is so characteristic of Handel's mature style; the Siciliana, in particular, has all the freshness of an early work. The second concerto shares its material with a number of works, as will be seen from the Appendix. Moreover, the 1st movement exists in two different concerto versions, published by Chrysander as (a) and (b) in volume xxi of the *Händel-Gesellschaft* edition, and printed as nos. 4 and 5 of the *Hallische Händel-Ausgabe* (vol. iv/12). Version (b) stems from an autograph fragment in the British Library (RM. 20. g. 13)—a Largo for two horns, two oboes, strings, and continuo. This horn version, which Hudson dates tentatively to *circa* 1720,[77] differs from the oboe concerto not only in orchestration, but also in key and tempo. It is written in F major, not B♭, and is marked Largo, not Vivace.

Handel's other oboe concerto—a charming work in G minor—was first published by J. Schuberth of Leipzig in 1863–4.[78] The title page of this nineteenth-century edition bears the following words: 'im Jahre 1703 in Hamburg componirt von G. F. Handel' and there is no reason to question the early date. Any doubts as to authenticity are dispelled by the 4th movement which begins with one of Handel's most characteristic generating motifs (found also

[75] Walsh's edition provides the only source for the second oboe concerto in Bb, although individual movements, borrowed from earlier works, do appear elsewhere. As for the first concerto, the manuscript copy preserved at the British Library (ADD. MS. 31576, ff. 79ʳ–82ʳ) is late (1770–5) and could, therefore, have been transcribed from the printed edition.

[76] See F. Hudson in the Foreword to vol. iv/12 of the *Hallische Händel-Ausgabe*, p. vii. Most other authorities (e.g. Chrysander, Seiffert, Lam) agree on an early dating.

[77] See ibid. viii.

[78] For further details see F. Hudson, 'Ein seltener Händel-Druck? Das Concerto g-moll für Oboe, zwei Violinen, Viola und Continuo', *Händel-Jahrbuch*, xiii–xiv (1967–8), 125–37.

at the start of op. 4, no. 3, 2nd movement).

Curiously, Handel's only known violin concerto remained unpublished in the eighteenth century; it was first issued by Chrysander in volume xxi of the *Händel-Gesellschaft* edition under the title *Sonata a 5*. From the type of paper used in the autograph source (GB-Lbm, RM. 20. g. 14, ff. 11–20), it can be established that Handel wrote the concerto during his stay in Italy; the work is contemporary with the opera *Agrippina* and can be dated to within a narrow band: 1709–10.[79] Although Handel may, of course, have written other violin concertos which are now lost,[80] one cannot discount the possibility that the *Sonata a 5* was the work performed by the noted violinist Matthew Dubourg in London on 18 February 1719, the advance publicity for which ran as follows: 'At Mr. Hickford's Great Room in James-Street near the Hay-market, on Wednesday next, being the 18th day of February, will be perform'd a Consort of Vocal and Instrumental Musick, by the best Hands. A new Concerto, Compos'd by Mr. Hendel, and perform'd by Mr. Matthew Dubourg . . .'[81] Handel was clearly influenced in this work by the type of concertos he encountered in Italy. The Finale is particularly Venetian in style: its sturdy ritornello would not be out of place in a Vivaldi concerto, its episodes are well defined, and the string writing is idiomatic throughout.

The Concertos 'a due cori'

Technically the three concertos 'a due cori'[82] are misnamed

---

[79] See F. Hudson's Foreword to vol. iv/12 of the *Hallische Händel-Ausgabe*, p. viii.

[80] For example: a flute concerto is listed under Handel's name in the Breitkopf Thematic Catalogue (cf. B. S. Brook, ed., *The Breitkopf Thematic Catalogue: the Six Parts and Sixteen Supplements 1762–1787* (New York, 1966), p. 100) and could possibly be by him, though the style of the incipit is more typical of Hasse than Handel.

[81] Advertised in *The Daily Courant* for 16 February 1719; reproduced in O. E. Deutsch, ed., op. cit., p. 83.

[82] These three concertos may be found in the *Händel-Gesellschaft* edition, vol. xlvii, pp. 130–58, 159–231 and Supplement (bound with vol. xlviii), pp. 203–41. The first has also been printed in the *Hallische Händel-Ausgabe*, vol. iv/12, no. 8.

in that they are written for *three* separate groups of instruments—one string and two wind ensembles. They are late works, written, it is thought, between 1744 and 1751,[83] and the first two concertos (in B♭ and F respectively) rely heavily on borrowed material. There is no attempt to disguise the borrowings which are taken from such popular works as *Messiah*, *Esther*, *Belshazzar*, and *Semele*. *Belshazzar* had been written as late as 1744 and a comparison of the chorus 'See from his post Euphrates flies' with the 3rd movement of the first concerto shows that the instrumental version was made direct from the oratorio.[84] The third concerto (in F major) also contains some borrowings (the overture shares its material with Handel's 'Fitzwilliam' Overture for two clarinets and horn; the Finale has material in common with *Partenope*) but the three middle movements appear to be original. Although there is still some controversy as to the priority of this work over the sixteenth organ concerto it seems likely that the full orchestral version was written first.[85]

Unfortunately we do not know for what occasion these double concertos were originally designed—whether for performance within the oratorios[86] or for some open-air function. The last possibility is attractive given the rich instrumentation and expansive content of the works. Each concerto has four or more movements and the material is broad and dignified—well suited to performance on a large scale.

---

[83] In the Preface to vol. xlvii of the *Händel-Gesellschaft* edition, Chrysander put the date of composition at between 1740 and 1750. Later he ascribed the concertos to the period after the Scottish rebellion, 1748–50 (F. Chrysander, 'Händel's Instrumental-kompositionen für grosses Orchester', *Vierteljahrsschrift für Musikwissenschaft*, iii (1887), 25). Seiffert, in his edition of the concertos, gives a date of between 1747 and 1751. It is possible, however, that the first of the double-orchestra concertos was written as early as 1744, see F. Hudson in the Foreword to vol. iv/12 of the *Hallische Händel-Ausgabe*, p. x.

[84] F. Hudson, Foreword to *Hallische Händel-Ausgabe*, vol. iv/12, p. x.

[85] See pp. 118 and note 63.

[86] A contemporary copy of the third concerto 'a due cori' is marked 'Concerto in the Oratorio of Judas Maccabaeus'. This does not prove, however, that Handel designed the concerto for that purpose in the first instance.

The Horn Concerto in D Major

Before going on to discuss the formal structure of Handel's concertos some mention must be made of the D major concerto for two horns and strings which Max Seiffert published under the title of Concerto Grosso no. 30 in 1939. This edition was based on a set of eighteenth-century manuscript parts (not in Handel's handwriting) which Seiffert had discovered in the Schlossarchiv of the Prince of Bentheim-Tecklenburg's residence at Rheda (MS. 616). The Prince's residence lay on the Hanover to Dusseldorf road, a route taken by Handel on his journeys from Germany to England, and Seiffert maintained that the composer used to break his journey there. This assertion, however, remains unproven. The only real evidence connecting the concerto with Handel comes from the presence of his name on one of the parts (and on the cover, though this is of a later date). Even so, Frederick Hudson, who prints the work as a Supplement to volume iv/12 of the *Hallische Händel-Ausgabe*, expresses grave doubts as to its authenticity on both stylistic and circumstantial grounds. He points out that although Handel made similar experiments with solo horn passages in certain early works (notably *Radamisto* and the 1715 and 1717 *Water Music* suites) the general style of this D major concerto is untypical. Furthermore, he draws attention to the fact that there is only one other Handel manuscript at Rheda (a copy of an operatic aria) and this, in itself, is curious if, as Seiffert claimed, Handel knew the Prince personally.[87]

3. General Planning, Movement Types

For the most part, Handel's concertos approximate more nearly to the 'da chiesa' plan with its regular alternation of slow and quick movements, than to the Venetian type. The majority of his organ concertos are cast in four-movement form (slow–fast–slow–fast) and the same arrangement is

[87] F. Hudson, Foreword to vol. iv/12 of the *Hallische Händel-Ausgabe*, p. xi.

found in the second and fourth concertos of the op. 6 set. Handel was, however, reluctant to be bound by any rigid formal scheme and there are many alternative designs—notably in the Grand Concertos some of which have five and six movements apiece. Within the 'da chiesa' framework there is often a tendency to pair slow and fast movements. Many of the slow movements are separated from the next Allegro only by a double bar line and frequently they prepare the listener for the quick movement by cadencing in the dominant, rather than the tonic, key.[88] This last technique is particularly effective since it provides a notional conclusion for the slow movement and, at the same time, focuses attention on what is to come. Two- or three-movement concertos are rare[89] and the arrangement of movements within these works is seemingly fortuitous. For although the three-movement concertos sometimes follow Venetian patterns[90] there are other schemes too, as in the violin concerto with its slow–slow–fast pattern.

Although Handel obviously preferred the 'da chiesa' to the Venetian plan this does not mean, of course, that the content of his concertos is always serious. Originally there had been a distinction between the solemn 'sonata da chiesa' form (i.e. suitable for church performance) and the dance-orientated 'sonata da camera' (fit for chamber use). But as dance movements found their way into the 'da chiesa' form with increasing frequency the distinction gradually disappeared, until, by the beginning of the eighteenth century, it was virtually obsolete. It comes as no surprise, therefore, to find Handel using various dance-derived movements in his concertos. These may either take the form of extra move-

[88] E.g. oboe concerto no. 1 in B♭ major. Handel adds two extra bars at the end of the third movement to make a perfect cadence in the dominant key. The next Allegro then follows in B♭.

[89] Op. 3, no. 6, has only two movements; examples of three-movement concertos include op. 3, no. 1, op. 4, no. 1, op. 4, no. 6, Op. 7, no. 6 (counting the *ad libitum* movement), and the violin concerto.

[90] As in op. 4, no. 6 which is arranged in the following manner: 'andante allegro'—Larghetto—'allegro moderato'.

ments, tacked on to a normal 'da chiesa' concerto, or they may form part of the four-movement structure itself.[91]

The presence of these dance-derived movements contributes to the unusually wide range of movement types found in the concertos. The op. 6 set alone is, as Lang puts it,

> . . . a fantastic jumble: French overture, Italian, French and English dances, *sonata da chiesa*, chamber duet, all freely mixed; then again we hear an aria or an accompanied recitative, theme and variations, fugue, etc. Some movements are entirely in the *concerto a quattro* style, that is, for orchestra alone without solo parts, others tend towards the solo concerto, still others belong rightfully in the domain of the suite, and some are decidedly symphonic. . . .[92]

And when one considers the concertos as a whole the wealth of variety becomes even more impressive. Some idea of this extraordinary richness can be gained from Table 3 which lists the separate movement types together with one representative example of each:

Table 3

Movement type	Example
Allegro in concerto style	Op. 6, no. 3, III
Allegro with figurative material	Op. 6, no. 5, III
Allegro with popular or 'folk' associations	Op. 3, no. 5, Finale
Allegro with rhythmic ostinato	Concerto 'a due cori' no. 2, V ('allegro ma non troppo')[1]
Allegro with strong contrasts of material	Op. 6, no. 5, V
Allegro with symphonic connections	Op. 4, no. 4, I
Motivic Allegro	Oboe concerto no. 2, Finale
Programmatic Allegro	Organ concerto no. 13, II
Dance-derived movements:	
(a) Allemande	Op. 6, no. 8, I
(b) Bourrée	Op. 7, no. 1, IV (Allegro)
(c) Chaconne	Op. 7, no. 1, I and II

[91] An example of the former is provided by op. 6, no. 9, which has six movements: Largo—Allegro—Larghetto—Allegro—Menuet—Gigue; the second category may be represented by op. 4, no. 3, which is a four-movement concerto with a gavotte-Finale.

[92] P. H. Lang, *George Frideric Handel* (London, 1966), p. 649.

(d)	Gavotte	Op. 7, no. 5, IV
(e)	Gigue	Op. 6, no. 9, VI
(f)	Hornpipe	Op. 6, no. 7, V
(g)	March	Organ concerto no. 16, Finale
(h)	Minuet	Op. 6, no. 9, V
(i)	Musette	Op. 6, no. 6, III
(j)	Polonaise	Op. 6, no. 3, IV
(k)	Sarabande	Oboe concerto no. 3, III
(l)	Siciliano	Oboe concerto no. 1, III

French Overture:

(a)	conventional type	Op. 6, no. 10, I
(b)	with non-fugal Allegro	Op. 6, no. 6, I

Fugal Allegro with figurative episodes	Op. 3, no. 3, II
Fugue	Op. 3, no. 2, III

Slow movements:

(a)	air	Op. 6, no. 10, III
(b)	chordal	Op. 6, no. 9, I
(c)	decorative	Op. 4, no. 2, III
(d)	figurative	Op. 3, no. 2, II
(e)	ground bass	Op. 7, no. 5, II
(f)	pastoral	Op. 3, no. 4, II (Andante)
(g)	short, modulatory	Op. 6, no. 12, IV
(h)	slow, with strongly contrasted material	Op. 6, no. 2, III
(i)	trio sonata type	Op. 6, no. 5, IV
(j)	variations	Op. 6, no. 12, III
(k)	'vocal' duet	Op. 6, no. 1, III

[1] Where the number of the movement alone might prove misleading, the tempo indication is included in parenthesis.

Handel's technique of re-using old material does, of course, contribute to the variety of these concerto movements. The symphonic Allegro which opens op. 4, no. 4, for example, was originally written as an orchestral introduction to the chorus 'Questo è il cielo' from *Alcina*. Transferred to its new context, the movement injects an exciting element of vitality and drama into the concerto genre. Unfortunately, however, not all the borrowings are integrated so successfully. Sometimes their original function is all too clear, as in the thin-textured Allemande of op. 6, no. 8, which sounds much more effective as a keyboard piece in suite no. 2 of Handel's third collection.

4. Formal Structure

The same diversity is apparent in Handel's treatment of form. In general terms, he relies less on stereotyped ritornello structures than his contemporaries, and places more weight on the form-building properties of motivic development. The course of a movement may be altered at any moment to suit the musical content and unorthodox procedures become the order of the day.

The Fugal Allegro

Handel's refusal to be restricted by convention is particularly noticeable in the fugal Allegros. These movements, which comprise one of the largest formal groups in the concertos, fall into two categories: the fugal Allegro with figurative episodes (i.e. the concerto fugue) and the strict fugue itself. Op. 3, no. 3, movement two is representative of the first type in that its solo recorder (or oboe) and first violin provide concertante interest. The exposition of the fugue subject takes place in the first eleven bars (bars being numbered from the beginning of the Allegro section), and this is followed by a solo episode which introduces new and highly figurative material. At bar 19 fragments of the original tutti material prepare the way for another statement of the fugue subject in the bass. From this point onwards there is a regular alternation between the two contrasting sections. The soloists have four main episodes during the course of the movement and the fugal section functions as a tutti ritornello:

Outline structure of op. 3, no. 3, movement two (Allegro)

Bar no.	Tutti/solo	Material	Key
1	Tutti	Fugal	G–D–G
12	Solo	Figurative	D
19	Tutti	Fugal	D

[93] This particular fugue subject was popular with Handel; it also occurs in the *Birthday Ode for Queen Anne* (2nd movement—'The day that gave great Anna birth'), in *Deborah* (the first chorus, at 'O grant a leader to our host'), and in the *Brockes Passion* (see the chorus 'Ein jeder sei ihm untertänig'). The entire movement is, of course, found in the seventh *Chandos Anthem*. (see Appendix A).

23	Solo	Figurative	G–E minor–G–E minor
35	Tutti	Fugal	E minor
37	Solo	Figurative (interrupted at bar 44 by one bar of tutti with material from the fugal section)	E minor–A minor–D–B minor
48	Tutti	Fugal	B minor– E minor–A–D–G
60	Solo	Figurative	G
65	Tutti	Fugal	G

Although there are several movements of this type in Handel's concertos, he preferred the genuine fugue in which there is no division into solo and ripieno groups and no alternation of contrapuntal/figurative material. Perhaps there were pragmatic reasons for this. A great many of these fugal movements were transferred from Handel's vocal or keyboard works and it was obviously quicker to make a straight-forward transcription than to recast them in concerto form. Admittedly the effect of such pieces within a concerto framework is somewhat monochrome, lacking as they do the colourful contrasts between concertino and ripieno instruments, but this is balanced, to some extent, by the more unified structure of the form. The main defect of the concerto fugue is that any cumulative effect that may be built up is weakened by the presence of unrelated solo episodes. There are no such problems of course in the orchestral fugue.

The op. 3 set again provides a representative example in the shape of the 3rd movement of no. 2. The exposition of this fugal Allegro is particularly characteristic in that the countersubject overlaps with the end of the fugue subject. Normally, of course, the first statement of the fugue subject would be unaccompanied but Handel frequently ignored this convention with good effect. The other point of interest concerns the arrangement of entries. All proceeds smoothly until the third bar when the viola rushes in with the first four notes of the fugue subject, creating a stretto with the bass instruments which present the whole theme two beats later. While a false entry of this type would not occasion comment in the middle or final section of a fugue, its presence at the very beginning of the exposition cannot be disregarded. The rhythm is disturbed (because the viola enters on beat three, not beat one), and the subsequent bass entry is made all the more emphatic:

EXAMPLE 4
Handel, op. 3, no. 2, 3rd movement, bars 1–6

After the exposition there is a short and rather conventional episode in which the interest is shared between the syncopations of the two upper parts and the steadily-moving bass line. The same type of material is used for the second episode (at bar 16ff.). Later in the movement, however, these 'interludes' between the various statements of the fugue subject become more original. At bar 29, for example, Handel introduces a striking idea, the essence of which is more homophonic than contrapuntal despite the exchange of motifs between first and second violins:

EXAMPLE 5
Handel, op. 3, no. 2, 3rd movement, bars 29–30

Theoretically, a passage of this kind has no place in a fugal movement since it halts the logical flow of part-writing and impedes the cumulative process. Yet Handel frequently introduced such passages into his fugues. If explanation is needed (and in Handel's case the musical result usually justifies the means) it must lie in his penchant for motivic development. Although the episodic idea (labelled (a) in Ex. 5) sounds new, it is in fact derived from the countersubject. The various stages of development may be traced from the first appearance of this motif in bar 3, where it serves as a decorative preparation for the suspension (see Ex. 4, second violin part), to bar 26, where the interval of the fourth is widened to a sixth, and finally, to bar 29 where the three-note motif detaches itself from the following suspension and is subjected to further changes of melodic outline (see Ex. 5). One other point must be stressed, this motif which assumes such great importance in the course of the movement is derived, as we have seen, not from the fugue subject itself, but from the countersubject. As P. H. Lang remarked when discussing Handel's vocal fugues: 'In some of his most magnificent fugues Handel does not pay much attention to the original theme; instead of developing it in the "correct" manner, he proceeds freely with snippets of thematic material, almost in a symphonic vein. If a motif strikes his fancy he will belabor it with gusto.'[94]

'Block' Movements

The dramatic contrast produced by the introduction of homophonic passages into movements of a predominantly contrapuntal nature is a familiar feature of Handel's music. He seemed to relish the juxtaposition of contrasting sections, whether the opposition was of the linear/vertical type just discussed or whether it stemmed primarily from the use of sharply differentiated blocks of material. Some of the non-fugal concerto movements actually derive their formal plan from the principle of dramatic confrontation. There can be little doubt, for instance, that in the 3rd movement of op. 6, no. 2, Handel intended there to be a direct contrast between the Largo section and the following 'larghetto andante, e piano'.[95] The resultant form can be represented in these terms:

Outline structure of op. 6, no. 2, 3rd movement

Bar no.	Key	Tutti/solo	Tempo	Material
1–9	B♭	Mainly bar by bar t/s alternation	Largo	A
10–17	B♭–F	Tutti with solo	Larghetto	B
18–26	F	Bar by bar t/s alternation	Largo	A
27–45	F	Tutti with solo	Larghetto	B
46–7	–C	Tutti with solo	Adagio	Adagio cadence

The two main sections (A and B) are based on strongly contrasted material, the first consisting of an opening flourish with bar-by-bar alternation of tutti and solo groups, the second being characterized by a smooth, repeated-note figure. This thematic opposition is of fundamental importance and the different tempo indications which appear at the beginning of each section serve merely to enhance it.[96]

[94] P. H. Lang, op. cit., p. 605.

[95] Cf. also W. Serauky, *Georg Friedrich Händel, sein Leben, sein Werk* (Kassel, 1956), pp. 442–3.

[96] Interestingly enough, Corelli's op. 6 set provides a parallel example. In the second concerto of this collection, 1st movement, an opening vivace section alternates with a contrasting allegro section, thus producing a very similar form to

A similar example occurs in the 5th movement of op. 6, no. 5. Here there is no change of tempo to underline the dramatic opposition but the individual sections are equally well defined:

Outline structure of op. 6, no. 5, 5th movement. (There is no division into concertino and ripieno groups in this movement)

Bar no.	Key	Material
1–4	D/G/D	A
5–8	D	B^1
9–14	D–A	B^2
15–18	A	A
19–22	A	B^1
23–36	A, modulating through F# minor to B minor	B^2
37–40	B minor	B^1
41–6	G–D	A
47–50	D/G/D	B^1
51–6	D/G/D	B^2
57–8	D	A
59–67	D/G/D	B^2
68–71	D	B^1
72–8	D	B^2
79–82	D	A

As will be seen from Example 6, sections A and B are differentiated not only by the type of melodic material used but also by rhythm and harmonic pace. The opening theme—which sounds remarkably Scarlattian[97]—moves in a two-quaver/crotchet pattern and is presented over a static bass. This is followed immediately by the livelier material of B^1; momentum is increased by the semiquaver movement of beats one and two, and then by the rapidly changing harmony at the end of each bar. Section B^2 becomes even more urgent, with constant semiquaver movement and a baroque running bass:

---

the one discussed. (The Corelli example is, however, complicated by the presence of an adagio section in the tonic minor and a final passage which is marked 'largo andante'.)

[97] See p. 157.

EXAMPLE 6

Handel, op. 6, no. 5, 5th movement, section A (bars 1–4); the
beginning of section B¹ (bars 5–7) and part of section B² (bar 10). (The
oboe parts are omitted)

The Ritornello Allegro

Although Handel was less reliant on ritornello structures
than many of his contemporaries, his concertos still contain
a fair proportion of these movements. It seems that he
associated the ritornello Allegro with the solo concerto
rather than the concerto grosso for there are proportionately
more ritornello structures in the organ and oboe concertos
than in the sets of concerti grossi. The op. 6 collection, for
example, contains only three such movements:[98] no. 3, 3rd

[98] Or four, if the somewhat irregular Finale of op. 6, no. 4, is regarded as a
ritornello movement.

movement; no. 6, 4th movement; and no. 9, 2nd movement. Furthermore, each of these movements is written in the manner of a solo concerto for, although the scores call for two soloists, in practice all the figurative passages are given to the first violin; the second merely provides an accompaniment. Indeed, taking the concertos as a whole, we find that Handel uses the ritornello Allegro only three times in a true concerto grosso context: in the opening movement of the C major concerto from *Alexander's Feast*, at the beginning of op. 3, no. 1, and in the 1st movement of op. 3, no. 6.

Handel's ritornello Allegros do not fall into any stereotyped pattern. Some are written in conventional concerto style, while in other movements—see, for example, the Finale of op. 3, no. 1—the ritornello principle is allied to material of a more dance-like character. As in J. S. Bach's concertos, so here the number of ritornello statements varies widely in different movements, although four statements represents the norm. It is often difficult to decide at what point the middle ritornelli begin, for the entry of the tutti does not always coincide with the return of the opening ritornello material and where there are several different sections in the first ritornello these are sometimes lifted out of context and presented as independent tutti passages later in the movement.

By comparison with J. S. Bach, Handel's opening ritornelli seem short and rather insubstantial. Most last for between six and twelve bars of $\frac{4}{4}$ (at an allegro tempo), though one or two are considerably longer than this. The simplest type of ritornello consists of two or three ideas heard in straight succession (cf. op. 6, no. 9, 2nd movement).[99] In the majority of cases, however, the repetition of the various sections creates a more sophisticated structure. The opening ritornello of op. 7, no. 3, 1st movement, for instance, is so arranged that the third section (C) returns to

[99] Here there are three clearly-defined sections: A (bars 1–18), complete with *pianoidée*; B(bars 18–24), a lively section characterized by downward-rushing scales, and C (bars 24–8), a simple Corellian progression which brings the ritornello to an uneventful conclusion.

round off the tutti statement, making an ABCDC pattern:

EXAMPLE 7

Handel, op. 7, no. 3, 1st movement, bars 1–10 (outer parts only)

In the above example, the four principal sections, though short, are clearly differentiated. The first phrase divides into antecedent and consequent (A and B), each having its own character, while the next phrase has a curious interpolation (bar 7) in the shape of a smooth, piano motif (D).

This idea of inserting a quiet contrasting motif into the ritornello gained ground during the second and third decades of the eighteenth century. Experimental examples occur in Vivaldi's concertos although he tended to use contrasts of mode and material rather than of dynamics.[100] Gradually the contrast motif, or *pianoidée*, became more formalized and a number of conventions grew up surround-

[100] E.g. Vivaldi's violin concerto in G RV 302, 1st movement.

ing its use. There would be a sudden lowering of dynamics, a thinning of texture to three parts: the upper voices would consort in thirds over a static bass and there would often be a darkening of tonality. Although Handel had little time for convention he did sometimes use the *pianoidée* in its orthodox form. There is a contrast motif in the ritornello of op. 4, no. 2, 2nd movement, which incorporates all the features mentioned above, and similar examples occur elsewhere.[101]

EXAMPLE 8

Handel, op. 4, no. 2, 2nd movement, bars 1–14 (short score)

[101] Other examples occur in op. 6, no. 9, 2nd movement (here only the piano mark is missing) and in op. 7, no. 5, 1st movement (the change of key is from G minor to F minor).

From the music historian's point of view, the inclusion of a quiet, contrasting motif within the ritornello was of considerable importance since it directly undermined the baroque doctrine of affections whereby a single affect (or mood) was maintained throughout a movement. Once contrast motifs had been introduced the way was open for the dramatic dualism of sonata form. Indeed, the *pianoidée* might almost be considered the ancestor of the classical second subject for it contained within itself the idea of a soft contrasting theme.

Since Handel's treatment of ritornello movements depends so greatly on the type of material with which he is working, it will be more fruitful to follow the course of one movement than to attempt any generalization. The movement selected for detailed analysis is the second Allegro from op. 6, no. 6. As will be seen from the following example, the style of the opening ritornello leaves little doubt that Handel was acquainted with the work of Albinoni and Vivaldi:

EXAMPLE 9
Handel, op. 6, no. 6, 4th movement, bars 1–6 (outer parts only)

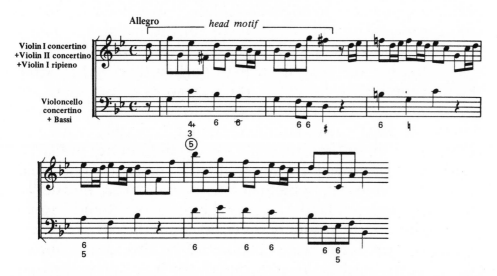

These bars represent only the first part of what is, for Handel, an unusually lengthy ritornello. Given the scale of this first tutti section it is not surprising to find Handel effecting some temporary movement away from the tonic key. The head-motif, a square, sturdy idea in G minor, is followed by a sequential passage leading to a restatement of the opening theme in the relative major. The second section of the ritornello (bars 6–12) confirms this modulation and at the same time introduces a typical Vivaldian flourish in the shape of forceful arpeggio movement for unaccompanied violins. There is then a caesura before the final part of the ritornello which is in G minor throughout and which starts with the original head-motif (bar 13).

The first solo episode is thoroughly Vivaldian in content, the solo violinist being given brilliant semiquaver figuration while the other string instruments provide a light, open-textured accompaniment (cf. bars 21ff.). The next appearance of the ritornello is at bar 35. However, the head-motif is not presented straight away. Handel rearranges his material so that this particular tutti section commences with the last few bars of the ritornello (the figurative section). We then move on to the second section with its arpeggio flourish until finally, at bar 42, the first part of the ritornello is reached. As regards key, this second ritornello statement springs a surprise: it begins regularly enough in D minor (the dominant) but moves into F major for the last few bars.

The second solo episode opens in similar fashion to the first, although the figuration is reworked (bars 51f.). After the first three bars, however, the tutti joins in and there are some rapid exchanges between solo and ripieno instruments. A third tutti statement, concerned only with the central portion of the ritornello, occurs in G minor at bar 59 and this is followed by another solo passage. The final ritornello statement, which begins at bar 70, is unusually free. Once again, Handel avoids the head-motif and begins the section with a totally new idea in the shape of an ascending chromatic scale. Thematically, this idea is out of place, yet its musical effect is superb for it creates a sense of rising excitement the results of which carry through to the end of the movement. To return to the head-motif, this is not heard in its complete form again. Instead, Handel takes the rhythm and basic melodic shape of the opening and subjects it to further development during the course of the final ritornello. At bars 80–4, therefore, we find a short development in which the head-motif is re-shaped to suit the all-important harmonic scheme (see the Neapolitan chord of bars 83–5):

EXAMPLE 10

Handel, op. 6, no. 6, 4th movement, bars 80–6 (outer parts only)

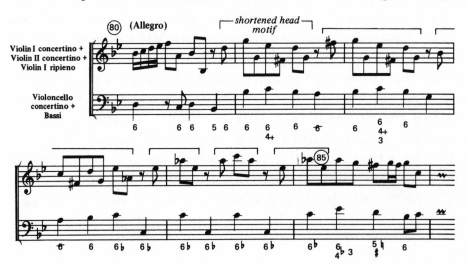

One further point must be mentioned in connection with the movement just discussed. It will be noticed that the penultimate ritornello is presented in the tonic key. By analogy with J. S. Bach's practice, this might lead us to expect some kind of final section with repetition of material from earlier solo episodes. In fact, no such repetition occurs. Looking at the concertos as a whole, the same pattern emerges: although the penultimate ritornello (of a four- or five-ritornello movement) will sometimes be in the tonic key,[102] solo material is seldom recapitulated at this point.[103]

Ritornello Structure in Slow Movements

For some reason Handel avoided the 'framed' slow movement popular with J. S. Bach and Vivaldi. Those slow movements (and they are few in number) which are constructed according to ritornello principles, therefore, have the full form. Typical in this respect is the opening Grave of the G minor oboe concerto. Although the movement is so short (29 bars in all) it contains four statements of the ritornello, in G minor, B♭ major, C minor and G minor respectively (bars 1–5, 13–14, 18–20, and 26–9). The structure 'works' because there is no clear distinction between tutti and solo material; a sharper contrast would have made the movement too episodic in style. What is perhaps the most curious example of Handel's ritornello form occurs in the opening 'larghetto, e staccato' of op. 4, no. 1. This movement appears to be based on two different ritornelli. The first (bars 1–7) is characterized by the upward-rushing scales of bar 2 and this vigorous opening contrasts strongly with the material of the other ritornello (bars 24–7) which is played *all'ottava* on the strings against a pedal note held in the upper stave of the organ part. Throughout, the ritornelli are presented in alternation so that one does not assume greater importance than the other.

[102] Another example occurs in the 1st movement of op. 4, no. 4.

[103] The 2nd movement of op. 4, no. 2, is interesting in that some figurative material from the first solo is heard between the fourth and fifth ritornelli (bars 26–8 are repeated, transposed into the home key, at bars 107–9). However, this does not represent Handel's normal practice.

Binary Movements

If anything, binary movements outnumber those in ritornello form. Binary form was, of course, germane to the
suite so that one would expect the dance movements to be
written in traditional bipartite form—and so they are, for
the most part.[104] But Handel also uses the form in movements which have no ostensible connection with the suite.
Sometimes the double bar line will be present; sometimes it
is discarded. In a sense its presence is irrelevant (if repeats are
omitted) for the listener recognizes binary structure by
virtue of its tonic/dominant: dominant/tonic key scheme
and by the characteristic (often symmetrical) arrangement
of material within each half.

It must be said that Handel makes little attempt to adapt
the form to the special requirements of the concerto genre.
In the 1st movement of op. 4, no. 6, for example, the tutti
makes only three important appearances: at the beginning
and end of the movement and at the end of the first half.
Obviously there is little to distinguish a movement such as
this from contemporary sonata pieces (and, indeed, some of
the concerto movements were so derived).[105]

For the 2nd movement of op. 6, no. 1, Handel adopts an
alternative, but no more satisfactory, solution: here it is the
soloists who are neglected, with only 8 independent bars out
of a total of 54. This movement, though so unequal in its
tutti/solo division, has an exceptionally well-balanced structure. It breaks into two parts at bar 28 despite the absence of
a double bar line. In bars 1–28, therefore, we have the first
section of a conventional binary-form movement, complete
with the traditional modulation from tonic (G) to dominant
(D) keys. The second half is particularly interesting since it
embraces a well-defined recapitulation section. Starting at

---

104 With the notable exception of the Musette from op. 6, no. 6, which is in a type
of rondo form: ABACADACA.

105 E.g. op. 4, no. 5, 2nd movement which derives from the recorder sonata op. 1,
no. 11 (see Appendix A). The sonata version is in straight-forward binary form but
in the concerto version Handel repeats the first five bars (and adds a double bar line)
to create a tutti/solo effect.

bar 39 with a restatement of the opening theme, this final section recapitulates all the principal material of the first half. It even ends in the same manner—with a transposed statement of bars 24–8. Within the concertos, this is the closest that Handel ever came to a sonata-form type of construction.

Before leaving the subject of Handel's binary-form movements a word must be said about those pieces which combine bipartite structure with other formal elements. One of the most curious, yet successful, of these hybrid movements is the Finale of op. 7, no. 2. Its underlying structure is clearly that of a binary-form movement with a double bar line dividing the two halves. The tonal scheme is also conventional in that we find the expected modulation from tonic to dominant and back. Superimposed upon this binary structure, however, are elements of both ritornello and 'block' form.

The movement opens with an eight-bar tutti statement, beginning as follows:

EXAMPLE 11
Handel, op. 7, no. 2, Finale, bars 1–4

The interest then passes to the solo organ part which introduces a new and completely different idea:

EXAMPLE 12
Handel, op. 7, no. 2, Finale, bars 8–11 (organ part only)

The contrast between these two themes is very marked; after the strong, incisive opening the paired quavers of the solo theme sound mellow and ingratiating. Here, then, we have the strongly contrasting sections associated with 'block' form. But the form is complicated further by the reappearance of the tutti at the end of the first half (bars 34ff.) presenting the original ritornello material. The second half of the movement opens with a repetition of the solo theme, now transposed from A to E major. There follows a short but powerful tutti entry which effects a modulation to B minor and the solo theme is resumed in a new key (bar 50). After a more figurative section for unaccompanied organ the tutti instruments present a new version of their ritornello in the home key. This heralds the start of a final section in which the solo theme is recapitulated (bars 74ff.).[106] The tutti instruments then bring the movement to an end with yet another variant of the ritornello.

An admixture of binary and variation form is sometimes used for Finales of a dance-like character. The idea is simple yet effective: Handel takes a normal binary-form movement and extends it by the addition of one or more variations. These variations, which follow the course of the original very closely, rely heavily on the conventional techniques of patterned figuration. The Finale of op. 3, no. 2, illustrates this point well: in the first variation the melody is preserved intact while the bass line is broken up into quavers (the old 'division' technique); throughout the second variation the oboes have the melody with the violins adding a decorative countersubject in the faster rhythm (triplet quavers). The progressive diminution of note-values (from the crotchets of the opening binary section to the triplets of variation two) was a traditional feature of early baroque variation movements, designed to combat the static, and necessarily repetitive, character of the form.

---

[106] As so often in Handel, the theme is given a varied restatement.

Ground Bass Movements

Discussion of these variation movements leads to a consideration of Handel's ground bass structures. Strict ostinato form is seldom found in his concertos, although the 2nd movement of op. 7, no. 5, with its constant repetition of a two-bar ground, provides an isolated, if uninspired, example. More typical are the first two movements of op. 7, no. 1, which, taken together, form a large-scale chaconne. Both movements are built on the same harmonic progression—an elaboration of the basic I–IV–V–I formula—but there is sufficient variety of treatment to justify separation: the first Andante is in $\frac{4}{4}$; the 2nd movement (also an Andante) presents the ground in triple time. It says much for Handel's powers of invention that our attention does not flag at some stage during the 197 bars. In fact, the musical interest is sustained by a variety of means: the inventive quality of the figuration, the subtle changes of orchestration and texture, the occasional migration of the ground from lower to upper parts, the flowing countersubjects—all these elements play a major part. They also compensate for the limited tonal range. Although on paper the key scheme of the 1st movement looks varied enough (E♭, F, G minor, C minor, B♭), in practice there are long stretches of static B♭ major tonality; similarly with the 2nd movement which begins in B♭ major and touches briefly on two darker keys (E♭ major and B♭ minor) before returning to the tonic.

'Da capo' Structures

Unlike J. S. Bach, Handel seldom used 'da capo' structures for his concertos. This might seem curious in one who was primarily a vocal composer and whose operas and oratorios abound with 'da capo' arias in the high baroque manner. Of course, operatic stars of the period expected—sometimes even demanded—this type of aria since it offered unparalleled opportunities to display their skill at ornamentation (the first part being decorated on repetition). Although the ABA form had severe limitations, to abandon it in opera would have been unacceptable during the 1720s. However, instrumental composers were under no obligation to use the form and it is conceivable that Handel's dislike of formalized structures led him to avoid it where he could. Of the three examples which occur in the concertos,[107] one is a dance movement (in simple minuet style); the other two combine 'da capo' and ritornello features. The most interesting of these ritornello movements is the Finale of op. 3, no. 5, an Allegro in ¢ time which, with its folk-like main theme, sounds curiously reminiscent of Telemann:

EXAMPLE 13
Handel, op. 3, no. 5, Finale, bars 1–12

Although there is no division into tutti/solo groups, and although almost every bar is derived from the material shown above, the movement has a strong ritornello flavour. Handel makes a distinction between *all'unisono* statements and those with some harmonic or contrapuntal colouring, so that the form may be represented as follows:

Outline structure of op. 3, no. 5, Finale

Section	Bar no.	Key	Material
Section A	1	D minor	Ritornello 1 (unison)
	12	D minor–F–A minor/D minor	Opening material 'developed' contrapuntally (see Ex. 23)
	66	D minor	Ritornello 2 (unison)
Section B	74	F–C/A minor	Based on a variant of the principal theme, the style being harmonic rather than contrapuntal
Section A	98	D minor	Ritornello 3 (unison)

107 These are: op. 3, no. 4, 4th movement; op. 3, no. 5, 5th movement; and op. 6, no. 11, Finale (hence also the Finale of organ concerto no. 14).

| 110 | D minor–F–
A minor/
D minor | Opening material 'developed'
contrapuntally |
| 164 | D minor | Ritornello 4 (unison) |

The idea of using a variant strain for the central section proves most effective here and illustrates once again Handel's unique powers of thematic manipulation. It is particularly interesting to see how he arrives at the variant. The essence of the original theme lies in its repeated four-note pattern (see Ex. 13) and this feature is retained in section B. But the direction of the motif is altered, the downward leap of a diminished fourth being replaced by a simple continuation up the scale:

EXAMPLE 14

Handel, op. 3, no. 5, Finale, bars 74–8 (beginning of section B)

This ability to develop and manipulate material lies at the centre of Handel's compositional technique. Motivic development of the type just discussed may occur in almost any movement, whatever its mode of construction.[108] It is this technique which so often transforms traditional fugal, ritornello, or 'da capo' structures into unique and living forms.

5. Stylistic Features

It is a commonplace that Handel was one of the most eclectic composers of the baroque period. His style reflects the rich variety of music with which he came into contact yet, at the same time, remains intensely personal. There is some unique and indefinable quality which both binds together the most disparate elements into the familiar

---

[108] In some exceptional movements—e.g. the Finale of the second oboe concerto in Bb major—motivic development provides the sole form-building element.

Handelian style and also lends a sense of unity to all his works. So great is this unifying force that sharply contrasting styles may occur within a single work without seeming incongruous. One of the most striking examples of this is provided by op. 6, no. 5. Among its six movements there is an opening French Overture (in the style of Lully), a Corellian Adagio, and a 5th movement whose string writing is obviously influenced by the clichés of the newly-developing symphony (see Ex. 6, section B^2). The eclectic nature of this work was fully appreciated by Burney who described it in the following terms:

The opening of this piece always impressed me with the idea of its being the most spirited and characteristic of all the movements that were written by HANDEL, or any other composer, on Lulli's model of Opera Overture; which seems to require a convulsive, determined and military cast. The two following movements . . . contain little more than the light and common-place passages of the times. The *Largo*, however, is an excellent piece of harmony and modulation, in Corelli's natural and sober style; and, in the next movement, we have a very early specimen of the symphonic style of Italy, in which rapid iterations of the same note are designed to contrast with something better, if not mere noise and *remplissage*, totally devoid of meaning, of which there are but too frequent instances. The subject of HANDEL'S movement is modern, marked and pleasing; and the base accompaniment of his iterations, bold and interesting. The finale, or minuet of this Concerto, has been so much admired by English composers of HANDEL'S school, as to have been frequently thought worthy of imitation.[109]

And it is not only in this concerto that we find such variety. Old and new techniques are used side by side and the distinctive national idioms of Italy and France (and even of those countries on the periphery of musical developments such as Poland and England) all enrich the Handelian style.

Handel's catholicity of taste was, to a large extent, a product of the type of musical education he received. In 1696 he began serious study with Zachau (or Zachow as the name is sometimes spelt), an organist and composer steeped in the traditions of German church music. Hawkins tells us

---

[109] C. Burney, *In Commemoration of Handel*, p. 57.

that his exercises consisted of 'the composition of fugues and airs upon points or subjects delivered to him from time to time by his master'.[110] But Zachau's teaching was not as narrow as this suggests. According to Mainwaring, he 'had a large collection of Italian and German music: he shewed him [Handel] the different styles of different nations; the excellencies and defects of each particular author'.[111]

Initially, it seemed that Handel was going to follow Zachau's profession for his first appointment was that of organist at the Domkirche, Halle. But he soon made his way to Hamburg, attracted, no doubt, by the strong operatic traditions of that city. He found employment at the famous opera house, first as a violinist, later as harpsichordist—a more responsible post. It was here that he heard the operas of Reinhard Keiser which made such a deep impression upon him;[112] here, too, in 1705, that his first opera, *Almira*, was performed. Having entered the operatic arena, it was only natural that he should make a 'pilgrimage' to the South, and so we find him, the following year, in Italy, gaining first-hand experience of the Italian style from such composers as Corelli, Carissimi, the two Scarlattis (father and son), Vivaldi, and Steffani (whom he succeeded as kapellmeister to the Elector of Hanover in 1710).[113] Although Handel's stay in Italy was relatively short its effects proved long-lasting. His appointment at Hanover, and his contacts with French,[114] and subsequently English,

[110] J. Hawkins, op. cit. v. 264.

[111] J. Mainwaring, op. cit., p. 14.

[112] Especially *Octavia* which Handel used extensively in his opera *Agrippina* and elsewhere, cf. M. Seiffert's preface to Keiser's *Octavia*, ed. F. Chrysander and published as Supplement 6 to the *Händel-Gesellschaft* edition (Leipzig, 1902).

[113] We do not know whether Handel ever met Vivaldi but it is almost certain that he was personally acquainted with the other great figure of the Italian concerto: Arcangelo Corelli. The anecdote of how Corelli reputedly failed to sight-read a passage in Handel's *Il Trionfo del Tempo* has been repeated by numerous biographers from Mainwaring to the present day; true or not, it is quite probable that Corelli directed the orchestra in the Rome performance of *Il Trionfo* and also *La Resurrezione* which was produced in the same year (1708) (see R. Gerber, 'Händel und Italien', *50 Jahre Göttinger Händel-Festspiele Festschrift Göttingen*, 1970 (Kassel, 1970), pp. 5–15).

[114] At Hanover (where Cambert's son-in-law Farinel was music director) and through Handel's friendship with Telemann.

music resulted in an overlay of other nationalistic idioms but did little to alter the basic orientation of his style which, from 1706 onwards, reflected his deep commitment to the Italian manner.

Another factor which contributed to the eclecticism of Handel's style was, of course, his habit of appropriating material from other composers' works. His plagiaristic activities—for there is no other word to describe them—are well-known and will be discussed in detail later on. The subject is important since it sheds light both on Handel's compositional technique and on the type of music known to him. Yet to discuss his borrowings at this point would only prove confusing, for it is not true that the composers from whom Handel borrowed material are necessarily those whose style was the most closely related to his own. If we consider the artistic relationship between Handel and Corelli, for example, it will be observed that although Handel borrowed very few actual themes from Corelli he was considerably influenced by the latter's general style. And the converse can also be true. Although Handel plundered Telemann's *Musique de Table* collection time and again for thematic inspiration, he seldom adopted what might be described as the Telemann style (the only exceptions being the folk-like Finale theme of op. 3, no. 5, and the Polonaise of op. 6, no. 3).

The Formation of a Style

Some account of Handel's early career has already been given and it seems appropriate therefore to discuss the effect which the various encounters with different types of music had on his own developing style. Leaving aside the very early period of study with Zachau, we come to his years at the Hamburg opera, then under the leadership of the brilliant, if somewhat unconventional, Reinhard Keiser.

There is little doubt that Handel's style owed much to the influence of Keiser. Borrowings apart, there are sufficient parallels in the sphere of movement-types, melodic phrases, instrumentation, and so forth to support this view. Keiser's

treatment of the French Overture and the Siciliana come
particularly close to Handel's; furthermore, there are
marked similarities between the melodic styles of the two
composers. The example given below (from Keiser's
Octavia) shows how closely the style corresponds and
underlines the danger of regarding this type of melody as
exclusively Handelian:

EXAMPLE 15
Keiser, *Octavia*, Trio following the duet 'Die trübe Wolke', bars
1–14[115]

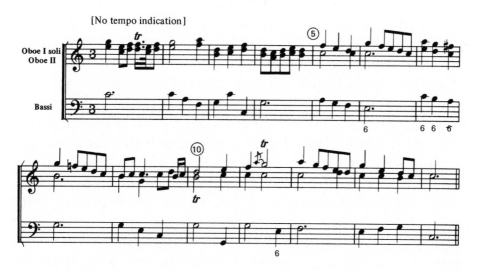

A comparable movement is the Finale of Handel's op. 3, no.
4, with its broad melodic lines and decisive harmony.
Although Keiser's curious use of the $^6_4$ (Ex. 15, bar 10, beat 3)
has no parallel in this particular movement, a remarkably
similar usage occurs in the Finale of Handel's *Alexander's
Feast* concerto (at bar 13).

After Hamburg came Italy, and Handel's knowledge of
musical styles was extended to include (among others) the
works of Corelli, Vivaldi, and Domenico Scarlatti. In point
of fact, it is not clear whether Handel's involvement with
the new Italian concerto dates from his stay in Italy or

[115] Example from Supplement 6 of the *Händel-Gesellschaft* edition, ed. F. Chrysander, p. 203.

whether it should more properly be placed after 1712 when he had already settled in England. He would probably have heard some of Vivaldi's early concertos in Italy for these may have been circulating before 1710 despite their relatively late publication date.[116] But it is debatable whether he encountered Corelli's op. 6 set before taking up residence in London. These twelve concertos were not published until 1714—the English edition followed one year later—and although it is possible that they, too, had circulated in manuscript form there is less evidence for this. (Muffat's famous claim[117] that he had heard some of Corelli's concertos in Rome in the early 1680s is often taken to refer to this op. 6 set; in fact, he could equally well have been describing a 'concertante-style' performance of some sonatas.)[118]

Corelli's importance for the general lay-out of Handel's op. 6 set has already been mentioned (see p. 101f). However, the resemblance between the two sets of concerti grossi (both incidentally, styled op. 6) goes much further than this. The ancestry of certain passages in Handel's set is all too clear: while not lifted straight from Corelli's op. 6, they stand in direct relation to it. Even where one is dealing with a conventional eighteenth-century formula the similarity of usage suggests that Handel knew the earlier work. Two separate examples are given below. In the first (Ex. 16) Handel takes over a typical Corellian progression in which a rising bass creates harsh dissonances against an ostinato figure in the upper parts; in the second example he adopts the Italianate device of voice-exchange over a repetitive chord-scheme:

[116] See W. Kolneder, 'Das Frühschaffen Antonio Vivaldi', op. cit. 254–62.

[117] See the multilingual preface to his *Auserlene mit Ernst und Lust gemengte Instrumentalmusik* (1701).

[118] M. Talbot, 'The Concerto Allegro in the Early Eighteenth Century', *Music and Letters*, lii (1971), 16.

[119] Example from the Augener edition of Corelli's op. 6, ed. J. Joachim and F. Chrysander (London, n.d.).

EXAMPLE 16

(a) Corelli, op. 6, no. 4, the $\frac{2}{4}$ Allegro, bars 72–5 (solo parts only);[119]

(b) Handel, op. 6, no. 11, 4th movement, bars 42–5 (solo violin parts and bass line only)

EXAMPLE 17

(a) Corelli, op. 6, no. 1, 2nd movement, the $\frac{4}{4}$ Largo, bars 17–18 (solo parts only);[120] (b) Handel, op. 6, no. 1, 5th movement, bars 16–19 (solo violin parts and bass line only)

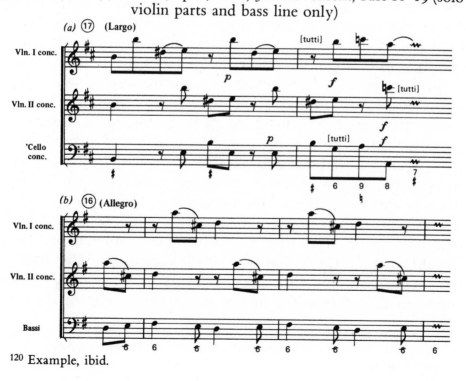

[120] Example, ibid.

There are, moreover, many further points of correspondence between the two sets. These include similarities of
figuration; passages where the harmonic interest centres on
just two chords heard alternately; contrapuntal writing in
which the upper parts have a series of suspensions over a
constantly-moving bass; frequent hemiola cadences in
triple-time movements; and a tendency to slow down
momentum at final cadence points, either by decreasing the
rate of harmonic pulse or by an abrupt adagio marking. Of
course, none of these features occurs exclusively in the
works of Corelli and Handel and it would be absurd to
suggest that Corelli was their sole author. Yet these formulas
occur so frequently in the latter's music that they have
become an inseparable part of his style. Following the
dissemination of Italian scores in the early eighteenth century the Corellian manner found many imitators, in England and, to a lesser extent, on the mainland of Europe as
well.

The influence of Vivaldi on some of Handel's Allegro
movements (e.g. op. 6, no. 6, 4th movement) has already
been mentioned. It is most apparent in the type of ritornelli
used and in the figurative episodes of solo concertos where
Handel, like Vivaldi, relies extensively on conventional
formulas. Several solo episodes in the organ and oboe
concertos, as also in the solo-concerto movements of the op.
6 set, are based on rising or falling sequences, series of
chords with roots a fifth apart, chains of suspensions,
passages in parallel thirds or sixths, or in close imitation, and
those stereotyped rythmic patterns which occur so frequently not only in Vivaldi's concertos but in many other
spheres of Italian baroque music as well.[121] In general,
Handel's string writing is less advanced than that of either
Vivaldi or J. S. Bach, but one or two idiomatic passages in
the virtuoso manner do occur—notably in his only violin
concerto (the 'Sonata'), in op. 3, no. 1: I, and in the 3rd

---

[121] The most common of these rhythmic/melodic motifs were (a) 𝅘𝅥𝅮𝅘𝅥𝅯𝅘𝅥𝅯𝅘𝅥𝅯, and
(b) both of which may be found in op. 4, no. 6, 1st movement, bars 32–3 and
53–4 respectively.

movement of op. 6, no. 3, from which the following example is taken:

EXAMPLE 18

Handel, op. 6, no. 3, 3rd movement, bars 33–4 (solo part only)

Among the other Italians whose work influenced Handel were Carissimi, Steffani, and the Scarlattis. Of these, the first two appear to have had most influence on Handel's *vocal* works and do not, therefore, concern us here; similarly with Alessandro Scarlatti whose influence is primarily apparent in the pastoral movements and lilting Siciliana arias of Handel's operas. But his son's music probably exerted some influence on Handel's instrumental style, as may be seen from Example 19:

EXAMPLE 19

(a) Domenico Scarlatti, *Essercizi*, no. 23, bars 1–2[122]

(b) Handel, op. 6, no. 5, 5th movement, bars 1–3

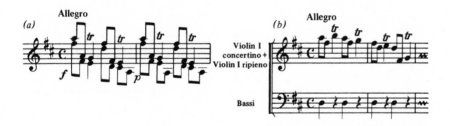

In the Scarlattian style also is the Finale to op. 6, no. 6, with its triplet rhythms, short phrases, and strange harmonic alignments:

[122] Longo 411. Cited in *Handel: a Symposium*, ed. G. Abraham, p. 206.

EXAMPLE 20
Handel, op. 6, no. 6, Finale, bars 29–36 (short score)

Again there is the problem of determining at what stage Handel became receptive to Scarlatti's influence. Although the two men met in Italy[123] there is little evidence that either influenced the other's style at that stage. Kirkpatrick, author of a standard biography on Domenico Scarlatti, sees a few similarities between the early works of Scarlatti and Handel,[124] but these examples stem more from the conventions of contemporary Italian music than from any direct relationship between their respective composers. Unfortunately, also, there is little information regarding the chronology of Scarlatti's early works so that it is impossible to say whether the young Handel was indebted to Scarlatti or vice versa.

One thing is certain, however: Scarlatti's music became extremely popular in England in the third and fourth decades of the eighteenth century. This was largely due to the efforts of Thomas Roseingrave[125] who had met Domenico in Italy in 1709 and had been much impressed by his virtuoso harpsichord playing. On his return to England,

[123] They became firm friends, see J. Mainwaring, op. cit., pp. 59–61.
[124] R. Kirkpatrick, *Domenico Scarlatti* (Princeton, 1953), p. 151.
[125] See R. Newton, 'The English Cult of Domenico Scarlatti', *Music and Letters*, xx (1939), 138–56.

Roseingrave began to promote Scarlatti's music:[126] in 1720 he supervised the production of *Narciso* at the Haymarket Theatre, and in 1739 he edited 'XLII Suites de Pièces Pour Le Clavecin. En deux Volumes. Composées par Domenico Scarlatti'. True, the *Essercizi*, another collection of thirty sonatas by Scarlatti, had been published in London earlier that year so that some of Scarlatti's sonatas were circulating in England shortly before Roseingrave's edition was produced. But whatever the source, it seems probable that Handel became intimately acquainted with Scarlatti's sonatas in 1739, i.e. just before writing his Grand Concertos.

Next to the Italian, French influences are the most conspicuous in Handel's work. The French Overture was, as its name implies, a stronghold of the style and Handel had a particular liking for this type of opening. Moreover, we find him—in the op. 3 set at least—using trio sections (for unaccompanied oboes and bassoon)[127] of the kind popular in French opera of the late seventeenth and early eighteenth centuries. And then there are the dances, many of which are of French origin. It is perhaps surprising that there are no examples of the fashionable Loure and Passepied in Handel's concertos, all the more so since these movements figure prominently in the orchestral music of that other Francophile, Georg Philipp Telemann. Yet the Gavottes, Minuets, and Bourrées which Handel uses so frequently are very French in style and close parallels for these movements may be found in such contemporary works as Rameau's *Les Indes Galantes* (1735).

It would be interesting to know how far Handel was influenced by Rameau but this subject has not been fully investigated to date. Rameau's biographer, Girdlestone, sees what could be a borrowing from Rameau's *Les Fêtes d'Hébé* in the opening theme of the chorus 'And the glory of the

---

[126] An advertisement in *The Daily Courant* for 25 March 1718 confirms that these activities had started before 1720, M. Tilmouth, 'A Calendar of References to Music in Newspapers published in London and the Provinces (1660–1719)', op. cit., p. 102.

[127] E.g. in op. 3, no. 4, 3rd movement, bars 13–14, 32.

Lord' in *Messiah*,[128] and we know (through Hawkins[129]) that Handel admitted an acquaintance with Rameau's music. Previously Hawkins's statement and the examples of Lullian influence in Handel have been rather a mystery, for there seemed no way in which he could have come into contact with French stage traditions (apart from any opportunities which his rapid journeyings through France might have afforded). But historians have long known that James Brydges, the first Duke of Chandos, had an extensive library, and the importance of this for Handel has been largely overlooked. For according to the catalogue of holdings drawn up in 1720 by one Mr. Noland, this library was particularly rich in French operatic scores of the Lullian period.[130] Given Handel's connections with the Duke we can surely assume that he had access to this valuable collection.

In recent years the question of English influences on Handel has again been raised.[131] Handel was questioned on the same topic himself and replied (somewhat peremptorily if Hawkins and Burney can be believed) that England had had no composers of worth when he arrived and that he never attempted to imitate English church music. Despite this, traces of Purcellian influence have been found in some of the later operas and oratorios and in a few earlier, mainly ceremonial, works such as *The Birthday Ode for Queen Anne* and the *Utrecht Te Deum*. These discoveries prompt one to consider the concertos from the same angle. Apart from the wider issues concerning the origins of the organ concerto, however, there is little evidence of English influence in Handel's instrumental music.[132] To be sure, the Hornpipe

---

[128] C. Girdlestone, *Jean-Philippe Rameau* (London, 1957), p. 345 note 1.

[129] J. Hawkins, op. cit. v. 386.

[130] C. H. Collins Baker and Muriel I. Baker, *The Life and Circumstances of James Brydges First Duke of Chandos* (Oxford, 1949), p. 137.

[131] In the following publications: E. H. Meyer, 'Händel und Purcell', *Händel-Jahrbuch*, v (1959), 9–26; F. B. Zimmerman, 'Handel's Purcellian Borrowings in His Later Operas and Oratorios', *Festschrift Otto Erich Deutsch zum 80. Geburtstag*, ed. W. Gerstenberg, J. La Rue and W. Rehm (Kassel, 1963), pp. 20–30, and 'Musical Borrowings in the English Baroque', *The Musical Quarterly*, lii (1966), 483–95.

[132] An exception to this is provided by the similarity of a theme from Purcell's

was a dance of English origin and an example occurs in Handel's op. 6 (no. 7, Finale). But those who claim this as evidence of English influence are forgetting that Handel based the movement on a 'Hornepippe' in Muffat's *Componimenti Musicali*. No significance can, therefore, be attached to this particular movement. The only passage which could be said to reflect English influence is found in the 1st movement of op. 7, no. 1, where the persistent dotted rhythms have all the gaiety of a Purcellian 'alleluia':

EXAMPLE 21

Handel, op. 7, no. 1, 1st movement, bars 43–5

But to labour the point would be misleading. Purcell's style was doubtless considered old-fashioned by the early eighteenth century and, in any case, as Dent reminds us, we should not expect 'to find in Handel any characteristics of Purcell's melody, for that is too much bound up with Purcell's lively feeling for the English language. Nor must we look for Purcell's original harmonies, for Handel had been trained in the traditional smooth Italian counterpoint, while Purcell's dissonances and irregular part-writing sprang from an older English tradition.'[133]

Contrapuntal and Harmonic Technique

The smooth Italian counterpoint to which Dent refers is an important feature of Handel's style. Whereas J. S. Bach created for himself a unique and highly complex contrapun-

Ode for St. Cecilia's Day (1692), and Handel's *Water Music*, see E. H. Meyer, 'Händel und Purcell', 12–13.

[133] E. J. Dent, 'English Influences on Handel', *The Monthly Musical Record*, lxi (1931), 227.

tal language, Handel was content, for the most part, to rely on traditional methods. That clarity was his main concern is evident from the following example; here the descending scale pattern—a familiar motif in Italian counterpoint since the days of Palestrina—is passed rapidly from voice to voice, yet the harmonic structure remains clear and consonant throughout:

EXAMPLE 22

Handel, op. 4, no. 1, 2nd movement, bars 2–5 (organ part only)

This last point is fundamental; clearly Handel believed that the movement of individual parts should not cloud or disrupt the basic chord scheme. Only on rare occasions—such as in the Andante from op. 6, no. 11, where the points of imitation create a strongly dissonant effect[134]—is linear movement given priority over harmony.

It will be noticed, from the example cited above, that Handel did not reserve imitative passages for fugal movements alone; he regarded counterpoint as simply another texture, to be used as and when the occasion arose. In several movements we find him exploiting the contrast between sections of chordal (or *all'unisono*) writing and more imitative material. Sometimes the imitation is used to expand the initial theme; so, after the strong unison opening of op. 3, no. 5, Finale (see Ex. 13), Handel sustains, or rather increases, momentum by repeating this theme in canon:

[134] Burney's comment on this movement is interesting: 'the symphony, or introduction, of the *andante*, is extremely pleasing; and no less remarkable for its grace, than the boldness with which the composer, in order to bring in the answers to points of imitation has used double discords, *unprepared*' (C. Burney, *In Commemoration of Handel*, p. 66).

EXAMPLE 23
Handel, op. 3, no. 5, Finale, bars 12–16 (short score)

Elsewhere the contrast of texture is accompanied by new thematic material—compare, for example, the decisive opening of op. 6, no. 11 (Finale), with the imitative and more pliant material of bars 10ff.

Bold, simple harmonic schemes lie at the root of Handel's style. He is heavily dependent on the three main triads of a key (tonic, dominant, subdominant) and is not afraid to use repetitive chord progressions where appropriate. Indeed, in some of the most effective pastoral movements the range of chords is deliberately restricted in order to convey a peaceful, languid atmosphere (see Ex. 24 overleaf). The simple chord structure of this example might well have proved monotonous in the hands of a lesser composer, but the melodic style and gentle harmonic accompaniment of this Andante are so well integrated and the movement of the bass so purposeful that one is aware only of the warm string sound and the lulling rhythms of the principal theme.

The high level of consonance displayed in Example 24 is typical of Handel's music as a whole for he employed dissonant passing notes with great caution and appoggiaturas scarcely at all. Moreover, in those few places where accented dissonances are used, the result is curiously uncharacteristic. So it is that the 1st movement of op. 6, no. 4, with its affettuoso marking, paired semiquavers, melodic dissonance, and rich harmonic colouring, sounds completely out of style; indeed, it is much more typical of Bach than Handel.

Another feature which distinguishes the harmonic style of

EXAMPLE 24
Handel, op. 6, no. 7, 4th movement, bars 1–4

Handel and Bach is their use of chromaticism. Whereas Bach was constantly exploring the possibilities of chromatic chords, Handel tended to avoid lengthy passages of chromaticism (though his choice of fugue subject sometimes led him to adopt a more intense idiom than normal, as in the 2nd movement of op. 6, no. 6). The only non-diatonic chord which Handel used with any frequency was the Neapolitan sixth and even here he preferred to treat the characteristic flattened second in a melodic (rather than harmonic) context. The flattened second plays a particularly prominent role in the 4th movement of op. 6, no. 4. Introduced first at bar 9 (see Ex. 25) the B♭s recur at several other points in the movement (bars 89–96, 104–6, 109–11, 119–20); each time they are presented with great emphasis so that their significance for the movement as a whole cannot be overlooked.

EXAMPLE 25
Handel, op. 6, no. 4, 4th movement, bars 9–14 (outer parts only)

Although Handel uses so few chromatic chords in his concertos, his harmonic range is broadened by the occasional use of unorthodox chord progressions. These often take the form of interrupted cadences. In bar 15 of the following passage the listener anticipates a cadence in E♭ major. But this perfect cadence is avoided at the last moment when Handel substitutes a C^7 chord for the expected tonic. A subtle type of false relation is at work here. For the E♮ (placed in the upper part for maximum effect) conflicts strongly with the E♭ (anticipated, not heard). As will be seen from Example 26 (on page 166), the whole progression is then repeated at a different pitch.

It must be emphasized that an example such as this is the exception rather than the rule. By and large, there are very few passages in the concertos which will bear comparison (from the harmonic point of view) with the colourful and imaginative harmony of the best of Handel's vocal works. It may well be, as Leichtentritt maintained, that 'complicated chromatic harmony and bold modulations had a meaning for Handel only in association with texts or situations, only

EXAMPLE 26
Handel, op. 6, no. 8, 1st movement, bars 14–18

when he was writing a lyric passage for a cantata or a dramatic scene for an opera'.[135]

Key Schemes and Modulation Technique

Although most of Handel's concerto movements contain nothing untoward in the realm of key relationships, mod-

[135] H. Leichtentritt, 'Handel's Harmonic Art', *The Musical Quarterly*, xxi (1935), 208–23.

ulations being restricted, for the most part, to closely-
related keys, his tonal schemes are occasionally extended to
include major/minor relationships of a more adventurous
type. Tonic major/minor changes are often associated with
the *pianoidée* sections of Handel's ritornelli. But this particular key relationship is not confined to such sections; it can
occur at almost any point in a movement provided there is
some rationale for its use. If we take the 2nd movement of
op. 4, no. 1, for instance, we find two important passages in
the tonic minor key (cf. bars 43–58 and 95–8). At first, it
may seem surprising that Handel has introduced these
passages since there is no justification for them in the
opening theme. Yet, looking at the concerto as a whole, his
reasoning becomes clear. The work opens with a solemn
'Larghetto, e staccato' in the key of G minor and presumably Handel was reluctant to follow this with a bright G
major Allegro without some reference to the original key.
(The fact that the last movement ends in G major (i.e. 'out
of key') is explained by its alleged connection with
Athalia.)[136]

The most effective of all these tonic major/minor changes
occurs in the 1st movement of op. 6, no. 1. This movement
begins with four decisive bars which put the basic tonality
of G major beyond doubt. Towards the end of the movement, however, the mood changes; B♮s are introduced and
the music droops down to a final cadence, ending inconclusively on a $^6_5$ chord (bass note F#). Burney's description,
which he produced for the Commemoration concerts of
1784, is as evocative as the movement itself: 'though it
begins with so much pride and haughtiness, it melts, at last,
into softness; and where it modulates into a minor key,
seems to express fatigue, langour, and fainting'.[137]

Although this tonic major/minor relationship is the one
most often used by Handel to add colour to a movement, he
has a marked predilection also for the juxtaposition of tonic

---

[136] See R. Fiske, 'Handel's Organ Concertos—do they belong to particular
Oratorios?', 14–22.

[137] C. Burney, *In Commemoration of Handel*, p. 102.

major and dominant minor keys (i.e. I/v). A typical example occurs in the Andante of his second oboe concerto in B♭ (bars 11–13). The key of F minor is reached via D minor, F major, and, finally, G minor and C minor. Modulation back to the home key of B♭ is then effected by raising the third of the F minor triad and so converting it into the normal dominant. For some reason Handel seemed to associate this particular key change with the tonality of B♭, most of the other examples being found in works of this key.[138]

Melodic Writing

So far, little has been said about the relationship between Handel's vocal works and the concertos. That they were closely linked is evident from the number of borrowings between the two (see Appendix A). Moreover, it is hardly surprising that Handel's experience as a composer of operas and oratorios should have had such a profound effect on his melodic style in particular. Certainly the melodic writing of the concertos seems better suited at times to voices than to instruments and this is true not only of the aria-like slow movements such as op. 6, no. 12, 3rd movement, but of some Allegros too. For even in fast movements the melodic lines contain few awkward leaps (with the exception of those solo episodes which are modelled on Vivaldi), and are often broken up into short phrases in the vocal manner.

One of the most striking features of Handel's vocal and instrumental music is its balance, particularly with respect to phrase structure. Whereas J. S. Bach favoured a smooth, continuous style, Handel tended to separate his phrases by means of rests. That he was a master of the caesura emerges from such examples as the popular Minuet from *Esther* (op. 4, no. 2, Finale). Here the breaks occur at precisely the right moment, emphasizing the regularity of the phrase structure and, at the same time, creating an air of anticipation:

---

[138] Compare also op. 6, no. 7, 4th movement (bars 27–9), and op. 4, no. 4, 2nd movement (bars 38–41).

EXAMPLE 27
Handel, op. 4, no. 2, Finale, bars 1–12 (organ part only)

Most of his dance (or pseudo-dance) movements have this clear, periodic phrasing. Yet irregular phrases are not avoided altogether. Three-, five-, and even nine-bar periods are occasionally introduced to break up the symmetry, and in most cases these asymmetrical phrases sound completely natural. The Sarabande from the G minor oboe concerto, for example, opens with a nine-bar statement. The first phrase ends at bar 4, but the next five bars form an indivisible unit. In this instance, as so often in Handel's music, the irregularity is an integral part of the phrase; it does not arise artificially through repetition.

EXAMPLE 28
Handel, oboe concerto in G minor, 3rd movement, bars 1–9 (oboe part only)

The bold, plain style of the above is characteristic of many of Handel's slow movements. How much decoration was added in performance we shall probably never know. The above-mentioned Sarabande would not offer much scope in this direction as its melodic line is too clearly defined; however, one or two of the organ concertos' slow movements are so short and insubstantial (e.g. the 3rd movement of no. 14 in A) that elaborate ornamentation would obviously be needed to make them effective at all. Unfortunately, we have little information about the type of decoration which might have been added to such movements, since Handel rarely wrote out his ornamentation in full. The only example we have is op. 4, no. 2, 3rd movement, which, with its florid organ part, could well reflect the improvised ornamentation technique of Handel himself.

6. The Question of Plagiarism

At some point in almost every discussion of Handel's music reference is made to his habit of borrowing material from other composers. And since a knowledge of his activities in this sphere is essential to a comprehensive understanding of his musical personality it seems appropriate, despite the wealth of literature on the subject,[139] to reconsider the question here.

That Handel borrowed very extensively from the works of other composers is an indisputable fact. As early as 1831 William Crotch listed the names of twenty-nine composers from whom Handel borrowed material at one stage or another,[140] and in the latter part of the nineteenth-century Chrysander published a six-volume Supplement to the *Händel-Gesellschaft* edition[141] containing those works by

---

[139] For the early literature on Handel's plagiarism see the summary in J. S. Shedlock, 'Handel's borrowings', *The Musical Times*, xlii (1901), 450–2, 526–8, 596–600. References to more recent publications are given in the course of the text.

[140] Crotch's list, published in the *Substance of several courses of Lectures on Music* (London, 1831), is as follows: Josquin de Près, Palestrina, Turini, Carissimi, Calvisius, Uria (Urio), Corelli, Alessandro and D. Scarlatti, Seb. Bach, Purcell, Locke, Caldare (Caldara), Colonna, Clari, Cesti, Kerl (Kerll), Habermann, Muffat, Kuhnau, Telemann, Graun, Mondeville, Porta, Pergolesi, Vinci, Astorga, Bononcini, and Hasse. To this list may be added the names of Keiser, Stradella, Erba, Lotti, Krieger, Poglietti, Mattheson, Buxtehude, and Pasquini, cf. J. S. Shedlock, op. cit.

[141] The first five volumes were published between 1888 and 1892; the sixth was

Erba, Urio, Stradella,[142] Clari, Muffat, and Keiser to which Handel was particularly indebted. The controversy, then, does not concern the fact of Handel's plagiarism but centres on the far more difficult questions of eighteenth-century attitudes and of why Handel needed this type of stimulus for his invention.

One has first to establish whether the borrowings were made openly or in secret. The chief advocate of this second view was Sedley Taylor who maintained that since Handel's enemies (and he had many in the theatrical world) did not bring a charge against him, they could not have known of the borrowings.[143] These arguments, however, were then considered and dismissed by Seiffert;[144] he observed that the whole question turned on the eighteenth-century view of plagiarism. If contemporary attitudes were more permissive in this respect than our own, then Handel's borrowings could have been made openly without fear of repercussions. The same line was pursued by P. Robinson[145] who demonstrated that some of Handel's continental models were known in England at the time. An organ canzona by Kerll, for example, had been printed by Walsh and Hare in 1719[146] and subsequently reissued around 1731; Handel used the same work, almost unaltered, in his oratorio *Israel in Egypt*. More recent research has unearthed some borrowings from English music too[147]—a dangerous course of action if Handel were bent on keeping his plagiaristic

---

brought out in 1902, after Chrysander's death.

[142] P. Robinson suggested that Handel was in fact the author of these three works (*Handel and his Orbit* (London, 1908), and 'Handel, or Urio, Stradella and Erba', *Music and Letters*, xvi (1935), 269–77, but his view has few supporters.

[143] S. Taylor, *The Indebtedness of Handel to Works by Other Composers* (Cambridge, 1906), pp. 177–8.

[144] M. Seiffert, 'Händels Verhältnis zu Tonwerken älterer deutscher Meister', *Jahrbuch der Musikbibliothek Peters*, xiv (1907), 41–57.

[145] 'Was Handel a Plagiarist?', *The Musical Times*, lxxx (1939), 573–7.

[146] The work was included in *A second collection of Toccates, vollentarys, and fugues . . . by Pasquini, Poglietti and others*. The Walsh publication was derived from a Roger publication of 1698–9 [Lesure's date] entitled *Toccates & suites pour le clavessin de Messieurs Pasquini, Poglietti & Gaspard Kerle*.

[147] See F. B. Zimmerman, 'Musical Borrowings in the English Baroque', 483–95, and 'Handel's Purcellian Borrowings in his Later Operas and Oratorios', pp. 20–30.

activities out of the public eye.[148]

Taking a broad view, it seems that eighteenth-century attitudes towards plagiarism were considerably more lenient than those of the nineteenth or twentieth centuries. Certainly the idea of forging new works from pre-existing material was not new; one thinks, for example, of the parody mass so popular in the Renaissance. Nearer the Handelian concept, however, was Purcell's use of ideas from Lully's stage works[149] for in this case the model was the work of a well-known recent composer. Handel's contemporaries also indulged in similar activities: even Bach, against whom charges of plagiarism are seldom levelled, used material from Handel's *Almira* in his cantata 'Wachet, betet',[150] and there is evidence that he knew the latter's *St. John Passion* of 1704 as well,[151] so that Handel was by no means alone in this.

But were all types of borrowing regarded as legitimate in the eighteenth century? The answer to this is not straightforward. Within certain limits, plagiarism was acceptable, but there was also a growing possessiveness among composers for which the competitive nature of the music publishing business was partly responsible. Both Mattheson and Scheibe, two of Germany's leading music critics, agreed that borrowing was permissible if the material was reworked and the finished product was held to be an improvement on the original. Both also were aware of some of Handel's borrowings, Mattheson having had personal experience of this.[152] While Mattheson's comments on

---

[148] In one case at least it seems obvious that Handel intended his borrowing to be recognized as such. Arne's famous ode 'Rule, Brittania' was first performed in 1740 and Handel, in his *Occasional Oratorio* of 1746, 'honoured Arne by quoting the first three bars of "Rule Brittania" to the words "War shall cease, welcome Peace . . ." This was undoubtedly an intentional and well-considered act . . .' (W. H. Cummings, 'Dr. Arne', *Proceedings of the Royal Musical Association*, xxxvi (1909–10), 81).

[149] Compare the famous Frost scene in Purcell's *King Arthur* (1691) with Act IV of Lully's *Isis* (1677); Lully had died only four years before *King Arthur* was written.

[150] See P. Robinson, 'Bach's Indebtedness to Handel's Almira', *The Musical Times*, xlviii (1907), 309–12.

[151] See id., 'Handel's influence on Bach', *The Musical Times*, xlvii (1906), 468–9.

[152] Mattheson accused Handel of having appropriated material from his opera

Handel's plagiarism are obviously coloured by his own, unfortunate, experience, Scheibe is both objective and unconcerned: 'Händel, although many times developing not his own thoughts but those of others, especially the inventions of Reinhard Kaiser, has manifested all the time a great understanding and a powerful deliberation, and assuredly has shown in all his pieces how refined and delicate his taste in the arts must be.'[153]

There is nothing to indicate that the English took a more puritanical view. Although the career of Handel's rival, Bononcini, was ruined by the disclosure that he had passed off a madrigal by Lotti as his own, the circumstances surrounding the incident are by no means clear; it is even possible that he was framed by his enemies. In any case, Bononcini's alleged misdemeanour differed from Handel's in that he had deliberately misled a distinguished body of musicians and scholars (The Academy of Ancient Music) into thinking that the madrigal was his own work.[154]

We come now to the second question: why did Handel need a stimulus of this kind? Several reasons have been put forward over the years. Professor Dent suggested that the illness which took him to the spa town of Aix-La-Chapelle in 1737 might have been responsible,[155] the implication being that after that date Handel no longer possessed the creative energy to invent new themes. While the majority of Handel's borrowings do indeed occur in music written after that date, one or two large-scale acts of plagiarism were perpetrated before this. These could hardly be explained in terms of an impending illness since the disorder was a stroke and, in any case, we are still left with a few examples of borrowings in the early Italian operas, chief among which is the reappearance of material from Keiser's *Octavia* in *Agrip-*

Porsenna (1702), see O. E. Deutsch, ed., *Handel*, p. 135 (translated from Mattheson's *Critica Musica* (Hamburg, 1722)).

[153] O. E. Deutsch, ed., op. cit., p. 620 (translated from Scheibe's *Der critischer Musikus*, 2nd edn. (Leipzig, 1745)).

[154] E. Walker, *A History of Music in England*, 3rd edn. revised and enlarged by J. A. Westrup (Oxford, 1952), p. 242.

[155] E. J. Dent, *Handel* (London, 1947), pp. 100ff.

pina (1709). It seems fairly obvious, therefore, that Handel acquired the habit as a young man and that his illness, if it had any effect at all, merely acted as a catalyst.

There are, however, two additional possibilities, the first of which was advanced by F. B. Zimmerman in his article on 'Musical Borrowings in the English Baroque'. Zimmerman draws attention to the many pressures which society exerted on eighteenth-century composers. They were expected to produce new works with great rapidity, for 'old' music had but limited appeal; and the situation in the opera house was even more difficult since a work was rarely presented in exactly the same form twice. Under these conditions a composer would surely be tempted to use borrowed material (from his own or another's work) and rework it as best he could.

It is worth emphasizing that Handel made no distinction between material borrowed from other composers and that borrowed from his own works; both were subject to exactly the same type of treatment. One often finds two or more movements based on the same theme, but otherwise totally independent of each other. If the 2nd movement of op. 4, no. 3, is compared with the Finale of the G minor oboe concerto it will be seen that, while the two openings correspond very closely (see Ex. 29), the movements follow a different course from the fourth bar onwards.

EXAMPLE 29

Handel, (*a*) op. 4, no. 3, 2nd movement, bars 1–4 (upper part only)

(*b*) oboe concerto in G minor, Finale, bars 1–4 (upper part only)

And this brings us to the other possible explanation of Handel's borrowings: could it be that he was always more concerned with the sucessful working-out and development of ideas than with the invention of new themes? Certainly the example mentioned above suggests this.

For his concertos, Handel drew primarily on the works of Telemann and Muffat. However, there are isolated cases of other borrowings. The extent to which Handel relied on borrowed material varies greatly, of course, with individual movements. Some concerto movements are exact replicas of their models but in other cases (as will be seen from Appendix A) Handel simply takes over the opening theme and very little else. When secondary material is also incorporated it is woven unobtrusively into the fabric of the new work. Typical in this respect is the 1st movement of op. 7, no. 6. Its model is the E♭ major concerto from Telemann's *Musique de Table* collection (Book three) and the beginning of both works is shown below:

EXAMPLE 30
(*a*) Handel, op. 7, no. 6, 1st movement, bars 1–8 (outer parts only)
(*b*) Telemann, *Musique de Table*, Book 3, no. 3, 1st movement, bars 1–8
(outer parts only)[156]

[156] Example from *Georg Philipp Telemann Musikalische Werke*, vol. xiv, *Tafelmusik Teil 3*, ed. J. P. Hinnenthal (Kassel, 1963), p. 63.

Although Handel has altered the direction of the opening arpeggio figure, changed the key of the piece, and substituted the direction Pomposo for Telemann's Maestoso, the relationship between the two passages is still very striking. Moreover, the possibility of coincidence is ruled out by the fact that an additional passage corresponds: in bars 63 and 64 Handel takes up a figure, highly characteristic of Telemann, which occurs in bar 12 of the *Musique de Table* concerto. The same technique is employed in the 1st movement of the fifteenth organ concerto (again based on a Telemann model—see p. 115), and in the 2nd movement of op. 7, no. 2, whose material has recently been shown to derive from an obscure ricercar by Gottlieb Muffat.[157]

7. Popularity and Influence of the Concertos

Evaluations of Handel's instrumental music by eighteenth-century writers are absurdly mixed, especially with regard to the Grand Concertos. Burney tells us that it was the fashion during Handel's lifetime 'to regard his compositions for violins, as much inferior to those of Corelli and Geminiani'.[158] This may be an accurate reflection of contemporary opinion; but it could equally well have been a thrust at his arch-rival, Sir John Hawkins, in whose *History* the following passage occurred: '. . . as to these twelve Concertos, they appear to have been made in a hurry, and in the issue fell very short of answering the expectations that were formed of them, and inclined men to think that the composition of music merely instrumental, and of many parts, was

[157] See S. Wollenberg, 'Handel and Gottlieb Muffat: a newly discovered borrowing', *The Musical Times*, cxiii (1972), 448–9.

[158] C. Burney, *In Commemoration of Handel*, pp. 105–6.

not Handel's greatest excellence.' Later in the same volume Hawkins expresses a similar view: 'His concertos for violin are in general wanting in that which is the chief excellence of instrumental music in many parts, harmony and fine modulation: In these respects they will stand no comparison with the concertos of Corelli, Geminiani, and Martin.'[159] But if some critics disapproved, the public did not. With similar works by Corelli and Geminiani (an Italian who had taken up residence in England), the op. 6 concertos provided the staple diet of many public concerts and private gatherings in London and the provinces. Their popularity declined only during the 1760s when the pre-classical symphony began to eclipse earlier types of orchestral music.

As for the organ concertos, Burney tells us that they 'long remained in possession of the first and favourite places, in the private practice and public performance of every organist in the kingdom'.[160] Certainly English composers were not slow to imitate Handel's example, and by the mid-century the organ concerto had become a feature of many dramatic entertainments. A 1753 performance was billed to include 'a concerto on the Organ by Mr. Stanley . . .'[161] and the *Public Advertiser* for 17 February 1761 carried the following notice: 'At the Theatre Royal in Drury Lane, this Day, will be performed a New Sacred Oratorio Call'd Judith. The music composed by Dr. Arne, with a Concerto on the organ . . .' From about 1740 onwards a spate of these concertos was published. Among the first English composers to produce such works were Harry Burgess (harpsichordist at the Drury Lane Theatre), Gladwin (the first organist at Vauxhall), and William Fenton (Prebendary of Hereford). During the 1740s and 1750s organ concertos were also written by Avison, Mudge, Edwards, J. C. Mantel, B. Cooke, T. Roseingrave, and Stanley;[162] later Arne took up the form. Only in the 1780s did the popularity of this type

---

[159] J. Hawkins, op cit. v. 358, 417.
[160] C. Burney, *A General History of Music*, iv. 664.
[161] See W. C. Smith, *Concerning Handel, His Life and Works* (London, 1948), p. 237.
[162] C. L. Cudworth, 'The English Organ Concerto', *The Score*, viii (1953), 53.

of concerto begin to wane; symptomatic of the decline is the fact that none of Handel's organ concertos was included in the Commemoration Concerts of 1784 although several works from both his op. 3 and 6 sets were performed.

It is, of course, true that Handel's instrumental music had considerable influence on some English composers. There is firm evidence for this not only in stylistic comparability but also in the shape of borrowed material.[163] A particularly interesting example occurs in an unpublished Overture in C major by William Boyce[164] where, as will be seen from Example 31, he appropriates a substantial part of the opening ritornello from Handel's *Alexander's Feast* concerto:

EXAMPLE 31

(a) Handel, *Alexander's Feast* concerto, 1st movement, bars 1–8 (outer parts only);

(b) Boyce, Overture in C major, opening bars of the fragment preserved in Bodleian MS. Don.d.146

[163] The theme of 'Away, away' from Arne's *Comus* resembles the opening of a chorus in *Athalia*, cf. J. Herbage, 'The Vocal Style of Thomas Augustine Arne', *Proceedings of the Royal Musical Association*, lxxviii (1951–2), 86.

[164] The earliest version of Handel's *Alexander's Feast* concerto (a 'Concerto per il Gravicembalo' in C) dates from around 1730—J. A. Fuller-Maitland and A. H. Mann, *Catalogue of the Music in the Fitzwilliam Museum Cambridge* (London, 1893), p. 97. According to librarians at the Bodleian Library, Oxford, the Boyce MS. is dated 1735–40 on the grounds of calligraphy.

But it is important that the extent of this influence should not be exaggerated. Obviously the oratorios were of immense importance as the prototype of a national art-form which was cultivated throughout the nineteenth century and on to the present day. And the same is true of the organ concertos, though the popularity of this genre faded as suddenly as it began. In the realm of string music, however, Handel's works were not always the favourite models. English composers tended rather to imitate the works of Corelli and Geminiani, while the more adventurous turned their attention (after 1764) to the 'galant' style of J. C. Bach and Abel. Between 1760 and the baroque revival of the early nineteenth century (in which Haydn and then Mendelssohn played a leading part) the Handelian style became progressively less influential. The reasons for this are clear enough. Although not totally unaffected by developments (in the concerto and other fields) which were taking place on the Continent during the 1730s and 1740s—he was obviously acquainted, for example, with the new symphonic style—Handel did not always choose to adopt or imitate the most recent stylistic trends. His use of a trio-sonata concer-

tino and his application of other Corellian methods in the
op. 6 set are explicable in terms of English fashions. But
other features also mark him out as a traditionalist. Chief
among these is the spirit of dignity and order which
pervades all his work. Although isolated traces of rococo
influence occur,[165] Handel's music is, in a sense, the very
antithesis of this style with its charming sentimentality and
concentration on detail at the expense of the whole. As
Hawkins put it: 'till they were taught the contrary by
Handel, none was aware of that dignity and grandeur of
sentiment which music is capable of conveying, or that
there is a sublime in music as there is in poetry'.[166]

[165] E.g. the opening theme of op. 6, no. 6, 5th movement with its scurrying
triplets, or the 'scotch snaps' of the Finale to the concerto from *Alexander's Feast*.
[166] J. Hawkins, op cit. v. 418.

III

Georg Philipp Telemann

1. Introduction; Telemann's Career

As a postscript to Telemann's autobiography which appeared in Mattheson's *Grundlage einer Ehren-Pforte* (Hamburg, 1740), the editor added the following couplet:

> A Lully fame has won: Corelli may be praised;
> But Telemann alone above all praise is raised.[1]

Such lavish commendation of Telemann was not unusual in the eighteenth century; it reflects the great esteem in which the composer was held by his contemporaries, and his music clearly had a wide following both in Germany and, to a lesser extent, in France. After about 1780, however, the musical public showed little interest in baroque or pre-classical works and most of Telemann's compositions were consigned, together with those of his contemporaries, to oblivion. But the resurgence of interest in J. S. Bach and Handel during the romantic period and the subsequent growth of musicology encouraged research into what were then regarded as the lesser figures of eighteenth-century music. From this point on Telemann's true stature began to emerge. It was decided to produce a collected edition of his works under the auspices of the *Gesellschaft für Musikforschung*, the first volume of which appeared in 1950, and soon there were indications that a full-scale Telemann revival was under way. Modern editions of his works flooded on to the market and his compositions began to figure prominently in concerts of baroque music. As more of his work became available so respect for Telemann grew until his present

---

[1] 'Ein Lulli wird gerühmt; Corelli lässt sich loben; Nur Telemann allein ist übers Lob erhoben', J. Mattheson, *Grundlage einer Ehren-Pforte*, p. 369. The metrical translation given in the text is from R. Rolland, *A Musical Tour through the Land of the Past*, tr. B. Miall (London, 1922), p. 97.

reputation as one of the leading composers of the early eighteenth century was firmly established.

Telemann had a long and productive career. Four years older than Bach and Handel, he outlived both. As a composer he was remarkably prolific, producing several operas (both comic and serious), a substantial number of sacred works and literally hundreds of instrumental pieces ranging from solos, duets, and trios to full orchestral works. Nor did he confine his activities to composition. His treatise *Sing-, Spiel- und Generalbass-Übungen* (Hamburg, 1733–4) proved an important addition to literature on the theory and practice of music, and the new periodical he launched in 1728 (*Der getreue Musik-Meister*) was one of the earliest publications of its kind to include complete printed compositions. Besides this he found time to write three autobiographical accounts which, being written at different stages of his career (1718, 1729, and 1739), provide valuable information for the historian.[2]

From these autobiographical accounts we gain a picture of an immensely active man. While still a Law student at Leipzig University (from 1701) he was composing operas and conducting his own Collegium Musicum and in 1704 he took on additional responsibilities as organist and director of music at Leipzig's Neukirche. Some time during the following year he became kapellmeister to Count Erdmann von Promnitz of Sorau. Then, in 1706, he resigned this position moving on to Eisenach where he was engaged as konzertmeister (i.e. principal violinist) of the Duke's private orchestra (1707).

---

[2] The first sketch (dated 14 Sept. 1718) stems from the Frankfurt period, and it was eventually published in Mattheson's *Grosse General-Bass-Schule* of 1731 (cf. pp. 160–71); the second account is contained in a letter from Telemann to J. G. Walther, 20 Dec. 1729, and its contents appeared in the latter's *Musicalisches Lexikon* of 1732 (cf. pp. 596–7); the third account was written in 1739 and published the following year in Mattheson's *Ehren-Pforte* (cf. pp. 354–69). (The first and third accounts have been reprinted in the Foreword to *Denkmäler deutscher Tonkunst*, xxviii, ed. M. Schneider (Leipzig, 1907), rev. edn. H. J. Moser (Weisbaden, 1958); the second account is reproduced in *Georg Philipp Telemann: Briefwechsel*, ed. H. Grosse and H. R. Jung (Leipzig, 1972), pp. 32–4. Hereafter references will be made to these more accessible sources.)

In the spring of 1712 Telemann signed a contract with the City Council of Frankfurt-on-Main accepting the post of organist at the Barfüsserkirche. Once again he became involved in a variety of other activities: he was for several years director and secretary of the Frauenstein Collegium Musicum, a society of music-loving amateurs which met regularly and gave weekly concerts. In addition to this, he became director of music at the church of St. Catherine's in Frankfurt and continued to fulfil commissions from the Duke of Saxe-Eisenach in his capacity as 'Kapellmeister von Haus aus', or 'external' kapellmeister.

The last forty-six years of Telemann's life—from 1721 until his death—were spent in Hamburg. His position as Cantor of the Johanneum (the local grammar school) and music director of the city's five principal churches was ostensibly a full-time appointment; yet once again we find him accepting offices in plurality. He continued to write music for the court of Eisenach, and in 1726 took the title 'Kapellmeister von Haus aus' to the Margrave of Bayreuth. Moreover he accepted extra commitments even within the city of Hamburg itself. In 1722 he signed an agreement with the management of the Hamburg opera to direct performances at the famous opera house; besides this he played a prominent part in the general musical life of the city, promoting, among other events, a series of concerts at the Drill Hall, Hamburg, where the public could hear cantatas, oratorios, and repeat performances of festival music. Once established in Hamburg Telemann travelled little, the only visit abroad which had any lasting impact on his music being an eight-month stay in Paris during 1737.[3]

2. The Concertos: Sources, Chronology, and Instrumentation

If we are to believe Telemann's own testimony, he had no

[3] Mennicke's theory that Telemann had made an earlier visit to France in 1707 (cf. *Hasse und die Brüder Graun als Symphoniker* (Leipzig, 1906), p. 93) rests on a misinterpretation of one of Telemann's remarks—see L. de la Laurencie, 'G. Ph. Telemann à Paris', *Revue de Musicologie*, xlii (1932), 77.

great love of the concerto. This admission is made in his first autobiographical sketch: 'Because it was a pleasant change, I also began to write concertos. Yet I must confess that deep down I did not care for them although I have composed a good many . . .'[4] It is significant that Telemann's lack of interest did not prevent him from cultivating the genre assiduously. Such detachment was typical of the eighteenth century when the likes and dislikes of an artist were of little consequence. Telemann himself was always vague about the exact number of works he had written and this, together with his wide application of the term 'concerto',[5] has created many problems for scholars.

Earlier this century it was thought that Telemann had written as many as 170 concertos. This was the figure given by Arnold Schering in 1905[6] and accepted by most subsequent writers. But, unfortunately, Schering had based his calculations on information in Eitner's *Quellen-Lexikon* and Eitner's list of concertos, it later emerged, contained several duplicated works. Schering's total was, therefore, much too high. Fortunately these and other misconceptions have been dispelled by Kross's recent monograph *Das Instrumentalkonzert bei Georg Philipp Telemann* (Tutzing, 1969). As a result of his studies we now possess, for the first time, a thematic catalogue of Telemann's concertos together with much valuable information regarding source material.

Kross's catalogue contains ninety-nine items. Most of the works listed are genuine concertos whatever their original function.[7] But there is one notable exception. Kross admits

---

[4] 'Alldieweil aber die Veränderung belustiget so machte mich auch über Concerte her. Hiervon muss bekennen dass sie mir niemahls recht von Herzen gegangen sind ob ich deren schon eine ziemliche Menge gemachte habe . . .', *Denkmäler deutscher Tonkunst*, xxviii, p. xiii.

[5] Both Telemann and J. S. Bach used the term 'concerto' in a very broad sense. The former's *Sechs Konzerte*, for example, are trio sonatas not orchestral works, cf. *Georg Philipp Telemann Musikalische Werke*, vol. xi, ed. J. P. Hinnenthal (Kassel, 1957).

[6] A Schering, *Geschichte des Instrumentalkonzerts*, p. 120.

[7] Two of the violin concertos (V. C(2) and V. a(1)) started life as sinfonias, the first serving as the Overture to *Der neumodische Liebhaber Damon* (first performed Hamburg, 1724) and the second as the Overture to *Emma und Eginhard* (Hamburg,

that the F major *Suiten-Konzert* for violin and strings is an 'Ouverture' with concertante elements, yet this work still appears in his catalogue even though Telemann's other concert-suites, many of which contain concertante features, are ignored. One suspects that Kross felt obliged to retain the F major work since it had been edited by Schering for the *Denkmäler* series[8] and had, for some years, passed as a 'representative' example of Telemann's concerto style.

The primary sources for Telemann's concertos may be divided into three categories: autographs, manuscript copies, and eighteenth-century editions. Only four of the concertos survive in autograph: the F major *Suiten-Konzert* mentioned above; a concerto in B♭ major for violin and strings dedicated to the Dresden violinist, Pisendel (V.B(3));[9] a concerto grosso in B minor for two flutes, 'calchedon' (i.e. chalcedon),[10] and strings, and a concerto grosso in D for the same combination. The concerto for Pisendel is the only manuscript to bear a date and this was completed on the 14 September 1719.

[Most of Telemann's concertos are preserved in contemporary copies rather than autographs, the largest collections being found at Darmstadt (Hessische Landes-und Hochschulbibliothek) and Dresden (Sächsische Landesbibliothek).] The Darmstadt copyists have been identified as

---

1728). Another violin concerto (V.B (2)) may have been intended for chamber performance since in one manuscript source (D-brd-DS 1042/6) it is entitled 'Sonata a tre Violini'. (The code used to identify individual concertos is that formulated by S. Kross, op cit., pp. 123–72: the solo instrument is listed first, then comes a letter indicating the key of the work (lower case for minor keys); finally, if it proves necessary to make a further distinction, a number is added. Thus, the two A minor violin concertos have the following code: V. a(1) and V. a(2). Although this sytem is clumsy and will become obsolete with the publication of the comprehensive *Telemann-Werke-Verzeichnis* now in progress, it is simpler than referring to the manuscript sources in full.)

[8] In *Denkmäler deutscher Tonkunst*, xxix–xxx, ed. A. Schering, pp. 103–95.

[9] See note 7 above for an explanation of the code used.

[10] The chalcedon, or colascione as it was more generally called, was a long-necked lute with five strings. It is specified in two concerti grossi by Telemann (C. gr. D and C. gr. h) and in the Dresden version of his E minor concerto for two flutes and strings. The spelling 'calchedon' which appears in the manuscript sources is an unusual, and possibly corrupt, variant.

Graupner, Endler, and Grünewald, all of whom were attached to the kapelle at some stage during Telemann's life-time. Several of the Darmstadt concertos are in score rather than parts—a significant point since at that date, when orchestras were directed from the first violin desk, from the harpsichord, or both, copyists seldom made a full score except for study purposes. The Dresden manuscripts are less informative; almost all of them are in parts and it has not proved possible to identify the copyists.

Very few of Telemann's concertos were printed during his life. Indeed, the three concertos which appeared in the *Musique de Table* collection of 1733 seem to be the only ones. To be sure, certain works were available from Breitkopf's at Leipzig,[11] but these were almost certainly circulated in manuscript copies.

Kross does not attempt to devise a chronology for Telemann's concertos—nor should he have done so given the scanty information available. Earlier scholars were more ambitious in this respect but their attempts to impose a chronological order on the concertos were hardly success-ful. The widespread acceptance of some of these theories, however, compels us to go over the ground again, if only to clarify the issue. One theory which gained credence during the early part of this century was that held by Arnold Schering. He suggested that the concertos preserved at Darmstadt were those written during Telemann's Frankfurt period (1712–21) whereas the Dresden concertos stemmed

---

[11] The Breitkopf catalogues advertise six concertos by Telemann. However, two of these—a D major concerto for two violas and a concerto for two 'Sampogne' (*The Breitkopf Thematic Catalogue: the Six Parts and Sixteen Supplements 1762–1787*, ed. B. S. Brook (New York, 1966), pp. 73, 113)—fall into the category of chamber music. The other four are as follows: the viola concerto in G major (*Breitkopf Catalogue*, p. 73); a concerto for two violas in A major (also p. 73)—this work does not appear in Kross's catalogue since there is no extant source for it; the flute concerto in D major (p. 100)—Kross catalogue Fl. D(2)—and a concerto in C minor for oboe and violin (p. 248). This last work has survived only in the keyboard arrangement made by Bach's friend J. G. Walther. It is interesting, incidentally, that Walther retained the original key of the work whereas Bach usually transposed his arrangements down a tone.

from his Eisenach period (*c.* 1707–12).[12] Although this
hypothesis seems reasonable on geographical grounds, it has
serious defects. Even within our limited sphere of knowledge, exceptions exist. The concerto which Telemann
wrote for Pisendel is dated 1719 and falls, therefore, in the
Frankfurt/Darmstadt category. However, the autograph
manuscript of this work is preserved, not at Darmstadt, but
at Dresden where, of course, Pisendel was employed.
Schering's theory also leaves a number of other questions
unanswered. What should one deduce from the many
concertos which are preserved in both libraries? Did Telemann abandon the concerto genre entirely after his move to
Hamburg in 1721? Could he not have sent concertos to his
friends at Dresden and Darmstadt as he himself received
music from the Berlin court?[13]

Attempts have also been made to date the concertos from
their instrumentation. Krüger maintained[14] that the concertos with chalcedon were designed for Frankfurt. Certainly
the church music which Telemann wrote for Frankfurt
often calls for a chalcedon[15] and on this count the theory
seems reasonable. But Krüger's other ideas are more
speculative. In the last autobiographical sketch Telemann
recalls playing double concertos with Pantaleon Hebenstreit, a notable violinst and the inventor of the improved
dulcimer to which he gave his name.[16] These concerts
probably took place during the Eisenach period (1707–12)
since both musicians were attached to the kapelle at that
time. Krüger argues from this that the concertos for two

---

[12] A Schering, *Geschichte des Instrumentalkonzerts* (Leipzig, 1905), p. 120.

[13] See p. 214.

[14] W. Krüger, *Das Concerto Grosso in Deutschland*, p. 90.

[15] C. Valentin, *Geschichte der Musik in Frankfurt am Main* (Frankfurt, 1906; reprint Wiesbaden, 1972), p. 229.

[16] '. . . I remember this Herr Hebenstreit's considerable skill on the violin, which surely placed him in the forefront of all other masters of that instrument; it was such that a few days before we were to play a concerto together I always locked myself in my room, fiddle in hand, shirt-sleeves rolled up, with something strong to oil my nerves, and gave myself lessons so that I could match up to his dexterity', *Denkmäler deutscher Tonkunst*, xxviii, p. xi; (from R. Petzoldt, *Georg Philipp Telemann*, tr. H. Fitzpatrick (London, 1974), pp. 27–8).

violins and strings were written at Eisenach, and he may, of course, be right. But as Professor Hutchings observes,[17] Telemann would also have required concertos for his Collegium Musicum concerts in Leipzig. It is, therefore, dangerous to assume that all the double violin concertos originated during the years 1707–12.

The shortcomings of these theories prompt one to consider stylistic evidence; but here again the results are far from conclusive. Burney once remarked that Telemann 'Like the painter Raphael, had a first and second *manner*, which were extremely different from each other. In the first, he was hard, stiff, dry and inelegant; in the second, all that was pleasing, graceful and refined.'[18] Although the concertos as a whole exhibit considerable variations of style, it is impossible to determine at what point in time this change occurred. Some writers would have us see a radical change of style after the year 1738 when Telemann returned from Paris. However, this is hardly credible since the *Musique de Table* concertos already display features of the new style and these were published in 1733—four years before Telemann's visit to France.

Various other factors also cloud the issue. So few of the concertos can be dated by external means[19] that it is impossible to draw any accurate conclusions regarding Telemann's stylistic development. Moreover, evidence from other areas suggests that Telemann made isolated experiments with different idioms, often varying his mode of expression according to the type of project in hand. Thus, his comic

---

[17] A. Hutchings, *The Baroque Concerto*, 3rd rev. edn. (London, 1973) p. 243.

[18] C. Burney, *The Present State of Music in Germany, the Netherlands and United Provinces,* 2nd edn. (London, 1775), ii. 244.

[19] Those concertos which can be dated were all written within fourteen years of each other: 1719, a concerto in Bb major for violin and strings (V. B(3)), dedicated to Pisendel; 1724, a concerto in C major for violin and strings (V. C(2)) which served as the Overture to *Der neumodische Liebhaber Damon* (Hamburg, 1724, see C. Ottzenn, *Telemann als Opernkomponist* (Berlin, 1902), pp. 18–26); 1728, see C. Ottzenn, for violin and strings (V. a(1)) which originally served as the Overture to Telemann's opera *Emma und Eginhard* (Hamburg, 1728, see C. Ottzenn, op. cit., pp. 55ff.); 1733, three concertos for various instruments published in the *Musique de Table* collections (Hamburg, 1733).

opera *Pimpinone* anticipates the *opera buffa* style of the 1730s and 1740s,[20] whereas some of his later (non-operatic) works, such as *Der Tag des Gerichts*, are written in a more conservative manner. Taking all these factors into consideration it is obvious that the stylistic analysis of Telemann's concertos will not provide an answer to problems of chronology.

Telemann was one of the few eighteenth-century composers who composed solo and grosso concertos in roughly equal proportions. Altogether, Kross lists forty-eight solo concertos in his thematic catalogue. However, the D major flute concerto (Fl. D(3)) and the F major recorder concerto are different versions of the same work, another concerto for flute or oboe in G major (Fl. G(1)) exists only in a fragmentary state, and a concerto in E minor is entered on two separate occasions, under both flute and violin concertos.[21] The number of complete solo concertos should, therefore, be reduced to forty-five. Besides the solo concertos there are fifty works for two or more soloists. Kross divides these into the following categories: double concertos (of which there are twenty-seven); *Gruppenkonzerte* i.e. concertos for more than two solo instruments (fifteen); genuine concerti grossi with a trio-style concertino (eight); and arrangements (two).[22]

The autobiographical accounts reveal that Telemann had, in his youth, learnt a variety of instruments including the clavier, violin, recorder, oboe, flute, 'schalümo' (?chalumeau[23]), gamba, double bass, and bass trombone.

[20] Telemann's *Pimpinone* was first performed at Hamburg in 1725; Pergolesi's celebrated intermezzo *La Serva Padrone*, which is written in a similar style, did not appear until 1733.

[21] In fact, as Kross establishes on p. 126 of his monograph, the work is for violin, not flute.

[22] Of the two clavier arrangements, one is anonymous, the other stems from J. G. Walther (see note 11, p. 186). On the general subject of Walther's keyboard transcriptions, see L. F. Tagliavini, 'Johann Gottfried Walther trascrittore'. *Analecta Musicologica*, vii (1969), 112–19.

[23] The chalumeau was a single-reed instrument whose appearance resembled that of the recorder. It had a certain localized popularity in parts of Germany and central Europe during the first half of the eighteenth century. For further information see H. Becker, 'Das Chalumeau bei Telemann', *Konferenzbericht der 3. Magdeburger Telemann-Festtage 1967*, ii. 68–76.

This experience was, of course, invaluable to him as a composer and orchestrator and may also have influenced his choice of solo instruments, for the concertos reveal a strong bias towards the violin, flute, and oboe. The statistics are as follows: there are twenty-two solo concertos for violin, eleven for flute, eight for oboe, two for oboe d'amore, two for recorder, and one apiece for the trumpet, horn, and viola. (In compiling these statistics the troublesome concerto in E minor mentioned above has been regarded as a violin concerto (see note 21, p. 189) and the concerto in G major for flute (or oboe) and strings has been placed among the flute concertos.) As for the double concertos, many of these are written for two similar instruments, so that one finds pairs of soloists—two flutes or two violins, oboe d'amore, chalumeaux, etc. In these concertos the two soloists are almost always treated as a unit, frequently playing the same material in parallel thirds or sixths.

The *Gruppenkonzerte* employ an outstandingly varied collection of solo instruments. Not only are there concertos for three (or more) similar instruments (i.e. three trumpets or four violins), but a number have unusual combinations of stringed and wind instruments within the concertino group. There is a concerto for two 'tromba selvatica' and two violins, and another for two oboe d'amore and cello; one for three horns and violin, and another for flute, oboe d'amore, and viola d'amore. These are but a few of the combinations used, other groupings being equally imaginative.

The concerti grossi, on the other hand, are nearly all scored for the same type of concertino. Here the solo group consists of two equal melody instruments (usually two flutes or two oboes) and a bass. The bass part does admit some variety, being designed sometimes for bassoon, sometimes for chalcedon, and, in one case, for violin.[24]

---

[24] The concerto grosso in E minor is scored for a concertino group of two flutes and solo violin. During solo episodes the violin functions as a *Bassetchen* or 'high bass', its part being written in the bass clef. For other examples of this notational device see pp. 272–3.

Turning to the ripieno group, we find that in most of Telemann's concertos the accompaniment is provided by strings and keyboard continuo alone. However, these traditional forces are often used in an original manner. Four-part writing is the norm for tutti passages, but there are other combinations besides the orthodox arrangement of two violins, viola, and bass. Some concertos (as, for example, the E minor double concerto for flute, violin, and strings) have a single violin part and two viola lines. In this Telemann may have been influenced by the orchestral music of certain French composers who favoured double viola parts. By contrast, a few of his concertos are written for a three-part ensemble comprising two violins and bass. This type of instrumentation occurs most often in solo concertos for flute or violin but there is no hard and fast rule that all flute or violin concertos omit the viola from the ripieno. Indeed, in one exceptional work—the violin concerto in F major—the ripieno consists merely of two viola parts (marked violetta and viola) and a bass line. Presumably Telemann did not wish any ripieno violinists to compete, on this occasion, with the solo violin tone.

At times, wind instruments enrich the sound of the ripieno group. The concerto in C major for two chalumeaux is accompanied by bassoons and strings, and in several of the concertos for two horns, oboes stiffen the texture. Yet one has the feeling that Telemann added these wind instruments indiscriminately, for their presence within the ripieno group can upset the delicate balance between soloist and orchestra. In one of the double violin concertos (2V.D (1)) the soloists are 'supported' by strings and trumpets (!), and the same type of instrumentation occurs in the double concerto for violin and cello which boasts ripieno parts for trumpet, three violins, two violas, and continuo.

3. General Planning; Movement Types

Approximately two thirds of all Telemann's concertos are cast in four-movement form and follow the standard 'da chiesa' pattern of alternating slow and fast movements. The remainder are written in the three-movement form associated with the Venetian concerto. Concertos with more than four movements are rare and are usually extensions of the 'da chiesa' plan with an additional movement at the beginning or end of the concerto.[25] This preference for the old four-movement concerto might seem curious, especially when one recalls Telemann's lively interest in contemporary musical developments. Yet it is intimately connected with his predilection for the *Gruppenkonzert* and concerto grosso forms. The ratio of four-movement to three-movement concertos in Telemann is approximately 2:1, as has already been stated, but the proportion varies according to the type of work in question. Whereas half the solo concertos are in three-movement form, all the concerti grossi have four movements apiece. These statistics support the theory that during this period composers tended to associate the 'da chiesa' arrangement with the concerto grosso, and the three-movement plan with the solo concerto.

Although the historical origins of the three- and four-movement concerto were quite distinct (the one evolving from the sinfonia, the other from the sonata), the two types had much in common. If one disregards the opening slow movement of Telemann's 'da chiesa' concertos, the remaining movements correspond almost exactly to those of the three-movement works. Two features serve to distinguish them: the first Allegro is slightly more severe in the 'da chiesa' than in the Venetian type, while the minuet Finale is virtually confined to the four-movement concertos. Apart from this, however, both genres share the same wide range of movement-types.

The opening movement of Telemann's 'da chiesa' concertos (i.e. the first slow movement) may be written in virtually any time signature, ranging from the common-

---

[25] E.g. the concerto in E minor for flute, violin, and strings which has the following arrangement of movements: (1) no tempo indication, but probably Moderato; (2) Adagio; (3) Presto; (4) Adagio; (5) Allegro.

place $\frac{4}{4}$ to the more exotic metres of $\frac{3}{8}$, $\frac{12}{8}$, and $\frac{6}{4}$. The choice of metre is more important than might be imagined in that Telemann appears to associate particular time signatures with particular movement-types. A compound-time signature, for example, often heralds a gentle, lilting movement, while imitative writing usually takes place in the $\frac{3}{2}$ movements. It is noticeable that despite Telemann's links with French music he seldom opens a concerto with a slow movement in French Overture style. Indeed, he goes out of his way to avoid all semblance of baroque pomposity. Several of his opening movements are headed 'Affettuoso', 'Soave', or 'Avec Douceur'—directions which reflect the intimate, slightly sentimental style of the music:

EXAMPLE I[26]

Telemann, concerto in G major for two violas, 1st movement, bars

1–4

In terms of length and weight the first Allegro was traditionally the most important movement of both the 'da chiesa' and the three-movement concerto. Telemann himself reveals a conventional preference for the concerto-style

[26] The sources from which examples are taken are listed in Appendix B.

Allegro based on strongly rhythmic themes. The incisive incipit of Example 2 is characteristic in this respect; moreover it illustrates how dependent the German concerto had become on the Italian style:

EXAMPLE 2

Telemann, concerto in E major for violin and strings, 2nd movement, bars 1–3

Next in popularity to the concerto-style Allegros come the contrapuntal movements. Some of these are fully-fledged fugues—see the 1st movement of the F minor oboe concerto (Ob. f(1))—but in many other cases Telemann adopts a more relaxed contrapuntal idiom in which the writing is imitative without being strictly fugal.

As far as the baroque concerto was concerned, the principal function of the slow movement was to provide a contrasting element in terms of mood, tempo, and, above all, key. Most of Telemann's major-mode concertos have slow movements in the relative minor, although the tonic minor and dominant keys are sometimes found as, exceptionally, is the relative minor of the dominant. For minor-mode concertos[27] (and these comprise roughly 38 per cent of the total) the relative major is the normal contrast key, but the tonic major is used on occasion and there are isolated examples of slow movements in the subdominant minor and in the relative major of the subdominant.

Besides providing this vital key contrast, the central slow movement may also afford a change of texture since Telemann, like Bach, sometimes reduces his instrumental forces at this point. One must, however, distinguish between the

---

[27] Of the eight oboe concertos, six are in minor keys. It seems that here, as also in his Passions, Telemann associated the instrument with dark tonalities, see G. Fleischhauer, 'Einige Gedanken zur Instrumentation Telemanns', *Konferenzbericht der 3. Magdeburger Telemann-Festtage 1967*, ii. 49.

'sonata-inspired' slow movement and the conventional exclusion of solo instruments from the slow movements of brass concertos. In the first case Telemann omits certain members of the ripieno group (usually all the upper strings) and leaves the movement to soloist(s) and bass alone. Having reduced the group to chamber music proportions, he adapts his style accordingly, often writing in the manner of the baroque solo or trio sonata:

EXAMPLE 3
Telemann, concerto in F major for recorder and gamba, 2nd movement, bars 1–3

It is in movements such as these that one sees most clearly the hold still exercised by the sonata on the eighteenth-century concerto.

Completely different factors were responsible for the omission of brass instruments in certain slow movements. During the first half of the eighteenth century trumpets and horns were generally barred from participating in the slow movements of orchestral works, partly because of their overpowering tone quality, and partly because of their natural limitations when playing in minor keys. Composers were, therefore, faced with two practical alternatives: they could either score the slow movements of their brass concertos for strings alone, or else they could retain some tutti/solo contrast by substituting a less strident solo instrument at this point. Telemann had recourse to both solutions on different occasions. Most of his slow movements are for strings alone, but in the D major concerto for three trumpets (3 Trp. D(1)) an oboe is taken out of the ripieno group and given the principal part in the Largo.

Later in the century, of course, composers became less timid in their use of brass instruments and it is interesting, in this connection, that Telemann himself allowed the solo horn to participate in the Largo of his D major horn concerto. This was, however, an isolated experiment and must be regarded as exceptional.

Although virtually any time signature may appear in the central slow movement, Telemann shows a preference for the traditional 'bel canto' signature of $\frac{3}{2}$. Sometimes this prompts him to write a solemn contrapuntal piece in the manner of an Italian trio sonata. In the following extract the severe imitative opening, the purposeful movement of the bass line, and the general harmonic scheme of bars 5 and 6 have the old-fashioned flavour of Corelli:

EXAMPLE 4

Telemann, concerto in D major for trumpet and strings, 3rd movement, bars 1–7

Other slow movements look forward rather than back. This is particularly true of the 'operatic' movements—the recitatives and arias—in which Telemann's belief that singing was of fundamental importance to music[28] found practical expression. Although recitative movements are not common, there are two examples in the oboe concertos (see

[28] 'Singen ist der Fundament zur Musik in alle Dingen. Wer die Composition ergreifft muss in seinen Sätzen singen. Wer auf Instrumenten spielt muss des Singens kündig seyn. Also präge man des Singen jungen Leuten fleissig ein.' From the 1718 account of his life, see *Denkmäler deutscher Tonkunst*, xxviii, p. viii.

the slow movements of Ob. d and Ob. f(2)).[29] Whether this was simply coincidence or whether Telemann's fine sense of instrumental colour was responsible, we shall probably never know. But the choice of instrument was felicitous for the plaintive tones of the oboe are well suited to these rhetorical outbursts. One of Telemann's recitative movements (the six-bar Adagio from the D minor oboe concerto) is given below in full. It will be seen from this that the soloist has a declamatory line throughout and the accompaniment with its curious chord progressions has all the richness and fluidity of its operatic prototype:

EXAMPLE 5
Telemann, oboe concerto in D minor, 3rd movement (string parts in short score)

In the aria-like slow movements the strings are often marked *pizzicato* to ensure the lightest possible accompani-

[29] Only the F minor concerto has a slow movement which is actually entitled 'recitativ accomp.', but the style of the Adagio from the D minor concerto is equally declamatory (see Ex. 5).

ment—a technique borrowed directly from operatic practice. One of the best examples of this type of movement occurs in the E minor concerto for flute, recorder, and strings. Here the two soloists present a cantabile melody of exquisite beauty against a delicate harmonic background:

EXAMPLE 6
Telemann, concerto in E minor for flute, recorder, and strings, 3rd movement, bars 4–8; (the first three and a half bars of this movement consist of a simple chordal introduction)

Historically, Telemann's use of this type of operatic movement is important, for the aria became increasingly important among instrumental composers of J. C. Bach's generation. The continuation of the tradition extends also into the later eighteenth century with the Mozartian *Romanza*.

Turning to the Finale, we find an intriguing mixture of old-established and more progressive movement-types. In some concertos Telemann still uses the traditional closing movement in $\frac{3}{8}$ time which was so popular with Vivaldi and his followers. There are also a number of movements in imitative or concerto style which differ little from those mentioned already in connection with the first Allegro. More interesting from our point of view, however, are the dance Finales (principally gigues and minuets), and those lively Presto movements in duple or quadruple time which were the ancestors of the classical Finale.

Most of Telemann's gigues belong to the Italian, rather than the French, category, and are therefore very different in style from the familiar Bachian models. At this period the Italian *Giga* was characterized both by its greater speed and vivacity, and also by its uncomplicated texture which contrasted sharply with the quasi-fugal content of the French type. Telemann's handling of these movements is surprisingly sophisticated for, although he will sometimes retain the conventional binary structure associated with the dance, he is equally prone to abandon all rigid schemes in the interests of free musical development. Characteristic in this respect is the Finale of his D major violin concerto (V.D.(2)) whose impressive opening, with its built-in orchestral crescendo, is shown at Example 7. Although the movement as a whole has elements of ritornello form—seen in the regular alternation of tutti and solo sections—the treatment of material is very free.

EXAMPLE 7
Telemann, violin concerto in D major (V.D.(2)), 4th movement, bars
1–4

The minuet Finale proved less popular with Telemann than the *Giga* but the few examples which he has left us are significant from the historical point of view: in the first place they are almost all genuine minuets, written in $\frac{3}{4}$ time—not the compromise $\frac{3}{8}$ favoured by so many transitional composers;[30] secondly, Telemann's themes by virtue of their simplicity and directness, foreshadow those of the classical (symphonic) minuet:

EXAMPLE 8
Telemann, concerto in D major for flute and strings (Fl. D (5)), 4th movement, bars 1–5

Interesting though these dance movements are, it is the presto Finales which display the greatest originality. In these movements Telemann casts off all restraints and writes with what appears to be a natural spontaneity. The melodic material is tuneful in style and often contains strong folk elements. Nowhere is this more apparent than in the exuberant Finale of the E minor concerto for flute, recorder, and strings.

EXAMPLE 9
Telemann, concerto in E minor for flute, recorder, and strings, 4th movement, bars 1–8 (outer parts only)

---

[30] The one exception is found in the last movement of Telemann's E minor concerto for two oboes and violin; this movement is entitled Menuett but is in $\frac{3}{8}$ time.

A rustic atmosphere is produced right at the beginning of this movement by the drone bass while the structure of the melody, with its constant repetition of short motifs and the occasional intrusion of ponderous minims (to emphasize weak beats), reveals the specific influence of Polish folk music.

4. The Structure of Allegro Movements

To anyone familiar with the structural principles of J. S. Bach's concertos, Telemann's use of form holds few surprises. It is true that there are a greater number of binary movements in Telemann's concertos, but this stems more from his love of dance-derived movements than from any 'progressive' inclination towards symphonic forms. Looking back over the eighteenth century as a whole, one cannot claim that Telemann was in the forefront of formal developments. Most of his ritornello movements lack a recapitulation section and those exceptional movements which combine ritornello and recapitulatory designs do not make any significant advance on the Bachian model.

Ritornello Movements

As one would expect in concertos of this period, ritornello movements form by far the largest category. These vary considerably in length and may have as few as three, or as many as five, statements of the ritornello. The ritornello itself is usually quite short (eight bars of $\frac{4}{4}$ being a fairly typical length) and its internal structure is uncomplicated. In some cases the ritornello seems to be woven in one piece—to evolve naturally from snippets of the opening thematic material. Other ritornelli have a more formal structure which can be analysed in conventional terms, e.g. head-motif, followed by a sequential section followed by a strongly cadential passage. In many cases Telemann's ritornelli consist simply of a head-motif and a sequential section, for he did not favour the endlessly-repeated cadence nor the *pianoidée* which, despite its virtues, could (and often did) degenerate into a meaningless cliché.

Ritornello form, although seemingly so inflexible, was, of course, capable of subtle variations as far as the internal arrangement of material and the thematic relationship between tutti and solo groups was concerned. In Telemann's case, after noting that he uses from three to five statements of the ritornello, further generalization becomes difficult since his movements vary so greatly in their detailed organization of material. The most advantageous course, therefore, is to discuss the structure of a few sharply contrasting movements, and to see what range of methods is applied.

The first Allegro from the well-known viola concerto represents the simplest type of ritornello form used by Telemann. The opening ritornello is short, consisting of a head-motif and sequential section alone:

EXAMPLE 10

Telemann, viola concerto in G major, 2nd movement, bars 1–7
(outer parts only)

There are three full statements of the ritornello in tonic, dominant, and tonic keys respectively (bars 1–7, 25–31, and 70–6)[31] and the intervening solo episodes are based partly on ritornello themes and partly on more figurative material. The viola dominates each solo episode, for the accompani-

---

[31] Modern edition by H. C. Wolff (Kassel, 1968).

ment is light and often entrusted to the bass instruments, or, less frequently, to the upper strings, alone.

Of a completely different order is the first Allegro from the E major concerto for flute, oboe d'amore, viola d'amore, and strings.[32] This movement begins with an expansive ritornello—twenty-eight bars in all. Despite its length there is no sectional division along conventional lines; Telemann allows the music to unfold continuously from the three principal motifs shown below:

EXAMPLE II

Telemann, concerto in E major for flute, oboe d'amore, viola d'amore, and strings, 2nd movement, bars 1–10 (outer parts only)

During the course of the movement the ritornello is heard four times: at bars 1–28 (E major), 60–70 (A major), 110–38 (B major), and 263–91 (E major). The second statement is greatly curtailed and the third, though it follows the opening tutti very closely, has some minor modifications. The last statement is unabridged. Apart from these structurally important ritornello statements the ripieno instruments also make a number of shorter references to ritornello material (as at bars 188–92, 198–203, 212–17, 223–30, 238–45, and 253–7). The first solo section opens with figurative material for the viola d'amore (see Ex. 12a) and this is followed by a

---

[32] Ed. F. Stein (Frankfurt, 1938).

'sigh' figure (Ex. 12b). Immediately thereafter Telemann introduces a slow-moving countersubject against the figurative material (Ex. 12c). Although essentially so simple, this countersubject proves important later in the movement. Indeed, these three motifs, together with an inverted ritornello figure and a new idea in descending thirds (cf. the oboe d'amore part at bars 54–6), supply virtually all the material for subsequent solo episodes.

EXAMPLE 12

Telemann, concerto in E major for flute, oboe d'amore, viola d'amore, and strings, 2nd movement: (a) bars 29–32, (b) bars 34–8, (c) bars 40–3

This movement is particularly well organized. However, it must be admitted that Telemann was not always so economical with his material. In numerous solo episodes he relies on commonplace figuration which bears little or no relationship to the principle thematic ideas. Passages of mere note-spinning occur frequently and cannot be justified on grounds of virtuosity alone since Telemann, unlike Bach and Vivaldi, rarely stretches the technical abilities of his soloists to the full.

Exceptionally one finds Telemann experimenting with recapitulatory designs. An example occurs in the first Allegro of the D minor concerto for two chalumeaux and strings.[33] The tonic key is re-established near the beginning of the third solo episode (at bar 64) and the remainder of the episode consists of repeated material, drawn initially from the opening of the first solo and subsequently from its conclusion:

Outline analysis of the 2nd movement of Telemann's D minor concerto for two chalumeaux and strings

Bar	Key	Tutti/Solo	Material
1	D minor	Tutti	Ritornello 1
12	D minor, modulatory, F	Solo	Commencing with an independent solo theme—A
38	F to C	Tutti	Ritornello 2
41	C, modulatory, A minor	Solo	Figurative
55	A minor	Tutti	Ritornello 3
60	A minor to D minor	Solo	At bar 64 there is a repeat of solo theme A in the tonic; at bar 70 Telemann introduces solo material from the end of the first solo section (bars 33–8) now transposed to the tonic
78	D minor	Tutti	Ritornello 4

The above format is, of course, very similar to that adopted by J. S. Bach for certain of his ritornello movements (see pp. 63–5). But there is one important difference: whereas Bach usually begins his final section with ritornello material, Telemann prefers to use solo themes at this point and the force of his 'recapitulation' is weakened accordingly.

Composite Ritornello Structures

Like Bach, Telemann combined ritornello principles freely with other modes of construction. Apart from straightforward ritornello movements, therefore, one also finds ritornello form linked with 'da capo' structures (as in the baroque aria) or providing the basis for many fugal movements in concertante style. Taking the 'da capo' structures first, we find that once again there is a distinction between the way in which Telemann and Bach handled the form. In

[33] Ed. H. Dechant (London, 1973).

the first Allegro from Telemann's triple concerto in A major (*Musique de Table*, Book 1)[34] there are three ritornello statements during the first section of the movement (at bars 1–30, 82–94, and 124–42), in tonic, dominant, and tonic keys respectively. The central section (bars 143–98) is based on contrasting material and the texture of the writing is lighter.[35] This section ends with a cadence in F# minor (bar 198) and the 'da capo' follows abruptly. Although the plan obviously resembles that found in the 1st movement of Bach's E major violin concerto (see pp. 66–7), one distinction can be drawn: there is no statement of the ritornello in the central section. This was Telemann's established practice and serves to distinguish his 'da capo' ritornello movements from those of J. S. Bach.

Most of the fugal movements in Telemann's concertos (and there are a significant number) may be classed as concerto fugues: that is to say, the contrapuntal tutti sections are relieved by more figurative episodes for the soloist and the initial exposition often functions as a ritornello, returning at strategic points throughout. The content of the solo episodes and their relationship to the opening fugue subject is unpredictable. The soloist may refer constantly to the fugue subject,[36] it may present a variant thereof,[37] or it may even avoid the fugal material altogether, as in the 2nd movement of Telemann's D major violin concerto (V. D(1)).[38] In this last instance Telemann obviously sought a sharp contrast between the five ritornello statements (which are all fugal) and the more brilliant solo episodes.

---

[34] Ed. J. P. Hinnenthal in *Georg Philipp Telemann Musikalische Werke*, vol. xii (Kassel, 1959).

[35] See Ex. 18a.

[36] See the Finale of Telemann's D major trumpet concerto ed. K. Grebe, (Hamburg, 1959).

[37] See the 1st movement of Telemann's F minor oboe concerto (Ob. f(1)), ed. F. Schroeder (London, 1958); the oboe presents a variant of the original fugue subject at the beginning of the first solo episode (bar 18).

[38] Ed. S. Kross in *Georg Philipp Telemann Musikalische Werke*, vol. xxiii (Kassel, 1973), pp. 25ff.

Exceptional Usages

Before leaving the subject of the ritornello movements some eccentricities must be mentioned. It will have been noticed, for example, that Telemann's key schemes do not always follow a conventional course. Sometimes the second ritornello is in the subdominant rather than the dominant, and frequently the dominant (or relative) key is only established during the course of the second ritornello. Occasionally also, Telemann breaks up the first solo episode with a 'mock' ritornello which commences in the dominant but which reverts suddenly to the tonic. (This happens in the 1st movement of the F major violin concerto (bars 21–6),[39] the second ritornello proper, which remains in the dominant key throughout, being delayed until bar 38.) All these examples are primarily concerned with tonal structure. However, there are more radical experiments which affect the whole organization of material, irrespective of key. Most startling in this respect are Telemann's occasional attempts to dispense with his final ritornello statement. The first Allegro of the G minor violin concerto provides a case in point. It begins with an assertive tutti passage of quite exceptional length—forty bars in all. This is followed by a solo episode and a second ritornello statement in C minor (at bar 117). After a further solo passage, however, the movement ends abruptly and the final Vivaldian flourish (bars 159 to the end), though effective in its own way, is no substitute for the expected ritornello statement.

Binary Movements

We come now to Telemann's binary movements, most of which are still connected either directly or indirectly with the dance. All the Minuets are, of course, written in binary form and so are a number of those Finales which have a light-hearted or popular content. Telemann was, however, notably reluctant to employ binary structures for more serious Allegro movements and the isolated experiments

[39] Ibid., pp. 90ff.

that he made in this direction were not always successful. In the first Allegro of his B minor violin concerto there is an uneasy alliance between baroque concerto style and binary form. This is a subjective assessment, it is true, but one is conditioned to expect ritornello structure in a movement of this kind and the bipartite form proves curiously disconcerting. In this respect the first Allegro of the third *Musique de Table* concerto is much more successful. Here both the style and the form of the movement derive from symphonic models; there is, therefore, no dichotomy between form and content.

Sometimes the organization of Telemann's more extended binary movements approaches that of what was later known as sonata form. His presto Finales are particularly interesting from this point of view, as may be seen from the following analysis:

Outline structure of the presto Finale from Telemann's F major violin concerto[40]

Bar	Key	Tutti/solo	Material	Additional comments
1	F	Tutti	A	Interrupted by the soloist at bars 9–12; a subsidiary idea (x) is introduced at bar 16
22	F to C	Solo + tutti accompaniment	B	= a contrasting second subject
48	C to D minor	Tutti	A′	Interrupted by a similar, though not identical, solo passage at bars 56–62; the subsidiary idea (x) returns at bars 62–7; this is followed by further development of the opening theme (bars 67–78)
78	D minor to F	Solo + tutti accompaniment	B′	Apart from transposition and other minor modifications the final section of both halves is identical (compare bars 36–48 with 86ff.)

It will be noticed that (as in many baroque suite movements) the final section of both halves of the movement

[40] Ed. S. Kross in *Georg Philipp Telemann Musikalische Werke*, vol. xxiii, pp. 101f.

correspond. The most striking feature, however, is not the amount of repetition involved—substantial though this is—but the presence of a strongly contrasted second subject. The key scheme also points towards the sonata for the second subject is heard first in the dominant (see bars 22ff.) and, subsequently, in the tonic key. Also significant is the organization of material at the beginning of the second half—the rudimentary development section. Here Telemann presents his head-motif in C major (the dominant) and then repeats it, immediately afterwards, in D minor. The disruptive effect of this abrupt tonal shift anticipates the modulatory techniques of later classical composers.

Rondo Form

The other form which occurs frequently in Telemann's lighter Finales is the rondo, or, to be more precise, the *rondeau*. The distinction is important for the French type of movement was extremely stylized. It had a clearly articulated refrain and its couplets also were cast in regular phrase lengths. A typical example of the *rondeau* Finale is found in the D major concerto for three trumpets (3 Trp. D(2)).[41] The movement is based on the following refrain which is heard five times altogether (at bars 1–8, 17–24, 33–40, 49–56, and 65–72):

EXAMPLE 13

Telemann, concerto in D major for three trumpets and orchestra (3 Trp. D(2)), presto Finale, bars 1–8

---

[41] Ed. G. Fleischhauer (Leipzig, 1968).

Since each of the intervening couplets is also eight bars long, the movement has all the symmetry of the traditional French *rondeau*.[42]

5. The Structure of Slow Movements

Some indication has already been given of the various types of slow movement cultivated by Telemann. From the point of view of form, most of these movements fall into one of the following categories: through-composed, ritornello, or ground bass structures. The trio-sonata and Siciliana movements are nearly always through-composed and rely heavily on the baroque technique of motivic expansion. Ritornello movements are less common. Occasionally, however, a slow movement will reflect the structure of an adjacent Allegro. This happens in the D minor concerto for two chalumeaux where the opening Largo is cast in exactly the same form as the subsequent ritornello movement.[43] There are a few examples also of the 'framed' slow movement in which a central solo section is enclosed by two identical tutti passages. Technically these movements could be represented by the scheme ABA, but in practice the tutti passages are so short (see, for example, the Largo of the oboe d'amore concerto in A major)[44] that the result is closer to ritornello, than to genuine 'da capo' form. As for the ground bass structures these are treated with great flexibility. The bass line, which is often in the nature of an ostinato rather than a strict ground, is allowed to modulate freely and may be subject to rhythmic alteration at any time. In the following passage contraction of the original phrase structure takes place during the very first repetition of the 'ground' (see bar 5) and this is not untypical:

EXAMPLE 14

Telemann, concerto in F major for recorder and strings, 3rd movement, bars 1–7

[42] Compare the Finale of J. S. Bach's E major violin concerto (BWV 1042); here the refrain and couplets are cast, for the most part, in sixteen-bar periods.

[43] See p. 205.

[44] Ed. F. Schroeder (London, *c.* 1962).

6. Stylistic Features

Stylistically, Telemann's music reflects all the tensions and contradictions of a transitional era. The concertos themselves display a considerable range of style: some make little advance on the type of material used by Muffat and Corelli; others derive their inspiration from Venetian models; some are written in the 'galant' manner and in certain other cases one may detect hints of the North German expressive style and even anticipations of Mozart. Yet the dangers of eclecticism are skilfully avoided for Telemann seldom mixes styles within individual concertos. One work will be written in the Corellian manner throughout, whereas another may lean towards Albinoni or Graun in all its movements. In each concerto, therefore, a certain stylistic unity is preserved.

There remains, however, a considerable disparity between the style of individual concertos as may be seen by comparing a few select works. Representative of the Corellian type is the concerto in A minor for two flutes and strings.[45] This work is cast in four-movement form and the material used in firmly rooted in the traditions of the Italian baroque. The opening of the 2nd movement (see Ex. 15) relies for its effect on the frequent use of suspensions, the

[45] Ed. F. Stein (Kassel, 1953).

repetition of two or three principal motifs, and the steadily-moving bass—all features associated with baroque music in general. Then at bar 5 comes a typical Corellian progression, characterized by harmonic tautology, imitation at the unison in the two upper parts, and step-wise movement in the bass:

EXAMPLE 15

Telemann, concerto in A minor for two flutes and strings, 2nd movement, bars 1–7

The oboe concerto in F minor (Ob. f(1))[46] provides an example of Telemann's Vivaldian manner. This work, which is (significantly) in three movements (Allegro —'largo e piano'—Vivace) has a more contemporary flavour than the flute concerto just discussed. Although the 1st movement is fugal, a homophonic style prevails during

[46] Ed. F. Schroeder (London, 1958).

the solo episodes. In the following extract from the last solo section the decorated internal pedal and the light, open texture produce a strikingly progressive effect:

EXAMPLE 16

Telemann, concerto in F minor for oboe and strings (Ob. f(1)), 1st movement, bars 80–5

The 2nd movement of the same concerto—a Siciliana in all but name—is notable for its elegant melodies and rich harmonic colouring. Venetian influence may, perhaps, be detected in the interjections of the bass part (see Ex. 27 on p. 226), for these descending scale figures, though not regular enough to constitute a true ostinato, perform a similar function. As for the Finale, this is the most Vivaldian movement of the whole concerto. It is a fine $\frac{3}{8}$ movement conspicuous for its clear textures and lively melodic writing.

The three concertos of the *Musique de Table* collection reveal yet another idiom in which Telemann was well versed, namely, the 'style galante'. The slow movement of the triple concerto in A major is particularly representative with its melting appoggiaturas and nervous rhythms. Rococo clichés are present in the shape of quaver syncopations (bar 2) and 'scotch snaps' (bar 4). The form taken by the cadence at bars 3–4 is also revealing in that the dominant note (E) is preceded by the sharpened fourth of the scale

(D#)—a cadential formula associated with much rococo and pre-classical music:

EXAMPLE 17

Telemann, concerto in A major for flute, violin, cello, and strings (*Musique de Table*, Book 1), 1st movement, bars 1–4

The expressive North German style makes only an occasional appearance in the concertos. This is surprising in view of the fact that Telemann visited Berlin on several occasions and corresponded not only with his godchild Emanuel Bach but also with a number of Emanuel's colleagues, including Agricola, C. H. Graun, Christoph Nichelmann, and J. J. Quantz. Moreover, we know that he kept in touch with artistic developments at Berlin. In 1756, for example, Emanuel Bach sent him a concerto by J. G. Graun and the content of Emanuel's letter makes it clear that Telemann had requested some such work.[47] This exchange

47 Bach's letter (dated 29 Dec. 1756) is printed in *Georg Philipp Telemann: Briefwechsel*, p. 372.

is significant, for included in volume xxiii of the *Telemann-Ausgabe* is a violin concerto in B♭ major whose central Adagio is so uncharacteristic of Telemann and so typical of Graun's decorated style that one might be led to question its authenticity. If genuine (and the editors voice no suspicions on this count) the work provides a striking example of the influence of North German music on Telemann. At the same time, however, it must be stressed that there are no parallels for this movement in the rest of Telemann's concertos.

On rare occasions Telemann's style anticipates that of the Viennese classical school. We do not know whether Mozart was acquainted with Telemann's published works or not, but there is a marked resemblance (despite the difference in tempo) between the 2nd movement of Telemann's first *Musique de Table* concerto and the Adagio of Mozart's flute quartet K. 285:

EXAMPLE 18

(*a*) Telemann, concerto in A major for flute, violin, cello, and strings (*Musique de Table*, Book 1), 2nd movement, bars 143–6; (*b*) Mozart, flute quartet in D major (K. 285), 2nd movement, bars 1–4

These last examples do much to expose the weakness in traditional assessments of Telemann's style. Both Schering and Krüger,[48] it will be recalled, classify Telemann as a Corellian concertist. Perhaps they were misled by the many superficial resemblances between the two composers—by Telemann's preference for the four-movement concerto and by his occasional use of rapid exchanges between the solo and ripieno groups. In fact, the Corellian manner was but one of a number of styles which Telemann could adopt at will. As Professor Hutchings rightly observes: 'Telemann, so far from fitting into a niche labelled "Corellian" represents the whole history of the concerto and other forms of French and Italian concert music as reflected in German composers from Muffat until after Quantz.'[49]

National Elements

It is evident, both from his music and from the autobiographical sketches, that Telemann had a keen ear for musical style. In his youth he had travelled considerable distances to attend performances of operatic and instrumental music. The pattern of his early professional career also proved stimulating in this respect for, by chance, he held a succession of posts which brought him into contact with the art-music and folk-culture of several different nations. Like

---

[48] See A. Schering, *Geschichte des Instrumentalkonzerts* and W. Krüger, *Das Concerto Grosso in Deutschland*.

[49] Arthur Hutchings, *The Baroque Concerto*, p. 237.

so many of his compatriots at that time, Telemann was fascinated by local colour, by the national elements in music. In a letter to J. G. Walther (dated 1729) he acknowledged his musical debt to three countries: Poland, France, and Italy.[50] It is important, therefore, to establish what impact these national styles had on his artistic development in general and on the concertos in particular.

Telemann came into direct contact with Polish music while in the service of Count Erdmann von Promnitz at Sorau. Some years later he described these experiences:

When the Court removed to Pless for six months, one of Promnitz's estates in Upper Silesia, I heard there, as I had done in Cracow, the music of Poland and the Hanaka region of Moravia in its true barbaric beauty. In the country inns the usual ensemble consisted of a violin tuned a third higher which could out-shriek half a dozen ordinary fiddles; a Polish bagpipe; and a regal. In respectable places, however, the regal was omitted and the number of fiddles and pipes increased; in fact I once heard thirty-six Polish pipes and eight Polish violins playing together. One would hardly believe the inventiveness with which these pipers and fiddlers improvise when the dancers pause for breath. An observer could collect enough ideas in eight days to last a lifetime. But enough; this music, if handled with understanding, contains much good material. In due course I wrote a number of grand concerti and trios which I clad in an Italian coat with alternating Allegri and Adagi.[51]

If this account had not been written, the concertos themselves would have provided ample evidence of Telemann's interest in Polish music. Drone basses occur in certain Finales (see Ex. 9) and Polish dance rhythms are also prominent. The manuscript source for one of the flute concertos (Fl. D (2)) is actually headed *Concertos Polonaise*—a fitting title for a work which opens in the following manner:

---

[50] 'Was ich in den *Stylis* der Musik gethan, ist bekandt. Erst war es der Polnische, dem folgete der Französ., Kirchen-Cammer-und Opern-Style u. was sich nach dem Italiänischen nennet, mit welchem ich denn itzo das mehreste zu thun habe', Telemann to J. G. Walther, (20 Dec. 1729) printed in *Georg Philipp Telemann: Briefwechsel*, p. 34.

[51] *Denkmäler deutscher Tonkunst*, xxviii, p. x (from R. Petzoldt, *Georg Philipp Telemann*, tr. H. Fitzpatrick, p. 25).

EXAMPLE 19

Telemann, concerto in D major for flute and strings (Fl. D(2)), 1st
movement, bars 1–4 (incipit)

Typical of Slavonic folk music is the limited range of pitch
and the paired crotchets which recur constantly between
quicker rhythmic patterns. Similar characteristics may be
observed in the Finale of Telemann's B minor violin
concerto[52] whose opening theme is also saturated with folk
elements.

Telemann's enthusiasm for French music developed early
in his career. While still a schoolboy at the Hildesheim
Academy he had travelled to Hanover and Brunswick to
hear orchestral performances in the French manner. A few
years later, at Sorau, we find him studying the works of
'Lully, Campra and other leading masters'. It was here, too,
that he wrote over two hundred 'Ouvertures' in the space of
two years.[53] We learn from the autobiographies that Telemann had a long-standing desire to visit France. By the time
this ambition was eventually realized (in 1737) some of his
works had already been published in the French capital[54] and
the Parisians were eager to meet him in person. That
Telemann was well acquainted with the subtler aspects of
French music is evident from his correspondence with C. H.
Graun over Rameau's declamation.[55] In these exchanges it is
significant that he supported the French method of declamation while Graun defended the Italian.

[52] Ed. S. Kross in *Georg Philipp Telemann Musikalische Werke*, vol. xxiii, (Kassel,
1973), pp. 198ff.

[53] *Denkmäler deutscher Tonkunst*, xxviii, p. x.

[54] On 6 April 1736 Le Clerc obtained a privilege for publishing some of
Telemann's works; the *Six Quatuors* were engraved later that year.

[55] This correspondence has been printed in *Denkmäler deutscher Tonkunst*, xxviii,
pp. lxv-lxxii. For an illuminating commentary, see R. Rolland, *A Musical Tour
through the Land of the Past*, pp. 124–9.

Much has been made of the influence of French music on Telemann and it is certainly true that his orchestral suites contain numerous dance movements of French origin. But the concertos are of a different order; on the whole they show few signs of French influence, examples being confined to the occasional use of terms such as *vivement, avec douceur*, etc. and the deliberate local colour of the C major *Concerto alla francese* (C. gr. C).

Unfortunately, Telemann is less informative on the question of Italian influence. We learn from the autobiographical sketches that he admired Corelli's work (along with that of Steffani and Caldara) but there is no specific reference to the Italian concerto style and the names of leading composers such as Albinoni and Vivaldi are not recorded at all. This is surprising given the impact of the Italian concerto in Germany. Yet one must not deduce too much from these omissions for the fact remains that Telemann's concertos are strongly Italianate in style. As one would expect, it is the violin concertos which reveal the full extent of his Italian debt. Several of the works published in volume xxiii of the *Telemann-Ausgabe* are built on the type of square-cut theme favoured by Albinoni (see Ex. 2), and the solo writing with its idiomatic crossing of strings and occasional double stopping has all the fire and brilliance of Vivaldi:

EXAMPLE 20
Telemann, concerto in F major for violin and strings, 1st movement,
bars 16–20

One might wonder why Telemann omitted Germany from his list, but there are reasons for this. In the first place

Germany was not a political or cultural entity in the
eighteenth century. In the second place the princes, electors,
and margraves who ruled the various states tended to
import their culture from Italy or France and this did little to
foster the development of an indigenous musical style.
Telemann himself never speaks of a German style in the
collective sense. Instead he refers to individual composers
whose music impressed him. We know, for example, that
during his Leipzig period he made a study of Kuhnau's
contrapuntal technique;[56] at the same time, he was studying
the art of melodic writing in collaboration with Handel.[57]
How much Telemann profited by the first exercise is
uncertain, for, although he had a great facility in counterpoint and fugue, one doubts whether this was acquired
through a study of Kuhnau's work alone. Nor may the
effect of his collaboration with Handel be assessed with any
great precision. Although he appears to emulate the Handelian manner in one or two places (see Ex. 21), there is not
enough evidence to suggest direct imitation:

EXAMPLE 21
Telemann, concerto in G major for violin and strings (V.G(1)), 2nd
movement, bars 1–5 (outer parts only)

---

[56] Johann Kuhnau (1660–1722) was organist at the city's two principal churches
while Telemann was in Leipzig. In 1701 he was appointed Cantor of St. Thomas's.

[57] '. . . in melodic movements, however, and their analysis, *Händel* and I were

Contrapuntal and Melodic Technique

That Telemann elected to study both the old contrapuntal technique (as represented by the works of Kuhnau) and the cantabile melodic style is significant because these two, seemingly contradictory, elements are of fundamental importance to his music. His fluent command of counterpoint is evident in a wide range of vocal and instrumental works. The six flute duos (op. 5), for example, contain whole movements in canonic form, and, although strict canon is not maintained for any length of time in the concertos, passages in a freer contrapuntal discipline are of frequent occurrence. In fact the type of counterpoint found in the concertos is often extremely simple. In the following example, for instance, each violin has the same passage in the manner of a round while the harmony remains static:

EXAMPLE 22

Telemann, violin concerto in D major (V.D(2)), 1st movement, bars 4–5 (the lower strings rest for two bars)

The same principle is used extensively elsewhere. Imitation is almost always at the octave or unison (except in a fugal context) and this in turn tends to cause harmonic tautology. Exact imitation is never forced. If a pattern will not fit, Telemann shows no hesitation about adapting the intervals of the original. Often, in such cases only the general melodic shape and basic rhythmic structure of a motif is retained:

constantly occupied, with frequent visits on both sides, and also with correspondence', *Denkmäler deutscher Tonkunst*, xxviii, pp. ix–x (trans. in O. E. Deutsch, ed., *Handel: a Documentary Biography*, p. 492).

EXAMPLE 23
Telemann, concerto in A major for flute, violin, cello, and strings
(*Musique de Table*, Book 1) 4th movement, bars 41–5 (solo flute and
violin part only)

Voice exchange and invertible counterpoint are two other devices which Telemann uses frequently in his concertos. As might be expected, these occur most often in solo episodes where two melody instruments of similar range are consorting. Specific examples may be found in the 2nd movement of the E minor concerto grosso for two flutes, violin, and strings[58] (bars 17–18) and in the Allegro of the third *Musique de Table* concerto for two *tromba selvatica*, two violins, and strings (compare bars 46–9 with 112–15).[59]

Telemann did not have an intuitive approach to melodic writing. His melodies always sound polished rather than spontaneous, except in movements of a folk nature where the melodic flow is unusually free. This sophistication reveals itself in a number of ways, but principally through the manipulation of phrase lengths and the subtle arrangement of melodic motifs within the phrase. Occasionally, for example, Telemann will create an asymmetrical phrase structure by overlapping his cadence bars with the begin-

[58] Ed. F. Schroeder (London, 1959).
[59] Ed. J. P. Hinnenthal, *Georg Philipp Telemann Musikalische Werke*, vol. xiv (Kassel, 1963), pp. 63 ff.

ning of a new phrase. This happens in the opening Allegro
of the G minor violin concerto.[60] As will be seen from the
following passage the eighth bar forms an integral part of
both the first and second phrases:[61]

EXAMPLE 24
Telemann, violin concerto in G minor, 1st movement, bars 1–19

Even the ingenuous Siciliana movements contain some
subtlety of phrasing and the internal construction of their
regular eight-bar periods may be extremely complex. The
melody given as Example 25 can be analysed in various
ways. Broken down into the smallest units we get the

---

[60] Ed. S. Kross, ibid., vol. xxiii, *Zwölfe Violinkonzerte* (Kassel, 1973), pp. 137ff.
[61] A similar technique of eliding phrases was developed by Mozart during the
later years of his life and proved a valuable foil to that regularity of phrasing which
had dominated the earlier part of the classical period, see C. Rosen, *The Classical
Style: Haydn, Mozart, Beethoven* (London, 1971), pp. 260ff.

arrangement 1,1,3,1,2; alternatively, one could see a two-bar, six-bar pattern. Either way, there is little hint of the 4,4 or 2,2,4 bar structure normally associated with the Siciliana:

EXAMPLE 25

Telemann, concerto in A major for oboe d'amore and strings, 2nd movement, bars 6–13

On close acquaintance it is possible to identify certain hallmarks in Telemann's melodic style. One of these, as Kross points out in his monograph,[62] is the frequent use of fourths. This interval is prominent in a number of concerto movements, including the 'allegro assai' from the E major violin concerto (see Ex. 2). Telemann also had a liking for 'horn' themes—two-part passages based mainly on the notes of the harmonic series (Ex. 26a). Moreover, he employed a characteristic decorative pattern in which the embellishment centred constantly on a single note (Ed. 26b):

EXAMPLE 26

Telemann, (a) concerto in A major for oboe d'amore and strings, 4th movement, bars 1–5, (b) concerto in E minor for flute, voilin, and strings, 2nd movement, bars 24–6 (outer parts only)

[62] S. Kross, *Das Instrumentalkonzert bei Georg Philipp Telemann*, p. 99.

Harmonic Practice

The significance of Telemann's statement, 'if nothing new is to be found in melody one must look for it in harmony',[63] must not be overrated. This remark was originally made during the course of a letter to C. H. Graun (dated 15 December 1751) in which Telemann was defending the French style of declamation. In context, the statement is reasonable enough. Out of context (and it has been bandied about by several writers) it can only mislead, for Telemann's instrumental style is not normally spiced with dissonant or unusual harmonic progressions. Indeed, most of his concertos are written in a rather bland harmonic idiom and such 'rich' passages as occur are concentrated in a small number of movements. These passages are, naturally, the most interesting yet it must be emphasized that in discussing them one is considering the exceptions rather than the norm.

Reference has already been made to the colourful 'largo e piano' from Telemann's F minor oboe concerto (Ob. f(1)) but it is worth describing the harmonic structure of the movement in greater detail here. After a fairly conventional opening, tension is built up in the baroque manner, with a rising chromatic bass (see Ex. 27, bars 13–16). Yet Tele-

---

[63] 'Ist in der Melodie nichts Neues mehr zu finden, so müsse man es in der Harmonie suchen', *Georg Philipp Telemann: Briefwechsel*, p. 285.

mann gives this traditional progression a new and unexpected twist. The bass line does not proceed smoothly from Ab to C; its general upward movement is counterbalanced by a series of descending scales. The climax of this section comes at bar 20 where, in order to delay the expected cadence, Telemann suddenly introduces a chromatic supertonic seventh chord on D:

EXAMPLE 27

Telemann, concerto in F minor for oboe and strings (Ob. f(1)), 2nd movement, bars 11–22 (ripieno parts are in short score)

Even more radical are his experiments with enharmonic change. A well-known example occurs in the Andante of the G major viola concerto.[64] This movement opens in E minor (as one would expect) but when the solo viola enters (bar 4) the music moves rapidly through the major keys of A, G, and D until, at bar 9, a B♭ is introduced which leads to a cadence in G minor (bar 10). Telemann then has to move out of this remote key into the dominant (B minor) and he does so by very simple means: the note B♭ becomes A♯ by enharmonic change and at bar 11 he is ready to present the second ritornello in the key of B minor.

EXAMPLE 28

Telemann, concerto in G major for viola and strings, 3rd movement, bars 8–11

Although these rich splashes of harmonic colour are more prevalent in slow movements than elsewhere, some chromatic touches may also be found in the Allegro movements. One of the most interesting passages occurs in the 2nd movement of the F major recorder concerto.[65] This binary-form Allegro opens with figurative material for the soloist in the home key. Then, at bar 18, comes a dramatic piano section in the minor mode (Ex. 29). During the course of this passage the steady descent of the bass line is twice interrupted (bars 19–20 and 21–2) by semitonal movement in the opposite direction:

[64] Ed. H. C. Wolff (Kassel, 1968).
[65] Ed. M. Ruëtz (Kassel, 1969).

EXAMPLE 29

Telemann, concerto in F major for recorder and strings, 2nd
movement, bars 18–22

This rather eccentric approach is characteristic of Telemann;
moreover, it sets him apart from J. S. Bach, who, though he
made frequent use of chromaticism, seldom disrupted the
logical movement of parts in quite this manner.

One further point must be mentioned before leaving the
subject of Telemann's harmonic practice and this concerns
the rate of chord change per bar. Baroque composers, for
the most part, favoured a quick harmonic pulse, this being
especially noticeable in the tutti sections of their concertos.
But with the style changes of the mid-eighteenth century
came a new and more relaxed approach: the time-scale of
progressions was expanded and harmonic rhythm slowed
down accordingly. Although the initial impact of this was
felt in the symphony, repercussions were soon apparent in
other fields. Telemann himself was one of the first concertists to experiment with the new manner. Normally, it is
true, he kept the styles of symphony and concerto quite
separate, but in one or two movements we see him transferring the broad, symphonic style[66] to the concerto.

[66] Slow harmonic rhythm became something of a cult in symphonies of the
mid-eighteenth century. An extreme example occurs in a work by the Mannheim

EXAMPLE 30

Telemann, concerto in E♭ major for two *tromba selvatica*, two violins, and strings (*Musique de Table*, Book 3), 1st movement, bars 1–6 (string parts in short score)

Not only is the harmonic pulse very slow (the tonic chord lasts for five bars), but the musical interest lies to a great extent in the texture rather than the melodic content. The *trombe* could obviously have doubled the violin part in places, given the triadic nature of the material, yet they are given their own line which cuts through the texture, counterbalancing the descending arpeggios of the string instruments at bars 2 and 4.

Orchestration and Texture

This leads us to consider the related questions of orchestration and texture, in which area Telemann was something of an innovator. His keen awareness of tone colour informed both his selection of instrumental forces and the way in which they were employed. The variegated composition of his concertino groups has already been mentioned; equally imaginative, however, was his decision to use the viola in a solo capacity for, although some comparable works were being written at that time, the idea of using the viola as a soloist in orchestral music was still in its infancy.

The use Telemann made of his resources again shows his

composer Anton Filtz; the Finale of his D major symphony (op. 2, no. 5) opens with no fewer than twenty-six bars over a pedal (see *Denkmäler der Tonkunst in Bayern*, iii¹, ed. A. Sandberger (Leipzig, 1902), pp. 168ff.).

fine sense of colour and his readiness to experiment with
unorthodox methods of scoring. Sometimes he gave independence to the most unlikely instruments, as in the following passage where the timpani are unusually prominent:

EXAMPLE 31
Telemann, concerto in D major for three trumpets, drums, and strings
(3 Trp. D(2)), 2nd movement, bars 14–17

In this extraordinary solo episode the drums, although still
linked with their traditional field-partners the trumpets, are
not regarded as mere ballast. It is they who provide the
effective bass line, for the basso continuo gives but minimal
support.

Even the more traditionally-scored concertos provide
some examples of Telemann's imaginative orchestration.

The delicate Andante from the A minor violin concerto (V. a(1))[67] has a filigree texture in which a short motif is passed down through the accompanying string instruments. Equally effective in this respect is the Siciliana from the triple concerto in E major which is shown below:

EXAMPLE 32

Telemann, concerto in E major for flute, oboe d'amore, viola d'amore, and strings, 3rd movement, bars 1–4 (short score)

[67] Ed. H. C. Wolff (Kassel, 1950).

Here the melody is given to the viola d'amore while the upper strings provide a harmonic accompaniment. The inspired touch comes at bar 2 when Telemann introduces a semiquaver triplet figure on the flute and oboe (in canon). The rests which separate each appearance of this figure give the movement a delightful open texture, more in keeping with classical than baroque style.

7. Telemann's Influence on Contemporary Composers; His Historical Importance Assessed

It remains now to discuss Telemann's position *vis-à-vis* his contemporaries and to assess his importance in the history of the concerto. Some aspects of the interrelationships between the three leading composers of the German high baroque—Bach, Handel, and Telemann—have already been investigated by Serauky.[68] The whole subject is fascinating, but not without its frustrations. For in a sense we have more information about their temporal, than their artistic, connections. We know, for instance, that during his Eisenach period (*c.* 1706–12) Telemann was in close touch with J. S. Bach and that he stood as godfather to Bach's son Carl Philipp Emanuel in 1714. Moreover, Bach's clavier arrangement of the G minor violin concerto (BWV 985) provides firm evidence that he was intimately acquainted with at least one of Telemann's concertos. When we turn to the music, however, we find surprisingly few connections. The two composers used the same modes of construction, it is true, but this in itself is insignificant; from the stylistic point of view their concertos have little in common. With Handel, on the other hand, the situation is slightly different: although we cannot judge the precise extent to which Telemann was influenced by the Handelian style,[69] there is considerable evidence on the other side. It can be inferred from Handel's activities as a plagiarist and his plundering of

---

[68] W. Serauky, 'Bach-Händel-Telemann in ihrem musikalischen Verhältnis', *Händel-Jahrbuch* [new series] i (1955), 72–101.

[69] See p. 220.

the *Musique de Table* set in particular that he was the main beneficiary of the friendship.[70]

Apart from his connections with Bach and Handel, Telemann was acquainted with many leading musicians in other German cities. He had links with the court of Dresden (through Pisendel), with Berlin (through Emanuel Bach and others), and with Darmstadt where a number of his Leipzig friends had found employment. As far as is known, Telemann's concertos made little impact at the first two centres; yet at Darmstadt they provoked an immediate response. Perhaps this was due to the close ties which existed between him and various members of the kapelle. The composers Christoph Graupner and Gottfried Grünewald and the wind-player Michael Böhm had all been active in Leipzig musical circles at the same time as Telemann; later, these three assisted him with performances of large-scale works at Frankfurt.[71] Moreover, these connections operated in both directions. Telemann's works were frequently performed at Darmstadt and the musicians there had access, so it appears, to several of his concertos. As we have seen, Graupner and Grünewald put a number of these works into score—possibly for study purposes; it comes as no surprise, therefore, to learn that the concertos inspired both respect and imitation at Darmstadt.

Telemann's influence is seen to best advantage in the concertos of Christoph Graupner (1683–1760).[72] Of Graupner's fifty surviving concertos, twenty-two are solo concertos and twenty-eight are for two or more solo

[70] Despite Handel's activities in this field the friendship between the two men remained unimpaired; they were still corresponding in December 1750 when Handel sent Telemann a crate of rare plants to augment his collection, see O. E. Deutsch, ed., op. cit., pp. 696–7.

[71] Musicians from Darmstadt participated in the performance of Telemann's 'Brockes' passion (first performed 1716) and of his festival cantata for the birth of Emperor Leopold's son. See E. Noack, 'G.Ph.Telemanns Beziehungen zu Darmstädter Musikern', *Konferenzbericht der 3. Magdeburger Telemann-Festtage 1967*, ii. 13–17.

[72] Although it is seldom possible to establish chronological priority, when all the circumstances are reviewed it seems likely that Telemann's concertos provided the model for Graupner and not vice versa.

instruments.[73] It is clear from these figures that he shared Telemann's liking for multiple soloists. Along with this went a preference for the older, four-movement concerto and an inclination to employ a colourful assortment of solo instruments. Frequently, too, one finds that pairing of similar instruments within the concertino group which is so characteristic of Telemann. The two passages shown below (Ex. 33) betray a remarkably similar approach. In both cases the solo instruments are paired according to type; the two flutes (or two oboes) move constantly in parallel thirds and each group answers the other antiphonally:

EXAMPLE 33

(a) Telemann, concerto in B♭ major for two flutes, two oboes, and strings, 2nd movement, bars 24–8; (b) Graupner, concerto in B♭ major for two flutes, two oboes, and strings, 1st movement, bars 40–4

[73] The autograph manuscripts of these concertos are preserved in the Hessiche Landes-und Hochschulbibliothek, Darmstadt. For a full discussion of Graupner's concertos see Martin Witte's unpublished dissertation, *Die Instrumentalkonzerte von Johann Christoph Graupner (1683–1760)* (Göttingen, 1963).

Perhaps it is no coincidence that these works are written in the same key and for the same orchestral forces. Hints of Telemann's style are also found in Graupner's C major concerto for two chalumeaux and strings,[74] and here again there is a concerto by Telemann in the same key and with identical instrumentation.[75]

Outside Germany Telemann's music naturally exerted less influence. The concertos in particular were not widely disseminated since so few had appeared in print. To be sure, the *Musique de Table* concertos must have been known in France, judging by the number of French subscribers to the set,[76] but three isolated works of this nature would hardly have had a profound effect on indigenous composers. Besides, the concerto as an art-form did not attract so many devotees in France as in Germany. Few composers cultivated it with any enthusiasm and of these only Michel Blavet[77] wrote works that are at all comparable with those of Telemann; the other leading instrumental composer of the time, Jean Marie Leclair (1697–1764), adopted a more Vivaldian approach.

The artistic merit of Telemann's work has long been a matter for debate. Some regard him as a composer whose work was marred by a 'fatal facility'[78] and who had an unfortunate propensity for writing music of a superficial and popular cast. This view is not a modern phenomenon; it can be traced right back to the eighteenth century. In 1774, for example, we find the German writer J. F. Reichardt remarking sourly that Telemann's 'first works are certainly different from his last, in which he is pleasing enough, and

---

[74] Graupner evidently shared Telemann's liking for 'horn' themes, cf. his C major concerto for two chalumeaux and strings (D-brd-DS, Mus. Ms. 411/41), 1st movement, bars 13–14.

[75] MS. copy at D-brd-DS, Mus. Ms. 1033/38; the score and parts of this Telemann concerto are in Graupner's hand.

[76] A facsimile of the original subscription list is reproduced in *Georg Philipp Telemann Musikalische Werke*, vol xiv, ed. J. P. Hinnenthal (Kassel, 1963).

[77] Blavet (1700–68), who was also a flautist, participated in the first public performance of Telemann's *Quatuors*.

[78] *Grove's Dictionary*, 5th edn., ed. E. Blom (London, 1954), viii. 370.

unfortunately pleasing to everybody'.[79] Hostile assessments
of this type probably sprang from Telemann's use of 'light'
themes and the way in which he combined these with the
'learned style'. If we look at the fugal movements of the
concertos, we find that, although some are based on austere,
scholastic themes,[80] others have fugue subjects of a dance-
like character. Typical in this last respect is the theme shown
at Example 34 which is given a full-scale exposition in the
traditional fugal manner:

EXAMPLE 34
Telemann, violin concerto in D major (V.D(1)), 2nd movement, bars
1–8 (solo violin part only)

It is certainly conceivable that such a curious fusion of
learned and popular elements might prove unacceptable to
some eighteenth-century critics. Moreover, Telemann's use
of folk music could also be construed as 'popularization',
for, although there was widespread interest in folk culture at
that time (an interest which manifested itself in numerous
publications of traditional songs and dances), composers
were, for the most part, reluctant to incorporate such
elements into art-music.[81]

Our present picture of Telemann is in a state of flux; as
research progresses, however, one point becomes clear:

---

[79] J. F. Reichardt, *Vertraute Briefe eines aufmerksamen Reisenden* (Berlin, 1774); cited
by A. Hutchings, op. cit., p. 249.

[80] See the 1st movement of the F minor oboe concerto (Ob. f(1)), modern edition
by F. Schroeder (London, 1958).

[81] After Telemann's death the incorporation of folk themes into the concerto
became increasingly common. J. C. Bach based the Finales of several of his keyboard
concertos on popular tunes and advertised the fact by retaining the original
song-titles. The 3rd movement of his op. 13, no. 4 (published 1777), for example, is
based on the Scottish air, 'The yellow haired laddie'. C. S. Terry, *John Christian Bach*,
2nd rev. edn. (London, 1967), p. 183.

given the remarkable stylistic range of his music, Telemann can no longer be classed as a baroque composer. In many ways his work forms a link between the baroque and classical periods. The break with tradition is not complete in that he still relies extensively on the figurative patterns and contrapuntal devices of the old manner. Yet his belief that melody was of supreme importance, his experiments with orchestration and texture, his synthesis of popular and learned styles, are all progressive traits. The tension between old and new which is so characteristic of Telemann is representative of the whole transitional era. In this respect he is one of the most typical composers of his age.

IV

Johann Adolf Hasse[1]

1. Introduction; Career

J. A. Hasse was one of the most successful and highly respected composers of the eighteenth century. A German by birth,[2] his early training inclined him towards the Italian operatic style. So successful was he in this idiom that he became the leading operatic writer of his age. His dramatic works, many of which were based on the libretti of the famous Italian poet Metastasio, were produced in all the operatic centres of Europe—from Naples and Venice to London, Paris, Dresden, and Berlin. In short, wherever there was a market for *opera seria* and facilities for its production, Hasse's operas held the stage, delighting audiences with their lyrical melodies and lucid textures. The dominant position occupied by Hasse's operas during the mid-eighteenth century emerges clearly both from lists of operatic productions (in which his name appears frequently) and from contemporary literature. No music historian, critic, or lexicographer writing between the years 1750 and 1780 could afford to ignore Hasse; indeed, most of these writers saw him as a figure of European stature whose works demanded extensive discussion. And since Hasse's laurels had been won in the theatre, it was only natural that contemporary assessments of his music should concentrate on the vocal works. In this climate, his instrumental productions were either disregarded completely or shrugged off as inconsequential.

Exactly the same emphasis is apparent in recent times.

---

[1] A paper on this subject was read to the Royal Musical Association in 1973, see 'The Concertos of Johann Adolf Hasse', *Proceedings of the Royal Musical Association*, xcix (1972–3), 91–103.

[2] Born Bergedorf near Hamburg in 1699.

Whereas Hasse's vocal music has been the subject of pain-staking research,[3] his instrumental works remain largely unexplored.[4] Furthermore, the extent of Hasse's involve-ment in this area has been consistently underestimated. Few of our standard reference manuals, for example, mention the fact that he wrote over sixty concertos—a fair number even by the gargantuan standards of the eighteenth century. It would appear, therefore, that instrumental music, and the concerto in particular, occupied a more important place in Hasse's creative output than has previously been acknow-ledged.

Since Hasse is the least-known figure of our five compos-ers, his career will be traced in some detail here.[5] Hasse's first appointment was that of tenor singer at the Hamburg opera in 1717. Four years later he made his debut as an operatic composer with *Antioco* at Brunswick. Following this he decided that an Italian visit was imperative. Unfor-tunately, biographical details concerning this period of Hasse's career are sparse, but it is known that he spent several years in Naples,[6] and that he studied composition first with the talented young composer Nicola Porpora (1686–1768), and subsequently with the doyen of Neapoli-tan opera, Alessandro Scarlatti (1660–1725). This second arrangement proved the more satisfactory. Under Scarlatti's

[3] See Gerber's authoritative study of the operas (R. Gerber, *Der Operntypus Johann Adolf Hasses und seine textlichen Grundlagen* (Leipzig, 1925)) and, more recently, Hansell's pioneer work on Hasse's non-operatic vocal music (S. H. Hansell, 'Sacred Music at the *Incurabili* in Venice at the Time of J. A. Hasse', *Journal of the American Musicological Society*, xxiii (1970), 282–301, 505–21); also, id., *Works for Solo Voice of Johann Adolph Hasse* (1699–1783), Detroit Studies in Music Bibliography no. xii (Detroit, 1968).

[4] The only major work published after 1900 to deal with Hasse's instrumental music is K. H. Mennicke's *Hasse und die Brüder Graun als Symphoniker* (Leipzig, 1906), and significantly this book discusses the overtures to dramatic works.

[5] Biographical details are available in the following publications: ibid., pp. 352–446; also, id., 'Johann Adolph Hasse: eine biographische Skizze', *Sammelbände der Internationalen Musik-Gesellschaft*, v (1903–4), 230–44, and 'Zur Biographie Joh. Adolph Hasse's', *SIMG*, v (1903–4), 469–75; M. Seiffert, 'Zur Biographie Johann Adolph Hasse's', *SIMG*, vii (1905–6), 129–31. See also S. H. Hansell, 'Sacred Music at the *Incurabili* in Venice at the Time of J. A. Hasse', 282–301, 505–21.

[6] Hasse was in Naples from *c.* 1724–30, S. H. Hansell 'Sacred Music at the *Incurabili* in Venice at the Time of J. A. Hasse', 284.

guidance Hasse became thoroughly versed in the Italian operatic style. Several of his works were staged successfully in Naples and Venice and he was given what appears to have been a titular appointment at the Royal Court of Naples.[7] Hasse acclimatized easily to the Mediterranean way of life. His total identification with the people and culture of the country was symbolized by his new style of signature: 'Giovanni Adolfo Hasse', and by his conversion to Catholicism. In 1730 the process of Italianization was carried one stage further by his marriage to Faustina Bordoni, the noted soprano.

But Germany still exercised some claims upon him. Already, in 1730 Hasse was designated in various opera libretti[8] as 'maestro di cappella' to the King of Poland and Elector of Saxony. Yet he and his wife did not move to Dresden immediately. They remained in Italy for much of 1730 and it is only in the summer of 1731 that we find them installed at the Saxon court. Although Hasse's official term of office at Dresden lasted from around 1730 to 1763, he was not resident in that city throughout the entire period. His operatic activities made travel desirable, if not absolutely essential, and he revisited Italy on several occasions, organizing concerts and directing performances of his operas. Fortunately, leave of absence was granted more readily in Dresden than at many other German courts. Furthermore, it seems that whenever Frederick Augustus II held court at Warsaw (in his capacity as King of Poland), Hasse was excused from attending. He was also free to accept additional appointments. So we find him in Venice during the year 1735–6 directing activities at the famous Conservatorio dell' Incurabili.[9] Other visits to Italy followed: in 1738–9

---

[7] In the libretto to Hasse's opera *Il Tigrane* (first performed 4 November 1729) Hasse is referred to as a supernumerary maestro of the Royal Court of Naples.

[8] S. H. Hansell, 'Sacred Music at the *Incurabili* in Venice at the Time of J. A. Hasse', 286.

[9] The first *documentary* evidence for his connection with the Venetian Conservatorio dell' Incurabili dates from 1736: in both the libretto and score of Hasse's opera *Alessandro nell'Indie* (produced in 1736), Hasse is entitled 'Maestro del Pio Ospital dell' Incurabili', see ibid. 287.

(when Hasse again rented a house at Venice), in the spring and summer of 1757, and in the summer of 1758.[10]

In 1763 Hasse's connections with Dresden terminated abruptly with the accession of a new Elector, Frederick Christian. Although allowed to retain the honorary title of Oberkapellmeister, he was effectively dismissed from Dresden[11] and moved to Vienna where he and his wife spent the next ten years. During this period Hasse threw himself with renewed vigour into operatic activities. Charles Burney, visiting the Austrian capital in 1772, declared that Hasse and Metastasio were in direct competition with Gluck and Calzabigi at that time.[12] It is clear also, from Burney's account, that Hasse was physically weak, suffering frequent bouts of gout and conscious of his diminished powers. The year after Burney's visit Hasse and Faustina retired to Venice where they passed the remaining years of their life.

2. The Concertos: Sources

Seventy separate concertos bearing Hasse's name[13] have survived to the present day in printed and/or manuscript form.[14] Unfortunately autograph manuscripts are exceedingly rare, the only known example being an unsigned flute

[10] Hasse may also have been in Venice from May 1748 to February 1749 when the Saxon court was again held at Warsaw. Furthermore, it is possible that he was in Italy during the years 1758–60 as several of his operas were produced in Naples at that time.

[11] The curious circumstances surrounding Hasse's abrupt departure from Dresden—he was discharged without the customary pension—have provoked much speculation. But it seems that the new Elector was simply motivated by economic expediency. Frederick Christian was in no position to maintain the splendid establishment of his predecessor, since the exchequer was greatly improverished following Frederick the Great's siege of Dresden.

[12] C. Burney, *The Present State of Music in Germany, the Netherlands, and United Provinces*, i. 237.

[13] This figure encompasses all those works which are entitled 'concerto' and which bear Hasse's name. It therefore includes those concertos where Hasse's authorship is open to dispute (see p. 248) and the sinfonias of op. 4 which Walsh published under the title of concertos (see p. 245).

[14] A further two works—the flute concertos in E minor and G major (Racc. I no. 2 and Racc. II no. 3) advertised by Breitkopf in 1763—are known from their thematic incipits only, *The Breitkopf Thematic Catalogue: the Six Parts and Sixteen Supplements 1762–1787*, p. 97.

concerto in G major, now housed in the Bodleian Library, Oxford.[15] The extreme scarcity of autograph concertos by Hasse is curious. However, it is known that he sustained great personal losses during Frederick the Great's bombardment of Dresden in 1760 and some of the concerto manuscripts may well have been destroyed at that time.[16] But if autograph manuscripts of the concertos are rare, contemporary copies are plentiful. Many of the works exist in two or more copies, and one concerto (op. 3, no. 10) has survived in no fewer than thirteen different sources. A detailed description of Hasse's concerto manuscripts cannot be given here: we must await the comprehensive thematic catalogue of Hasse's work which is being prepared in the United States. But some general guide to the location of sources may prove helpful. Contemporary copies of the concertos are to be found in many European centres including Berlin, Brussels, Darmstadt, Dresden, Karlsruhe, London, Paris, Rostock, Schwerin, and Wolfenbüttel.[17] The most important collections, however, are at Stockholm, Uppsala, and Lund. These Swedish libraries[18] possess between them over eighty handwritten copies of Hasse's concertos, all dating from the eighteenth century. Duplications are numerous, but the very proliferation of copies gives an indication of Hasse's popularity as a concertist.

In addition to these manuscript sources, there are several printed collections of Hasse's concertos which stem from the mid-eighteenth century. The first set was issued around 1740 by Gerhardo Friderico Witvogel of Amsterdam under

[15] MS. Mus. c. 108. Even here there is some doubt concerning the authenticity of the autograph. Although the calligraphy is indeed similar to Hasse's own, the manuscript is not signed by him. However, there are two notes added in a different hand which state that the work is in Hasse's handwriting (see fo. 56ᵛ and fo. 59). Since these additions date from the eighteenth century they must carry some weight.

[16] It is, of course, possible that the autograph manuscripts of some concertos may reappear. The original scores of several of Hasse's operas were presumed lost for many years but have recently been rediscovered at the Giuseppe Verdi Library, Milan.

[17] Manuscripts are preserved at the following libraries: D-ddr-Bds; B-Bc; D-brd-DS; D-ddr-Dlb; D-brd-KA; GB-Lbm; F-Pc; D-ddr-ROu; D-ddr-Sws; D-brd-W.

[18] S-Skma; S-Uu; S-L.

the title: 'Sei Concerti/Tre a Due Flauti Traversieri/e Tre a Flauto Solo/Violino Primo, Violino Secondo/Alto Viola/Violoncello e Cimbalo,/Del Signor/GIOVANNI ADOLFFO HASSE,/Opera Prima.'[19] As the title makes clear, this set consisted of six concertos, three for two flutes (nos. 1, 3, and 5), and the remainder for solo flute and string accompaniment. Curiously, the first work in the set was subtitled 'Oratorio' in the individual parts. This may explain its strange construction, for the work is cast in a two-movement form ('allegro moderato' and 'andante vivace') with a shortened restatement of the allegro material tacked on to the Andante. Presumably it was designed as an overture to one of Hasse's oratorios although the original has not been traced. Apart from this, the other concertos of op. 1 look genuine enough. Indeed, two of them (nos. 2 and 4) reappear in another collection of Hasse's concertos: Walsh's op. 3.[20]

John Walsh was Hasse's main publisher in England. By 1740 he had already issued a number of Hasse's works and in the spring of 1741 he brought out a collection of twelve concertos for solo flute and string orchestra entitled: 'TWELVE/CONCERTOS/IN SIX PARTS,/For a GERMAN FLUTE, Two VIOLINS,/a TENOR, with a THOROUGH BASS for/the HARPSICHORD or VIOLONCELLO./Compos'd by Signor/GIOVANNI ADOLFFO HASSE./Opera Terza./London.'[21]

We do not know how Walsh acquired these concertos in the first instance. He may well have obtained them direct from Hasse who is said to have visited London briefly in 1734. One thing seems clear, however: it is unlikely that the composer had much to do with the preparation of this

---

[19] This publication is completely different from the op. 1 which Walsh had published in 1739 and which consisted of six sonatas or trios for two German flutes, or two violins, and bass.

[20] Op. 1, no. 2 = op. 3, no. 1; op. 1, no. 4 = op. 3, no. 10.

[21] The set was advertised on 19 February 1741 (see W. C. Smith and C. Humphries, A Bibliography of the Musical Works published by the firm of John Walsh during the years 1721–1766, p. 180). Despite the title, one concerto, op. 3, no. 4, contained parts for two flutes.

edition. The set contains numerous signs of haste and carelessness, ranging from discrepancies of dynamic and tempo indications, to the omission of a few bars' rest for certain instruments. Moreover, there are some odd editorial alterations. Arnold Schering suggested that the viola part of the op. 3 set was, in all probability, an editorial addition,[22] and his theory is substantiated by an examination of the relevant manuscript sources. Ten of the twelve concertos which make up Walsh's op. 3 set have survived in manuscript form, and of these, nine are scored for flute and three-part string ensemble—that is, they dispense with the viola part.[23] The one exception (op. 3, no. 8) is not of crucial importance to the argument: although it is scored for a four-part string ensemble, the additional string part is entitled 'violetta in violino'[24] and no definite conclusions may be drawn from so enigmatic a heading. The other remarkable feature of Walsh's edition, and, indeed, of all his subsequent editions of Hasse's concertos, is the designation on the title page of a thorough bass for the harpsichord *or* violoncello. The normal late baroque procedure was, of course, to employ at least two instruments on the bass line: a string bass (usually the cello) and a keyboard instrument for realizing the figures. This was almost certainly what Hasse envisaged, for the phrase 'cembalo e violcello' (harpsichord *and* cello) occurs frequently in his concerto manuscripts. Significantly, this same phrase appears on the bass part of Walsh's op. 3 set. Why, then, does the title page call for harpsichord *or* cello? There are two possible explanations: either Walsh and his colleagues mistranslated the Italian, or else they deliberately altered the designation to aid sales.

The next set of Hasse's 'concertos' to be issued by Walsh was advertised later that same year—on 24 October 1741.

---

[22] A. Schering in the Foreword to *Denkmäler deutscher Tonkunst*, vol. xxix-xxx, pp. xxiii-xxiv.

[23] The fact that op. 3, nos. 1 and 2, are listed in the Breitkopf catalogues (for 1763 and 1766 respectively) as having a viola part is not necessarily significant since these incipits may well have derived from the Walsh publication (see *The Breitkopf Thematic Catalogue: The Six Parts and Sixteen Supplements 1762–1787*, pp. 97, 244).

[24] MS. in S-Skma, Fb0-R.

The full title of this publication (op. 4) was 'Six/CON-CERTOS/For VIOLINS, FRENCH HORNS or HOBOYS etc./with a Thorough Bass for ỹ HARP-SICHORD/or VIOLONCELLO/in Eight Parts/Compos'd by Sig^r:/GIOVANNI ADOLFFO HASSE./Opera Quarta./London.' In fact, Walsh's description is inaccurate, for the set contains no concertos as such. It is simply a collection of sinfonias from various operatic works which Hasse had composed during the 1730s. Although Schering made this point at the turn of the century,[25] he did not identify the overtures in question. It has, however, proved possible to trace the operatic connections of all but one of these concertos, as the following list reveals:

Op. 4 Opera	Librettist	Date of first known performance[26]
No. 1 *Asteria*	Pallavicini	Dresden, 3 August 1737[27]
No. 2 *Senocrita*	Pallavicini	Dresden, 27 February 1737
No. 3 *Cleofide*	Metastasio and Boccardi	Dresden, 13 September 1731
No. 4 *Artaserse*	Metastasio	Venice, Carnival 1730
No. 5 *Cajo Fabricio*	Zeno	Rome, end of year 1731
No. 6 Unidentified[28]		

The fact that these sinfonias were issued under a misleading title is less important than might be imagined since terminology was, at that stage, notoriously imprecise. We learn from Rousseau's dictionary, for instance, that the word 'concerto' had a wide range of meanings. The term could refer to a symphony executed by the entire orchestra, although it was increasingly used in the modern sense—to signify an orchestral composition with one or more solo parts.[29] A similar ambiguity was inherent in the musical

[25] A. Schering, *Geschichte des Instrumentalkonzerts*, p. 124 note.

[26] Information concerning librettists and dates of performance is taken from K. H. Mennicke, *Hasse und die Brüder Graun als Symphoniker*, pp. 493–5, 500–25.

[27] Op. 4, no. 1, proved immensely popular; it was issued separately several times during the eighteenth century under such titles as 'A Favourite Concerto' and even found its way into *The Piano-Forte Magazine*, vol. ii, no. 7 (1797).

[28] The sixth concerto differs from the others in two main respects: it is constructed in the manner of a French overture and has no wind parts.

[29] Rousseau's definition of the term concerto is as follows: 'Mot Italien francisé, qui signifie généralement une Symphonie faite pour être executée par tout un Orchestre; mais on appelle plus particulièrement *Concerto* une Pièce faite pour

genres themselves. During the middle years of the century
the sinfonia and concerto were very closely related from a
stylistic point of view. Tutti/solo contrast could, and often
did, occur in the symphony[30] although the solo episodes
were seldom as extended as in a concerto. The distinguishing feature of the sinfonia at this time was its richer
instrumentation (wind instruments were frequently added
to the ensemble), and the prevalence of binary (rather than
ritornello) structures. Although the distinction between
sinfonia and concerto became more pronounced as the
century advanced, it was not until the 1770s that this process
was finally rationalized. Terminology then became more
precise as composers distinguished more effectively between the various types of orchestral music: the concerto,
the symphony proper, and the symphony with solo parts
(now entitled 'sinfonia concertante').[31]

Walsh advertised his next set of Hasse's concertos (op. 6)
in the *General Evening Post* for 3–5 December 1745. These
works do appear to be genuine concertos despite the fact
that binary forms are more prevalent than in the op. 3 set.
The full title of the publication is as follows: 'SIX/CON-
CERTOS/IN SIX PARTS./For a GERMAN FLUTE. Two
VIOLINS,/a TENOR, with a THOROUGH BASS for
the/HARPSICHORD or VIOLONCELLO./Compos'd
by Signor/GIOVANNI ADOLFFO HASSE./Opera

---

quelque Instrument particulier, qui joue seul de tems en tems avec un simple
Accompagnement, après un commencement en grand Orchestre; et la Pièce
continue ainsi toujours alternativement entre le même Instrument récitant, et
l'Orchestre en Choeur. Quant aux *Concerto* où tout se joue en Rippieno, et où nul
Instrument ne récite, les François les appellent quelquefois *Trio*, et les Italiens
Sinfonie.' J. J. Rousseau, *Dictionnaire de Musique* (Paris, 1768; first published Geneva,
1767), p. 112.

[30] See, for example, Haydn's trilogy of symphonies nos. 6, 7, and 8 (*Le Matin, Le
Midi, Le Soir*) which he wrote in 1761. For a full discussion of the concertante
element in Haydn's early symphonies see H. C. Robbins Landon, *The Symphonies of
Joseph Haydn* (London, 1955), pp. 233ff.

[31] It must be admitted, however, that the dividing line between the concerto and
the sinfonia concertante was always thin; a work such as Mozart's sinfonia
concertante for violin, viola, and orchestra of 1779 differs little from his concertos
proper.

Sexta./London.' This was the last important set of Hasse's concertos to be published by Walsh. Another collection, entitled 'SIX CONCERTOS Set for the Harpsichord or Organ, Compos'd by Signor GIOVANNI ADOLFFO HASSE. London' is of no great significance since it consists merely of transcriptions from the op. 3 and 4 sets.[32]

3. Dating, Authenticity, Instrumentation, and Related Questions

It is not possible at present to devise an effective chronology for Hasse's concertos. Most of the manuscript sources are undated and such information as derives from water-marks is often imprecise. The weight of available evidence does, however, suggest that Hasse's concertos belong to an early stage of his career: some of the Swedish manuscripts, for example, could not have been written after 1768. Moreover, stylistic evidence points in the same direction. Hasse's late style sometimes approached that of the Viennese classical school, as in parts of his opera *Ruggiero* (1771),[33] but there are few hints of so progressive an idiom in the concertos. From internal evidence it seems probable that the majority of his concertos were composed at an early stage—perhaps during the 1730s and 1740s. With the printed concertos, of course, the problem of dating is less acute, for here, at least, we have a *terminus ante quem*. In this connection, it is significant that all the printed sets of concertos were first issued during the 1740s. Once again, therefore, a relatively early date of composition is implied.

Some questions of authenticity also arise. This is only to be expected when dealing with orchestral music of the eighteenth century. In a pre-copyright era the determined activities of an unscrupulous composer, copier, or publisher could pass unchecked. Besides, the very similarity of concerto incipits made the correct attribution of anonymous

---

[32] No. 1 = op. 4, no. 1; No. 2 = op. 3, no. 5; No. 3 = op. 3, no. 3; No. 4 = op. 3, no. 6; No. 5 = op. 3, no. 8; No. 6 = op. 3, no. 2.

[33] See H. Engel, 'Hasse's Ruggiero und Mozarts Festspiel Ascanio', *Mozart-Jahrbuch*, i (1960/1), 29–42.

manuscripts a hazardous occupation. Thus, a concerto might be assigned to Hasse in one source, and to Pergolesi or Vivaldi in another. R. Meylan, in a valuable article on eighteenth-century wind concertos (flute, oboe) of doubtful origin,[34] mentions thirteen concertos by Hasse where the attribution is open to debate. Of these, four concertos were published by John Walsh—as op. 3, nos. 2, 3, and 11, and op. 6, no. 6—and the remainder are known only from manuscript sources. One should not assume that these thirteen works are necessarily unauthentic; each case must be judged separately. On stylistic grounds, it seems likely that the three doubtful concertos[35] of op. 3 were, in fact, written by Hasse. The same is true of most of the manuscript concertos listed by Meylan; they contain nothing alien to Hasse's style. On the other hand, there is good reason to doubt the authenticity of op. 6, no. 6, for the solo writing is more brilliant than normal and the melodic material is equally uncharacteristic. Since this concerto also exists in a manuscript bearing Scherer's name,[36] there must be serious doubts as to Hasse's authorship. In a few cases, the question of authenticity has been resolved by scholars working in other fields: for example, the G major concerto which Breitkopf advertised under Hasse's name in 1766[37] is now known to be by Vivaldi, not Hasse,[38] and discoveries of a similar nature may well follow as we glean more information about the many concertists active in the eighteenth century.

[34] R. Meylan, 'Documents douteux dans le domaine des concertos pour instruments à vent au XVIIIe siècle', *Revue de musicologie*, xlix (1963), 47–60.

[35] The attributions are as follows: op. 3, no. 2, to Hasse and Anon.; op. 3, no. 3, to Hasse and Pikel; op. 3, no. 11, to Hasse and Pergolesi.

[36] Little is known of Scherer apart from the fact that several instrumental works bearing his name were circulating during the mid-eighteenth century.

[37] As Racc. IV no. 1, *The Breitkopf Thematic Catalogue: the Six Parts and Sixteen Supplements 1762–1787*, p. 244.

[38] A copy of this concerto bearing Vivaldi's name has been found in the famous Giordano collection at the Bibloteca Nazionale, Turin. No manuscript bearing Hasse's name has ever been traced and indeed Breitkopf had already advertised the concerto under Vivaldi's name in 1763. The work is obviously by the Italian composer and appears in Ryom's catalogue as no. 436.

Most of Hasse's concertos are scored for a single flute (flauto traverso) and strings.[39] There are, however, a few double concertos: three concertos of op. 1 employ two flutes, as does the fourth concerto of the op. 3 set. In addition, there is a manuscript concerto for flute and bassoon in E minor, and a double concerto for two flutes in Bb major.[40] None of these works falls into the concerto grosso category. In the op. 1 set the two flutes are treated as a pair rather than as individual soloists. Since they consort in parallel thirds or sixths for long stretches the general effect differs little from that of a solo concerto. A slightly different approach is adopted in some concertos from the op. 6 set. Here Hasse occasionally shares the interest between his solo flute and a concertante violin (the latter being drawn from the ripieno group, as in some of Vivaldi's flute concertos). The only 'concerto' with more than two soloists is found at Dresden in the Sächisiche Landesbibliothek.[41] Scored for the unusual combination of chalumeau, oboe, bassoon, and cembalo, this work is, in fact, a concertized sonata and not a concerto at all.

Although Hasse evidently preferred to write for the flute, there are a few solo concertos for other instruments. Among these are two works for Hasse's own instrument (the harpsichord), two for violin, two for oboe, and one for mandolin.[42] It must be emphasized, however, that the vast majority of these works also survive in versions for flute and strings and may, therefore, be arrangements of flute concertos. The possibility is a real one, for in the few cases where comparative dates are available, precedence lies with the flute concertos.

The manuscripts of the two cembalo concertos are both

---

[39] One concerto (MS. at S-Skma, FbO-R) is for 'flauto traverso d'amore'.

[40] The concerto for flute and bassoon is preserved at S–L, Engelhart collection 102; two manuscripts of the Bb concerto are housed at S-Skma, see also p. 250.

[41] MS. Mus. 2477.0.4.

[42] The printed horn concerto mentioned by Gerber (E. L. Gerber, *Neues historisch-biographisches Lexikon der Tonkünstler*, 1812–1814, facsimile edition by O. Wessely (Graz, 1966), ii. 517) has not, as yet, been traced; it could be that Gerber was referring to one of the op. 4 set 'For Violins, French Horns or Hoboys'.

preserved at Wolfenbüttel.[43] But on inspection the G major concerto for obbligato cembalo and strings (no. 126 in Vogel's library catalogue[44]) proves to be another version of a flute concerto which was published twice in eighteenth-century collections—as op. 1, no. 2, and as op. 3, no. 1. The A major concerto at Wolfenbüttel also exists in two versions: (i) for unaccompanied cembalo (Vogel no. 127) and (ii) for flute and strings (MS. at Stockholm in the Kungliga Musikaliska Akademiens Bibliothek). There are further complications with this second cembalo concerto in that it was advertised by Breitkopf in 1766 as a violin concerto. However, no manuscript of the violin version has been traced. The same is true for Hasse's other 'violin' concerto. Breitkopf advertised this work on two separate occasions: once in 1763 as a concerto in B♭ major for two flutes and strings and subsequently, in 1767, as a violin concerto in G major,[45] yet no manuscript sources for the violin version are known to exist. The two surviving copies both give the key of the work as B♭ major and the instrumentation in each case is for two flutes and strings.[46] The fact that Breitkopf's catalogues are notoriously inaccurate as far as instrumentation is concerned together with the absence of source material makes it unlikely that Hasse conceived these concertos for violin. However, violinists may well have appropriated suitable flute or oboe concertos for their own use. Solo instruments of matching range were still considered to be interchangeable at this period and performers were uninhibited by the type of purist strictures in force today.

Manuscript sources do, however, exist for Hasse's two oboe concertos. The G major flute concerto published as op.

[43] In the Herzog-August Bibliothek.

[44] E. Vogel, *Die Handschriften nebst den Älteren Druckwerken der Musik-Abteilung der Herzogl. Bibliothek*, part viii of O. von Heinemann, *Die Handschriften der Herzoglichen Bibliothek zu Wolfenbüttel* (Wolfenbüttel, 1890), p. 23f.

[45] *The Breitkopf Thematic Catalogue: the Six Parts and Sixteen Supplements 1762–1787*, pp. 98, 278.

[46] MSS. at S-Skma, Fb0-R.

1, no. 6, and advertised by Breitkopf in 1763 (Racc. II no. 1)[47] survives in six different manuscripts, two of which indicate that the solo part may be played on an oboe. In one case the instructions are ambiguous: the work is headed 'Concerto per il Oboe ô Flauto Trav. Solo in F'; but in the other source, the oboe alone is given as soloist.[48] For Hasse's other oboe concerto[49] there is no equivalent flute version. However, the authenticity of this work is doubtful: two sources name D. de Micco as the author;[50] furthermore the style of the concerto is not altogether typical of Hasse. Controversy also surrounds the mandolin concerto. A manuscript source of this work is preserved in the Deutsche Staatsbibliothek, Berlin, and the flute version was published by Walsh as op. 3, no. 11. Yet Hasse's authorship is not absolutely certain for Breitkopf attributes the flute version to Pergolesi.[51]

Concerning the instrumentation of Hasse's concertos, it is noteworthy that the majority of the manuscript concertos are scored for a three-part string ensemble, the viola being omitted. This type of scoring was prevalent in Italy during the 1720s and 1730s. The records of Cardinal Ottoboni's establishment at Rome show a gradual decline in the number of viola players during the first two decades of the century, and after 1720 violas are frequently absent from the lists altogether.[52] A similar trend may be observed in the work of Neapolitan composers. Many Neapolitan solo concertos were written for a three-part string ensemble consisting merely of violins and bass. There is no viola part,

---

[47] *The Breitkopf Thematic Catalogue: the Six Parts and Sixteen Supplements 1762–1787*, p. 97.

[48] These two manuscripts are at S-Skma. The location of the other four manuscripts is as follows: MS. (G major) at S-Skma, FbO-R; MS. (F major) at S-L, Kraus collection 123; two MSS. (both F major) at S-Skma.

[49] D-brd-DS.

[50] MSS. at D-brd-KA and S-Skma. See R. Meylan, 'Documents douteux dans le domaine des concertos pour instruments à vent au XVIIIᵉ siècle', 53.

[51] *The Breitkopf Thematic Catalogue: the Six Parts and Sixteen Supplements 1762–1787*, p. 100.

[52] S. H. Hansell, 'Orchestral Practice at the Court of Cardinal Pietro Ottoboni', *Journal of the American Musicological Society*, xix (1966), 398–403.

for example, in Leo's six cello concertos, nor in Porpora's flute concertos.[53] Some scholars have seen the origins of this three-part texture in the baroque trio sonata with its dual melody line and supporting bass. Recent opinion, however, takes the view that this type of instrumentation resulted from the fundamental changes (i.e. simplification) of style which were taking place in Italian music at that time.[54]

One of the most difficult questions concerning Hasse's concertos is for whom, and for what purpose, they were originally intended? Unfortunately neither the manuscripts nor the printed editions give any direct information on this subject since they contain no dedicatory notes or prefaces. The fact that Hasse chose to write for the flute may be significant, although one must remember that this instrument was enjoying widespread popularity among amateur musicians of the day. It has been suggested that the concertos were designed for Frederick the Great—an amateur flautist of considerable ability. But although Frederick certainly admired Hasse's music there is no documentary evidence to support this view, and the lack of such evidence is particularly disturbing when one considers the wealth of contemporary literature concerning Frederick and his circle. Other possibilities arise: some of the concertos could have been written for performance in Italy. We know that instrumental concertos were sometimes inserted between the acts of dramatic works in Italian theatres. Von Uffenbach relates that Vivaldi performed violin concertos between the acts of his operas, and we learn from the same source that Pisendel played one of Vivaldi's concertos as interlude music during a theatrical performance at Venice.[55] Hasse could, therefore, have utilized his flute concertos in like manner. It is also possible that he wrote some concertos for

[53] D. Green, 'Progressive and Conservative tendencies in the violoncello concertos of Leonardo Leo', in *Studies in Eighteenth-Century Music*, ed. H. C. Robbins Landon in collaboration with R. E. Chapman (London, 1970), pp. 261–71.

[54] S. H. Hansell, 'Orchestral Practice at the court of Cardinal Pietro Ottoboni', 402.

[55] See W. Kolneder, *Antonio Vivaldi: His Life and Work*, p. 149.

the talented ladies of the Venetian Conservatorio dell' Incurabili—an institution with which he was connected at various stages of his life. Yet, if this were so, one would expect him to have written for a wider range of solo instruments, for the girls were expert on all manner of musical instruments, both wind and stringed. Another possibility is that the concertos were designed for Dresden, possibly for Quantz, who was (intermittently) a member of the orchestra from 1718 until 1741.[56] Attractive though this theory is, there are difficulties in accepting it. The Dresden opera orchestra was one of the largest in Europe. We learn from Rousseau's dictionary that in 1754 it consisted of eight first violins, seven second violins, four violas, three cellos, three double basses, two flutes, five oboes, five bassoons, two horns ('Cors de Chasse'), and two harpsichords, with the optional addition of trumpets and drums.[57] Hasse, as director, had all these resources at his disposal. And if the concertos were composed for this illustrious group of musicians, it is curious that he did not exploit his resources to the full; all the more so, since a composer like Vivaldi, when writing specifically for Dresden, was careful to score his concertos more richly than usual.[58] In short, none of the above hypotheses is entirely satisfactory, but each is worthy of consideration.

4. General Planning

Those who seek the rich textures of J. S. Bach or the colour and vitality of Vivaldi will be disappointed in Hasse's concertos, for his work falls neither within the German tradition nor within the aesthetic framework of the baroque period. His style is essentially simple and elegant, with the emphasis on lyrical melody and clear textures. Most of his concertos are short, unpretentious works which make few

[56] Hasse first met Quantz in Naples in 1725 when he secured the latter an introduction to Alessandro Scarlatti.

[57] See Plate G, Figure 1, in J. J. Rousseau, *Dictionnaire de Musique*.

[58] See, for example, Pincherle nos. 359 and 383—M. Pincherle, *Antonio Vivaldi et la musique instrumentale*, vol. 2 *Inventaire-Thématique*, pp. 56, 58), RV 576, 577.

demands on performer or audience. Some are marred by extreme rigidity of form or by poverty of invention, but others prove unexpectedly charming by virtue of their fresh melodies and mellifluous sound.

In view of Hasse's long stay in Italy and his known allegiance to the Italian style, it comes as no surprise to find him adopting the formal principles of the Venetian concerto. Models for this type of work were readily available to him, not only in Italy, but also at Dresden where the Vivaldian manner was firmly entrenched.[59] Hasse, like Vivaldi, preferred a three-movement form. Within this sinfonia-like scheme, his movements follow a predictable course: an opening Allegro in common time is succeeded by a short slow movement, often in the relative minor or subdominant key, and the work is rounded off by a lively Finale in $\frac{3}{8}$ metre. Only exceptionally does one come across a four-movement concerto. Sometimes these works are extensions of the three-movement plan, as in op. 3, no. 8, where Hasse has added a final Minuet to his basic scheme. Elsewhere the four-movement concerto traces its ancestry back to the 'concerto da chiesa'. This is clearly the case with op. 3, no. 9, whose austere movements are arranged in the traditional slow–fast–slow–fast pattern.

Although the occasional four-movement concerto reveals links with the 'concerto da chiesa', there is little cross-fertilization from the old 'concerto da camera'. The only dance movement to appear in Hasse's concertos is the Minuet, and this occurs infrequently. The Gigue is seldom

[59] The Venetian concerto was popular in Dresden long before Hasse took over as kapellmeister. Quantz recalled that he first came into contact with Vivaldi's concertos at Pirna, near Dresden, in 1714 (J. J. Quantz, autobiography in F. W. Marpurg, *Historisch-Kritische Beyträge zur Aufnähme der Musik*, 5 vols. (Berlin, 1754–60; facsimile, Hildesheim, 1970), i. 205) and Franz Benda informs us that when a choir boy in Dresden during the 1720s he knew Vivaldi's concertos by heart (F. Benda, autobiography in J. A. Hiller, *Lebensbeschreibungen berühmter Musikgelehrten und Tonkünstler neuerer Zeit* (Leipzig, 1784), i. 34). The initial impetus may have come from Pisendel, a violinist who had joined the orchestra in 1712, spent a period studying with Vivaldi in Italy (1717), and later became konzertmeister at Dresden, a post he held from 1728 until his death in 1755 (or thereabouts—the exact date is not known).

used. In fact, the complete absence of movements in compound time is one of the most striking features, even the Siciliana—so common in Vivaldi—being excluded from the general design.[60]

5. Formal Structure

As far as the formal structure of individual movements is concerned, Hasse, like Vivaldi, is heavily reliant on ritornello principles. In most concertos ritornello form provides the foundation of all three movements and is often handled in an unimaginative and stereotyped fashion. A particularly disconcerting example occurs in op. 3, no. 7. Here the first and last Allegro movements follow an almost identical course: even the position and keys of the tutti interruptions correspond.[61] This is an extreme case, yet it must be admitted that Hasse often treats ritornello form as a rigid frame for musical ideas rather than as a living organism capable of growth and change. The danger of monotony is ever present in so formalized an approach and Hasse does not always avert it. In addition to these ritornello structures, there are a limited number of binary-form movements. The Minuet is automatically cast in binary form, as befits a dance movement; more significant is the presence of bipartite structures in a few slow movements and Finales. Apart from this, however, other formal schemes are virtually non-existent: neither rondo nor 'da capo' forms occur at all.

Ritornello Structure in Allegro Movements

Although there are marked differences of mood and style

---

[60] The slow movement of op. 3, no. 6, has the lilting rhythms and lyrical melody of a Siciliana but is written in $\frac{3}{8}$ (not $\frac{6}{8}$). The barring is orthodox. (Certain other Neapolitan compositions, notated in $\frac{3}{8}$ metre but with bar lines occurring after every sixth quaver are effectively in compound time. For details of this specifically Neapolitan tradition see H. Hell, *Die Neapolitanische Opernsinfonie in der ersten Hälfte des 18. Jahrhunderts* (Tutzing, 1971), p. 193.)

[61] In both movements there is a series of tutti interruptions in the keys of E minor, D major, and C major. See 1st movement, bars 74–7, 79–81, 83–6; 3rd movement, bars 91–4, 98–101, 105–8.

between the first and last movements of Hasse's concertos, their formal structure has much in common. It is possible, therefore, to discuss both types of movement under the same heading. The majority of Hasse's Allegro movements are cast in straight-forward ritornello form with three or four statements of the ritornello. Key structure follows conventional procedures: in a three-ritornello movement the statements appear in the tonic, dominant, and tonic keys respectively, and in a four-ritornello movement the most common key-scheme is: tonic, dominant, relative minor, and tonic.[62] The various ritornello statements are not identical; indeed it is often only the first and last tutti sections which correspond in every detail. Middle statements of the ritornello are usually shortened, and Hasse takes the opportunity to vary his tutti material at this point, either by developing one or two of the ritornello motifs or by presenting the various sections of the ritornello in a different order. This technique was, of course, taken over directly from the Vivaldian concerto. Between the ritornello statements come two (or three) solo episodes. Here the texture is often lighter, for Hasse, like Tartini, prefers to drop the string bass and continuo from the ensemble, leaving the accompaniment to upper strings alone. As a result of this, the full orchestral tutti plays a rather insignificant role in his concertos; it has little to do except present the ritornello statements and make occasional interjections into solo episodes. In passing, it should perhaps be mentioned that tutti interruptions are more prevalent in the second (or third) solo sections than in the first. This is somewhat unusual. Both Vivaldi and J. S. Bach, for example, allowed the tutti to harass the soloist from the start. The position of the cadenza *fermata* in Hasse's concerto movements is also of interest. It may be placed either before the final ritornello,[63] or (more significantly) within it,[64] the second practice being,

---

[62] Minor key concertos are extremely rare.

[63] As in op. 3, no. 7, 3rd movement.

[64] As in op. 3, no. 6, 3rd movement. Hasse did not write out his cadenzas in full; he merely indicated their position by means of a *fermata*.

of course, the one adopted by composers of the Viennese classical school during the latter part of the century.

The opening ritornello often falls into a number of different sections, this sectional division being more apparent in the first movements than in the Finales. The break between sections may even be emphasized by a *fermata*, as in the following example, although so definite a gap is unusual for Hasse:

EXAMPLE I[65]

J. A. Hasse, op. 3, no. 4, 1st movement, bars I to II (first violin part)

Normally Hasse's ritornelli fall into three or four parts. The four-part ritornello consists of an opening motif or phrase, a sequential section, a contrast motif, and a final cadential passage. The tripartite ritornello is based on a similar ground plan, but lacks one of the middle sections—the sequential passage or the contrast motif. Both schemes were in fairly general use from about 1730 onwards, the four-part ritornello being especially prevalent during the middle of the century among composers of the Berlin school.[66] Since the various sections of the ritornello have their own character and function, each will now be examined in turn.

It is obvious that the nature of the head-motif, or opening phrase, will vary from movement to movement. Yet some general observations may be made. The traditional 'call to attention'—often a brief triadic motif such as that which opens J. S. Bach's E major violin concerto—is still found in

---

[65] The Walsh edition provides the text for most of the examples. Details of those few concertos which have been reprinted in modern times are given in Appendix C.

[66] See H. Uldall, *Das Klavierkonzert der Berliner Schule* (Leipzig, 1928), p. 19.

some concerto movements by Hasse, (as in the 1st movement of op. 3, no. 1) but is less common than one might expect. Several of his Allegro movements open, not with the flamboyant gestures of the baroque, but with lilting melodic material:

EXAMPLE 2

J. A. Hasse, op. 3, no. 8, 1st movement, bars 1–4 (violin part only)

After the initial motif or theme, the four-part ritornello continues with a sequential section. This is often the place for semiquaver figuration and fast harmonic rhythm. The writing is more brilliant now and, indeed, this passage is occasionally entrusted to the soloist who thus makes an independent (and hence unorthodox) contribution to the opening tutti section.[67] The third part of the ritornello introduces an element of contrast. This section is obviously related to the traditional type of *pianoidée* which has been discussed already in connection with Handel's concertos and which later became an important feature of the Berlin concerto. Hasse's contrast sections have all the conventional attributes: the lyrical melodic line is often doubled at the third or sixth; the bass line is static and consists of reiterated quavers; the key darkens, often changing to the tonic minor mode. Curiously, though, this section is seldom marked piano by Hasse and the texture is not always thinned. The last part of the ritornello serves to re-establish the home key and to emphasize the cadence. There are usually two or more perfect cadences in the tonic before the ritornello eventually comes to an end. Indeed the repetitious nature of this section can prove irritating to modern listeners.

A typical example of Hasse's ritornello structure is given below. The four sections are labelled as follows: head-

---

[67] See op. 3, no. 8, 1st movement, bars 4–7.

motif = A, sequential section = B, contrast motif = C, and cadential section = D.

EXAMPLE 3 *Four-part ritornello structure*
J. A. Hasse, op. 3, no. 7, 1st movement, bars 1–17 (outer parts only)

In this particular example the solo flute doubles the violin part throughout the opening ritornello as was customary in concertos of the baroque period. Elsewhere, however, one can see indications that this tradition was on the wane for Hasse does not always include his soloist in ritornello sections. The flute rests throughout all three ritornello statements in the 1st movement of op. 3, no. 10, and is absent from the texture for long stretches in certain other

movements also. Occasionally the soloist makes a limited
contribution to ritornello passages, playing everything
within its range, but resting when forced to do so. This is
presumably what happens in op. 3, no. 8, where the flute
part descends to middle C in the first tutti of the opening
movement. The note was below the compass of most flutes
at that time, and as if to reassure the soloist, Walsh inserts
the word 'Viol.' under the flute part at that point. Historically, the omission of the soloist from tutti sections is of
considerable significance and Hasse's concertos provide an
early, though by no means isolated, example of a practice
that was to become widespread later in the century.

The first solo section usually opens with some reference
to ritornello themes. Sometimes the soloist makes but a
brief allusion to ritornello ideas before embarking on independent material. More often, however, there is a restatement of the opening theme with different instrumentation.

EXAMPLE 4
J. A. Hasse, op. 3, no. 3, 1st movement; (*a*) bars 1–3, (*b*) bars 12–15
(beginning of the first solo episode)

A comparison of the two passages reproduced above will illustrate Hasse's procedure. He merely transfers the bass line from the basso continuo to one of the upper parts. The solo flute then presents the melody without competition, and the original middle part is either omitted completely (as here) or else placed on the second violins. Thus, although the tutti material remains essentially unaltered, there is a change of tone colour for the solo section and a lighter, more transparent texture is created.

The sharp distinction between tutti and solo sections in Hasse's concertos depends more on contrasting textures than on thematic contrast. But on those few occasions when the soloist does present a new and independent theme, one can detect a definite change of mood. In the 1st movement of op. 3, no. 6, for example, the suave lyricism of the solo theme contrasts strongly with the robust opening:

EXAMPLE 5
J. A. Hasse, op. 3, no. 6, 1st movement; (*a*) bars 1–2, (*b*) bars 21–4
(flute part)

Examples of this type of thematic dualism may be found in the concertos of both J. C. Bach and Mozart. Indeed, the idea of constructing a movement on two strongly con-strasted themes became so widespread that nineteenth-century theorists came to regard it as a *sine qua non* of sonata structure.

During the course of the first solo episode Hasse makes the customary modulation to the dominant key (or to the relative major in the rare minor-key concertos). This modulation is then confirmed by the tutti with their second ritornello statement. Although this section is often only loosely connected with the previous tutti, the head-motif and cadential passages from the first ritornello are still clearly recognizable. The second solo episode (and the third, where this is present) continues on much the same lines as the first. The solo writing is, however, slightly more brilliant and the key structure becomes more flexible. Yet the modulations cannot be termed adventurous and there is no feeling of tonal achievement when the tonic is eventually regained.

In Hasse's solo episodes one may observe a gradual movement away from the figurative writing of the baroque concerto towards the more melodic style of the pre-classical era. This is not to say that he abandoned the Vivaldian type of solo episode entirely; there are several instances where the flute is given figurative passages to show off the performer's technique. Yet Hasse obviously found difficulty in sustaining this type of writing. His phrases are too short to be effective, and the figuration changes so rapidly that the episode is apt to splinter into a number of disconnected fragments.

EXAMPLE 6

J. A. Hasse, op. 3, no. 7, 3rd movement, bars 133–47 (short score)

More successful in this respect is the first solo episode of the
1st movement of op. 3, no. 8. Here the material is melodic
rather than figurative and the short phrases do not create
such a disjointed effect. The syncopations and the arch-like
melodic lines are both characteristic of Hasse's style. In fact
these mannerisms occur in so many of his solo
episodes—irrespective of the principal thematic ideas—that
it is sometimes difficult to distinguish one Allegro movement from another.

EXAMPLE 7

J. A. Hasse, op. 3, no. 8, 1st movement, bars 20–7 (flute part only)

Arriving at the last ritornello statement, we find this is
often an exact replica of the first. Sometimes, however,
Hasse varies the tutti passage slightly by giving the soloist
an independent part during the final cadence bars. This
happens in several Allegro movements including op. 3, no.
3 (1st movement and Finale), op. 3, no. 7 (Finale), and op. 3,
no. 11 (1st movement). The independent solo part is modest
enough, yet the technique is effective in that it re-establishes
the primacy of the solo instrument. And since the soloist
would normally be doubling the violin part at this point in a
movement, its independence has added force.

The majority of Hasse's Allegro movements are cast in straight-forward ritornello form of the type discussed above. Exceptionally, however, more sophisticated methods of organization are used. One of the most interesting examples occurs in the Finale of op. 3, no. 6.[68] On first acquaintance this appears to be an ordinary ritornello movement. There are three statements of the ritornello, in D, A, and D major respectively. But the middle statement modulates from the dominant to the remote key of C# minor, ending with emphatic repeated quavers on the note C#. Immediately afterwards—at bar 165—the soloist announces important ritornello material in the home key of D major; no attempt is made to soften the harsh effect of this startling key change. The abrupt return to the tonic, coupled with the recurrence of ritornello themes in the solo part, gives the impression that we are at the start of a recapitulation section. And this impression is heightened at bar 225 when the final ritornello is interrupted by a short solo passage recapitulating material from the end of the solo section (compare bars 116ff. with bars 225ff.). The key structure at this point shows an affinity with that of sonata form, since the solo material has been transposed from dominant to tonic for its reappearance here. Although there are obvious similarities between this type of formal organization and that of sonata form as found in the late eighteenth-century concerto, one must not press the analogy too far. Hasse never uses a full recapitulation section. He merely effects a return to the tonic key at some point prior to the final ritornello and thereafter includes a short repetition of solo material. His tentative experiments in this field remain far less significant than those of J. S. Bach or of the Neapolitan-based Leonardo Leo.[69]

The Slow Movements

From the structural point of view Hasse's slow movements

---

[68] Modern edition by R. Engländer (London, 1953).

[69] See D. Green, 'Progressive and Conservative tendencies in the violoncello concertos of Leonardo Leo', p. 269.

are considerably more varied than his fast movements.
Although ritornello form still predominates there is a
greater flexibility of treatment: the number of ritornello
statements varies from two to four according to the length
and scope of individual movements; moreover, the ritornello is sometimes treated as a theme for development
rather than as a true rondo.[70] The musical argument thus
unfolds more spontaneously than in many of the quick
movements. Besides the ritornello structures, there are
some binary and through-composed movements. The slow
movement of op. 6, no. 2, is in pure binary form with a
characteristic tonic–dominant/dominant–tonic key scheme
and with no hint of a recurring tutti section. Of even greater
interest are the through-composed movements (e.g. the
Largo of op. 3, no. 11, the Andante of op. 6, no. 1, the
Adagio of op. 3, no. 3) where the only form-building
element is that of motivic development. Here we see Hasse
grappling for once with individual problems of structure
rather than forcing his ideas into a formal straight-jacket.

Hasse's slow movements also exhibit a surprisingly wide
range of moods. Dry, brittle ritornello movements with
sharp dotted rhythms (see Example 8).

EXAMPLE 8
J. A. Hasse, op. 3, no. 1, 2nd movement, bars 1–3 (short score)

contrast strongly with those expressive slow movements in
which a more intense and emotional atmosphere is gener-

[70] See the Andante of op. 6, no. 5, where the second and final ritornellos are free
developments of the first.

ated. Sometimes the mood will change abruptly during the course of a movement. This happens in the Adagio of op. 3, no. 4—a curious ritornello movement which opens with a poignant syncopated phrase in Hasse's most expressive manner but which becomes more conciliatory in tone as it progresses:

EXAMPLE 9
J. A. Hasse, op. 3, no. 4, Adagio, bars 1–9 (outer parts only)

Although there are a few subsequent references to the minor mode these are short-lived and the movement ends on a lilting, pastoral note.

Interrelations Between Movements

Before leaving the subject of Hasse's concerto form some account must be taken of his experiments with thematic unification. For although he did not view the concerto as a cyclic form he made isolated attempts to relate certain movements by thematic means.[71] To be sure, it is not always possible to determine whether these relationships are intentional or not. In op. 6, no. 1, for example, the outer movements are based on similar themes:

EXAMPLE 10
J. A. Hasse, op. 6, no. 1; (*a*) 1st movement, bars 1–4; (*b*) 3rd movement, bars 1–8 (first violin part only)

but since triadic themes were a commonplace in instrumental music of the mid-eighteenth century (and before) the resemblance could well be coincidental. However, a more remarkable example occurs in op. 6, no. 5. The work opens as follows with an Allegro movement in G major:

EXAMPLE 11
J. A. Hasse, op. 6, no. 5, 1st movement, bars 1–6 (first violin part only)

Towards the end of this movement (at bar 130) Hasse introduces a decorative version of the Allegro theme ('x' in Ex. 12a) which bears a marked resemblance to the opening of the following Andante:

[71] The same technique is found in certain isolated concertos by Vivaldi and in some of Padre Martini's symphonies, see W. Kolneder, *Antonio Vivaldi: His Life and Work*, p. 62; also H. Brofsky, 'The Symphonies of Padre Martini', *The Musical Quarterly*, li (1965), 663.

EXAMPLE 12

J. A. Hasse, op. 6, no. 5; (*a*) 1st movement, bars 129–33 (flute part only); (*b*) 2nd movement, bars 1–4 (first violin part only)

Although the two passages are not absolutely identical—they differ in tempo and mode—they are strikingly similar. Moreover, since the cadential material of bars 138–9 also reappears in the Andante (at bars 12–13) there can be little doubt that this was a deliberate, if rather unorthodox, attempt to relate the two movements by thematic means.

6. Stylistic Features of the Concertos

Handel's biographer, John Mainwaring, on hearing Hasse's music in London wrote: 'He is remarkable for his fine elevated air, with hardly so much as the shew of harmony to support it. And this may serve not only for a character of HASSE in particular, but of the Italians in general at the time we are speaking of.'[72] There are two points of interest here. First, Mainwaring makes no distinction between Hasse and his fellow Italian composers. This is understandable, since Hasse was universally regarded as the champion of Italian music.[73] Secondly, by drawing attention to Hasse's 'fine elevated air' with its delicate accompaniment, Mainwaring has isolated the most important single element in Hasse's music. This concentration on melody is fundamental to all Hasse's work. In both vocal and instrumental music his one aim was to present the melodic line as clearly as possible without obtrusive accompaniment figures or distracting countermelodies.

[72] J. Mainwaring, *Memoirs of the Life of the Late George Frederic Handel*, p. 117.
[73] Contemporary writers invariably associated Hasse's music with the Italian tradition—see, for example, F. W. Marpurg, *Historisch-Kristische Beyträge zur Aufnahme der Musik*, i. 22.

It must be stated at the outset that Hasse's approach to melodic writing has more in common with pre-classical techniques than with baroque methods. Yet some traces of the older style remain. In the 2nd movement of op. 6, no. 4, for example, the solo episodes are all related: each episode begins with the same idea but develops in a slightly different manner. This technique was a prominent feature of the baroque concerto. Examples may be found in J. S. Bach—notably in the solo episodes of the 1st movement of his A major clavier concerto (BWV 1055). In most cases, however, Hasse rejects this type of motivic expansion in favour of a more periodic style. Like many composers of the transitional era he tended to think in short phrase lengths. And while he preferred to cast his melodies in two-, four-, or eight-bar phrases, some themes are less uniform. Irregularity of phrase structure is found most often in the slow movements, many of which are based on three- or five-bar themes. These asymmetrical phrases are sometimes caused by simple repetition, as in the 2nd movement of op. 6, no. 3:

EXAMPLE 13
J. A. Hasse, op. 6, no. 3, 2nd movement, bars 1–5 (first violin part only)

More often, however, the irregularity forms an integral part of the whole. In the following passage the three-bar phrases, together with the exotic melodic intervals, create a most original effect:

EXAMPLE 14
J. A. Hasse, op. 3, no. 12, 2nd movement, bars 1–10 (first violin part only)

The interval of the diminished third, so prominent in the foregoing example, appears fairly frequently in Hasse's melodic lines. So also does the augmented second (see Ex. 19, bars 31 and 38). Hasse's predilection for these particular intervals may stem from his years in Naples where he must surely have come into contact with native folk music. Neapolitan culture was quite distinct from that of other Italian cities, for it had absorbed a variety of influences from both East and West. An oriental flavour is present in many of Naples' street songs and it was this exotic quality that in turn influenced the art-music of eighteenth-century Neapolitan composers.

In Hasse's melodic gifts lie, paradoxically, both his strength and his weakness. By concentrating so exclusively on the melodic line other aspects of musical composition inevitably suffer. Contrapuntal devices such as imitation or voice exchange are renounced with unusual rigour, and on the rare occasions when Hasse includes a fugal movement in his concertos the result is disappointing. The sort of stereotyped figures used may be seen in the following example. Neither the subject nor countersubject shows much inventive skill, the part writing is awkward and the crossing of the two violin parts at various points serves little useful purpose (see Ex. 15). After this exposition the fugal texture is abandoned although a half-hearted attempt to write contrapuntally is made later in the movement.

Hasse was far more at his ease with homophonic movements in which he could indulge his natural inclination for purely melodic writing. Most of his concerto movements are written in the treble-dominated style. Textures are thin and clear, especially in solo episodes where the accompaniment is often entrusted to upper strings alone and where the

EXAMPLE 15

J. A. Hasse, op. 6, no. 4, 1st movement, bars 1–12 (the flute rests throughout the opening ritornello)

soloist is given the lightest possible support. In these sections Hasse makes no pretence at thematic accompaniment, nor does he vary the texture with imitative writing.

The accompanying parts move in uniform rhythms for much of the time, their sole task being to supply an unobtrusive harmonic background for the soloist. The texture of ritornello sections is richer but equally lucid. Even here, there are seldom more than three real parts in operation although extensive doubling conceals the fact. This unwillingness to write in more than three real parts at any given time is extremely characteristic of Hasse. It occasioned comment from no less a person than Emanuel Bach who, according to Burney, 'once wrote word to Hasse, that he was the greatest cheat in the world; for in a score of twenty *nominal* parts, he had seldom more than three *real* ones in action; but with these he produced such divine effects, as must never be expected from a crowded score'.[74]

Exceptionally, Hasse resorts to even thinner textures. The slow movement of op. 6, no. 1, is scored for flute and first violins only, all other parts being marked *tacet*. The flute has the melody while the violins provide a simple, non-melodic bass line. Written in the F clef, it will be seen from the following example that their part requires transposition up an octave (or two, where appropriate):[75]

EXAMPLE 16
J. A. Hasse, op. 6, no. 1, 2nd movement, bars 1–4

This strange notation was, presumably, intended to apprise

[74] C. Burney, *The Present State of Music in Germany, the Netherlands, and United Provinces*, ii. 253.

[75] A similar example is found in the first violin part of Telemann's concerto grosso in E minor. See S. Kross, *Das Instrumentalkonzert bei Georg Philipp Telemann*, p. 169.

the violinists of their new and unusual role as 'bass' instruments. That the performance of these 'high bass' lines was a recognized part of violin technique emerges from the following passage in Quantz's *Versuch*:

If a concertante part is accompanied only by violins, each violinist must pay close attention to whether he has a plain middle part to play, one in which certain little phrases alternate with the concertante part, or a high bass part. In a middle part he must greatly moderate the volume of his tone. If he has something which alternates with the solo, he may play more strongly, and in the high bass he may play still more strongly, especially if he is at some distance from the soloist, or from the listeners.[76]

It is significant that in a movement such as the one discussed above Hasse omits the keyboard continuo from the texture. The same trend may be observed in certain other movements where the direction 'senza cembalo' is found.[77] Moreover, the custom of dropping the conventional bass instruments (cellos, basses, and keyboard) from solo episodes further reduced the importance of the continuo in his work. Taking a broad view, we can see that this was part of a general movement undermining the dominance of the keyboard continuo which was gaining momentum in the 1730s and 1740s and to which a number of composers, including the Italian concertists Vivaldi and Tartini, contributed. In retrospect this development appears to have been inevitable, for reaction against baroque music also implied a reaction against the continuo style on which it was based. In practice, however, it took over half-a-century before the tenacious thorough-bass influence was finally eclipsed.

One of the most perceptive contemporary appraisals of Hasse's style is found in Burney's *Present State*: 'His modulation is, in general, simple, his melody natural, his accom-

---

[76] J. J. Quantz, *Versuch einer Anweisung die flute traversière zu spielen*, p. 205; English translation by E. R. Reilly in J. J. Quantz, *On Playing the Flute* (London, 1966), p. 236.

[77] E.g. the Adagio of op. 3, no. 3, Walsh edition, 'violoncello e cembalo' part.

paniments free from confusion; and leaving to fops and
pedants all that frights, astonishes, and perplexes, he lets no
other arts be discoverable in his compositions, than those of
pleasing the ear, and of satisfying the understanding.'[78] This
penetrates to the heart of the matter, for although Hasse
seldom theorized about his work, it is evident that in his
aesthetic system simplicity was synonymous with beauty.
His harmonic language is extremely consonant, even by
eighteenth-century standards. Harsh discords are avoided
lest they interrupt the smooth euphony of his style, and
very few rich chords are admitted to Allegro movements,
the only flashes of colour being those which come from
melodic chromaticism[79] or major/minor key contrasts. As
one would expect, the slow movements are more adventurous harmonically, but even here an impressive opening is
liable to give way to the simple interchange of tonic and
dominant chords over a static bass line:

EXAMPLE 17

J. A. Hasse, op. 3, no. 2, 2nd movement, bars 1–5 (short score)

As far as the key schemes of individual movements are

---

[78] C. Burney, op cit. i. 319.

[79] Hasse's use of melodic chromaticism for linking phrases (e.g. op. 3, no. 6, 1st
movement, bars 34 and 36) anticipates the Mozartean style.

concerned, Hasse makes few departures from conventional practice. Tonic and dominant key areas are used for long stretches, and excursions to other keys tend to be brief and insignificant. In the second solo section—traditionally the place for wider-ranging modulation—Hasse's limitations become obvious: he seldom uses any but the most closely related keys[80] (i.e. tonic, dominant, subdominant, and their relative minors) and his modulation technique is often clumsy. Yet, on the credit side, one has to admit that he employs major/minor contrasts with great skill and sensitivity. These changes of mode, being decorative rather than functional, may occur at any point in his concerto movements. A characteristic example, in which Hasse uses the minor mode to lend a new and darker shading to his melodic material, is given below:

EXAMPLE 18

J. A. Hasse, op. 3, no. 8, 1st movement, bars 27–31 (short score)

This type of writing points up Hasse's close relationship with Southern traditions, for the rapid alternation between major and tonic minor modes was a specifically Italian trait; Pergolesi was much addicted to it as also were his fellow operatic composers of the 1730s. And although these composers did not fully appreciate the expressive possibilities of the device (as Schubert was later to do) their audiences evidently found it moving. Thus Charles de Brosses could write that the Italians 'hardly ever compose in the minor mode; almost all their airs are written in the major; but into

---

[80] The modulation to the key of the leading note in the Finale of op. 3, no. 6, is quite exceptional.

these they mix, without anyone expecting it, some phrases in the minor which surprise and strike the ear to the point where the heart is affected'.[81]

Although Hasse employs expressive devices such as these, his music is concerned more with balance and line than with the portrayal of strong emotions. Accordingly he tends to avoid sharp contrasts of dynamics[82] despite the fact that these were fashionable in Italy during the middle of the eighteenth century. J. F. Reichardt, seeking to explain why neither Hasse nor Graun 'employed the now so fashionable alternations of forte and piano, in which every other note is either strong or weak', put it down to 'their proper feelings or fine taste'.[83] Certainly, if contemporary reports are accurate, Hasse was never guilty of startling his listeners or exceeding the bounds of good taste. Even his operatic music seems more charming than dramatic.

So far, little has been said about the relation between Hasse's concertos and the rest of his work, but the fact that he was primarily an operatic composer did of course have far-reaching effects on his instrumental style. Operatic influence is particularly strong in the aria–like slow movements which are found in some concertos. It is in these movements, where the solo flute becomes a substitute for the human voice, that Hasse's melodic gifts are displayed to best advantage. The following passage from the Andante of op. 6, no. 5, gives some idea of his fluent style; the melody is simple, yet elegant, the phrases are beautifully balanced, and the lines rise and fall with exquisite grace:

[81] *Le Président de Brosses en Italie: lettres familières écrites d'Italie en 1739 et 1740 par Charles de Brosses*, ed. M. R. Colomb, 2nd ed. (Paris, 1858), ii. 380 (tr. M. F. Robinson, *Naples and the Neapolitan Opera* (Oxford, 1972), p. 111).

[82] Occasionally, however, one does find an example of rapid alternation between forte and piano, e.g. the opening theme of op 3, no. 10, modern edition by A. Schering in *Denkmäler deutscher Tonkunst*, vol. xxix–xxx, p. 33.

[83] J. F. Reichardt, *Briefe eines aufmerksamen Reisenden* (Frankfurt and Leipzig, 1774; translated by O. Strunk, *Source Readings in Music History from Classical Antiquity to the Romantic Era* (London, 1952), 702–3).

EXAMPLE 19

J. A. Hasse, op. 6, no. 5, 2nd movement, bars 18–38 (flute part only)

This movement illustrates with particular force the felicitous application of general operatic methods to instrumental
music. Occasionally, also, one finds Hasse taking over more
specialized vocal techniques. In several slow movements
from the op. 3 set, for example, the solo flute enters with a
held note while the tutti instruments repeat the ritornello
material underneath (e.g. op. 3, no. 1, 2nd movement). This
type of solo entry is borrowed directly from vocal music
and the singer would doubtless have embellished the note
with a *messa di voce*—a gradual swelling and diminishing of
the tone.

7. Hasse's Historical Position Assessed

Throughout this chapter Hasse's association with Italian
traditions has been stressed. He was obviously influenced by
the Vivaldian concerto with its sinfonia-like scheme and
ritornello structures. But although his use of form is closely
related to Vivaldi's, the style of his concertos is more
progressive. To be sure, the two composers still have much
in common: thin-textured accompaniments, repeated
quaver figures, the rapid veering from major to minor

modes, and the use of syncopated themes are almost as
prevalent in Vivaldi's concertos as in Hasse. Yet Hasse was
the more *avant-garde* of the two. Many of his concerto
movements reveal the melodic and rhythmic clichés of the
transitional era. Their graceful melodies, short phrases,
triplet decorations, slow harmonic rhythm, and constant
cadencing are all harbingers of a new style in which
elegance, not dignity, reigns supreme. It is significant that
towards the end of the 1730s Vivaldi's work was thought
old-fashioned by comparison with his young rival. The
Frenchman, Charles de Brosses, writing from Venice in
1739, remarked: 'To my great surprise I found that he
[Vivaldi] is not so highly esteemed as he merits in this
country, where everything is *à la mode*, where his works
have been heard for too long now, and where the previous
year's music is no longer a draw. Today the famous Saxon
[i.e. Hasse] is the man of the moment.[84]

Hasse's concertos bear the hallmarks of that new melodic
style which emerged in certain regions of Italy during the
late 1720s. Unfortunately, neither the term 'rococo' nor
'galant' is precise enough to distinguish between the different transitional styles which sprang up in various parts of
Europe towards the close of the baroque period. The new
Italian style with its emphasis on pure melody and its
rejection of more intellectual elements seems to have originated among a certain group of composers all of whom
were trained or active in Naples. After the recent spate of
polemical articles on this subject one hesitates to use the
term 'Neapolitan school', yet disputes over terminology[85]
must not be allowed to obscure the fact that an important

[84] From a letter to M. de Blancey, 29 August 1739: *Le Président de Brosses en Italie:
lettres familières écrites d'Italie en 1739 et 1740 par Charles de Brosses*, i. 215.

[85] H. C. Wolff, 'The Fairy Tale of the Neapolitan Opera', in *Studies in
Eighteenth-Century Music*, ed. H. C. Robbins Landon in collaboration with R. E.
Chapman (London, 1970), pp. 401–6; also H. Hucke, 'The Neapolitan Tradition in
Opera' in *Report of the Eighth Congress of the International Musicological Society New
York 1961* (Kassel, 1961), i. 253–77; and E. O. D. Downes, 'The Neapolitan
Tradition in Opera', ibid., pp. 277–84 and ii. 132–4.

group of composers was trained in Naples during the first half of the eighteenth century and that these composers shared a common idiom. Hasse may be counted among this group, which includes Vinci, Sarri, Leo, Feo, Porpora, and Pergolesi, for he spent six formative years in the city (from *c.* 1724 to 1730). Confirmation of Hasse's position within this school is supplied by his vocal and instrumental works alike. It has already been shown that the instrumentation of many of his concertos reflects Neapolitan traditions; stylistically also, they are of the same lineage. For their most pronounced characteristics—the treble-dominated style, three-part writing, aria-like slow movements, and avoidance of compound-time signatures—all find a counterpart in Neapolitan opera of the 1720s and 1730s.[86]

As regards the impact of Hasse's concertos on those of contemporary composers, little concrete evidence is available. But it seems likely that they exerted some influence over Quantz whom Hasse had met in Naples as a young man and with whom he worked at Dresden. Although Quantz's concertos are written in the 'mixed' style they have some obvious Italian traits. Moreover, Quantz's theoretical writings[87] suggest a knowledge of Hasse's concerto technique. Quantz himself may have provided Hasse's initial link with Berlin, for in 1741 he moved to Potsdam at the command of his royal flute pupil Frederick the Great. We do not know whether Hasse's concertos were actually performed by Frederick, but the Prussian leader certainly admired his music: several of his operas were produced at Berlin and in 1753 the composer made a personal visit to the city. That Frederick absorbed something of Hasse's manner is evident from the style of the 'first' royal flute concerto. The extract which follows comes from the end of the opening ritornello and shows the constant cadencing and triplet decorations familiar also in Hasse—in fact there is a close parallel between Frederick's concerto and Hasse's op. 3, no. 1, as Example 20 reveals:

---

[86] See M. F. Robinson, *Naples and Neapolitan Opera*, pp. 107ff.
[87] As evidenced by the *Versuch*.

EXAMPLE 20

(a) Frederick the Great, flute concerto no. 1 in G major,[88] 1st movement, bars 24–31 (short score); (b) J. A. Hasse, op. 3, no. 1, 1st movement, bars 13–18

If Riemann is correct in saying that Johann Stamitz spent some time in Dresden prior to 1743,[89] then Hasse's instrumental music may have influenced that of the early Mannheim school. Certainly Stamitz's G major flute concerto[90] has points of similarity with Hasse's work, especially with regard to its light textures and general melodic style. It may also be significant that syncopated themes feature prominently in Stamitz's early symphonies. Apart from this, however, there is little evidence that Hasse's music was

[88] Modern edition by P. Spitta in *Friedrichs des Grossen: Musikalische Werke* (Leipzig, 1889; reprinted New York, 1967), iii. 3.

[89] See the Foreword to *Denkmäler der Tonkunst in Bayern*, iii¹ (Leipzig, 1902), p. xxv, note 1.

[90] Modern edition by W. Lebermann in *Das Erbe Deutscher Musik*, li, *Flötenkonzerte der Mannheimer Schule* (Wiesbaden, 1964).

directly influential at Mannheim: neither his concertos nor his sinfonias show any trace of thematic dualism within the opening phrase or of the built-in crescendo—both distinguishing characteristics of the Mannheim style. It seems likely, therefore, that any similarities between the style of Hasse and Stamitz should be attributed first and foremost to a common source of inspiration—namely, the operatic idiom of the mid-eighteenth century—rather than to any personal contact between the two men.

The idea that Hasse's music exerted some influence on the young Mozart must not be overlooked, although it seems likely that Mozart's admiration for Hasse rested more on his theatrical works than on the lesser-known instrumental music. Despite their difference in age, the two composers regarded each other with deep respect. Mozart spoke warmly of Hasse's operas and *Il Sassone*, for his part, showed great affection and admiration for the young Mozart.[91] During the autumn of 1771 the careers of these two men crossed, when both were involved with the preparation of operatic festivities in Milan. It is, perhaps, symbolic that Hasse's last opera, *Ruggiero*, should have been produced in Milan at the same time as Mozart's little intermezzo *Ascania in Alba*, for the two composers had a similar approach to their art. Yet it must be stressed that the operatic works of late Hasse and early Mozart are more closely related than their instrumental music. Mozart never mentions Hasse's concertos in his letters, nor was he noticeably influenced by them. More congenial and up-to-date models were available to him in the concertos of J. C. Bach and Schobert.

Hasse's artistic relationship with the other great figure of classical music, Joseph Haydn, is of much the same order. Once again, there is evidence that Haydn admired Hasse but little evidence of direct imitation. We know that in 1767 the Austrian master sent off a newly-composed *Stabat Mater* for Hasse to see 'with no other intention than that in case, here and there, I had not expressed adequately words of such great importance, this lack could be rectified by a maestro so successful in all forms of music', and that Hasse responded by writing him a glowing testimonial which Haydn valued greatly.[92] Yet stylistic connections between the two are not obvious. Haydn's early concertos are written after the Viennese fashion, with highly ornamental parts for the soloist.

[91] In one of his letters to Ortez Hasse wrote: 'Il giovine Mozard è certamente portentoso per la sua età, ed io pure lo amo infinitamente', see *Mozart: die Dokumente seines Lebens*, ed. O. E. Deutsch (Kassel, 1961), p. 120.

[92] *The Collected Correspondence and London Notebooks of Joseph Haydn*, ed. H. C. Robbins Landon (London, 1959), pp. 8, 20.

One cannot claim, therefore, that Hasse's concertos were of seminal influence. Yet they remain of interest to both musicians and historians. A few are worthy of revival, although in many cases the quality of individual movements is disturbingly uneven. On the historical side, the concertos excite greater interest: they provide an example of the concerto in its 'pre-pre-classical' state and an illustration of the continuing influence of opera on the concerto genre. Whether this close association with opera was entirely beneficial is a matter for debate. Burney thought not. In the *General History* he wrote:

Indeed, Vinci, Hasse, Pergolesi, Marcello, and Porpora, the great luminaries of vocal compositions, seem never to have had any good thoughts to bestow on music, merely instrumental. Perhaps the superiority of vocal expression requires fewer notes in a song than a sonata; in which the facility of executing many passages that are unfit for the voice, tempts a composer to hazard everything that is new. Thus the simplicity and paucity of notes, which constitute grace, elegance, and expression in vocal Music, render instrumental, meagre and insipid.[93]

At this stage a clear distinction was opening up between composers who were successful in the opera house and those who excelled in the sphere of instrumental music. Tartini recommended composers to specialize in one or the other,[94] the implication being that it was impossible to succeed in both areas simultaneously. Hasse chose to concentrate on operatic music and his instrumental works were profoundly affected by this decision. It was only towards the end of the century that the conflict between the operatic and instrumental style was finally resolved—in the concertos of Mozart.

[93] C. Burney, *A General History of Music*, iv. 546.
[94] W. Kolneder, *Antonio Vivaldi: His Life and Work*, p. 161.

V

Carl Philipp Emanuel Bach

1. Introduction; Career

Four of J. S. Bach's most gifted sons—Wilhelm Friedemann, Carl Philipp Emanuel, Johann Christoph Friedrich, and Johann Christian—were important figures in the history of the concerto, and all four showed a distinct preference for the newly established keyboard concerto. Emanuel Bach was the most prolific concertist of the group. During a long and successful career he produced no fewer than fifty-two keyboard concertos. The majority of these works stem from the Berlin period (1740–68), when Bach[1] was court cembalist to Frederick the Great. Thereafter, the rate of production declines. Only eleven additional concertos were composed between 1768 and Bach's death twenty years later. This decline appears to be directly linked with his departure from Berlin. Around the middle of the eighteenth century the Prussian capital was a thriving centre for instrumental and vocal music. Many of the composers surrounding Frederick the Great were prominent concertists: J. J. Quantz, C. H. and J. G. Graun, and Franz and Georg Benda were all active in this sphere. Moreover, there was a small but lively group of composers who paid special attention to the keyboard concerto. This group included Bach, Nichelmann, and Schaffrath. In the enclosed atmosphere of court life these three composers were thrust into close contact with each other. It was largely due to their activities that Berlin gained recognition as the principal centre for the keyboard concerto in North Germany.

Emanuel's connections with the Berlin school must be seen in relation to his whole career. As a member of the

---

[1] Throughout this chapter the unqualified surname 'Bach' refers to Emanuel, not to his father.

Bach household, he was naturally surrounded by a musical environment from his youth onwards. Although Bach's autobiography[2] is not over-informative regarding the events of these early years, it yields one or two intriguing details. We learn, for example, that Bach received instruction in clavier playing and in the elements of composition from his father, and that he had the stimulating experience of meeting all those distinguished musicians and composers who visited Johann Sebastian's house on their way through Leipzig. As for his formal education, Emanuel was a pupil at the famous Thomasschule during the time of his father's cantorship. Subsequently, he enrolled as a law student at Leipzig University, and three years later (in 1734) moved to Frankfurt-on-the-Oder to continue his academic studies. Here Bach became a prominent figure in musical circles, writing and directing works not only for the local Musik Akademie but also for all manner of public and ceremonial occasions. On completing his law studies in 1738 Emanuel left Frankfurt for Berlin to enter the service of Crown Prince Frederick, later known as Frederick the Great.

Bach joined the Prussian kapelle as a cembalist and we are told that he had the honour of accompanying Frederick's flute playing during the first flute solo played at Charlottenburg after the Prince's accession.[3] But any satisfaction initially derived from Bach's appointment was soon dispelled. There are indications that he did not find his position wholly congenial. When Burney visited Bach in Hamburg during the year 1772, Emanuel remarked that he enjoyed more tranquillity and independence there than at court.[4] And our suspicion of his earlier discontent is further aroused

[2] Bach's autobiographical sketch was originally published in the German edition of Charles Burney's *The Present State of Music in Germany, the Netherlands, and United Provinces*, i.e. C. Burney, *Tagebuch einer musikalischen Reise*, translated into German by C. D. Ebeling (Hamburg, 1772–3; facsimile edition by R. Schaal (Kassel, 1959)), iii. 199–209. For an English translation of the autobiography see W. S. Newman, 'Emanuel Bach's Autobiography', *The Musical Quarterly*, li (1965), 363–72.

[3] C. Burney, *Tagebuch*, iii. 200.

[4] C. Burney, *The Present State of Music in Germany*, ii, 252.

by the fact that Bach made repeated efforts to gain employment elsewhere before eventually leaving Berlin for Hamburg in 1768.[5]

Bach's dissatisfaction was probably occasioned by several factors. In the first place, the artistic climate at Berlin was not particularly progressive. For although, as a young man, Frederick had championed advanced Italian music, his taste did not develop over the years. Consequently, by 1750 he was still an admirer of the Italian style that had been in vogue some twenty years earlier, and would take little account of more recent stylistic developments. Royal approval was, however, bestowed on the operas of C. H. Graun, Agricola, and Hasse, and on the ensemble music of Quantz, whose works provided the staple fare at Frederick's daily concerts. According to Nicolai,[6] Quantz wrote three hundred flute concertos which were performed by Frederick in rotation. To be fair, these concertos are not uniformly dull; but such an unvaried diet could scarcely promote a stimulating musical atmosphere at court.

Bach may also have been dissatisfied with his own status in Berlin. He was evidently not considered a prestigious member of the kapelle, as the pay rolls indicate. Whereas Quantz received 2,000 thalers per annum, together with additional perquisites, Bach's initial salary amounted to 300 thalers only. And when Christoph Nichelmann was appointed in 1744 to share Bach's duties as cembalist, he was offered double Bach's stipend.[7] It has been suggested that there was personal antagonism between the Prussian ruler and Bach, and there may be some truth in this. Certainly Frederick failed to appreciate the peculiar talents of Emanuel. And Bach, for his part, made no effort to conceal his low opinion of Frederick's musicianship.[8] Given all these

[5] When J. S. Bach died in 1750 Emanuel applied unsuccessfully for the cantorship at Leipzig; three years later he was considering moving to Zittau.

[6] C. F. Nicolai, *Anekdoten von König Friedrich II. von Preussen, und von einigen Personen, die um ihm waren* (Berlin and Stettin, 1788–92), vi. 149.

[7] K. Geiringer, *The Bach Family: Seven Generations of Creative Genius*, p. 340.

[8] E. E. Helm, *Music at the Court of Frederick the Great* (Oklahoma, 1960), pp. 174–5.

circumstances, it is not surprising to find Bach contemplating a move.

The opportunity finally came in the summer of 1767, with the death of Bach's godfather, Georg Philipp Telemann. Bach immediately applied for his position at Hamburg. The situation in this republican city, although so different from the enclosed atmosphere of Berlin, was not altogether unfamiliar to Bach. Formerly, he had maintained a correspondence with Telemann, supplying him, on occasion, with the latest music from the Prussian court.[9] Telemann, for his part, had recommended Emanuel as his most suitable successor—advice which the burghers duly accepted. After some difficulty Bach obtained his release from Berlin and was officially installed as Cantor of the Johanneum on 19 April 1768. Although dismissed from Frederick's service, links with the Prussian royal family were not entirely severed for Princess Amalia (Frederick's sister) retained Bach as her personal kapellmeister.

Historians rightly stress the change of circumstances between Bach's life in Hamburg and his earlier years in Berlin. Certainly the two posts were very different. At Hamburg Bach was no longer accountable to an individual patron. He therefore enjoyed a greater measure of artistic and personal freedom and this freedom is, to a certain extent, reflected in the numerous experimental works produced during the Hamburg period. Yet, on another level, Bach's way of life remained unchanged. Court duties had not taken up the whole of his attention in Berlin. He had been active in the city as a composer, teacher, and promoter of private and public concerts. And he had a wide circle of friends among the intellectual élite.[10] A similar picture emerges of Bach's life in Hamburg. Here, his circle of friends included the most distinguished thinkers and writers of the day, among them Lessing, Klopstock, Gerstenberg, Pastor Sturm, and Ebeling. Apart from this select group,

[9] On one occasion Bach sent Telemann a concerto by J. G. Graun, p. 214 note 47.
[10] K. Geiringer, op. cit., p. 342.

however, the ordinary citizens of Hamburg showed little interest in good music and Bach complained bitterly about their lack of taste.[11]

Although Emanuel's position at Hamburg involved the composition of much sacred music, his real interest lay elsewhere—in keyboard writing. While at Berlin, he had produced a theoretical treatise on the art of keyboard playing. This study, which was published under the title *Versuch über die wahre Art das Clavier zu Spielen*,[12] became a standard textbook on the subject. It was read by many leading composers (Haydn included) and was still considered relevant at the turn of the century.[13] But Bach was not merely, or even primarily, a theorist. He was renowned both for his exceptional skill in improvization and for his highly original keyboard compositions. During the course of his artistic career, he produced a wealth of sonatas, rondos, fantasias, and dances for the keyboard.[14] And the same predilection for keyboard writing is found in the concertos, all of which were composed or, in a few cases, later adapted for keyboard soloists.

2. The Concertos: Function, Sources, Instrumentation, Chronological Grouping

Given Bach's abilities as a performer, one might imagine that the concertos were designed for his own use. However, this was not necessarily so, for as Bach himself remarked: 'Among my works, especially those for clavier, there are only a few trios, solos and concertos that I have composed in complete freedom and for my own use.'[15] Some of the concertos may have been written for his pupils, although there is no indication to this effect. It seems likely that Bach

---

[11] C. Burney, *The Present State of Music in Germany*, ii. 251–2.

[12] 2 vols. (Berlin, 1753, 1762).

[13] In 1801 Beethoven recommended the *Versuch* as a primer for the young Czerny.

[14] Bach's compositions for solo keyboard are discussed in a monograph by P. Barford, *The Keyboard Music of C. P. E. Bach* (London, 1965).

[15] In C. Burney, *Tagebuch*, iii. 209; translation from W. S. Newman, 'Emanuel Bach's Autobiography', 363–72.

was aiming at a more general market. There were, after all, numerous amateur musicians in Berlin and Hamburg, and many of Emanuel's solo keyboard works were designed for this sector of the public.[16] Moreover, the six concertos of Wq. 43[17] were certainly published with amateurs in mind, as is evident from the advance publicity:

At the request of many amateurs of music six easy harpsichord concertos by Capellmeister C.Ph.E. Bach are to be published. Without losing any of their appropriate brilliance these concertos will differ from the other concertos of this composer in so far as they are more adapted to the nature of the harpsichord, are easier both in the solo part and the accompaniment, are adequately ornamented in the slow movements and are provided with written-out cadenzas.[18]

Sources

These six works were not the only Bach concertos to be printed during the composer's lifetime. In his autobiographical sketch of 1773, Emanuel cites nine concertos which he personally knew to have been published, namely: Wq. nos. 11, ?14, ?167, and the six concertos of Wq. 43.[19] To this list one must add Wq. 25, which was published in 1752 at the expense of one 'Balthas' Schmid' of Nuremberg,[20] and a

[16] E.g. the sonatas 'mit veränderten Reprisen' and the collections of sonatas, free fantasias, and rondos 'für Kenner und Liebhaber'.

[17] Throughout this chapter the numbering system adopted for Bach's works is that of A. Wotquenne, *Thematisches Verzeichnis der Werke von Carl Philipp Emanuel Bach* (Leipzig, 1905).

[18] This advertisement appeared in the *Hamburgische Unpartheiische Correspondent*, no. 69 (April 1771) and is trans. in L. Crickmore, 'C. P. E. Bach's Harpsichord Concertos', *Music and Letters*, xxxix–xl (1958–9), 237.

[19] Wq. nos. 11 and 43 can be identified positively from Bach's information. He also cites a flute concerto in E major (published by Winter in 1760). No such work is known, but since Winter published an E major *cembalo* concerto in that year it is possible that Bach had forgotten the exact instrumentation of the published version and was referring to Wq. 14. Emanuel also mentions a flute concerto in B♭ major published by Schmidt of Nuremberg in 1752. Unfortunately no copy of this publication has survived but it was probably an edition of Wq. 167, for which a manuscript source is still extant. See W. S. Newman, 'Emanuel Bach's Autobiography', 368.

[20] Although this concerto is not mentioned by Bach in his autobiography it is included in the *Verzeichnis des musikalischen Nachlasses des verstorbenen Capellmeisters Carl Philipp Emanuel Bach* published by his widow at Hamburg in 1790; see H.

few works which found their way to France and England: Wq. 2 (Huberty, Paris, advertised 1762); Wq. nos. 12, 25, and 14 (Walsh, London, c. 1765); and Wq. nos. 18, 24, and 34 (Longman Lukey and Co., London, c. 1775). Discounting duplications, fifteen Bach concertos were printed during his lifetime. In addition, many of his concertos were available from the Leipzig publishing firm of Breitkopf. The Breitkopf catalogues record the incipits of twenty-eight such works—Wq. nos. 32, 8, 20; 34, 29, 18; 16, 19; 6, 5, 24; 28, 26, 33; 2, 10, 27; 12, 17, 35; 46; 1 (listed under Sebastian Bach), together with the six concertos of Wq. 43.[21] Inclusion in these catalogues did not necessarily imply printed publication, since Breitkopf normally distributed their music in manuscript form. (It appears that only those items marked 'intagliate' in the catalogues were definitely available in print.)

Instrumentation

The majority of Bach's keyboard concertos were designed for solo harpsichord and orchestra.[22] Bach referred to these works variously as concertos for 'Cembalo', 'Clavier', or 'Flügel'. But this inconsistency simply reflects the imprecise nature of eighteenth-century terminology. Of the three terms used by Bach, only the latter, Flügel, referred specifically to the harpsichord. The other two were generic terms[23] which covered a range of keyboard instruments, including both harpsichord and clavichord. It is, however, extremely unlikely that Bach's concertos were ever played on the clavichord. This small keyboard instru-

---

Miesner, 'Philipp Emanuel Bachs musikalischer Nachlass', *Bach-Jahrbuch*, xxxv (1938), 103–36; xxxvi (1939), 81–112; xxxvii (1940–8), 161–81.

[21] *The Breitkopf Thematic Catalogue: the Six Parts and Sixteen Supplements 1762–1787*, pp. 132, 292, 479. (Breitkopf also includes the incipit of an F minor concerto (Racc. III no. 2) under Emanuel's name, but this work is now thought to have been written by his brother Wilhelm Friedmann, see p. 340.)

[22] There is also, following the tradition of J. S. Bach's 'Italian' concerto, a solitary concerto for keyboard alone (Wq. 112, no. 1; published 1765).

[23] The term cembalo usually referred to the harpsichord; however, on certain occasions it could refer also to the clavichord. The term clavier was even more general.

ment was not normally used in orchestral music owing to its delicate tone. In addition, there are sound historical reasons for believing that the standard continuo instrument of baroque ensemble music—the harpsichord—was simply elevated from the role of accompanist to soloist. It is inconceivable that the harpsichord should have been supplanted in the concerto (of all genres) by a softer-toned rival.

Exceptionally, Bach calls for other solo keyboard instruments in his concertos. The two works listed as nos. 34 and 35 in Wotquenne's thematic catalogue, were entered in Bach's *Nachlass* (1790) as concertos for organ or clavier.[24] And the surviving autograph of Wq. 34 is simply inscribed 'Concerto per il Organo'. As in the majority of his organ sonatas, so here Bach was thinking in terms of the chamber organ. There is no pedal part and no modification of keyboard style. Of Bach's double concertos, one (Wq. 46) is for two harpsichords, while the other (Wq. 47) is for the unusual combination of fortepiano and harpsichord.[25] A word must now be said about Wq. 47 for this work is unique in many respects. Bach's last concerto, it is the only one which expressly calls for the fortepiano. The two solo instruments are treated equally throughout and there is no idiomatic distinction between their parts. Indeed, one should hardly expect any significant difference of treatment, for at this stage in their development the two instruments sounded not unalike. The tone of the eighteenth-century fortepiano with its thin strings and leather hammers was much lighter and more metallic than that of today's concert grand. When Bach's concerto is performed on historically authentic instruments, the work does not develop into a contest between two unequal assailants, but rather illustrates how much closer the sound of the fortepiano was to the harpsichord than to the resonant modern grand.

[24] H. Miesner, op. cit. 124.

[25] Some experiments with this unusual combination had been made in France by J-Fr. Tapray during the 1770s. His 'Symphonie Concertante pour le Clavecin et le piano, avec Orchestre, . . . op. VIII' was advertised in February 1778 and this was followed shortly by two comparable works. See G. Favre, *La Musique française de piano avant 1830* (Paris, 1953), p. 14.

Wq. 47 was written in 1788,[26] just before Bach's death. Its existence raises the whole question of Bach's attitude towards the fortepiano. Why was he so slow to utilize the new instrument in his concertos? Bach was certainly acquainted with the fortepiano in Berlin, for Frederick the Great possessed a fine collection of instruments by the famous maker Silbermann. It was these pianos that J. S. Bach tried on his historic visit to Berlin in the spring of 1747. But Emanuel Bach's keyboard music at this time was still ostensibly designed for the harpsichord.[27] Only in the 1780s, with the second volume of the collection 'Für Kenner und Liebhaber' did Bach (or his publisher) actually begin to designate works for the fortepiano. Since no keyboard concertos originated between the years 1778 and 1788 we cannot tell whether he would have introduced the new instrument as a soloist at this point or not. The fact remains, however, that certain other composers had changed to the fortepiano a full ten years earlier. Emanuel's stepbrother, Johann Christian Bach, employed the new instrument in his concertos from the early 1770s onwards.[28] And by 1788 the majority of Mozart's piano concertos had been composed: only K. 595 remained to be written. The reason for Emanuel's caution is unclear. But it must be remembered that his conservative attitude was shared by many other members of the Berlin school.

Several of Bach's keyboard concertos also exist in versions for other solo instruments. The relationships between these works are set out in Table 4:

[26] The MS. of Wq. 47, recently re-discovered in the Bibliothek of the Berlin Sing-Akademie, bears the inscription: 'Im Jahr 1788 verfertiget'. Although the score is autograph, this inscription has been added in another hand. However, the concerto is assigned to the same year in Bach's *Nachlass* catalogue, see E. R. Jacobi, 'Das Autograph von C. Ph. E. Bachs Doppelkonzert in Es-dur für Cembalo, Fortepiano und Orchester (W47, Hamburg 1788)', *Die Musikforschung*, xii (1959), 488–9.

[27] It is, of course, possible that Bach's early sonatas were sometimes played on the fortepiano since performers tended to use whichever keyboard instruments were to hand.

[28] The first set of concertos by J. C. Bach (op. 1, 1763) was written 'pour le Clavecin', but from the second set onwards (op. 7, *c.* 1770) J. C. Bach wrote 'per il Cembalo o Piano e Forte'.

Table 4

Keyboard concerto	Corresponding version(s)
Wq. 22	For flute[1]
Wq. 26	(i) for flute (Wq. 166); (ii) for cello (Wq. 170)
Wq. 28	(i) for flute (Wq. 167); (ii) for cello (Wq. 171)
Wq. 29	(i) for flute (Wq. 168); (ii) for cello (Wq. 172)
Wq. 34	For flute (Wq. 169)
Wq. 39	For oboe (Wq. 164)
Wq. 40	For oboe (Wq. 165)

[1] The flute version of Wq. 22 is not recorded in Wotquenne's catalogue. It is, however, mentioned by H. Uldall in *Das Klavierkonzert der Berliner Schule und ihres Führers Philipp Emanuel Bach*, p. 57. The manuscript of the flute version is in D-Bds and a modern edition (for flute) has recently been issued—see Appendix D.

Unfortunately, it is not always possible to determine the priority of the different versions. In one case (Wq. 34 (169)), there is firm evidence that the clavier concerto preceded the version for flute. Uldall[29] states that in the autograph score of Wq. 34 the cembalo part has been crossed out and the flute part added in Bach's own handwriting. But, for the most part, one has to rely on stylistic evidence alone. Wq. 26, 28, and 29 pose a problem as the adaptations have been made with considerable skill and the solo lines differ according to the separate requirements of flute, cello, or keyboard. In Wq. nos. 22, 39, and 40, however, the solo parts are more closely related and the nature of the thematic material suggests that Bach may have intended these works originally for wind instruments rather than the harpsichord.[30] One must also take into account the following passage from the autobiography where Bach states that his compositions at that time (i.e. prior to 1773) included 'forty nine concertos for clavier and other instruments, which last, however, I have also arranged for clavier'.[31] This suggests

[29] H. Uldall, op. cit. 56.

[30] The main theme of Wq. 165, 1st movement, for example, is far better suited to the oboe than to the keyboard.

[31] '. . . 49 Concerten fürs Clavier und andere Instrumente, (welche letzten ich aber auch aufs Clavier gesetzt habe)', C. Burney, *Tagebuch*, iii. 207. The English

that, in certain cases, the keyboard version was indeed the later.

Turning now to the composition of the ripieno group, one is aware of the gradual augmentation of forces common to most forms of orchestral music in the mid–eighteenth century. Bach's Berlin concertos are almost all scored for soloist and string accompaniment (with continuo support), whereas all the concertos of the Hamburg period (1768–88) require additional wind instruments. Only five of the Berlin concertos (namely Wq. nos. 27, 35, 37, 38, and 46) have tutti parts for wind. In one case, Wq. 38 (1763), the flute parts are marked *ad libitum* and are clearly not essential to the whole. And in several other instances it appears that Bach added the extra wind parts at a later date. This view is supported by the fact that one of the concertos, Wq. 27, exists in two quite distinct versions. The autograph score calls for cembalo and strings alone. This is evidently the earlier version, for it reveals the signs of stress associated with the process of composition. The other version demands much larger resources: cembalo, strings, two trumpets (or horns), two oboes, two flutes, and timpani. That these additional wind parts are authentic is shown by the following entry in Bach's *Nachlass* catalogue: 'No. 28. D. dur. B(erlin). 1750. Clavier, 2 Hörner, 2 Violinen, Bratsche und Bass, und nach belieben, 3 Trompeten, Pauken, 2 Hoboen und 2 Flöten.'[32] It is not clear whether the *Nachlass* date refers to the original or revised version. E. N. Kulukundis, the editor of this concerto,[33] argues for the former interpretation by drawing a parallel between Wq. 27 and Wq. 37: Wq. 37 exists in an autograph manuscript to which horn parts were later appended by Bach; the additional wind parts were written

---

translation is from W. S. Newman, 'Emanuel Bach's Autobiography', 371. (Newman apparently assumes that Bach is referring to a clavier reduction of the orchestral parts, but this interpretation seems unnecessarily obtuse.)

[32] H. Miesner, 'Philipp Emanuel Bach musikalischer Nachlass', *Bach-Jahrbuch*, xxxv (1938), 123. (The reference to a third trumpet appears to be erroneous.)

[33] Wq. 27 has recently been issued in a modern edition, ed. E. N. Kulukundis (Madison, 1970), see vol. ii of *Collegium Musicum: Yale University*, second series.

on a different type of paper and were obviously added at a time when Bach's handwriting was deteriorating. Since the calligraphy of these parts is inconsistent with the date given for the concerto in the *Nachlass* (i.e. 1762), Kulukundis assumes that, in the case of Wq. 37, the *Nachlass* date refers to the time of composition rather than to that of later revisions, and he argues, by analogy, that the same is probably true for Wq. 27. Further evidence to suggest that wind parts were added after the completion of these Berlin concertos is provided by Wq. 35 (1759). Here the surviving score is notated in two separate hands. The solo cembalo and string parts are written by a copyist, while the horn parts are in Bach's own handwriting,[34] and were presumably, therefore, a later addition.

We do not know the precise date at which Bach revised these concertos. However, it is probable that most of the revised versions stem from the Hamburg, rather than the Berlin, period. The explanation for this must be sought, not in the move to Hamburg itself, but in the changing attitudes of the time. During the middle years of the century, that is 1740–60, most composers were content with a ripieno of strings only for their keyboard concertos. This was clearly a matter of preference, not of external restrictions: for example, horn players were permanent members of Frederick's kapelle, yet few Berlin concertos composed during the 1740s or 1750s required their services. It was only towards the end of the 1760s that the idea of writing for a larger orchestra spread from the symphony to the keyboard concerto. Bach's gradual augmentation of the ripieno group must therefore be seen as part of a general trend, the timing of which happened to coincide with his departure from Berlin.

All Bach's Hamburg concertos require a basic orchestra of strings and two horns. The horns are used primarily to reinforce the tutti in Allegro movements, but are sometimes

---

[34] See J. R. Stevens, 'The Keyboard Concertos of Carl Philipp Emanuel Bach', unpublished Doctoral dissertation (Yale, 1965), p. 235.

retained for the slow movements as well.[35] Many of the Hamburg concertos also require two flutes. However, these instruments tend to be employed as substitutes for the horns; they play a prominent part in certain slow movements (notably in Wq. 43, nos. 2–6) but seldom appear in the first or last Allegro. Only in Wq. 41 and 47 are the flutes used in conjunction with the horns. Whereas Bach's treatment of the brass instruments is thoroughly up-to-date—his horns supply inner harmony notes in the best symphonic tradition—his treatment of the flutes is, on the other hand, surprisingly conservative. In the slow movements they tend merely to double the violin parts and it is only in Bach's last concerto (Wq. 47) that they are allowed to present independent melodic material.[36] Precisely why Bach chose to employ this particular combination of wind instruments, i.e. flutes and horns, is not clear. The general preference in contemporary symphonies was for oboes and horns, rather than flutes. Yet Bach deliberately avoids this arrangement both in his concertos and in the Sonatinas, a related genre. That Bach was not averse to the tone-colour of the oboe *per se* is self-evident, for several of his symphonies contain oboe parts; moreover, he wrote two concertos for the instrument. Yet, for the ripieno group he preferred the less strident tones of the flute. One can but suggest that he was concerned lest the delicate sound of the harpsichord should be swamped by the powerful combination of oboes and horns within the orchestral tutti.

Chronological Grouping

The earliest known concerto by Emanuel Bach (Wq. 1) dates from 1733 or thereabouts, and the last concerto (Wq. 47) was composed in 1788. His concertos are, therefore, spread over a period of fifty-five years. Most writers divide the works into three groups according to their date

---

[35] E.g. Wq. 41 and 47.

[36] In the 1st movement of Wq. 47 the flutes are used to present important melodic material (see bars 15–17, 19–22). For details of a modern edition, see Appendix D.

and place of composition. The first category consists of three works only—Wq. nos. 1–3. These concertos were all written prior to Bach's Berlin period; Wotquenne dates them 1733, 1734, and 1737 respectively. The vast majority of concertos fall within the second group, comprising all those works which Bach wrote while attached to the Berlin court (from 1738–68). During his early years in Berlin Bach produced a steady stream of concertos at the rate of one or more a year. After 1751 however, his output became more erratic:[37] he composed a group of six concertos between 1753 and 1755 (Wq. nos. 29–34), an isolated work in 1759 (Wq. 35), and a further group of concertos between the years 1762 and 1765 (Wq. nos. 36–40). Towards the end of the Berlin period Bach's interest in the clavier concerto waned. This decline became even more pronounced at Hamburg, for during these last twenty years of his life Bach produced only another eleven concertos (Wq. nos. 41–2, the six concertos of Wq. 43, Wq. nos. 44–5, and Wq. 47).

Both Geiringer and Crickmore,[38] in their studies of Bach's concertos, adopt this tripartite division of his works. But it has certain disadvantages. For although Wq. 1–3 originated in the pre-Berlin period, all three works were subsequently revised during the 1740s and it is these revised versions alone that have come down to us. In practical terms, there is little difference between Wq. 1–3 and other concertos written at the start of the Berlin period. Furthermore, to draw too dramatic a contrast between the Berlin works and those of the Hamburg period is also misleading. For these Hamburg concertos, although experimental in nature, grow out of Bach's earlier works. The discussion which follows, therefore, will deal first with the concertos as a whole, and then proceed to note the special features of the eleven Hamburg concertos.

---

[37] Some writers, notably Jane R. Stevens (op. cit.) subdivide the Berlin period around the years 1751–3 but this results in a number of artificial distinctions being imposed.

[38] K. Geiringer, *The Bach Family: Seven Generations of Creative Genius*; L. Crickmore, 'C. P. E. Bach's Harpsichord Concertos', 227–41.

3. General Planning

Most of Bach's concertos are cast in traditional, three-movement form with the arrangement: fast–slow–fast. The only exceptions occur during the Hamburg period: Wq. 43, no. 4, for example, has four movements in the manner of a classical symphony, and two other concertos written at around the same time have slow introductions.[39] The opening movement is normally an Allegro ('allegro di molto', allegretto, etc.) of sizeable proportions and considerable vitality. Bach follows this with an intensely serious slow movement. His favourite tempo marking here is Adagio or Largo rather than Andante. Frequently, muted strings are required for all or part of the slow movement. This was in keeping with baroque traditions, but whereas a composer like J. S. Bach had reduced the number of instruments participating in the slow movement, the next generation of composers preferred to mute the orchestral strings.[40] For the Finale, Bach employed two principal movement-types: a lively movement in $\frac{6}{8}$ time which had affinities with the old-style Gigue, and the $\frac{2}{4}$ Allegro which was rapidly gaining in popularity at that time. The $\frac{3}{8}$ Finale is not common, and the Minuet is never used by Bach as a final movement. Given the frequency with which Bach employs the Minuet elsewhere, its virtual exclusion from the concertos is particularly interesting.[41] Another type of movement which figures prominently in Bach's clavier works but which is rarely found in the concertos is the Rondo.[42] There are no rondo Finales in Emanuel's concertos, despite the precedent afforded by Sebastian's E major violin concerto (BWV 1042). (Bach's avoidance of both the Minuet and

[39] Wq. 41 (1769) and Wq. 43, no. 5 (1772).

[40] Especially Nichelmann—see D. F. Lee, 'Christoph Nichelmann and the early clavier concerto in Berlin', *The Musical Quarterly*, lvii (1971), 644.

[41] A Minuet appears as the penultimate movement of Wq. 43, no. 4 but this is the only time Bach employs the Minuet in his concertos.

[42] Straight-forward rondo form occurs only once: in the central movement of Wq. 43, no. 2. However, Uldall (*Das Klavierkonzert der Berliner Schule*, p. 51) sees a type of rondo construction in the 3rd movement of Wq. 44 and in the 2nd movement of Wq. 45.

rondo Finale stems from his position within the North German school. There were, at this stage, two distinct schools of concerto composition in Germany, one indigenous to the North of the country and the other to southern states. Few Berlin composers, for instance, favoured either the Minuet or rondo Finale, although both these genres were popular in Austria and the South German territories. The majority of Bach's concertos are rooted in northern traditions; it is only the later works which reflect his growing interest in the South German style.)

As far as key structure is concerned, Bach's Berlin concertos offer few surprises. Major keys predominate,[43] and the two outer movements are always based in the home key of a work. Tonal contrast is provided by the slow movement which is usually in the opposite mode. Thus, in major-key concertos, the preferred tonality for the central movement is either the tonic minor,[44] relative minor, or (less frequently) the mediant minor, while for concertos in a minor home key the preferred tonality is the relative major, submediant major, or (occasionally) the tonic major. The eleven Hamburg concertos exhibit an even wider range of key relationships between movements, as will be apparent later.

4. Ritornello Structures

Bach's Allegro movements are nearly all cast in ritornello form, other formal schemes being extremely rare. Yet Bach did not take over baroque ritornello principles without modification. He experimented with a number of recapitulatory designs which were superimposed on the basic ritornello structure.[45] In fact, Bach's concept of ritornello form was closer to that of the classical era than to the baroque. Most of his Allegro movements include a final

[43] Two out of every three of Bach's Berlin concertos are in the major mode.

[44] It is noticeable that as the years progressed Bach employed the tonic minor more sparingly in his slow movements, preferring the relative minor or subdominant keys.

[45] For a detailed discussion of these experiments see J. R. Stevens, op. cit.

recapitulatory section in which material from the beginning of the movement and/or from the opening of the first solo section is brought back in the tonic key. This is followed by a repeat in the tonic of material from the end of the first solo (previously heard in the dominant or relative key), and the movement is brought to a close with the final ritornello statement. The analogy with sonata principles may be pressed further, for in certain concerto movements by Bach there is a lengthy middle section where important ideas are presented and developed in various keys.[46] Thus, in a four-ritornello movement by Bach, the first solo episode corresponds broadly to the exposition, the second to the development, and the final solo to the recapitulation of classical sonata form. This type of analysis is not wildly anachronistic, for towards the end of the eighteenth century theorists such as Heinrich Koch were themselves describing the concerto in terms of symphonic (i.e. sonata) form.[47]

Although the general outline of Bach's concerto form is comparable to that of the classical composers, there are important differences of detail. First, his concerto movements contain fewer clearly articulated themes. In particular, the important modulation from tonic to dominant which takes place during the first solo episode is not necessarily accompanied by new thematic material. Occasionally Emanuel introduces a lyrical theme at this point (after the manner of J. C. Bach), but he may equally well continue with figurative passages for the soloist in the new key. Secondly, his recapitulations carry far less weight than in the Mozartean concerto. The recapitulation is not presented as the inevitable outcome of the development section; there is little preparation for the return and no distinctive *Ruckführung* as in some of Mozart's works. But perhaps the most striking difference between Bach's concerto form

[46] E.g. Wq. 35, 1st movement, especially bars 69–87, where Bach exploits the contrast between his tutti and solo themes. Details of a modern edition are given in Appendix D.

[47] See J. R. Stevens 'An 18th-Century Description of Concerto First-Movement Form', *Journal of the American Musicological Society*, xxiv (1971), 85–95.

and that of the classical era lies in the number of ritornello statements used. Bach preferred four statements whereas Mozart, and other composers working within Viennese conventions, tended to employ three ritornello statements only—at the beginning and end of a movement, and between the exposition and development sections.[48]

The majority of Bach's Allegro movements then have four statements of the ritornello. These statements are organized according to various ground plans, the two principal schemes being outlined below:[49]

Scheme A

Ritornello 1	Tonic
Solo 1	Tonic to dominant (tonic to relative).[50]
Ritornello 2	Dominant or, exceptionally, the subdominant (relative, or less frequently, the subdominant minor)
Solo 2	Modulatory
Ritornello 3	Key various—*not* the tonic
Solo 3	Modulatory
Recapitulation	Tonic; this section usually *begins with the tutti*
Ritornello 4	Tonic

Scheme B

Ritornello 1	Tonic
Solo 1	Tonic to dominant (tonic to relative)
Ritornello 2	Dominant (relative)
Solo 2	Modulatory
Ritornello 3	Key various, *modulating to the tonic*[51]
Recapitulation	Tonic; this section usually *begins with the solo*
Ritornello 4	Tonic

One of the most important points to emerge from the above is the key of the penultimate ritornello. In Bach's four-ritornello movements, the penultimate ritornello

---

[48] It is true that one sometimes finds remnants of the extra ritornello in Mozart but its importance had been reduced significantly by that stage.

[49] Examples of these formal schemes may be found in the following concerto movements: Scheme A—Wq. 23, 3rd movement; Scheme B—Wq. 40, 3rd movement. Both works are available in modern edition, see Appendix D.

[50] Keys in parenthesis apply to minor mode concertos.

[51] This section often ends on a dominant chord so that the recapitulation may follow with added tonal force, see Wq. 40, 3rd movement, bar 256.

statement never begins in the tonic key, although it may modulate to that key later, as in Scheme B. The deliberate avoidance of the home key at this particular point is highly characteristic of Bach's concerto form. It is at this stage in a movement also that the main divergence between the two ground plans occurs. Whereas in Scheme A the return to the home key is not accomplished until the final solo episode, in Scheme B, the tonic is re-established towards the end of the penultimate ritornello statement. Under Scheme B, the third solo section is normally omitted.[52] so that the penultimate ritornello leads directly into the recapitulation.

The recapitulation itself may be ushered in either by the soloist or by the ripieno (or, on occasions, by both groups acting antiphonally). The actual instrumentation is unimportant; what determines the position of the recapitulation is the presentation, in the tonic, of material from either the beginning of the opening ritornello, or the start of the first solo section.[53] If, as happens sometimes under Scheme A, the tutti presents a substantial portion of the opening ritornello at the beginning of the recapitulation, there is obviously a case for regarding the movement as in five-ritornello form.[54]

Very occasionally a concerto movement will have five or more genuine statements of the ritornello. These are exceptional movements in which Bach enlarges his basic ground plans by inserting additional sections. The Finale of Wq. 27 is a case in point:

Outline structure of Wq. 27, 3rd movement

Bar	Section	Key
1	Ritornello 1	D
56	Solo 1	D to A

[52] Exceptions to this general principle are rare. An instance may be found in Wq. 14, 3rd movement, where the third ritornello modulates to the tonic but is succeeded by another modulatory solo passage before the start of the recapitulation.

[53] In many cases, of course, this material will be identical.

[54] In the 1st movement of Wq. 34 the tutti section commencing at bar 241 may be regarded either as the beginning of the recapitulation (as in scheme A), or as an additional ritornello statement.

91	Ritornello 2	A
113	Solo 2	A, modulatory, A
137	Ritornello 3	A modulatory to E minor
146	Solo 3	E minor modulatory to B minor
202	Ritornello 4	B minor to D
216	*Recapitulation* (begun by solo)	D
276	Ritornello 5	D

Here we are dealing with an extended version of Scheme B. Bach has simply inserted two additional sections (ritornello 3 and its attendant solo episode) into his basic plan. Little else is altered. The penultimate ritornello (in this case, ritornello 4) still modulates from a related key to the tonic, and still leads directly into the (solo) recapitulation.

Having established the broad outlines of Bach's concerto form, we are now in a position to concentrate on finer details. The opening ritornello is often of considerable length—fifty bars of $\frac{4}{4}$ in a moderate allegro tempo is not unusual for Bach. These extensive tuttis usually consist of several different sections, each with its own individual character and specific function. In the early Berlin concertos, the various sections are sometimes set apart from each other as in the following example from Wq. 6:

EXAMPLE 1[55]

Emanuel Bach: Wq. 6, 1st movement, bars 8–13 (short score)

[55] The sources from which examples are drawn are listed in Appendix E.

Here the first section is separated from the *pianoidée* by means of a *fermata* (bar 11).

Several of Bach's ritornelli have the four sections of a typical Berlin concerto: head-motif, contrast motif (known variously as the *pianoidée* or *Kontrastglied*), sequential section, and cadence bars—sections which, following Uldall's classification,[56] may be referred to as A, B, C, and D respectively. The head-motif naturally sets the tone for the entire movement. It may be a lyrical idea, phrased in regular periods, or a striking motif conceived in the symphonic manner. Some of the earlier concertos (e.g. Wq. 6 and 23) open with impetuous themes which foreshadow the wild thematic material of later Viennese *Sturm and Drang* compositions.[57] The second section of the ritornello is usually characterized by a sudden lowering of dynamics and by the introduction of contrasting material. The conventional *pianoidée* with its static bass line in reiterated quavers and its short melodic phrases in parallel thirds or sixths, is found in a number of Bach's concertos, including some of the late works (e.g. Wq. 43, no. 1, 1st movement, bars 9–12). Yet it is not the only type of contrast motif employed by Bach. The main *pianoidée* of Wq. 29, 3rd movement (see bars 17–23), is based on smooth suspensions familiar from late baroque music while the cantabile lyricism of the *pianoidée* in the 1st movement of Wq. 171 seems more typical of Johann Christian, than Emanuel Bach:

EXAMPLE 2

Emanuel Bach, Wq. 171, 1st movement, bars 8–12 (short score)

---

[56] H. Uldall, 'Beiträge zur Frühgeschichte des Klavierkonzerts', *Zeitschrift für Musikwissenschaft*, x (1927–8), 146.

[57] Such as Mozart's G minor symphony (K. 183) of 1773, or Haydn's symphony no. 45 (*The Farewell*) of 1772. For a discussion of the *Sturm und Drang* movement as

The sequential section of the ritornello, particularly in Bach's early concertos, tends to rely on baroque formulas—naturally enough, since the technique of sequential *Fortspinnung* was itself an important feature of the older style. It is in this section that one is most aware of Bach's debt to the past. The bass line frequently moves in a succession of fifths, and occasionally one finds all the apparatus of the *stile antico* with its passages of imitation and chains of suspensions:

EXAMPLE 3
Emanuel Bach, Wq. 6, 3rd movement, bars 5–9

The final section of the ritornello often refers back to the head-motif, thus imparting a nicely rounded form to the ritornello as a whole. This section is strongly cadential in feeling, although Bach seldom repeats the actual cadence bars—he is more concerned with the approach to the cadence than with its conclusion. Various methods are employed to enhance the effect of the final cadence. One of the more conventional ploys is to present the last few bars in unison. Alternatively the cadence may be approached and then avoided at the last moment, this type of delaying tactic being extremely characteristic of Bach. Occasionally an

reflected in music, see B. S. Brook 'Sturm und Drang, and the Romantic Principle in Music', *Studies in Romanticism*, ix/4 (1970), 269–84.

emphatic ending is thrown into sharp relief by the introduction of quiet contrasting phrases a few bars earlier.[58] Sometimes the tonic cadence is preceded by an excursion to a related key. This often takes the form of an interplay between the sharpened and natural fourth degree of the scale, as in the following extract:

EXAMPLE 4

Emanuel Bach, Wq. 2, 3rd movement, bars 33–7 (first violin part only)

Here the presence of an A♮ gives the impression that the music is veering towards the dominant key (B♭ major). The effect is, however, purely transitory and is neutralized by the reintroduction of A♭.

This passage prompts one to examine the key structure of Bach's ritornelli more closely, for although the first ritornello statement begins and ends in the same key—the tonic—there may be several transitory modulations *en route*. The *pianoidée* section, for example, may be presented in the tonic, dominant, or submediant key; occasionally also it appears in the tonic minor. And the sequential section is inherently prone to modulation, although it usually cadences in the home key. There is some distinction between the key schemes adopted for the ritornelli of the opening movement and those employed in the Finale. The most common transitional keys for the opening ritornello of the 1st movement are the dominant (in a major-key movement) and relative (in a minor-key movement). In Bach's Finales, on the other hand, the tonic minor is prominent. Indeed, the opposition between major and minor modes is sometimes exploited with highly dramatic effect. In the first ritornello of Wq. 165, 3rd movement, there is a sudden

---

[58] E.g. Wq. 6, 1st movement, bars 41–5.

switch to the tonic minor at bar 35; the home key is then reinstated after a dramatic general pause:

EXAMPLE 5
Emanuel Bach, Wq. 165, Finale, bars 32–45 (the two outer parts only)

While many of Bach's ritornelli contain all four of the sections discussed above, i.e. head-motif, *pianoidée*, sequential section, and cadence bars, the arrangement of these sections is not stereotyped. Uldall's ABCD plan is simply one of a number of possible arrangements. Sometimes the *pianoidée* is placed after the sequential section, not before (ACBD); at other times the contrast phrase is omitted altogether in favour of a simple tripartite structure (ABD). Sections may also be repeated, either in the same key, or transposed,[59] so that there is considerable variety of construction. The 1st movement of Wq. 14, for instance, has the following plan for its initial ritornello statement: ACBAC, while the first tutti section of Wq. 35, 1st movement, is more symmetrical: ACBCA'. The opening ritornello of this last concerto movement is reproduced in full since it provides an excellent example of Bach's compositional techniques:

[59] In Wq. 165, 1st movement, the head-motif returns in the dominant (Bb, modulating to F minor) at bar 21 of the first ritornello. A similar passage, now firmly anchored in the dominant, reappears thirteen bars before the end of this opening tutti section.

EXAMPLE 6
Emanuel Bach, Wq. 35, 1st movement, bars 1–22 (short score)

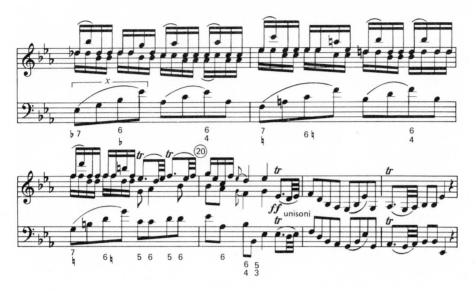

The head-motif (A) is a four-bar phrase of unusual suavity. The quieter repetition of this phrase is then interrupted by a sequential section (C) which, with its bustling semiquavers for the upper strings, is reminiscent of the early symphonic style. Next, the *pianoidée* (B) is heard in the tonic at bars 12–16. This section is immediately recognizable by virtue of its light texture, lower dynamic marking, simple harmonic scheme, and melodic lyricism. At bar 17 there is a return to the sequential material (C) and the ritornello is concluded by two bars (marked *all' unisono*) in which there is a direct reference to the head-motif (A′). But there is another point of interest besides the rondo-like construction. Bach attempts to unify the ritornello so that the various sections, while retaining their separate identity, also have an affinity with each other. He achieves this unity by means of motivic relationships. The sequential section, for example, utilizes a fragment from the head-motif as an accompaniment figure (x). Similarly, the principal idea of the *pianoidée* section germinates from a cell (figure y) already present in the cadence of bar 4. This desire for unification becomes even more marked in Bach's later concertos as we shall see.

The opening ritornello then consists of several different sections which may be organized in a variety of ways.

Subsequent ritornello statements are merely shortened versions of the original.[60] This general point may be illustrated by reference to our previous model—the 1st movement of Wq. 35. Here the four ritornello statements are arranged as follows:

Plan of material used in the ritornello statements of Wq. 35, 1st movement

Ritornello	Bar	Key	Material
1	1–6	E♭	A
	7–12	Modulatory to E♭	C
	12–16	E♭	B
	17–20	Modulatory to E♭	C
	20–2	E♭	A'
2	50–6	B♭	A
	57–62	Modulatory to B♭	C
	62–4	B♭	B
	64–6	B♭	A'
3	101–5	Modulatory to C minor	C
	105–9	C minor to E♭	A' extended
4	142–3	E♭	A
	144–9	Modulatory to E♭	C
	149–51	E♭	A'

It will be noticed that the first ritornello never returns complete, although the second statement repeats a substantial portion of the opening tutti; the *pianoidée* occurs in the first and second ritornelli, but not thereafter; the third ritornello is by far the shortest, lasting a mere eight bars; and the final tutti restates material from the beginning and end of the first ritornello. This arrangement is typical of many concerto movements by Bach, in that, with the exception of the final tutti, the ritornello statements decrease in length as the movement progresses. The same tendency may be observed in concertos by other Berlin composers. However, the full significance of this trend only emerges in the light of subsequent developments: by the classical period the 'third' ritornello had shrunk even further—often to the point of extinction.

---

[60] Exceptionally, however, Bach allows the tutti to develop the initial material in the course of a movement. An example occurs in Wq. 165, 1st movement, where the third ritornello statement (bars 225ff.) is a free development of ritornello motifs.

Before moving on to the solo episodes of Bach's Allegro movements, it seems appropriate to pause and consider the role of the soloist in tutti sections. Throughout the late baroque period the keyboard soloist was, of course, expected to provide the continuo during tutti sections of a concerto. However, during the course of Emanuel's lifetime the custom was gradually dying out. Evidence of this can be found in his own concertos. It is unlikely, for example, that Bach required his soloist to play throughout the shorter tutti passages, since the end of the solo phrase often overlaps with the entry of the ripieno.[61] Furthermore, there is evidence that the cembalo was sometimes omitted from lengthier tutti passages. The printed version of Wq. 14 (published in Berlin in 1760) has rests in the cembalo part throughout the main ritornello statements. Admittedly, the orchestral parts are also sketched in, but these must be a cue—if not why would the printer have added rests at all? The following passage from Bach's *Versuch* may possibly have some bearing on this matter: 'There are many things in music which, not fully heard, must be imagined. For example, in concertos with full accompaniment, the soloist always loses those passages that are accompanied fortissimo and those on which the tutti enters.'[62] Perhaps Bach decided that as the soloist could rarely be heard in loud tutti sections anyway, it might be more realistic to omit the cembalo altogether at such points.

Solo Episodes

When the soloist takes over at the start of the first solo episode, he generally makes some allusion to ritornello ideas in the original key. Frequently the soloist repeats the head-motif unaltered before veering off with his own material. Sometimes, however, the opening of the ritornello

---

[61] As in Wq. 43, no. 2, 1st movement, bar 64, see the eighteenth-century edition (Hamburg, 1772). Two bars later the solo and tutti lines are even less compatible.

[62] C. P. E. Bach, *Versuch*, i. 68–9. The translation is from C. P. E. Bach, *Essay on the true art of playing keyboard instruments*, tr. and ed. by W. J. Mitchell, 2nd edn. (London, 1951), p. 106.

theme is embroidered by the cembalist, as in the following example:

EXAMPLE 7

Emanuel Bach, Wq. 14, 1st movement (beginning of the first solo episode)

(The head-motif of the preceding ritornello is appended for comparison)

Occasionally a substantial portion of the ritornello is repeated at the beginning of the first solo episode in which case the material may be divided between the solo and ripieno groups. The most extended example of this occurs in the 1st movement of Wq. 23 where the ritornello material is given a 'double exposition'—once by the orchestral tutti (ritornello 1) and then antiphonally by the soloist and ripieno. It is interesting that in these antiphonal passages the soloist tends to embroider ritornello ideas while the ripieno confines itself to a plain restatement of the opening tutti (see bars 44ff.).

In some cases, of course, the first episode starts, not with ritornello motifs, but with a new and entirely independent solo theme.[63] The example below is taken from the 1st movement of Wq. 11 where there is a striking (and rather atypical) contrast between the vigorous ritornello theme (a) and the more lyrical solo phrase (b):

---

[63] Only rarely does the soloist present figurative material at this point.

EXAMPLE 8

Emanuel Bach, Wq. 11, 1st movement: (*a*) bars 1–5 (first violin part only); (*b*) bars 30–3 (cembalo part only)

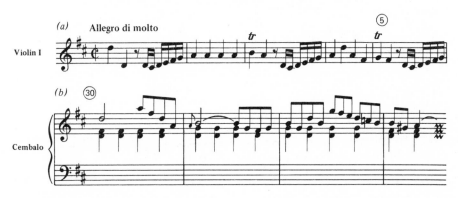

As this solo episode progresses Bach makes the customary modulation from tonic to dominant (or relative) keys in preparation for the second ritornello statement. The modulation is normally effected half-way through the episode and the cadence is followed either by a continuation of figurative material, or by a fresh theme[64] in the new key. This was the point at which classical composers introduced their lyrical second subject. Bach's procedure is slightly different, for although his 'second subjects' are thoroughly compelling they are not usually of the cantabile type associated with J. C. Bach and Mozart. He preferred stronger, more angular ideas as the following extract reveals:

EXAMPLE 9

Emanuel Bach, Wq. 6, 1st movement, bars 68–76

[64] Very occasionally, the second subject is based on previously heard material. This is the case in Wq. 35, 1st movement, where the *pianoidée* from the opening ritornello is pressed into service as a second subject—compare bars 12ff. with 42ff.

Although the second solo episode often begins in similar fashion to the first,[65] it serves a slightly different purpose. Bach is now less concerned with the presentation of melodic material than with the display element. Here the soloist can exhibit the full range of his or her technical ability. The keyboard writing is skilful and includes a variety of idiomatic figures which lie well under the fingers. Particularly characteristic are the series of broken chords which Bach distributes neatly between the hands.[66] A similar accent on virtuosity marks the third solo section, when one is present.

In all Bach's solo episodes the tutti plays an important role. Like his father, Emanuel seizes every opportunity to lace these sections with ritornello motifs—either in the form of tutti interruptions or as a thematic accompaniment to solo work. Throughout, it is noticeable that the development of ritornello ideas is entrusted to the ripieno rather than to the soloist. A typical example occurs in the second solo episode of Wq. 23, 3rd movement. Here Bach distorts the head-motif of the ritornello and uses it to create a pseudo-contrapuntal texture for the ripieno group. The motif is presented both in its original rhythmic form (x) and in augmentation (y). In a passage such as this it is the orchestral parts that are of supreme importance—the keyboard player merely adds an ornamental arabesque to the whole:

EXAMPLE 10
Emanuel Bach, Wq. 23, 3rd movement: (a) ritornello head-motif (first violin part only); (b) bars 196–201 (full score)

[65] As in Wq. 35, 1st movement—compare bars 23ff. with 67ff.
[66] E.g. Wq. 23, 3rd movement, bars 405–18.

The Final Section

We turn now to the final section of Bach's ritornello movements—the so-called recapitulation. Here the strict rules governing the alternation of solo and tutti sometimes break down, for this section may begin either with the ripieno, with the soloist or, occasionally, with the two groups acting antiphonally (as in Wq. 23, 1st movement, bars 253ff.). The actual arrangement of material, however, follows a more predictable course. After an initial reference to ritornello ideas there is some repetition of material from the beginning of the first solo section.[67] Then one of the figurative passages returns. This material is usually culled from the first solo episode (as in Wq. 34, 1st movement—compare bars 74ff. with 279ff.), but may also derive from the second solo (as in Wq. 6, 1st movement—compare bars 152ff. with 238ff.). Just before the final ritornello Bach recapitulates, in the tonic key, material from the end of the first solo section. This necessarily involves transposition from dominant to tonic keys. The parallel with sonata form is obvious and becomes especially pronounced when, as in the 1st movement of Wq. 25, a true 'second subject' from the end of the first solo is recapitulated in the home key.

While most ritornello movements by Bach have a final section on these lines, the generalizations do not, of course, apply in every single case. On the one hand there are movements such as the opening Allegro of Wq. 29 where the final (tonic) section can scarcely be termed a recapitulation at all. There is some repetition of material in a dominant/tonic relationship, it is true,[68] but not enough to distinguish its form from that of a progressive Vivaldian movement. The beginning of the recapitulation is ill defined and the whole section has more in common with an additional solo episode than with a genuine restatement of

[67] If the soloist has presented an independent theme at the beginning of the final solo section this theme will always be recapitulated by the soloist—never given to the ripieno alone or split up between the two groups.

[68] Bars 56–9 are transposed from the dominant to the tonic for the 'recapitulation', see bars 163–6. Details of a modern edition are given in Appendix D.

material. At the other end of the scale, there are movements such as the first Allegro of Wq. 23 where almost every bar of the final section has been heard at some earlier point.[69] And, inevitably, there are hybrid movements standing midway between these two extremes. In such cases the final section is partly based on repeated material and partly devoted to fresh solo figuration, the last movement of Wq. 35 providing an example.[70]

The Cadenza

Towards the end of the final section there will frequently be a *fermata* for the cadenza.[71] As in the classical concerto, so here Bach pauses on a second inversion chord.[72] The approach to the cadenza is also surprisingly progressive with the bass line rising a semitone:

EXAMPLE 11
Emanuel Bach, Wq. 14, 1st movement, approach to the cadenza
(cembalo part)

The original publisher of this concerto, Winter, did not supply any cadenzas—understandably since at that time (1760) a written-out cadenza was still the exception rather than the rule, performers being expected to improvise (or 'pre-compose') their own. Yet we have some guide as to the

---

[69] Only six bars (270–5) of this recapitulation section are newly composed.

[70] Bars 207–17 contain fresh figurative material for the soloist.

[71] Occasionally the cadenza is inserted before the recapitulation, as in the Finale of Wq. 34.

[72] For an assessment of Bach's role in the development of the cadenza, see H. Knödt, 'Zur Entwicklungsgeschichte der Kadenzen in Instrumentalkonzert', *Sammelbände der Internationalen Musik-Gesellschaft*, xv (1914), 375–419.

type of improvisation envisaged. There exists, in the Library of the Brussels Conservatoire, a collection of eighty candenzas to Bach's concertos.[73] Although the manuscript is not autograph its contents are likely to be authentic since it forms part of the famous Westphal collection.[74] Internal evidence also favours Bach's authorship, for the cadenzas were obviously written by a keyboard player with outstanding improvisatory ability; moreover, they are similar in style to those cadenzas which Bach supplied for the printed edition of his Wq. 43 set (Hamburg, 1772). From all this material some general points emerge. Bach seldom utilizes recognizable melodic fragments in his cadenzas; indeed, he goes out of his way to avoid any relationship between the cadenza material and that of the movement in question. His purpose is simply to introduce within the strict framework of concerto form, a fantasia-like interlude. The rhapsodic nature of the following example, with its non-melodic content and free rhythm is highly characteristic of Bach's cadenza style. Pre-composed, it is artfully designed to give an impression of spontaneity:

EXAMPLE 12
Emanuel Bach, Wq. 43, no. 1, 1st movement, bars 181–5

---

[73] B–Bc (U. no. 5871).

[74] Johann Jakob Heinrich Westphal (d. 1825) was an avid collector of Bach's music. His copies probably derive from those in Bach's own library since he was personally

5. Slow Movements

Structurally, the slow movements of Bach's concertos are closely related to the quick ones, in that the ritornello principle is of paramount importance to both. Yet there is, naturally, some modification of design. As the tempo of a movement decreases so it is essential for the ritornello structure to be compressed. Bach's slow movements are therefore more concise: no movement contains more than four ritornello statements and a few have only three main tutti sections—in tonic, dominant (relative), and tonic keys. While the majority of slow movements have a recapitulation of sorts, this section is not particularly extensive. Furthermore, the beginning of the recapitulation is sometimes obscured, for the return to tonic tonality does not necessarily coincide with the reappearance of essential material. As a rule, there are fewer independent solo themes in Bach's slow movements than in the Allegros. The soloist is heavily dependent on ritornello material, and the technique of ornamental variation assumes greater significance.[75]

The amount of ornamentation in the solo part varies considerably from work to work. In one case, there are two versions of the solo part for the same slow movement (Wq. 25). The plainer version was published by Balthasar Schmid of Nuremburg in 1752. The other, more elaborate

---

acquainted with the composer (see C. H. Bitter, *Carl Philipp Emanuel Bach und Wilhelm Friedemann Bach und deren Brüder* (Berlin, 1868), ii. 305). For further information concerning Westphal, see M. Terry, 'C. Ph. E. Bach and J. J. H. Westphal—a Clarification', *Journal of the American Musicological Society*, xxii (1969), 106–15.

[75] Uldall cites as an example the slow movement of Wq. 33 where the soloist adds delicate embellishments to the ritornello theme, see H. Uldall, *Das Klavierkonzert der Berliner Schule und ihres Führers Philipp Emanuel Bach*, pp. 39–40.

version has survived in two manuscript sources, both of which have claims to authenticity.[76] A short extract from both versions is given below. Those familiar with Bach's sonatas 'mit veränderten Reprisen' will recognize the distinctive style of ornamentation employed here:

EXAMPLE 13

Emanuel Bach, Wq. 25, 2nd movement, bars 26–9, cembalo part: (a) in the printed (unelaborated) version; (b) as it appears in the manuscript GB-Lbm (K. 7, i. 10)

6. The Hamburg Concertos

During the years at Berlin Bach developed and perfected the structural methods outlined above. After the move to Hamburg, however, there was a noticeable change of approach. He became more inclined to experiment, more receptive to influences from other parts of Europe. This desire to experiment is most prominent in the six concertos of Wq. 43. These works, published in October 1772, were composed with amateurs in mind,[77] yet from the point of view of structure, they are among the most adventurous

---

[76] Preserved at GB-Lbm (K. 7, i. 10) and B-Bc (U. no. 14, 885). The Brussels copy is contained in a book of keyboard pieces reputedly copied from Bach's autographs. The London copy (which is virtually identical) was acquired from the library of F. Gehring, L. Crickmore, 'C. P. E. Bach's Harpsichord Concertos', 238.

[77] See p. 289.

concertos ever written by Bach. Thereafter the urge to
innovate diminished, and Bach's last concerto (Wq. 47),
although advanced in style and unique in its combination of
solo instruments, is disappointingly conventional in structure.

While stressing the experimental nature of the eleven
Hamburg concertos, one must not forget their relationship
to Bach's earlier works. For example, the fast movements of
these late concertos are still based on ritornello principles.
This remains true even of Wq. 43, no. 2, where the Finale
purports to be in binary form.[78] Ritornello structure also
provides the basis for the opening movement of this concerto despite its rapid alternation of tempo from 'allegro di
molto' to andante. On the surface, the slow movements of
the Wq. 43 set appear more revolutionary, for on several
occasions Bach omits the final ritornello.[79] But this is not
innovation for its own sake: many of the slow movements
are designed to lead straight into the Finale and a closing
ritornello would only impede the link.

The Linking of Movements

The linking of movements is, in fact, one of the most
striking features of the Hamburg concertos. To be sure,
Bach had already made tentative experiments along these
lines during the Berlin period: the Adagio of Wq. 31 ends
inconclusively, thus preparing us for the last movement
which Bach intended to follow without a break;[80] and a
similar procedure may be observed in Wq. 30 where the
central movement is only separated from the Finale by a
brief, measured rest. But during the Hamburg period these
experiments became standard practice. In Wq. 41, 44, and
47, for instance, the last two movements are joined, and in

[78] See Crickmore's analysis, which brings out the duality of the sonata/ritornello
structure, in 'C. P. E. Bach's Harpsichord Concertos', 233f.

[79] Not, however, in Wq. 43, no. 2, where a final statement of the ritornello is
needed to complete the rondeau scheme, see p. 325.

[80] In the autograph manuscript of Wq. 31 (D- Bds (Mus. ms. P. 352)) the
following instructions appear at the end of the 2nd movement: 'Das Allegro fällt
nach diesem Adagio, ohne den geringsten Zwischenraum sogleich ein'.

the six concertos of Wq. 43 each movement leads directly into the next. The link passages take various forms. In some cases (as also in Wq. 30) Bach simply uses an imperfect cadence to bridge the movements; this device is effective up to a point, but can sound a little gauche. Other concertos have a more sophisticated transitional passage during which Bach effects a modulation to the key of the following movement. Occasionally Bach's link passages display remarkable ingenuity, as in Wq. 43, no. 1, where the transition from the 1st movement to the 2nd is inspired. During the opening ritornello of this concerto the following passage occurs:

EXAMPLE 14
Emanuel Bach, Wq. 43, no. 1, 1st movement, bars 18–21 (cembalo part only)

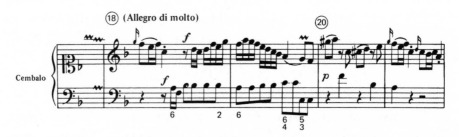

When, at the end of this movement, Bach is approaching the Andante, he simply repeats his ritornello passage; but the G# appoggiatura of the original is now treated as an essential note and becomes, by enharmonic change, the first A♭ of the slow movement:

EXAMPLE 15
Emanuel Bach, Wq. 43, no. 1, bars 194–7 (cembalo part only)

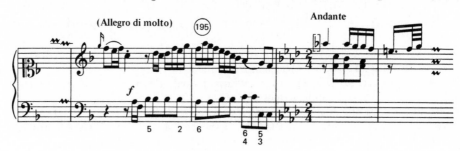

The linking of movements is symptomatic of Bach's new approach. Previously he seemed to regard the concerto as a motley collection of individual movements with no overall unity. During the Hamburg period, however, he became more concerned with the total impression of a work and with the unification of its separate parts. The linking of movements provided temporal continuity throughout a concerto and was, therefore, important. Even more fruitful, however, was the integration of movements through thematic cross reference.

Thematic Integration

Bach's penchant for thematic integration had emerged early in his career. We have already seen how he unified the various sections of the ritornello by this method while at Berlin. After his move to Hamburg, Bach employed the technique in a wider arena, using thematic relationships between movements to unify the concerto as a whole. There are several examples in the six concertos of Wq. 43. The slow introduction of Wq. 43, no. 5, commences with a theme which later forms the basis of the central slow movement, and in Wq. 43, no. 3, the opening theme of the first Allegro recurs during the course of the Larghetto. This last example is the more subtle of the two, for the slow movement opens with unrelated material (*b*) and the Allegro theme (*a*) does not reappear until bar 16 (*c*).

EXAMPLE 16
Emanuel Bach, Wq. 43, no. 3 (cembalo part only); (*a*) 1st movement, bars 1–3; (*b*) 2nd movement, bars 1–4; (*c*) 2nd movement, bars 16–19 (variant of (*a*))

Even more radical is the thematic unification of Wq. 43, no. 4. The whole structure of this work is unconventional. Superficially there appear to be four movements, but the first Allegro is incomplete. Bach has, in fact, divided the opening movement into two portions, the second of which is presented at the end of the concerto—after a Larghetto and a 'tempo di menuetto'. As if to emphasize the curious structure of this work, Bach brings back the main themes of the Larghetto and Minuet during the Finale. Two comparable examples spring immediately to mind: first, Mozart's piano concerto K.271 (1777) in which a Minuet movement is interpolated into the Finale, and secondly, the famous recitative section of Beethoven's Choral Symphony with its reminiscence of themes from earlier movements.

It was during the Hamburg period also that Bach began to experiment with the slow introduction. Two of the late concertos have introductions of this type: Wq. 41 (1769) and Wq. 43, no. 5 (1772). The slow introduction was, presumably, an import from the symphony. Haydn had, of course, experimented with the symphonic slow introduction as early as 1761 or thereabouts,[81] although it only became an established part of his technique in the 1780s and 1790s. The transference of the slow introduction from symphony to concerto was attempted sporadically by composers in the

81 E.g. the opening of symphonies nos. 6 and 7, could all be construed in this fashion.

1770s but met with little general acceptance. And by 1793 the German author Koch still regarded it as a novelty.[82]

Bach's growing desire for strange and novel effects is reflected in the key schemes of these late concertos, for the types of relationship used are noticeably more adventurous than before. The most revolutionary concerto in this respect is, again, Wq. 43, no. 4. The work opens with an Allegro in C minor; this is followed by a slow movement in D minor: the Minuet reverts to E♭, but the tonal balance is further disturbed by the Finale which begins in F minor before modulating back to the home key of C minor. Other concertos reveal Bach's predilection for supertonic relationships and for keys a third apart.[83] The slow movement of Wq. 43, no. 2, in D is in the supertonic key (E minor). Furthermore, within this Andante movement there is an inspired contrast between the tonal stability of the tutti sections (all three ritornello statements are in E minor) and the two solo episodes, which are in E and G major respectively. This results in a rondo-like structure in which the three primary key areas (E minor, E major, and G) play an immensely important role:

Outline structure of Wq. 43, no. 2, 2nd movement

Bar[84]	Key	Section	Material
318	E minor	Tutti	Ritornello (A)
324	E	Solo	(B)
340	E minor	Tutti	Ritornello (A)
346	G	Solo	(B)
362	E minor	Tutti	Ritornello (A)
367	E minor to D	Tutti	Link phrase

---

[82] 'Man hat seit kurzem angefangen, auch dem ersten Allegro des Concertes einen solchen kurzen Einleitungssatz von langsamer Bewegung und von ernsthaftem Charakter vorher gehen zu lassen, der bey den modernen Sinfonien gebräuchlich', H. C. Koch, *Versuch einer Anleitung zur Composition*, 3 vols. (Rudolstadt and Leipzig, 1782–93; reprint 1969), iii. 335.

[83] Wq. 43, no. 3, and Wq. 47 have a similar key scheme, the three movements of each concerto being cast in E♭, C, and E♮ major respectively.

[84] Bar numbers are reckoned from the beginning of the entire concerto.

7. Sonatina Influence

Several writers, including Geiringer and, more recently, Jane Stevens, have observed similarities between Bach's Hamburg concertos and the Sonatinas for solo keyboard instrument(s)[85] and orchestra which he composed towards the end of his Berlin period (1762–4). Some account must therefore be given of these rather strange works. Although the instrumentation of the Sonatinas recalls that of a conventional concerto the actual treatment of solo and ripieno groups is very different. Occasionally the soloist may achieve independence by virtue of idiomatic figuration, but for the most part the soloist co-operates with the ripieno in the joint presentation of material. In fact, Bach's Sonatinas are more closely related to the Austrian Divertimento than to the traditional concerto. The number of movements varies widely in individual works—one Sonatina has no fewer than eight movements—and the forms used (i.e. binary, rondo) are those of the suite. Other features which suggest kinship between the Sonatina and the Divertimento are the tonal unity within individual works (all movements in any one Sonatina being in the same key); the prevalence of dance movements, particularly the Minuet; and a certain levity of style more properly associated with popular music. These works are not, therefore, genuine concertos, a fact which Bach implicitly acknowledged by his choice of title.

How far, then, are Bach's Hamburg concertos comparable to his Sonatinas? There are a number of obvious similarities between the two. In the first place, their instrumentation corresponds: most of the Sonatinas are scored for solo keyboard, strings, flutes, and horns, and the Hamburg concertos share this instrumentation. In the second place, it appears that Bach transferred certain Divertimento-like forms from the Sonatinas to the late concertos. The central movement of Wq. 43, no. 2, as we

---

[85] Ten are for one solo instrument; the other two (Wq. 109, 110) are for two keyboard instruments. Although Wotquenne lists fifteen Sonatinas in his catalogue, three are duplications (compare Wq. nos. 101, 104, 105 with nos. 106, 107, 108).

have seen, has affinities with rondo form. In the same way, the Minuet now makes its début (as the penultimate movement of Wq. 43, no. 4). Exceptionally, also, Bach admits binary structures to other parts of the concerto, the Finale of Wq. 43, no. 2, being in a rare combination of ritornello and binary form.[86] And the evidence is augmented by a number of smaller points such as the tonal unity of Wq. 43, no. 5, whose three movements are all in the same key, and the 'popular' character of certain concerto themes:

EXAMPLE 17

Emanuel Bach, Wq. 43, no. 6, 3rd movement, bars 1–4 (cembalo part only)

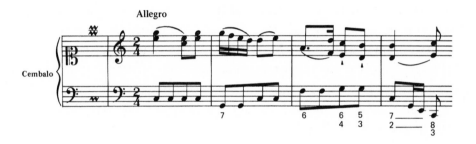

In all these respects[87] there is some measure of correspondence between the Sonatinas and the Hamburg concertos which is not present in concertos of the Berlin period.

Yet we must look beyond the Sonatinas to find the ultimate source of inspiration for these late concertos. In 1756 the Austrian composer Georg Christoph Wagenseil (1715–77) visited Berlin during a European concert tour. We do not know which of Wagenseil's works were performed in the Prussian capital, but some manuscript copies of his music found their way into the famous Thulemeier collection at Berlin and may well have been known to Bach. One of the works in the Thulemeir collection is a Diver-

[86] There is no precise parallel for this hybrid since Bach avoids ritornello structures in his Sonatinas.

[87] Jane Stevens tries to show that the break-down of tutti/solo opposition which occurs in the recapitulation sections of several late concertos is related to the special treatment of solo and tutti instruments in the Sonatinas (J. R. Stevens, *The Keyboard*

timento in A major for obbligato cembalo and strings (two violins and bass).[88] Since the Divertimento was not indigenous to North Germany,[89] scholars have inferred that it was Wagenseil who inspired the composition of Bach's Divertimento-like Sonatinas. In addition, it is likely that Bach knew some of Wagenseil's concertos, for his friend Grave possessed many such works by contemporary Viennese composers.[90] Even a cursory examination of Wagenseil's concertos will show that they exhibit several features characteristic of Bach's Hamburg works. They are written, as one would expect, in the South German tradition and possess a light-hearted quality more akin to the Divertimento than to the concerto proper. The Minuet appears with some frequency, and binary forms also gain admittance on occasion. It seems plausible, therefore, that both the Sonatinas and the Hamburg concertos represent the fruits of Bach's acquaintance with the southern style—a style which, by the 1770s, had established itself over much of Europe and was the direct precursor of the Viennese classical idiom.

8. Stylistic Features

Although the concertos span fifty-five years of Bach's working life, they are remarkably consistent in style. To find such consistency among the very early works of a composer is particularly surprising. However, two factors must be taken into account. First, the original versions of

---

Concertos of Carl Philipp Emanuel Bach). However, rapid alternation between solo and ripieno groups is already latent in Bach's earlier concertos—witness the dialogue between cembalo and orchestra in the 1st movement of Wq. 23.

[88] No. 283 in the collection, see R. Eitner, 'Thematischer Katalog der von Thulemeier'schen Musikalien-Sammlung in der Bibliothek des Joachimsthal'schen Gymnasiums zu Berlin', Supplement to *Monatshefte für Musikgeschichte*, xxxi (1899, reprint New York, 1960). The Divertimento in question is dated 3 July 1763. Bach's Sonatinas were written between 1762 and 1764.

[89] Its true home was Vienna. The concertante Divertimento was cultivated not only by Wagenseil but also by the young Haydn, see work-group xiv of A. van Hoboken, *Joseph Haydn: Thematisch-bibliographisches Werkverzeichnis*, vol. i. (Mainz, 1957).

[90] See H. Engel, *Das Instrumentalkonzert*, vol. i. (Wiesbaden, 1971), p. 217.

Wq. 1–3 have disappeared, so that there are no genuine examples of Bach's earliest concerto style. Secondly, and this may have some bearing on the first point, we know that Bach deliberately destroyed a number of his more youthful works.[91] This is obviously unfortunate from the historian's point of view as it becomes difficult to chart the exact course of his early development.

In the absence of hard facts, speculation becomes a tempting, if hazardous, occupation. One might reasonably expect Bach to have modelled his earliest works on the concertos of Tartini and his followers,[92] which were then in fashion. Superficially, this appears to be the case, for certain early concertos by Bach (notably Wq. 5, 1st movement, written 1739, revised 1762) do exhibit the rhythmic and melodic clichés of the Italian galant idiom. Yet, at the same time, the complexity and emotionalism of Bach's early concertos is utterly foreign to the Italian manner. The colourful, expressive elements associated with the *Empfindsamkeit* style are present early on, as the following brief extract from Wq. 2 reveals. Here, already, is the upward appoggiatura (F#) so characteristic of Bach's mature style. Here, too, the poignant false relations between outer parts (E♭–E♮) at the approach to the cadence:

EXAMPLE 18

Emanuel Bach, Wq. 2, 1st movement, bars 35–6 (cembalo part)

---

[91] In a letter (dated 1786) to J. J. Eschenburg of Brunswick, Bach stated that he had burnt several early manuscripts, E. F. Schmid, *C. P. E. Bach und seine Kammermusik* (Kassel, 1931), pp. 75–7.

[92] One of Tartini's pupils was J. G. Graun, Frederick's konzertmeister in Berlin and Bach's colleague.

Although Bach could, and sometimes did, adopt other styles, he found the expressive manner most congenial.[93] Even towards the end of his life, when attempting to assimilate the influences of South German music, he never wholly abandoned his earlier methods. Wq. 47 was written in 1788 at the height of the classical period. Yet it is curiously ambivalent in style. The following passage is typical: while the melody itself displays the smooth contours and equable rhythms of the classical idiom, the short-breathed phrase structure recalls the limitations of the earlier galant style. Nor is Bach's expressive manner far away. In the fifth bar the stable C major tonality suddenly gives way with the intrusion of a Bb, played forte in the bass part. It is clear from this passage that, although Bach was striving towards a more classical style, the eccentricities of his earlier manner persisted.

EXAMPLE 19

Emanuel Bach, Wq. 47, 2nd movement, bars 1–8 (short score)

Bach's views on aesthetics are well documented both in the autobiography and in the *Versuch*. His central doctrine

---

[93] Charles Burney, in a discussion of Bach's keyboard playing, wrote: 'he possesses every style; though he chiefly confines himself to the expressive', *The Present State of Music in Germany*, ii. 271.

emerges clearly: 'music primarily must touch the heart'.[94] And his views on performance were similar: 'A musician cannot move others unless he too is moved. He must of necessity feel all of the effects that he hopes to arouse in his audience, for the revealing of his own humour will stimulate a like humour in the listener'.[95] These pronouncements on the nature of music are all commensurate with a romantic view of art. Moreover, to judge from contemporary reports, Bach, the performer, cut a romantic figure. Burney described his improvisations in the following terms:

After dinner, which was elegantly served, and chearfully eaten, I prevailed upon him to sit down again to a clavichord, and he played, with little intermission, till near eleven o'clock at night. During this time, he grew so animated and *possessed*, that he not only played, but looked like one inspired. His eyes were fixed, his underlip fell, and drops of effervescence distilled from his countenance.[96]

The same sensitivity characterizes Bach's compositions. In his concertos, particularly those of the Berlin period, he uses all possible resources to stir the emotions of his audience. Many of the more expressive movements draw their inspiration from vocal models. There is a striking, if also exceptional, example of this in the Adagio of Wq. 31 (1752). Here the solo cembalo is given an impassioned recitative in free rhythm which the orchestra interrupts from time to time with considerable dramatic force. The rhetorical effect is enhanced by the use of violent dynamic contrasts within these tutti sections (ranging from *pp* to *ff*) and by abrupt changes of tempo (from adagio to presto).[97] Other slow movements are modelled on the aria. In a movement such as the 'adagio sostenuto' from Wq. 35, the exquisite cantabile writing has its roots in vocal technique:

---

[94] See Bach's autobiography in C. Burney, *Tagebuch*, iii. 209.
[95] C. P. E. Bach, *Essay on the true art of playing keyboard instruments*, p. 152.
[96] C. Burney, *The Present State of Music in Germany*, ii. 270.
[97] See H. Uldall, *Das Klavierkonzert der Berliner Schule*, p. 39.

EXAMPLE 20

Emanuel Bach. Wq. 35, 2nd movement, bars 1–4 (short score)

The transference of this song-like idiom to the keyboard did, of course, create certain difficulties, for the harpsichord lacked the sustaining power of voices and strings. That the problem exercised Bach to a considerable degree is evident from his autobiography where he states that his 'chief effort, especially in recent years, has been directed towards both playing and composing as songfully as possible for the clavier, notwithstanding its lack of sustaining power. This is not at all easy if the ear is not to be left too empty and the noble simplicity of the melody is not to be disturbed by too much bustle.'[98]

The writing of cantabile melodies was, however, only one method of achieving an expressive style. Many of Bach's Allegro movements make their impact by other, more direct means. In the 1st movement of Wq. 23 the irregular phrase structure of the opening theme, its wide leaps, dramatic trill figures, and vital dotted rhythms all combine to produce an impression of impetuosity. And the drama is reinforced by abrupt dynamic contrasts. This is not the ornamental dynamic shading of the rococo, with its excessively rapid vacillation between extremes;[99] the dynamic contrasts here are all dependent on the nature of the material used. So, in bar 9 the lengthy appoggiatura is played pianissimo, while the precipitous melodic descent of bar 11 is marked forte:

[98] C. Burney, *Tagebuch*, iii. 209. Trans. from W. S. Newman, 'Emanuel Bach's Autobiography', 372.

[99] The ornamental use of dynamics is occasionally encountered in Bach's early works, see Wq. 6, 1st movement, bars 64–5, where almost every crotchet bears a separate dynamic marking.

EXAMPLE 21

Emanuel Bach, Wq. 23, 1st movement, bars 1–14 (short score)

The extended appoggiatura of the previous example directs our attention to another facet of Bach's style—his predilection for expressive melodic dissonance. A great variety of melodic dissonance is found in his music, including appoggiaturas, suspensions, anticipations, and changing note patterns. Of these, the first and last are the most prevalent. The appoggiatura, which Bach once described as among the 'most essential' of ornaments,[100] appears in all shapes and guises (rising, falling, chromatic, diatonic, brief, extended) with plain or ornamental resolutions. It is often used in conjunction with conventional rhythmic patterns (♪♫♪ or ♫♪) to produce the pathetic sighs of 'galant' music. The changing note formula is responsible for

[100] 'Die Vorschläge sind einer der nöthigsten Manieren', C. P. E. Bach, *Versuch*, i. 55.

a particularly idiomatic turn of phrase which occurs frequently in Bach's work and is capable of extreme poignancy:

EXAMPLE 22
Emanuel Bach, Wq. 43, no. 2, 2nd movement, bars 326–7

A rhythmic variant of this same melodic pattern (a) is an important thematic element in the opening movements of Wq. 32 and 25.

Bach's expressive style depends, for the most part, on melodic, rather than harmonic, dissonance. That is to say, the dissonances are normally concentrated in the leading (upper) part. But his harmonic writing, although surprisingly consonant, lacks neither direction nor colour. The richness of his harmonic palette may be illustrated by the following extract from the slow movement of Wq. 171, where augmented sixth chords and diminished triads abound:

EXAMPLE 23
Emanuel Bach, Wq. 171, 2nd movement, bars 1–6 (short score)

In the above, the sense of harmonic purpose is strong and there is a logical progression to cadence points. Occasionally, however, Bach introduces a 'directionless' passage for special effect. During the central movement of Wq. 165, for example, there is a prolonged drift of chromaticism. Here a sense of order is maintained only by the linear movement of the outer parts (see bars 11–16). Sometimes, too, the stability of the harmonic pulse is deliberately undermined. In the following example Bach exploits the conflict between the metric stress (which occurs on every first and fourth quaver) and a superimposed cross-rhythm generated by the sophisticated use of suspensions:[101]

EXAMPLE 24

Emanuel Bach, Wq. 26, 2nd movement, bars 8–10

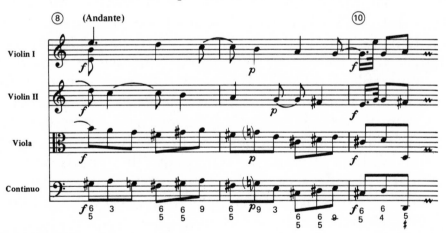

A passage such as this shows just how far Bach was prepared to go in his search for new and moving effects.

[101] The first two suspensions are quite regular, but from the last beat of bar 8 onwards three of the four dissonances occur on weak quaver beats.

9. Bach's Relationship to the Contemporary Scene

In its own day, Bach's style was considered rather strange and unorthodox. Any links between his music and that of earlier periods either escaped the attention of contemporary critics or did not occasion comment. Burney recommended Bach's compositions enthusiastically, with the proviso that 'the style of this author is so uncommon, that a little habit is necessary for the enjoyment of it'.[102] A similar attitude is reflected in the following passage, where Burney compares Bach and Domenico Scarlatti:

Both were sons of great and popular composers, regarded as standards of perfection by all their contemporaries except their own children, who dared to explore new ways to fame. Domenico Scarlatti, half a century ago, hazarded notes of taste and effect, at which other musicians have but just arrived, and to which the public ear is but lately reconciled; Emanuel Bach, in like manner, seems to have outstript his age.[103]

Burney's comparison is helpful—not least for its recognition that Bach and Domenico Scarlatti, as sons of distinguished composers, were placed in a comparable situation. Nor was that situation entirely enviable since each was forced to come to terms with the achievement of his father. According to Forkel, both Emanuel and his elder brother Friedemann 'admitted that they were driven to adopt a style of their own by the wish to avoid comparison with their incomparable father'.[104] This may be true, although the question of Emanuel's artistic relationship to his father is not a simple one. Sebastian's influence was surely inescapable, especially in Bach's early years. We have some confirmation of this in Emanuel's statement: 'In composition and keyboard playing I never had any other teacher than my father.'[105] Furthermore, Emanuel's respect is evidenced both

---

[102] C. Burney, *The Present State of Music in Germany*, ii. 266.

[103] Ibid. ii. 272–3.

[104] J. N. Forkel, *Johann Sebastian Bach: his Life, Art, and Work*, p. 104.

[105] C. Burney, *Tagebuch*, iii. 199. The translation is from W. S. Newman, 'Emanuel Bach's Autobiography', 366.

by his conscious appropriation of J. S. Bach's ideas,[106] and by
an anonymous letter to the *Allgemeine deutsche Bibliothek* of
1788 (vol. lxxxi) comparing the respective merits of Handel
and J. S. Bach—a letter which was almost certainly written
by Emanuel himself.[107]

There is no doubt that Emanuel knew some of his father's
keyboard concertos for a copy of J. S. Bach's clavier
concerto in D minor (BWV 1052) in Emanuel's hand still
exists today.[108] Moreover, there are certain similarities between their concertos: both Sebastian and Emanuel
favoured a thematic accompaniment to solo sections, using
motifs from the ritornello in the ripieno parts, and both
relished rapid exchanges between solo and ripieno instruments. Stylistic similarities are less marked, as one would
expect from composers of a different generation. But
Emanuel's predilection for subdominant colouring at the
beginning of a work, his spasmodic use of contrary motion
passages, and his penchant for auxiliary-note patterns in
accompaniment, all point to Sebastian's influence. Occasionally, too, Emanuel's keyboard style resembles that of his
father. The idiomatic figuration reproduced below is found
also in J. S. Bach's C minor Prelude (BWV 847) from Book
One of the *Forty-Eight Preludes and Fugues*:

EXAMPLE 25

Emanuel Bach, Wq. 23, 3rd movement, bars 255–8 (cembalo part
only)

---

[106] Emanuel incorporated the 'Sicut locutus' fugue from Sebastian's *Magnificat*
into his *Einchöriges Heilig* (Wq. 218), see K. Geiringer, 'Artistic Interrelations of the
Bachs', *The Musical Quarterly*, xxxvi (1950), 369–70.

[107] See D. Plamenac, 'New Light on the last years of Carl Philipp Emanuel Bach',
The Musical Quarterly, xxxv (1949), 565–87, especially 575–87.

[108] P. Kast, *Die Bach-Handschriften der Berliner Staatsbibliothek*, Tübinger Bach-
Studien, Heft 2/3 (Trossingen, 1958), p. 84.

There was, however, much that Emanuel rejected in his father's music. He held the 'modernist' view that natural melody was of prime importance, and counterpoint merely an outmoded historical relic. In conversation with Burney, Emanuel

spoke irreverently of canons, which, he said, were dry and despicable pieces of pedantry, that any one might compose, who would sacrifice his time to them; but it was ever a certain proof to him, of a total want of genius, in any one that was fond of such wretched studies, and unmeaning productions.

He asked if I had found many great contra-puntists in Italy; and upon my answering in the negative, he replied, nay, if you had, it would have been no great matter; for after counterpoint is well known, many other more essential things are wanting to constitute a good composer.[109]

Bach's avoidance of contrapuntal *forms* in the concertos is absolute:[110] there are no fugal movements as such. Yet he admitted certain other contrapuntal elements. As we have seen, imitative textures sometimes figure in the sequential section of a ritornello, and the development of ritornello material by the ripieno group often involves some measure of imitation. The picture that emerges, therefore, is complex. Emanuel did not break completely with the past, although he was obviously in sympathy with the new ideals of his own generation.

This raises the broader issue of Emanuel's artistic relationship to his contemporaries and since a large part of his life was spent among the composers and musicians of Frederick the Great's court it seems reasonable to consider first his position in relation to this particular group. As far as aesthetics were concerned, Bach shared Quantz's views on the efficacy of a singing melody, and on the expressive nature of music. 'That which does not come from the heart does not easily reach the heart',[111] wrote Quantz in his

[109] C. Burney, *The Present State of Music in Germany*, ii. 252–3.

[110] Although Bach avoided fugal movements in the concertos he wrote several keyboard fugues, mainly for inclusion in Marpurg's collections. See P. Barford, *The Keyboard Music of C. P. E. Bach*, pp. 20ff.

[111] 'Denn was nicht vom Herzen kömmt, geht auch nicht leichtlich wieder zum

treatise on flute playing (1752), and this sentiment was echoed by Bach in his own *Versuch*.[112] Turning to the concerto genre itself, one finds certain similarities of structure between Bach's concertos and those of his colleagues at Berlin. The four-ritornello form predominates, and many Allegro movements exhibit some type of recapitulation within the final section. Several turns of phrase are also held in common. The changing-note formula is important in concertos by Bach and Quantz,[113] and semiquaver 'sigh' figures are in fairly general use. Furthermore, there are standardized keyboard figurations which recur with some frequency; both Nichelmann and Emanuel Bach, for example, use similar patterns for their solo episodes.[114]

Historians have tended to regard Emanuel Bach as the leader of the Berlin school. This is an accurate reflection of his musical stature, but scarcely of his position *vis-à-vis* the school itself. In the first place, Bach was not a founder member of the school. Indeed, it is probable that he himself was influenced, initially at any rate, by developments at the Prussian court. We know that the keyboard concerto was cultivated at Berlin prior to Bach's arrival,[115] so that Bach was definitely not responsible for its introduction there. In the second place, Bach's style of writing was not wholly representative of the Berliners who preferred a simpler, more Italianate idiom. The dichotomy between the two styles was apparent to Charles Burney who observed: 'Though M. Bach continued near thirty years at Berlin, it

---

Herzen', J. J. Quantz, *Versuch einer Anweisung die flute traversière zu spielen*, p. 138. The translation is by E. R. Reilly in J. J. Quantz, *On Playing the Flute* (London, 1966), p. 163.

[112] See p. 331.

[113] See the opening theme of Quantz's A minor flute concerto (GB-Lbm Additional 33295):

[114] One concerto by Nichelmann has been attributed (wrongly) to C. P. E. Bach in two separate sources. See D. A. Lee, *The Works of Christoph Nichelmann: Thematic Index*, Detroit Studies in Music Bibliography, no. 19 (Detroit, 1971), pp. 17, 38–9.

[115] There is a keyboard concerto by one of the Graun brothers which is dated 1737. H. Uldall, *Das Klavierkonzert der Berliner Schule und ihres Führers Philipp Emanuel Bach*, p. 3. (Uldall's specific attribution of this concerto to K. H. Graun rests on the flimsiest of evidence.)

cannot be supposed that he was perfectly contented with his situation. A style of music prevailed, totally different from that which he wished to establish.'[116]

It follows, therefore, that Emanuel's music was not particularly influential within the Berlin school. Yet Bach's ultra-emotional approach was shared by certain other composers—notably by his own next of kin. Emanuel's elder brother, Wilhelm Friedemann Bach, also wrote in the expressive manner of the *Empfindsamkeit*. In fact their styles correspond so closely that an F minor concerto by Friedemann was for many years attributed to Emanuel himself.[117] It is impossible to determine whether C. P. E. Bach influenced Wilhelm Friedemann or vice versa. But in the case of Johann Christoph Friedrich Bach (1732–95) there is little doubt that it was Emanuel who influenced his later concerto style. Friedrich—or the Bückeburg Bach as he is called—was among the subscribers to Emanuel's Wq. 43 set, and these works obviously affected him to some extent. Two of Friedrich's concertos (in A and F major) dating from around 1787, have the same instrumentation as Bach's later works: i.e. strings, flutes, and horns, and the style of his E♭ major concerto (1792) comes close to that of the *Empfindsamkeit*.[118] As for the youngest member of the group, Johann Christian Bach, he was taken under Emanuel's protection after the death of their father. During these years in Berlin (1750–?6)[119] he wrote concertos whose structure was related to those of Emanuel Bach,[120] even if their style veered more to the Italianate manner of the Grauns. It must

[116] C. Burney, *The Present State of Music in Germany*, ii. 268.

[117] There are two sources for this work, one with the following inscription, 'riveduto del Sgr. Em. Bach', and one bearing the name of W. F. Bach. The concerto has been issued in a modern edition (under W. F. Bach), ed. W. Smigelski (Hamburg, 1959).

[118] See H. Wohlfarth, *Johann Christoph Friedrich Bach* (Bern, 1971), pp. 160–70.

[119] There is some doubt as to when J. C. Bach actually left Berlin, but we know that he was in Milan in 1757.

[120] An early (*c.* 1752) concerto in B♭ major by J. C. Bach has four ritornello statements, the third of which modulates from the submediant to the tonic after the fashion of Emanuel's Scheme B (see p. 301). E. J. Simon, 'The Double Exposition in the Classic Concerto', *Journal of the American Musicological Society*, x (1957), 111–18.

be said, however, that on leaving Berlin Christian Bach broke away from his brother's influence entirely. The six concertos of op. 1 (published in London in 1763)[121] were written after his stay in Italy and demonstrate clearly the effects of his conversion to Italian methods.

It is more difficult to assess Emanuel Bach's relationship to composers of the Viennese classical school. Haydn certainly knew some of Bach's works. According to Griesinger he was much impressed early in his career by the Prussian sonatas (published in 1742),[122] and later in life he acquired a number of Emanuel's compositions, including one of the double concertos.[123] Yet it is doubtful whether Bach's concertos had any direct bearing on those of Haydn. In fact, the extent of his influence on Haydn's music in general has probably been exaggerated,[124] for although one or two of Haydn's early keyboard sonatas reveal a detailed knowledge of Bach's style,[125] few other examples are forthcoming. Basically there is a wide gulf separating Bach and Haydn. The latter may have been initially attracted to the *Empfindsamkeit*, but his own style was firmly rooted in the different traditions of Austro–Italian music.

As for Haydn's influence on Bach, this question is beset with uncertainties, for we do not know how much Viennese music was circulating in North Germany at that time. A few scraps of information are, however, available. When van Swieten was Ambassador to the Prussian court in the 1770s, for example, the Berliners were eager to obtain Viennese music;[126] moreover, some members of the Esterháza kapelle

---

[121] C. S. Terry, *John Christian Bach*, p. 182.

[122] See V. Gotwals, *Haydn: Two Contemporary Portraits*, a translation of the *Biographische Notizen über Joseph Haydn* by G. A. Griesinger and of the *Biographisches Nachrichten von Joseph Haydn* by A. C. Dies (Madison, 1968; first published 1963), p. 12.

[123] See E. F. Schmid, 'Joseph Haydn und Carl Philipp Emanuel Bach', *Zeitschrift für Musikwissenschaft*, xiv (1932), 309–10.

[124] See A. Peter Brown, 'The Earliest English Biography of Haydn', *The Musical Quarterly*, lix (1973), 339–54.

[125] E.g. the slow movement of no. 11 (Hob. xvi/2), ed. C. Landon in *Haydn: Sämtliche Klaviersonaten*, vol. 1 (Vienna, 1966).

[126] *The Collected Correspondence and London Notebooks of Joseph Haydn*, ed. H. C. Robbins Landon (London, 1959), p. 20.

are known to have visited Berlin and Hamburg in 1783.[127] Bach himself, anxious to refute allegations that he had criticized Haydn's work, wrote: 'Based on reports which have come to me from Vienna and even from personnel of the Esterháza orchestra, I must believe that this worthy gentleman [i.e. Haydn], whose work still gives me much pleasure, is certainly my friend in the same way that I am his.'[128] Intimations of Haydn's influence appear in Bach's last concerto (Wq. 47). The Finale is based on the following theme:

EXAMPLE 26
Emanuel Bach, Wq. 47, 3rd movement, bars 1–8 (first violin part only)

and later in the movement we find Bach tossing this head-motif from part to part in Haydn's most playful manner:

EXAMPLE 27
Emanuel Bach, Wq. 47, 3rd movement, bars 175–80

[127] E. F. Schmid, op. cit. 306.
[128] C. P. E. Bach's reply to the allegations is dated 14 September 1785 and appears in the *Hamburger Unpartheiischer Correspondent*, no. 50 (1785). The original is reproduced in E. F. Schmid, op. cit. 305. The translation is from A. Peter Brown, 'The Earliest English Biography of Haydn', 344–5 note.

The other great figure of the classical period, Mozart, does not appear to have been influenced by C. P. E. Bach. One of Mozart's early concerto arrangements (K.40, July 1767) has a Finale based on Emanuel's keyboard piece 'La Boehmer' (Wq. 117), but that fact alone is insignificant. When, in later life, Mozart became more intimately acquainted with the music of the Bach family, it was Emanuel's fugues that attracted his attention,[129] not his concertos. Indeed, Mozart never mentions Bach's concertos although presumably he had access to some of them through Baron van Swieten.[130] Wolfgang's early mentor was, of course, J. C. Bach, and it was to this member of the Bach family that he owed the greatest debt. The three keyboard concertos of K.21b (formerly K.107) are all based on sonatas by the London Bach;[131] yet, to our ears, the arrangements sound entirely Mozartean, so close is the identity of style.

It was once fashionable to stress Emanuel Bach's influence on Beethoven. However, all that can be safely said here is that Beethoven owed something to Bach in the realm of rhythmic vitality, drama, unorthodox key schemes, and expressive power. Some of Beethoven's unconventional procedures were, indeed, anticipated by Bach: in Wq. 43, no. 1, for instance, Bach allows the soloist to open the slow movement—a device which Beethoven employed at the beginning of the 1st movement of his Fourth Piano Concerto. However, other composers besides Beethoven had also experimented along these lines.

---

[129] See Mozart's letter to his father (Vienna, 10 April 1782): 'I go every Sunday at twelve o'clock to Baron van Swieten, where nothing is played but Handel and Bach. I am collecting at the moment the fugues of Bach—not only of Sebastian, but also of Emanuel and Friedemann'; English version from *The Letters of Mozart and His Family*, tr. and ed. by E. Anderson, vol. iii (London, 1938), p. 1192.

[130] Baron van Swieten had been a subscriber to Bach's Wq. 43 set. For further information regarding his artistic relationship with Mozart see E. Olleson, 'Gottfried van Swieten: Patron of Haydn and Mozart', *Proceedings of the Royal Musical Association*, lxxxix (1963), 63–74.

[131] See E. J. Simon, 'Sonata into Concerto: a study of Mozart's first seven concertos', *Acta Musicologica*, xxxi (1959), 170–85.

In many respects the spirit of Bach's music is more closely related to the romantic, than to the classical, ethos. For some reason, as Geiringer remarked, he 'showed but little interest in, or understanding for, the steady growth of classical feeling in music'.[132] This is curious, since the classical style was already well established during the later years of his life. The new style was, however, essentially a product of the Austrian school, and Emanuel may have been temperamentally disinclined to adopt it. It is useless to speculate whether Bach might have embraced classicism had he lived a few years longer. The style of his last concerto, written in 1788 when Bach was seventy-four, suggests that he was moving in this direction, but for the greater part of his life he remained faithful to the ideals of the *Empfindsamkeit*, developing what was, in effect, a highly individual style.

[132] K. Geiringer, *The Bach Family*, pp. 353–4.

Appendix A

The concertos of G. F. Handel: borrowed and re-used material

The relationship between different versions of the same material is indicated as follows:

A = correspondence of head-motif only

B = more extensive borrowing but still an independent working

C = fairly close correspondence for much of the piece but with some radical alterations

D = close correspondence throughout but allowing for minor changes (e.g. slight variations in length, or melodic line, or inner parts)

E = identical (except for possible discrepancies of key or instrumentation).

For many of the works exact composition dates are not known; the priority of the different versions is not, therefore, discussed in this appendix.[1] All items listed in the right-hand column are self-borrowings (or anticipations) unless otherwise stated.

Concerto	*Other appearances of the same material*
Op. 3, no. 2, in B♭ major **HG xxi, 15–26; HHA iv/11,** **25–46**	
3rd movement (B♭ major, common time C, Allegro)	(1) *Brockes Passion*, Sinfonia, 1st movement (B♭ major, C, Allegro). Relationship = D (exact except for the addition of a four-bar introduction in the *Passion*)
	(2) *Six Fugues or Voluntary's for the Organ or Harpsicord*, no. 3 (B♭ major, C, no tempo indication). Relationship = B
4th movement (B♭ major, ⅜, no tempo indica- tion)	(1) *Alessandro*, Act 1, duet, 'Placa l'alma' (G major, ⅜, Allegro). Relationship = A
	(2) op. 1, no. 7 (sonata for recorder and figured bass), 5th movement (C major, ⅜,

[1] In certain isolated cases a firm priority has been established; for these, the reader is referred to Chapter II.

Allegro). Relationship = A

[A variant of this theme appears in op. 3, no. 6, 2nd movement; also in op. 7, no. 4, 3rd movement, in Suite no. 3 (First Collection), 6th movement, in *Il Pastor Fido* (first version), Overture, 6th movement (Finale)]

Op. 3, no. 3 in G major
HG xxi, 27–35; HHA iv/11,
49–62

1st movement
(G major, C, 'largo e staccato')

(1) Chandos Anthem no. 7: 'My Song shall be alway', Sonata (instrumental introduction), 1st movement (G major, C, 'largo, e staccato'). Relationship = E

(2) op. 4, no. 3, 1st movement (G minor, C, Adagio). Relationship = A. (Bars 1–4 of op. 3 = bars 1–2 of the organ concerto)

[Compare also Corelli's op. 6, no. 4, 1st movement which opens in a similar fashion]

2nd movement
(G major, C, Allegro)

(1) Chandos Anthem no. 7: 'My Song shall be alway', Sonata, 2nd movement (G major, C, Allegro). Relationship = E

(2) *Brockes Passion* no. 38 (chorus): 'Ein jeder sei ihm untertänig' (D major, C, Allegro). Relationship = B

(3) *Deborah*, Act 1, first chorus: 'Immortal Lord of earth and skies' at the words 'O grant a leader to our host' (D major, C, Andante). Relationship = B

(4) *Birthday Ode for Queen Anne*, 2nd movement ('solo e coro'): 'The day that gave great Anna birth' (D major, C, Allegro). Relationship = A

3rd movement
(E minor, C, Adagio)

Te Deum no. 2 in B♭ major, chorus: 'We believe that Thou shalt come to be our judge' (E minor, C, Adagio). Relationship = D

4th movement
(G major, C, Allegro)

(1) *Six Fugues or Voluntary's for the Organ or Harpsicord*, no. 2 (G major, C, no tempo indication). Relationship = E. (The keyboard fugue has one extra bar in the

middle; the omission of this bar from the concerto was, however, probably accidental)

(2) Chandos Anthem no. 9: 'O Praise the Lord with one consent', first chorus: 'O Praise the Lord with one consent' at the words 'Let all the servants of the Lord' (Eb major, C, 'andante con moto'). Relationship = A

Op. 3, no. 4 in F major
HG xxi, 36–44; HHA iv/11,
65–76

2nd movement
(F major, ⅜, Andante)

Concerto in G major for solo keyboard (?arrangement) (HHA, iv/17), no. 23, 2nd movement (G major, ¾, Andante) Relationship = D. (The op. 3 version lacks the final 3-bar Adagio cadence of the keyboard concerto movement)

3rd movement
(D minor, C, Allegro)

[Opening theme is similar to that found in *Acis and Galatea*, part 2, Trio: 'The flocks shall leave the mountains']

4th movement
(*a*) Minuetto Alternativo
(F major, ¾, Minuetto Alternativo)

(1) 'Courante e due Menuetti' for harpsichord (Third Collection), second Menuetto (F major, ¾, Menuetto 2). Relationship = D

(2) *Aylesford* no. 9 (F major, ¾, Menuet). Relationship = D

(3) op. 1, no. 5 (sonata for recorder and figured bass), 5th movement (G major, ¾, Menuetto). Relationship = C

4th movement
(*b*) Minuetto Alternativo
(F major, ¾, Minuetto Alternativo)

Aylesford no. 62 (F major, ¾, Menuet). Relationship = D

Op. 3, no. 4 in F major
(first printing)
HG—; HHA iv/11, 105–22

2nd movement
(F major, ₵, Allegro)

[Opening theme is similar to that found in *Acis and Galatea*, part 1, Sinfonia]

Op. 3, no. 5 in D minor
HG xxi, 45–53;
HHA iv/11, 79–90

1st movement
(D minor, ¾, no tempo indication)

Chandos Anthem no. 2: 'In the Lord put I my trust', instrumental introduction, 1st movement (D minor, ¾, no tempo indication). Relationship = E

2nd movement
(D minor, C, Allegro)

(1) Chandos Anthem no. 2: 'In the Lord put I my trust', instrumental introduction, 2nd movement (D minor, C, Allegro). Relationship = E.

(2) Suite no. 6 (First Collection), 3rd movement (F♯ minor, C, Allegro). Relationship = B

4th movement
(D minor, C, 'allegro ma non troppo')

Chandos Anthem no. 6 (first version): 'As Pants the Hart for Cooling Streams', Sonata (instrumental introduction), 2nd movement (E minor, C, Allegro). Relationship = E

Op. 3, no. 6 in D major/D
minor
HG xxi, 54–60;
HHA iv/11, 93–102

2nd movement
(D minor, ⅜, Allegro)

(1) op. 7, no. 4, 3rd movement (D minor, ⅜, Allegro). Relationship = D

(2) *Il Pastor Fido* (first version), Overture, 6th movement (Finale) (D minor, ⅜, no tempo indication). Relationship = C

(3) Suite no. 3 (First Collection), 6th movement (D minor, ⅜, Presto). Relationship = C

[A variant of this theme appears in op. 3, no. 2, 4th movement; also in *Alessandro*, Act 1, duet, 'Placa l'alma' and in op. 1, no. 7, 5th movement]

Op. 6, no. 1 in G major
HG xxx, 1–15;
HHA iv/14, 1–26

1st movement
(written originally for *Imeneo*)
(G major, C, 'a tempo Giusto')

The *Occasional Oratorio*, Sinfonia to Part 3, 1st movement (G major, C, no tempo indication). Relationship = E

3rd movement
(E minor, ¾, Adagio)

(1) The *Occasional Oratorio*, Overture (to Act 1), 3rd movement (B minor, ¾,

Adagio). Relationship = A

(2) op. 1, no. 2 (sonata for recorder and figured bass), 3rd movement (E♭ major, 3/2, Adagio). Relationship = A

(3) op. 4, no. 3, 3rd movement (E♭ major, 3/2, Adagio). Relationship = A

[As G. Abraham points out (*Handel: a Symposium* (London, 1954), p. 268 note), the idiom derives from Stradella—see Eurinda's aria, 'Sepellitevi' in *Floridoro*]

5th movement
(G major, §, Allegro)

[Reminiscent in a general way of Domenico Scarlatti—see G. Abraham, op. cit., p. 204]

Op. 6, no. 4 in A minor
HG xxx, 46–59;
HHA iv/14, 73–88

4th movement
(A minor, 3/4, Allegro)

Imeneo, Act 2, Clomira's aria, 'È si vaga del tuo bene' (version A) (A minor, 3/4, Andante). Relationship = C

Op. 6, no. 5 in D major
HG xxx, 60–76;
HHA iv/14, 91–116

1st movement
(D major, 3/4, 'larghetto, e staccato')

(1) *Ode for St. Cecilia's Day*, Overture, 1st movement (D major, 3/4, 'larghetto, e staccato'). Relationship = C

(2) Gottlieb Muffat, *Componimenti Musicali*, no. 1, 4th movement (Courante) (C major, 3/4, no tempo indication).

Relationship = A (bars 3–5 of the concerto correspond to bars 2–4 of the Muffat)

2nd movement
(D major, C, Allegro)

Ode for St. Cecilia's Day, Overture, 2nd movement (D major, C, Allegro). Relationship = D

5th movement
(D major, C, Allegro)

[Opening theme resembles that of Domenico Scarlatti's sonata in D, *Essercizi* no. 23 (Longo 411)—see Ex. 19 of Chapter II]

6th movement
(D major, 3/4, Menuet)

Ode for St. Cecilia's Day, Overture, 3rd movement (D major, 3/4, no tempo indication). Relationship = C

[There is also a slight resemblance between this movement and Gottlieb Muffat's *Componimenti Musicali*, no. 3, 5th movement (Menuet)]

Op. 6, no. 6 in G minor
HG xxx, 77–94;
HHA iv/14, 119–50

2nd movement
(G minor, C, 'a tempo giusto')

(1) Chandos Anthem no. 10: 'The Lord is my light', chorus, 'They are brought down and fall'n' (G minor, C, 'a tempo ordinario'). Relationship = A

(2) *O Numi eterni* (solo cantata), 6th movement 'Alla salma infedel' (G minor, ¾, Larghetto). Relationship = A (subject varied slightly)

3rd movement
(E♭ major, ¾, Larghetto)

The *Occasional Oratorio*, Sinfonia to Part 3, 2nd movement (Musette) (E♭ major, ¾, Larghetto). Relationship = E

5th movement
(G minor, ⅜, Allegro)

[Slight resemblance in spirit to op. 4, no. 2, 4th movement]

Op. 6, no. 7 in B♭ major
HG xxx, 95–106;
HHA iv/14, 153–66

5th movement
(B♭ major, ¾, Hornpipe)

[Resembles slightly Gottlieb Muffat's *Componimenti Musicali*, suite 4, 10th movement (Hornpipe)]

Op. 6, no. 8 in C minor
HG xxx, 107–17;
HHA iv/14, 169–82

1st movement
(C minor, C, Allemande)

Suite no. 2 (Third Collection), 1st movement (Allemande) (G minor, C, no tempo indication). Relationship = A

3rd movement
(C minor, C, Andante Allegro)

[A similar four-note head-motif is found in *Agrippina*, Act 1, quartet: 'Il tuo figlio']

4th movement
(E♭ major, ¾, Adagio)

Giulio Cesare, Act 3, Cleopatra's aria, 'Piangerò la sorte mia' (E major, ⅜, no tempo indication). Relationship = A

5th movement
(C minor, ¹²⁄₈ Andante)

[Resembles in spirit *Giulio Cesare*, Act 1, duet, 'Sonnata a lagrimar']

[As S. Sadie points out (*Handel Concertos* (London, 1972), pp. 49–50), some phrases in this movement resemble those in *Messiah* (cf. the *Pastoral* symphony and 'He shall feed his flock']

6th movement
(C minor, ¾, Allegro)

[Resembles in general style Gottlieb Muffat's *Componimenti Musicali* no. 1, 5th movement (Air)]

Op. 6, no. 9 in F major
HG xxx, 118–32;
HHA iv/14, 185–202

1st movement (F major, ¾, Largo)	[The bass line of this movement bars 1–7 corresponds to that at the beginning of Serse's aria, 'Ombra mai fù', from *Serse*, Act 1]
2nd movement (F major, C, Allegro)	Organ concerto no. 13, 2nd movement (F major, C, Allegro). Relationship = C [Reminiscent of *Serse*, Act 2, Atalanta's aria, 'Dirà che amor per me']
3rd movement (D minor, §, Larghetto)	Organ concerto no. 13, 3rd movement (D minor, §, Larghetto). Relationship = D
4th movement (F major, C, Allegro)	*Imeneo*, Overture, 2nd movement (G major, C, Allegro). Relationship = E
5th movement (F minor, ⅜, Menuet)	*Imeneo*, Overture, 3rd movement (G minor, ⅜, Menuet). Relationship = E

Op. 6, no. 11 in A major
HG xxx, 148–67;
HHA iv/14, 225–48

1st movement (A major, C, 'andante larghetto e staccato')	Organ concerto no. 14, 1st movement (A major, C, 'largo e staccato'). Relationship = D
3rd movement (F♯ minor, C, 'largo e staccato')	Organ concerto no. 14, 3rd movement (F♯ minor, C, Grave). Relationship = E
4th movement (A major, ¾, Andante)	Organ concerto no. 14, 2nd movement (A major, ¾, Andante). Relationship = D
5th movement (A major, C, Allegro)	Organ concerto no. 14, 4th movement (A major, C, Allegro). Relationship = E

Op. 6, no. 12 in B minor
HG xxx, 168–80;
HHA iv/14, 251–66

3rd movement (Aria) (E major, ¾, 'larghetto e piano')	[Similar in spirit to *Berenice*, Overture, 3rd movement (Minuet)]
5th movement (B minor, C, Allegro)	Zachow, keyboard suite in B minor[2] (no. 66 of *Gesammelte Werke für Tasteninstrumente*, ed. H. Lohmann (Wiesbaden, 1966)), 4th movement (Fuga finalis) (B minor, C, no tempo indication). Relationship = A (the first two bars of the fugue subjects correspond almost exactly)

---

[2] I am indebted to Mr. David Nicholls for this information.

Concerto grosso in C Major
(Alexander's Feast)[3]
HG xxi, 63–82

1st movement (C major, C, Allegro)	Boyce, Overture in C major (C major, C, no tempo indication). Relationship = B (cf. Chapter II, Ex. 31)
3rd movement (C major, C, Allegro)	[The opening theme bears a slight resemblance to that of the keyboard sonata in C major (Third Collection, no. 12); the similarity would be unremarkable were there not also connections between the 4th movement of the concerto and the sonata—see below]
4th movement (C major, C, 'andante, non Presto')	Keyboard sonata in C major (Third Collection, no. 12, 3rd movement (Gavotte) (C major, ₵, 'non troppo Presto'). Relationship = E for the first two sections. (The concerto then has an extra variation from bar 30 to the end)

Op. 4, no. 1 in G minor/G
major HG xxviii, 3–21;
HHA iv/2, 2–33

4th movement (G major, ⅜, Andante)	[This movement appears (minus its second variation and in the key of F major) in an early MS. version of the trio sonata op. 5, no. 6 (GB-Lbm R.M. 19.f.6), but not in the published version]

Op. 4, no. 2 in B♭ major
HG xxviii, 22–32;
HHA iv/2, 36–52

1st movement (B♭ major, C, 'a tempo ordinario, e staccato')	Sileti venti (motet for solo soprano), 'Symphonia' (B♭ major, C, Largo). Relationship = B
2nd movement (B♭ major, C, Allegro)	Op. 2, no. 3 (trio sonata), 4th movement (B♭ major, C, Allegro). Relationship = C. (The course of the two movements is the same as regards ritornello material but the solo sections of the organ version are mostly new)

---

[3] A keyboard version of this concerto—for 'Gravicembalo'—is listed by J. A. Fuller-Maitland and A. H. Mann: *Catalogue of the Music in the Fitzwilliam Museum* (London, 1893), p. 97.

4th movement
(B♭ major, ⅜, 'allegro,
ma non Presto')

[There is a slight resemblance in spirit to
op. 6, no. 6, 5th movement]

Op. 4, no. 3 in G minor
HG xxviii, 33–42;
HHA iv/2, 54–69

1st movement
(G minor, C, Adagio)

Bars 1–2. Op. 3, no. 3, 1st movement (G
major, C, 'largo, e staccato'). Relationship = A. (Bars 1–2 of the organ concerto = bars 1–4 of the concerto grosso)
[Compare also Corelli's op. 6, no. 4, 1st
movement which opens in a similar fash-
ion]

Bars 3–4. Op. 2, no. 6 (trio sonata), 1st
movement (G minor, C, Andante). Relationship = A

Bars 3ff. *Rinaldo* (first version), Act 2,
Armida's aria, 'Ah Crudel!' (G minor, C,
Largo). Relationship = B

Bars 3ff. *Rinaldo* (second version), Act 2,
Almirena's aria, 'Ah Crudel!' (G minor, C,
Largo). Relationship = B

2nd movement
(G minor, ¾, Allegro)

(1) op. 2, no. 5 (trio sonata), 4th movement
(G minor, ¾, Allegro). Relationship = B

(2) oboe concerto in G minor, 4th movement (G minor, ¾, Allegro). Relationship = A

(3) no. 18 of *Einzelne Suiten und Stücke,
zweite Folge*, ed. T. Best, *HHA* iv/17 (Kassel, 1975), 2nd movement (A minor, ¾,
Allegro). Relationship = A
[A variant of the same theme appears in op.
2, no. 2, 4th movement, and in op. 1, no. 4,
4th movement]

3rd movement
(E♭ major, ¾, Adagio)

(1) The *Occasional Oratorio*, Overture, 3rd
movement (B minor, ¾, Adagio). Relationship = A

(2) op. 1, no. 2 (sonata for recorder and
figured bass), 3rd movement (E♭ major, 3/2
Adagio). Relationship = A

(3) op. 6, no. 1, 3rd movement (E minor, ¾,
Adagio). Relationship = A
[As G. Abraham points out (*Handel: a
Symposium* (London, 1954), p. 268 note),
the idiom derives from Stradella—cf.

Eurinda's aria, 'Sepellitevi' in *Floridoro*]

4th movement
(Gavotte) (G minor,
¢, Allegro)

(1) op. 1, no. 2 (sonata for recorder and figured bass), 4th movement (G minor, C, Presto). Relationship = D

(2) op. 1, no. 1a (sonata for recorder and figured bass), 5th movement (E minor, C, Presto). Relationship = C

(3) op. 7, no. 5, 4th movement (G minor, C, Gavotte). Relationship = C

(4) *Agrippina*, Act 1, Agrippina's aria, 'Non hò cor che per armarti' (C minor, C, 'Staccato'). Relationship = A

[A variant of this theme occurs in op. 1, no. 1a, 2nd movement and this variant is itself foreshadowed in Corelli's op 5, no. 8, 3rd movement (Sarabanda). A similar theme also appears at the beginning of Georg Muffat's Concerto no. 4, 4th movement (Aria) (see his *Auserlesene mit Ernst und Lust gemengte Instrumentalmusik* (1701)]

Op. 4, no. 4 in F major
HG xxviii, 43–57;
HHA iv/2, 72–92

1st movement
(F major, C, Allegro)

Alcina, Act 1, chorus, 'Questo è il cielo' (second version) (F major, C, Presto). Relationship = B

4th movement
(F major, C, Allegro)

The Triumph of Time and Truth (1737 revision of the Roman cantata *Il Trionfo del tempo*), Act 3, chorus, 'Hallelujah' (F major, C, no tempo indication). Relationship = B

[In one copy of the concerto the Finale leads directly into the choral 'Hallelujah']

Op. 4, no. 5 in F major
HG xxviii, 58–62;
HHA iv/2, 94–101

The whole concerto uses the same material as op. 1, no. 11 (sonata in F major for recorder and figured bass)

1st movement
(F major, ¾, Larghetto)

Op. 1, no. 11, 1st movement (F major, ¾, Larghetto) Relationship = E (but there is no Adagio marking over the last two bars of the sonata movement)

2nd movement
(F major, C, Allegro)

Op. 1, no. 11, 2nd movement (F major, C, Allegro). Relationship = D. (In the concerto version Handel repeats the first five bars to create a tutti (and adds a double bar line) solo effect)

3rd movement (D minor, $\frac{12}{8}$, 'alla Siciliana')

Op. 1, no. 11, 3rd movement (D minor, $\frac{12}{8}$, Siciliana). Relationship = D. (In the concerto Handel has added two bars as an introduction)

4th movement (F major, $\frac{12}{8}$, Presto)

Op. 1, no. 11, 4th movement (F major, $\frac{12}{8}$. Allegro). Relationship = D. (In the concerto Handel has added two bars introduction, two bars at the close of the first part of the binary form, and a further two bars at the end of the movement)

Op. 7, no. 1 in B♭ major
HG xxviii, 73–89

1st movement (B♭ major, C, Andante)⎱ on the
leading to   ⎰ same
2nd movement   ⎱ ground
(B♭ major, $\frac{3}{4}$, Andante)

[A similar ground occurs in Suite no. 7 (First Collection), 6th movement (Passacaille)]

4th movement (Bourrée) (B♭ major, ₵, Allegro)

Gottlieb Muffat, *Componimenti Musicali* suite no. 4, 5th movement ('La Hardiesse') (B♭ major, $\frac{2}{4}$, Allegro). Relationship = A. (Compare bars 2–4 of the concerto with bars 4–7 of the Muffat)

Op. 7, no. 2 in A major
HG xxviii, 90–101

2nd movement (A major, C, 'a tempo ordinario')

Gottlieb Muffat, ricercar no. 28 from an unpublished MS. at the Library of the Minoritenkonvent, Vienna (MS XIV 712)[4] (F major, ₵, no tempo indication). Relationship = B

3rd movement (A major, C, Allegro)

Gottlieb Muffat, *Componimenti Musicali*, suite no. 6, 6th movement ('La Coquette') (G major, $\frac{2}{4}$, no tempo indication). Relationship = A

Op. 7, no. 3 in B♭ major
HG xxviii, 102–14

1st movement

[Opening phrase is similar to that of the

---

[4] See S. Wollenberg, 'Handel and Gottlieb Muffat: a newly discovered borrowing', 448–9.

(B♭ major, C, Allegro)

1st movement
(B♭ major, C, Allegro)

2nd movement
(B♭ major, ¾, Spiritoso)

'Hallelujah' chorus, *Messiah*, part 2. The concerto's opening bars were an afterthought; the movement was planned to begin in the present third bar]

[According to S. Sadie (*Handel Concertos* (London, 1972), p. 59) the fugue subject is borrowed from Habermann]

Op. 7, no. 4 in D minor
HG xxviii, 115–25

1st movement
(D minor, C, Adagio)

The single concerto movement for two organs in D minor (D minor, C, Adagio). Relationship = D. (The two-organ version has an extended ending involving a nine-bar cadential passage as opposed to the original two-bar close)

2nd movement
(D major, C, Allegro)

Telemann, *Musique de Table*, Book 2, Overture in D major, 4th movement (Air 1) (D major, C, Tempo giusto). Relationship = B

3rd movement
(D minor, ⅜, Allegro)

(1) op. 3, no. 6, 2nd movement (D minor, ⅜, Allegro). Relationship = D

(2) *Il Pastor Fido* (first version), Overture, 6th movement (Finale) (D minor, ⅜, no tempo indication). Relationship = C

(3) Suite no. 3 (First Collection), 6th movement (D minor, ⅜, Presto). Relationship = C

[A variant of this theme appears in op. 3, no. 2, 4th movement, also in *Alessandro*, Act 1, duet, 'Placa l'alma' and in op. 1, no. 7, 5th movement]

Op. 7, no. 5 in G minor
HG xxviii, 126–34

1st movement
(G minor, C, 'allegro ma non troppo, e staccato')

4th movement
(G minor, C, Gavotte)

[The phrase introduced at bar 5 is similar to that at the beginning of the trio sonata op. 2, no. 1, 1st movement]

(1) op. 4, no. 3, 4th movement (G minor, ₵, Allegro). Relationship = C

(2) op. 1, no. 2 (sonata for recorder and figured bass), 4th movement (G minor, C, Presto). Relationship = C

(3) op. 1, no. 1a (sonata for recorder and figured bass), 5th movement (E minor, C, Presto). Relationship = C

(4) *Agrippina*, Act 1, Agrippina's aria, 'Non hò cor che per armarti' (C minor, C, 'Staccato'). Relationship = A

[A variant of this theme occurs in op. 1, no. 1a, 2nd movement and this variant is itself foreshadowed in Corelli's op. 5, no. 8, 3rd movement (Sarabanda). A similar theme also appears at the beginning of Georg Muffat's Concerto no. 4, 4th movement (Aria) (see his *Auserlesene mit Ernst und Lust gemengte Instrumentalmusik,* 1701)]

Op. 7, no. 6 in B♭ major
HG xxviii, 135–40

1st movement
(B♭ major, ¾, Pomposo)

Telemann, *Musique de Table,* Book 3, concerto in E♭ major for two Waldhornen and strings, 1st movement (E♭ major, ¾, Maestoso). Relationship = B

Single concerto movement for two organs in D minor
HG xlviii, 51–6;
HHA iv/12, 87–94

See under op. 7, no. 4, 1st movement

Organ concerto no. 13 in F major
HG xlviii, 2–13;

1st movement
(F major, C, Larghetto)

Op. 5, no. 6 (trio sonata) 1st movement (F major, C, Largo). Relationship = D

2nd movement
(F major, C, Allegro)

(1) op. 6, no. 9, 2nd movement (F major, C, Allegro) Relationship =C

(2) Kerll, *Capricio Kuku* (G major, C, no tempo indication). Relationship = A (Compare bars 27–30 of the concerto with bars 1–3 of the Kerll—see Chapter II Example 2)

3rd movement
(D minor, §, Larghetto)

Op. 6, no. 9, 3rd movement (D minor, §, Larghetto). Relationship = D

4th movement
(F major, C, Allegro)

Op. 5, no. 6 (trio sonata), 4th movement (F major, C, Allegro). Relationship = C

Organ concerto no. 14 in A major
HG xlviii, 14–28

The whole concerto uses the same material as op. 6, no. 11 in A major

1st movement (A major, C, 'largo e staccato')

Op. 6, no. 11, 1st movement (A major, C, 'andante larghetto e staccato'). Relationship = D

2nd movement
(A major, ¾, Andante)

Op. 6, no. 11, 4th movement (A major, ¾, Andante). Relationship = D

3rd movement
(F♯ minor, C, Grave)

Op. 6, no. 11, 3rd movement (F♯ minor, C, 'largo e staccato'). Relationship = E

4th movement
(A major, C, Allegro)

Op. 6, no. 11, 5th movement (A major, C, Allegro). Relationship = E

Organ concerto no. 15 in D minor
HG xlviii, 57–67;
HHA iv/12, 69–84

1st movement
(D minor, ¾, Andante)

Telemann, *Musique de Table*, Book 1, no. 5, 1st movement (B minor, 𝄴, cantabile). Relationship = B

2nd movement
(D minor, ⅜, Andante)

Telemann, *Musique de Table*, Book 1, no. 5, 4th movement (B minor, ⅜, Allegro). Relationship = A

Organ concerto no. 16 in F major ('Ouverture')
HG xlviii, 68–100

1st movement
(F major, C, no tempo indication)

(1) Third concerto 'a due cori', 1st movement ('Ouverture') (F major, C, no tempo indication). Relationship = E

(2) Fitzwilliam Overture for two clarinets and corno di caccia, 1st movement (D major, C, Andante). Relationship = A

2nd movement
(F major, ¾, Allegro)

Third concerto 'a due cori', 2nd movement (F major, ¾, Allegro). Relationship = E

3rd movement
(F major, C, 'allegro ma non troppo')

Third concerto 'a due cori', 3rd movement (F major, C, 'allegro ma non troppo'). Relationship = E

4th movement
(D minor, 3/2, Adagio)

Third concerto 'a due cori', 4th movement (D minor, 3/2, Adagio). Relationship = E

5th movement
(F major, ¾, Andante)

Third concerto 'a due cori', 5th movement (F major, ¾, 'andante larghetto'). Relationship = E

6th movement
(F major, 12/8, Allegro)

(1) Third concerto 'a due cori', 6th movement (F major, 12/8, Allegro). Relationship = D (Exact for first part but the 'due cori' concerto has an extra D minor middle section and 'da capo' marks)

(2) *Partenope*, Act 1, Rosmira's aria, 'Io segno sol fiero' (F major, 12/8, Allegro). Relationship = B

7th movement (Marche) (F major, ₵, Allegro)	(1) *Judas Maccabaeus*, Act 3, March (after 'See, the conqu'ring hero comes' (G major, ₵, March). Relationship = E
	(2) Gottlieb Muffat, *Componimenti Musicali*, suite no. 6, 7th movement (Air) (G major, ₵, Vivace). Relationship = A

'Second' oboe concerto in B♭
HG xxi, 91–7;
HHA iv/12, 47–62
Version (a)

1st movement (B♭ major, C, Vivace)	(1) Chandos Anthem no. 8: 'O Come let us sing unto the Lord', Sonata (instrumental introduction), 1st movement (A major, C, Andante). Relationship = E
	(2) version (*b*) *HG* xxi, 98–9; *HHA* iv/12, 63–6 single movement (F major, C, Largo). Relationship = B
2nd movement (B♭ major, ₵, Allegro 'Fuga')	(1) Chandos Anthem no. 8: 'O Come let us sing unto the Lord', Sonata (instrumental introduction), 2nd movement (A major, ¾, Allegro). Relationship = E
	(2) op. 2, no. 4 (trio sonata), 4th movement (F major, C, Allegro). Relationship = C
3rd movement (B♭ major, C, Andante)	(1) Chandos Anthem no. 5: 'I will Magnify thee' (first version), Overture, 1st movement (A major, C, Andante). Relationship = E
	(2) op. 5, no. 1 (trio sonata), 1st movement (A major, C, Andante). Relationship = E
	(3) *Sonata a cinque*, 1st movement (B♭ major, C, Andante). Relationship = B
	(4) Chandos Anthem no. 5; 'I will Magnify thee' (second version), ritornello of 1st movement, alto aria, 'I will Magnify thee' (A major, C, Andante). Relationship = B
	(5) *Belshazzar*, Act 3, Cyrus' aria, 'I will Magnify thee' (A major, C, Andante). Relationship = B
	(6) no. 22 of *Einzelne Suiten und Stücke, zweite Folge*, ed. T. Best, *HHA* iv/17 (Kassel, 1975) (G minor, C, Larghetto). Relationship = A
4th movement (B♭ major, ¾, Allegro)	(1) Chandos Anthem no. 5; 'I will Magnify thee' (first version), Overture, 2nd movement (A major, ¾, Allegro). Relationship = E

(2) op. 5, no. 1 (trio sonata) 2nd movement (A major, ¾, Allegro). Relationship = E

**Oboe concerto in G minor
HG xxi, 100–7;
HHA iv/12, 3–16**

4th movement
(G minor, ¾, Allegro)

(1) op. 4, no. 3, 2nd movement (G minor, ¾, Allegro). Relationship = A

(2) op. 2, no. 5 (trio sonata), 4th movement (G minor, ¾, Allegro). Relationship = A

(3) no. 18 of *Einzelne Suiten und Stücke, zweite Folge*, ed. T. Best, *HHA* iv/17 (Kassel, 1975), 2nd movement (A minor, ¾, Allegro). Relationship = A

[A variant of the same theme appears in op. 2, no. 2, 4th movement and in op. 1, no. 4, 4th movement]

**Sonata a cinque in B♭ for
solo violin, oboes, strings, and
continuo
HG xxi, 108–16;
HHA iv/12, 29–44**

1st movement
(B♭ major, C, Andante)

(1) 'Second' oboe concerto in B♭ major version (*a*), 3rd movement (B♭ major, C, Andante). Relationship = B

(2) *Belshazzar*, Act 3, Cyrus' aria, 'I will magnify thee' (A major, C, Andante). Relationship = B

(3) Chandos Anthem no. 5: 'I will Magnify thee' (first version), Overture, 1st movement (A major, C, Andante). Relationship = B

(4) Chandos Anthem no. 5: 'I will Magnify thee' (second version), ritornello of 1st movement, alto aria, 'I will Magnify thee' (A major, C, Andante). Relationship = B

(5) op. 5, no. 1 (trio sonata), 1st movement (A major, C, Andante). Relationship = B

(6) no. 22 of *Einzelne Suiten und Stücke, zweite Folge*, ed. T. Best, *HHA* iv/17 (Kassel, 1975) (G minor, C, Larghetto). Relationship = A

First concerto 'a due cori' in
B♭ major
HG xlvii, 130–58;
HHA iv/12, 97–128

1st movement
(B♭ major, C, no tempo
indication)

Alexander Balus, Overture, 1st movement
(slow section only) (D major, C, no tempo
indication). Relationship = E

2nd movement
(B♭ major, ¾, 'allegro ma
non troppo')

Messiah, part 1, chorus: 'And the glory of
the Lord' (A major, ¾, Allegro). Relationship = D. (There is a 14-bar cut in the
middle of the concerto)

3rd movement
(B♭ major, C, Allegro)

Belshazzar, Act 2, chorus: 'See from his
post Euphrates flies' (B♭ major, C, 'allegro
ma non presto'). Relationship = D. (The
length is the same but there are minor
differences in melodic and inner parts)

4th movement
(G minor, ¾, Largo)

Ottone, Act 2, Teofane's aria, 'S'io dir
potessi' (G minor, ⅜, Largo). Relationship = A

5th movement
(B♭ major, C, 'a tempo
ordinario')

Semele, Act 1, chorus: 'Lucky omens bless
our rites' (B♭ major, C, 'a tempo
ordinario'). Relationship = D. (The concerto is shortened) Leading to . . .

6th movement
(B♭ major, ₵, 'alla breve
moderato')

Semele, Act 1, next chorus (B♭ major, ₵,
'alla breve moderato'). Relationship = E

7th movement
(Minuet) (B♭ major, ⅜, no
tempo indication)

Lotario, Act 2, Clodomiro's aria, 'Non
t'inganni la speranza' (F major, ⅜, Allegro).
Relationship = B

Second concerto 'a due
cori' in F major
HG xlvii, 159–202

1st movement
(F major, C, Pomposo)

Esther (1720 version), aria for an Israelite,
'Jehovah crown'd with glory bright' (F
major, C, Maestoso). Relationship = C

2nd movement
(F major, ¾, Allegro)

Esther (1720 version), chorus: 'he comes, he
comes' (to first double bar) (F major, ¾,
'allegro moderato'). Relationship = D

3rd movement
(F major, C, 'a tempo giusto')

Messiah, part 2, chorus: 'Lift up your heads'
(F major, C, 'a tempo ordinario'). Relationship = C

4th movement
(D minor, ¹²⁄₈, Largo)

Esther (1720 version), chorus: 'Ye sons of
Israel, mourn' (C minor, ¹²⁄₈, Adagio). Relationship = E

5th movement
(F major, ¾, 'allegro ma
non troppo)'

Birthday Ode for Queen Anne (1713), duet,
'Let rolling streams their gladness show' (G
major, ¾, no tempo indication). Relationship = A (the ground basses correspond)

6th movement
(F major, C, 'a tempo
ordinario')

The *Occasional Oratorio*, Act 1, chorus:
'God found them guilty, let them fall' (F
major, C, Andante). Relationship = B.
(Only the tutti sections of the concerto are
taken from the oratorio movement)

Third concerto 'a due cori' in F major
HG xlvii, 203–41

For 1st–5th movements see
under organ concerto no. 16

6th movement
(F major, ¹²⁄₈, Allegro)

(1) organ concerto no. 16, 6th movement
(F major, ¹²⁄₈, Allegro). Relationship = D
(exact for the first part, but the 'due cori'
concerto has an extra D minor middle
section and 'da capo' marks)

(2) *Partenope*, Act 1, Rosmira's aria, 'Io
segno sol fiero', (F major, ¹²⁄₈, Allegro).
Relationship = C (i.e. there is a closer relationship between this aria and the concerto
'a due cori' than between it and the organ
version)

Unlike organ concerto no. 16
there is no final March

Appendix B

The concertos of G. P. Telemann: sources of examples in Chapter III

All works listed are by Telemann unless otherwise indicated.

Ex.1: concerto in G major for two Violetten, strings, and continuo, ed. Kurt Flattschacher (Heidelberg, 1966).

Ex.2: concerto in E major for violin, strings, and continuo, ed. Siegfried Kross, *Georg Philipp Telemann Musikalische Werke*, vol. xxiii, *Zwölf Violinkonzerte* (Kassel, 1973), pp. 57ff.

Ex.3: concerto in F major for recorder, gamba, strings, and continuo, MS. 1034/43, Darmstadt (Hessische Landes-und Hochschulbibliothek).

Ex.4: concerto in D major for trumpet, strings, and continuo, ed. Karl Grebe (Hamburg, 1959).

Ex.5 concerto in D minor for oboe, strings, and continuo, ed. Hermann Töttcher, keyboard reduction (Hamburg, 1953).

Ex.6: concerto in E minor for flute, recorder, strings, and continuo, ed. Herbert Kölbel (Kassel, 1969), Hortus Musicus no. 124.

Ex.7: concerto in D major for violin, strings, and continuo, ed. Siegfried Kross, *Georg Philipp Telemann Musikalische Werke*, vol. xxiii, *Zwölf Violinkonzerte* (Kassel, 1973), pp. 45ff.

Ex.8: concerto in D major for flute, strings, and continuo, MS. 5600, Brussels (Conservatoire Royal de Musique, Bibliothèque).

Ex.9: concerto in E minor for flute, recorder, strings, and continuo, ed. Herbert Kölbel—see under Ex. 6.

Ex.10: concerto in G major for viola, strings, and continuo, ed. Hellmuth Christian Wolff (Kassel, 1968), Hortus Musicus no. 22.

Ex.11: concerto in E major for flute, oboe d'amore, viola d'amore, strings, and continuo, ed. Fritz Stein (Frankfurt, 1938).

Ex.12: as Ex. 11.

Ex.13: concerto in D major for three trumpets, drums, and orchestra, ed. Günter Fleischhauer (Leipzig, 1968).

Ex.14: concerto in F major for recorder, strings, and continuo, ed. Manfred Ruëtz (Kassel, 1969), Hortus Musicus no. 130.

Ex.15: concerto in A minor for two flutes, strings, and continuo, ed. Fritz Stein (Kassel, 1953), Nagels Musik-Archiv no. 167.

Ex.16: concerto in F minor for oboe, strings, and continuo, ed. Felix Schroeder (London, 1958), Eulenburg no. 1214.

Ex.17: concerto in A major for flute, violin, cello, strings, and continuo, ed. J. P. Hinnenthal, *Georg Philipp Telemann Musikalische Werke*, vol. xii, *Tafelmusik*, Book 1 (Kassel, 1959), pp. 51ff.

Ex.18: as Ex. 17.

Ex.19: concerto in D major for flute, strings, and continuo ('Concerto Polonoise'), MS. Stockholm (Kungliga Musikaliska Akademiens Bibliotek).

Ex.20: concerto in F major for violin, strings, and continuo, ed. Siegfried Kross, *Georg Philipp Telemann Musikalische Werke*, vol. xxiii, *Zwölf Violinkonzerte* (Kassel, 1973), pp. 90ff.

Ex.21: concerto in G major for violin, strings, and continuo, ibid., pp. 106ff.

Ex.22: concerto in D major for violin, strings, and continuo, ed. Siegfried Kross—see under Ex. 7.

Ex.23: concerto in A major for flute, violin, cello, strings, and continuo, ed. J. P. Hinnenthal—see under Ex. 17.

Ex.24: concerto in G minor for violin, strings, and continuo, ed. Siegfried Kross, *Georg Philipp Telemann Musikalische Werke*, vol. xxiii, *Zwölf Violinkonzerte* (Kassel, 1973), pp. 137ff.

Ex.25: concerto in A major for oboe d'amore, strings, and continuo, ed. Felix Schroeder (London, *c*. 1962).

Ex.26(*a*): as Ex. 25.

26(*b*): concerto in E minor for flute, violin, strings, and continuo, ed. (as a flute concerto) by Felix Schroeder (London, 1962), Eulenburg no. 1244.

Ex.27: concerto in F minor for oboe, strings, and continuo, ed. Felix Schroeder—see under Ex. 16.

Ex.28: concerto in G major for viola, strings, and continuo, ed. Hellmuth Christian Wolff—see under Ex. 10.

Ex.29: concerto in F major for recorder, strings, and continuo, ed. Manfred Ruëtz—see under Ex. 14.

Ex.30: concerto in E♭ major for two *tromba selvatica*, two violins, strings, and continuo, ed. J. P. Hinnenthal, *Georg Philipp Telemann Musikalische Werke*, vol. xiv, *Tafelmusik*, Book 3 (Kassel, 1963), pp. 63ff.

Ex.31: concerto in D major for three trumpets, drums, and orchestra, ed. Günter Fleischhauer—see under Ex. 13.

Ex.32: concerto in E major for flute, oboe d'amore, viola d'amore, strings, and continuo, ed. Fritz Stein—see under Ex. 11.

Ex.33(*a*): concerto in B♭ major for two flutes, two oboes, strings, and continuo, ed. Karl Michael Komma, *Das Erbe deutscher*

Musik, Reihe I, Bd. 11, *Gruppenkonzerte der Bachzeit* (Leipzig, 1938), pp. 26–55.

33(*b*): C. Graupner, Concerto in B♭ major for two flutes, two oboes, strings, and continuo, ed. Arnold Schering, *Denkmäler deutscher Tonkunst*, vol. xxix–xxx, *Instrumentalkonzerte deutscher Meister* (Leipzig, 1907; revised edition by Hans Joachim Moser, Wiesbaden, 1958), pp. 196–220.

Ex.34: concerto in D major for violin, strings, and continuo, ed. Siegfried Kross, *Georg Philipp Telemann Musikalische Werke*, vol. xxiii, *Zwölf Violinkonzerte* (Kassel, 1973), pp. 23ff.

Appendix C

The concertos of J. A. Hasse: modern editions arranged by date of publication

Flute concerto in B minor (Op. 3, no. 10), ed. A. Schering in *Denkmäler deutscher Tonkunst* vol. xxix–xxx (Leipzig, 1907; revised by H. J. Moser (Wiesbaden, 1958)), pp. 33–61.

Mandolin concerto in G major (compare the flute version, op. 3, no. 11),[1] ed. H. Neeman (Berlin 1938).

Flute concerto in D major (op. 3, no. 6), ed. R. Engländer, *Eulenburg Miniature Scores* no. 1203 (London, 1953).

Flute concerto in G major (op. 3, no. 5), ed. R. Engländer, *Nagels Musik-Archiv* no. 194 (Kassel, 1957).

Flute concerto in A major, ed. W. Mohr, *Banchetto Musicale*, no number (Heidelberg, 1964).

Oboe concerto in F major, ed. H. Töttcher and K. Spannegel (Hamburg, 1966).

[1] See p. 251.

Appendix D

The concertos of C. P. E. Bach: modern editions arranged by Wotquenne number

Wq. 6, harpsichord concerto in G minor, ed. F. Oberdörffer (Kassel, 1952).

Wq. 22, flute concerto[1] in D minor, ed. K. Redel (Munich and Leipzig, 1959); also ed. J-P. Rampal (New York, 1969).

Wq. 23, harpsichord concerto in D minor, ed. A. Schering, *Denkmäler deutscher Tonkunst*, xxix–xxx (Leipzig, 1906; revised H. J. Moser, Wiesbaden, 1958), pp. 62–102; also ed. G. Wertheim (Wiesbaden, 1956); also ed. G. Darvas (Budapest, 1968).

Wq. 26 (Wq. 166, Wq. 170), concerto in A minor for harpsichord (or flute, or cello) and strings, ed. W. Altmann (London, 1954).

Wq. 27, harpsichord concerto in D major, ed. E. N. Kulukundis, *Collegium Musicum Yale University*, second series, ii (Madison, 1970).

Wq. 29 (Wq. 168, Wq. 172), concerto in A major for harpsichord (or flute, or cello) and strings, ed. H. M. Kneihs (London, 1967).

Wq. 33, harpsichord concerto in F major, ed. F. Oberdörffer (Kassel, 1952).

Wq. 34, organ concerto in G major, ed. H. Winter (Hamburg, 1964).

Wq. 35, organ concerto in E♭ major, ibid.

Wq. 43, no. 2, harpsichord concerto in D major, ed. L. Landshoff (Wilhelmshaven, 1967).

Wq. 43, no. 5, harpsichord concerto in G major, ed. H. Riemann (reduction for two keyboards) (Leipzig, 1897).

Wq. 47, concerto in E♭ major for harpsichord, fortepiano, and orchestra, ed. E. R. Jacobi (Kassel, 1958).

Wq. 164, oboe concerto in B♭ major, ed. O. Kaul (Munich, 1965).

Wq. 165, oboe concerto in E♭ major, ed. H. Töttcher and K. Grebe (Hamburg, 1959).

Wq. 168, flute concerto in A major, ed. J-P. Rampal (New York, 1954); also ed. H. M. Kneihs (Zurich, 1968).

Wq. 169, flute concerto in G major, ed. J-P. Rampal (New York, 1960).

Wq. 171, concerto in B♭ major for cello (or viola) and strings, ed. P. Klengel (Leipzig, 1931); also ed. W. Schulz (Leipzig, 1938).

[1] See Chapter V, Table 4, note 1.

Appendix E

The concertos of C. P. E. Bach: sources of examples in Chapter V

All works listed are by Bach.

Ex.1: Wq. 6, harpsichord concerto in G minor, ed. F. Oberdörffer (Kassel, 1952).

Ex.2: Wq. 171, concerto in B♭ major for cello (or viola), strings, and continuo, ed. P. Klengel (Leipzig, 1931).

Ex.3: Wq. 6—see under Ex. 1.

Ex.4: Wq. 2, harpsichord concerto in E♭ major, published by Huberty (Paris, advertised 26 April 1762).

Ex.5: Wq. 165, oboe concerto in E♭ major, ed. H. Töttcher and K. Grebe (Hamburg, 1959).

Ex.6: Wq. 35, organ concerto in E♭ major, ed. H. Winter (Hamburg, 1964).

Ex.7: Wq. 14, harpsichord concerto in E major, published by G. L. Winter (Berlin, 1760).

Ex.8: Wq. 11, harpsichord concerto in D major, published by Balthasar Schmid (Nuremberg, 1745).

Ex.9: Wq. 6—see under Ex. 1.

Ex.10: Wq. 23, harpsichord concerto in D minor, ed. A. Schering, *Denkmäler deutscher Tonkunst*, xxix–xxx (Leipzig, 1906; revised H. J. Moser, Wiesbaden, 1958), pp. 62–102.

Ex.11: Wq. 14—see under Ex. 7.

Ex.12: Wq. 43, no. 1, harpsichord concerto in F major, published in Hamburg (1772).

Ex.13(a) Wq. 25, harpsichord concerto in B♭ major, published by Balthasar Schmid (Nuremberg, 1752).

  13(b) Wq. 25, harpsichord concerto in B♭ major, MS. at GB-Lbm K. 7, i. 10.

Ex.14: Wq. 43, no. 1—see under Ex. 12.

Ex.15: Wq. 43, no. 1—see under Ex. 12.

Ex.16: Wq. 43, no. 3, harpsichord concerto in E♭ major, published in Hamburg (1772).

Ex.17: Wq. 43, no. 6, harpsichord concerto in C major, published in Hamburg (1772).

Ex.18: Wq. 2—see under Ex. 4.

Ex.19: Wq. 47, concerto in E♭ major for harpsichord, fortepiano, and orchestra, ed. E. R. Jacobi (Kassel, 1958).

Ex.20: Wq. 35—see under Ex. 6.

Ex.21: Wq. 23—see under Ex. 10.

Ex.22: Wq. 43, no. 2, harpsichord concerto in D major, published in Hamburg (1772).

Ex.23: Wq. 171—see under Ex. 2.

Ex.24: Wq. 26, harpsichord concerto in A minor, ed. W. Altmann (London, 1954).

Ex.25: Wq. 23—see under Ex. 10.

Ex.26: Wq. 47—see under Ex. 19.

Ex.27: Wq. 47—see under Ex. 19.

Select Bibliography

ABER, ADOLF, 'Studien zu J. S. Bachs Klavierkonzerten', *Bach-Jahrbuch*, x (1913), 5–30.

ABRAHAM, GERALD ed., *Handel: a Symposium* (London, 1954).

ALDRICH, PUTNAM, 'Bach's Technique of Transcription and Improvised Ornamentation', *The Musical Quarterly*, xxxv (1949), 26–35.

AVISON, CHARLES, *Essay on Musical Expression* (London, 1752).

BACH, CARL PHILIPP EMANUEL, *Versuch über die wahre Art das Clavier zu Spielen*, 2nd edn., 2 vols. (Berlin, 1759); first published 1753, 1762). Tr. and ed. William J. Mitchell under the title: *Essay on the true art of playing keyboard instruments*, 2nd edn. (London, 1951; first published 1949).

The Bach Reader, ed. Hans T. David and Arthur Mendel, revised with supplement (London, 1966; first published 1945).

BARCLAY SQUIRE, WILLIAM, *Catalogue of the King's music library, Part I: The Handel Manuscripts* (London, 1927).

BARFORD, PHILIP, *The Keyboard Music of C. P. E. Bach considered in relation to his musical aesthetic and the rise of the sonata principle* (London, 1965).

BECK, HERMANN, 'Das Soloinstrument im Tutti des Konzerts der zweiten Hälfte des 18. Jahrhunderts', *Die Musikforschung*, xiv (1961), 427–35.

BECKER, HEINZ, 'Das Chalumeau bei Telemann', *Konferenzbericht der 3. Magdeburger Telemann-Festtage 1967*, ed. G. Fleischhauer and W. Siegmund-Schultz (Magdeburg, 1969), ii. 68–76.

BERGER, JEAN, 'Notes on Some 17th-Century Compositions for Trumpets and Strings in Bologna', *The Musical Quarterly*, xxxvii (1951), 354–67.

BESSELER, HEINRICH, 'Bach als Wegbereiter', *Archiv für Musikwissenschaft*, xii (1955), 1–39.

——, 'Zur Chronologie der Konzerte Joh. Seb. Bachs', *Festschrift Max Schneider zum achtzigsten Geburtstag,* ed. Walther Vetter (Leipzig, 1955), pp. 115–28.

——, 'Markgraf Christian Ludwig von Brandenburg', *Bach-Jahrbuch,* xliii (1956), 18–35.

——, ed., *Sechs Brandenburgischen Konzerte: Kritischer Bericht,* Johann Sebastian Bach: Neue Ausgabe Sämtlicher Werke, vii/2 (Kassel, 1956).

BITTER, C. H.,*Carl Philipp Emanuel und Wilhelm Friedemann Bach und deren Brüder*, 2 vols. (Berlin, 1868).

BLUME, FRIEDRICH, 'Die formgeschichtliche Stellung der Klavierkonzerte Mozarts', *Mozart-Jahrbuch*, ii (1924), 81–107.

——, *Johann Sebastian Bach im Wandel der Geschichte* (Kassel, 1947). Tr. Stanley Godman under the title: *Two Centuries of Bach: an account of changing taste* (London, 1950).

——, 'J. S. Bach's Youth', *The Musical Quarterly*, liv (1968), 1–30.

BOAS, HANS, 'Über Joh. Seb. Bachs Konzerte für drei Klaviere', *Bach-Jahrbuch*, x (1913), 31–8.

BONACCORSI, A., 'Contributio alla storia del Concerto grosso', *Rivista Musicale Italiana*, xxxix (1932), 467–92.

BOURKE, JOHN, 'Frederick the Great as Music-lover and Musician', *Music and Letters*, xxviii (1947), 63–77.

BOYDEN, DAVID D., 'When is a Concerto Not a Concerto?', *The Musical Quarterly*, xliii (1957), 220–32.

BROOK, BARRY S., ed., *The Breitkopf Thematic Catalogue: the Six Parts and Sixteen Supplements 1762–87* (New York, 1966).

DE BROSSES, CHARLES, *Le Président de Brosses en Italie: lettres familières écrites d'Italie en 1739 et 1740 par Charles de Brosses*, ed. M. R. Colomb, 2nd edn., 2 vols. (Paris, 1858; first published 1836).

BÜTTNER, HORST, *Das Konzert in den Orchestersuiten Georg Philipp Telemanns* (Wolfenbüttel and Berlin, 1935).

BUKOFZER, MANFRED F., *Music in the Baroque Era from Monteverdi to Bach* (London, 1948; first published New York, 1947).

BUNGE, RUDOLF, 'Johann Sebastian Bachs Kapelle zu Cöthen und deren nachgelassene Instrumente', *Bach-Jahrbuch*, ii (1905), 14–47.

BURNEY, CHARLES, *The Present State of Music in Germany, the Netherlands, and United Provinces*, 2nd edn., 2 vols. (London, 1775; first published 1773). Tr. C. D. Ebeling under the title: *Tagebuch einer Musikalischen Reisen*, 3 vols. (Hamburg, 1773; facsimile edn. by Richard Schaal, Kassel, 1959).

——, *An Account of the Musical Performances in Westminster-Abbey, and the Pantheon, May 26th, 27th, 29th; and June the 3rd, and 5th, 1784. In Commemoration of Handel* (London, 1785).

——, *A General History of Music from the earliest ages to the present period*, 4 vols. (London, 1789).

CARLYLE, THOMAS, *History of Friedrich II. of Prussia, called Frederick the Great*, 6 vols. (London, 1858–65).

CARRELL, NORMAN, *Bach's 'Brandenburg' Concertos* (London, 1963).

——, *Bach the Borrower* (London, 1967).

CARSE, ADAM, *The History of Orchestration* (New York, 1964; first published London, 1925).

——, *The Orchestra in the XVIIIth Century* (Cambridge, 1940).

CHRYSANDER, FRIEDRICH, *G. F. Händel*, 3 vols. (Leipzig, 1858, 1860, and 1867).

——, 'Händels zwölf Concerti grossi für Streichinstrumente', *Allgemeine musikalische Zeitung*, xvi (1881), 81–3, 97–9, 113–15, 129–32, 145–8.

——, 'Händels Instrumentalkompositionen für grosses Orchester', *Vierteljahrsschrift für Musikwissenschaft*, iii (1887), 1–25.

CLAUSEN, HANS DIETER, *Händels Direktionspartituren 'Handexemplar'*, Hamburger Beiträge zur Musikwissenschaft, Band 7 (Hamburg, 1972).

CLERCX, SUSANNE, 'La forme du Rondo chez Carl Philipp Emanuel Bach', *Revue de musicologie*, xvi (1935), 148–67.

COLE, MALCOLM S., 'Rondos, proper and improper', *Music and Letters*, li (1970), 388–99.

COLLINS BAKER, C. H. and BAKER, MURIEL I., *The Life and Circumstances of James Brydges First Duke of Chandos* (Oxford, 1949).

CRICKMORE, LEON, 'C. P. E. Bach's Harpsichord Concertos', *Music and Letters*, xxxix–xl (1958), 227–41.

CROTCH, WILLIAM, *Substance of several courses of lectures on music read in the University of Oxford, and in the metropolis* (London, 1831).

CUDWORTH, CHARLES, 'The English Organ Concerto', *The Score*, viii (1953), 51–60.

——, 'Handel and the French Style', *Music and Letters*, xl (1959), 122–31.

DADELSEN, GEORG VON, *Bemerkungen zur Handschrift Johann Sebastian Bachs seiner Familie und seiner Kreises*, Tübinger Bach-Studien, Heft i (Trossingen, 1957).

——, *Beiträge zur Chronologie der Werke Johann Sebastian Bachs*, Tübinger Bach-Studien, ed. W. Gerstenberg, Heft iv/5 (Trossingen, 1958).

——, 'Telemann und die sogennante Barockmusik', *Musik und Verlag: Karl Vötterle zum 65. Geburtstag am 12. April 1968 (Vötterle Festschrift)*, ed. Richard Baum and Wolfgang Rehm (Kassel, 1968), pp. 197–205.

DAFFNER, HUGO, *Die Entwicklung des Klavierkonzerts bis Mozart* (Leipzig, 1906).

DAHLHAUS, CARL, 'Bachs konzertante Fugen', *Bach-Jahrbuch*, xlii (1955), 45–72.

——, 'Versuch über Bachs Harmonik', *Bach-Jahrbuch*, xliii (1956), 73–92.

——, 'Bach und der „linear Kontrapunkt" ', *Bach-Jahrbuch*, xlix (1962), 58–79.

DART, THURSTON, 'Bach's "Fiauti d'Echo" ', *Music and Letters*, xli (1960), 331–41.

DAVISON, ARCHIBALD THOMPSON, *Bach and Handel: the consummation of the baroque in music* (Cambridge, Mass., 1951).

DAYMOND, EMILY R., 'Carl Philipp Emanuel Bach', *Proceedings of the Royal Musical Association*, xxxiii (1906–7), 45–52.

DEAN, WINTON, *Handel's Dramatic Oratorios and Masques* (London, 1959).

DELANEY, MARY, *The Autobiography and Correspondence of Mary Granville, Mrs. Delaney*, ed. the Rt. Hon. Lady Llanover, 3 vols. (London, 1861).

DENT, EDWARD J., *Alessandro Scarlatti: His Life and Works*, new impression with preface and additional notes by Frank Walker (London, 1960; first published 1905).

——, 'English Influences on Handel', *The Monthly Musical Record*, lxi (1931), 225–8.

——, *Handel* (London, 1947; first published 1934).

DEUTSCH, OTTO ERICH, ed., *Handel: A Documentary Biography* (London, 1955).

——, ed., *Mozart: die Dokumente seines Lebens*, Neue Mozart-Ausgabe (Kassel, 1961).

DOUNIAS, MINOS, *Die Violinkonzerte Giuseppe Tartini als Ausdruck einer Künstlerpersönlichkeit und einer Kulturepoch* (Munich, 1935).

DOWNES, EDWARD O. D., 'The Neapolitan Tradition in Opera', *Report of the Eighth Congress of the International Musicological Society, New York, 1961*, 2 vols. (Kassel, 1961), i. 277–84 and ii. 132–4.

DÜRR, ALFRED, 'Zur Chronologie der Leipziger Vocalwerke J. S. Bachs', *Bach-Jahrbuch*, xliv (1957), 5–162.

EDWARDS, OWAIN, 'English String Concertos before 1800', *Proceedings of the Royal Musical Association*, xcv (1968–9), 1–13.

EITNER, ROBERT, 'Thematischer Katalog der von Thulemeier'schen Musikalien-Sammlung in der Bibliothek des Joachimsthal'schen Gymnasiums zu Berlin', Supplement to *Monatshefte für Musikgeschichte*, xxxi (1899; reprint New York, 1960).

ELLER, RUDOLF, 'Zur Frage Bach-Vivaldi', *Bericht über den internationalen musikwissenschaftlichen Kongress Hamburg 1956*, ed. W. Gerstenberg, H. Husmann, H. Heckmann (Kassel, 1957), 80–5.

——, 'Die Entstehung der Themenzweiheit in der Frühgeschichte des Instrumentalkonzerts', *Festschrift Heinrich Besseler zum sechzigsten Geburtstag* (Leipzig, 1961), pp. 323–5.

——, and HELLER, KARL, Foreword to vol. vii/6 of the Neue Bach-Ausgabe, *Konzerte für drei und vier Cembali* (Kassel and Basle, 1975).

ENGEL, HANS, *Das Instrumentalkonzert* (Wiesbaden, 1971; first published Leipzig, 1932).

EPPSTEIN, H., 'Zur vor-und Entstehungsgeschichte von J. S. Bachs

Triplekonzert a moll (BWV 1044)', *Jahrbuch Staatlichen Institut Musikforschung*, 1970(1971), 34–44.

FALCK, MARTIN, *Wilhelm Friedemann Bach* (Lindau, 1956).

FAUCHIER-MAGNAN, ADRIEN, *The Small German Courts in the Eighteenth Century*, tr. M. Savill (London, 1958) from the original French version (Paris, 1947).

FEDERHOFER, HELLMUT, 'Bemerkungen zum Verhältnis von Harmonik und Stimmführung bei Johann Sebastian Bach', *Festschrift Heinrich Besseler zum sechzigsten Geburtstag* (Leipzig, 1961), pp. 343–50.

FERAND, E. T., 'Marcello: A. oder B.?', *Die Musikforschung*, xii (1959), 86.

FISCHER, W., *Verschollene Solokonzerte in Rekonstruktion: Kritischer Bericht*, Neue Bach-Ausgabe, vii/7 (Supplement) (Kassel, 1971).

——, 'Wiedergewonnene Solokonzerte Johann Sebastian Bachs: Bemerkungen zum Supplement der Neuen Bach-Ausgabe', *Musica*, xxv/2 (1972), 133–4.

FISKE, ROGER, 'Handel's Organ Concertos—do they belong to particular Oratorios?', *The Organ Yearbook*, iii (1972), 14–22.

FITZPATRICK, HORACE, 'The Austro-Bohemian School of Horn-Playing, 1680–1830, Its Players Composers, Instruments, and Makers: the Evolution of a Style', Univ. of Oxford D.Phil. thesis, 1965; published in a different version as *The Horn and Horn-Playing and the Austro-Bohemian tradition from 1680–1830* (London, 1970).

FLEISCHHAUER, GÜNTER, 'Die Musik Georg Philipp Telemanns im Urteil seiner Zeit', *Händel-Jahrbuch*, xiii–xiv (1967–8), 173–205; xv–xvi (1969–70), 23–73.

——, 'Einige Gedanken zur Instrumentation Telemanns', *Konferenzbericht der 3. Magdeburger Telemann-Festtage 1967*, ed. G. Fleischhauer and W. Siegmund-Schultz (Magdeburg, 1969), ii. 49.

FLUELER, MAX, *Die Norddeutsche Sinfonie zur Zeit Friedrichs der Grosse, und besonders die Werke Ph. Em. Bachs*, Dissertation (Berlin, 1908).

FORKEL, JOHANN NIKOLAUS, *Johann Sebastian Bach: his Life, Art, and Work*, tr. and ed. Charles Sanford Terry (London, 1920; first published Leipzig, 1802).

GECK, MARTIN, 'Gattungstraditionen und Altersschichten in den Brandenburgischen Konzerten', *Die Musikforschung*, xxiii (1970), 139–52.

GEIRINGER, KARL, 'Artistic Interrelations of the Bachs', *The Musical Quarterly*, xxxvi (1950), 363–74.

——, in collaboration with Irene Geiringer, *The Bach Family: Seven Generations of Creative Genius* (London, 1954).

——, in collaboration with Irene Geiringer, *Johann Sebastian Bach: the Culmination of an Era* (London, 1967).

GERBER, RUDOLF, *Bachs Brandenburgische Konzerte: eine Einführung in ihre formale und geistige Wesenart* (Kassel and Basle, 1951).

——, 'Händel und Italien', *50 Jahre Göttinger Händel-Festspiele Festschrift Göttingen*, 1970 (Kassel, 1970), pp. 5–15.

GIAZOTTO, REMO, *Tomaso Albinoni 'Musico di violino dilettante veneto' (1671–1750)* (Milan, 1945).

GIEGLING, FRANZ, *Giuseppe Torelli: ein Beitrage zur Entwicklungsgeschichte des italienisches Konzerts* (Kassel and Basle, 1949).

GIRDLESTONE, CUTHBERT, *Mozart's Piano Concertos* (London, 1958).

GÖLLNER, THEODOR, 'J. S. Bach and the tradition of keyboard transcriptions', *Studies in Eighteenth-Century Music: a Tribute to Karl Geiringer on his Seventieth birthday*, ed. H. C. Robbins Landon in collaboration with Roger E. Chapman (London, 1970), pp. 253–60.

GRADENWITZ, P, 'The Symphonies of Johann Stamitz', *The Music Review*, i (1940), 354–63.

GREEN, DOUGLASS, 'Progressive and Conservative tendencies in the violoncello concertos of Leonardo Leo', *Studies in Eighteenth-Century Music: a Tribute to Karl Geiringer on his Seventieth birthday*, ed. H. C. Robbins Landon in collaboration with Roger E. Chapman (London, 1970), pp. 261–71.

GRESS, JOHANNES, 'Händel in Dresden (1719)', *Händel-Jahrbuch*, ix (1963), 135–51.

GROSSE, HANS, *Telemanns Aufenthalt in Paris* (Leipzig, 1965).

GROUT, D. J., *A Short History of Opera*, 2nd edn. (New York and London, 1965).

HÄFNER, KLAUS, 'Ein bisher nicht beachteter Nachweis zweier Konzerte J. S. Bachs', *Bach-Jahrbuch*, lx (1974), 123–5.

HALM, AUGUST, 'Über J. S. Bachs Konzertform', *Bach-Jahrbuch*, xvi (1919), 1–44.

HANSELL, SVEN HOSTRUP, 'Orchestral Practice at the Court of Cardinal Pietro Ottoboni', *Journal of the American Musicological Society*, xix (1966), 398–403.

——, 'Sacred Music at the *Incurabili* in Venice at the Time of J. A. Hasse', *Journal of the American Musicological Society*, xxiii (1970), 282–301, 505–21.

VON HASE, HERMANN, 'Carl Philipp Emanuel Bach und Joh. Gottl. Im. Breitkopf', *Bach-Jahrbuch*, viii (1911), 86–104.

HAUSWALD, GUNTER, 'Der Divertimento-Begriff bei Georg Christoph Wagenseil', *Archiv für Musikwissenschaft*, ix (1952), 45–50.

HAWKINS, SIR JOHN, *A General History of the Science and Practice of Music*, 5 vols. (London, 1776).

HAYES, WILLIAM, *Remarks on Mr Avison's essay on musical expression* (London, 1753).

HELL, HELMUT,. *Die Neapolitanische Opernsinfonie in der ersten Hälfte des 18. Jahrhunderts* (Tutzing, 1971).

HELM, ERNEST EUGENE, *Music at the Court of Frederick the Great* (Oklahoma, 1960).

HERING, HANS, 'Bachs Klavierübertragungen', *Bach-Jahrbuch*, xlv (1958), 94–113.

HEUS, ALFRED, 'Die Dynamik der Mannheimer Schule', *Zeitschrift für Musikwissenschaft*, ii (1919–20), 44–54.

HIGBEE, DALE, 'Bach's "Fiauti d'Echo" ', *Music and Letters*, xliii (1962), 192–3.

HIRSCH, PAUL, 'Über die Vorlag zum Klavierkonzert in d=moll', *Bach-Jahrbuch*, xxvi (1929), 153–74.

——, 'Nachtrag zu dem Beitrag "Über die Vorlag zum Klavierkonzert in d=moll" ', *Bach-Jahrbuch*, xxvii (1930), 143–4.

Historical Manuscripts Commission, 12th report, appendix, part ix: The Beaufort Manuscripts (London, 1891).

HOFFMANN, A. and REDLICH, H. F., Foreword to vol. iv/14 of the Hallische Händel-Ausgabe, *Zwölf Concerti Grossi Opus 6* (Kassel, 1961).

HOFFMANN, ADOLF, *Die Orchestersuiten Georg Philipp Telemanns* (Wolfenbüttel and Zurich, 1969).

HOFFMAN–ERBRECHT, L., 'Der "Galante Stil" in der Musik des 18. Jahrhunderts', *Festschrift für Erich Schenk* (Graz, 1962), pp. 252–9.

HUCKE, H., 'The Neapolitan Tradition in Opera', *Report of the Eighth Congress of the International Musicological Society New York 1961* (Kassel, 1961), i. 253–77.

HUDSON, FREDERICK, 'Concerning the Watermarks in the Manuscripts and early Prints of G. F. Handel', *The Music Review*, xx (1959), 7–27.

——, Foreword to vol iv/11 of the Hallische Händel-Ausgabe, *Sechs Concerti Grossi Opus 3* (Kassel, 1959).

——, *Sechs Concerti Grossi Opus 3: Kritischer Bericht*, Hallische Händel-Ausgabe, iv/11 (Kassel, 1963).

——, 'Ein seltener Händel-Druck? Das Concerto g-moll für Oboe, zwei Violinen, Viola und Continuo', *Händel-Jahrbuch*, xii–xiv (1967–8), 125–37.

——, Foreword to vol. iv/12 of the Hallische Händel-Ausgabe, *Acht Concerti* (Kassel, 1971).

HUTCHINGS, ARTHUR J. B., 'The Keyboard Concerto', *Music and Letters*, xxiii (1942), 298–311.

——, *The Baroque Concerto*, 3rd rev. edn. (London, 1973; first published 1959).

——, 'The English Concerto With or For Organ', *The Musical*

Quarterly, xlvii (1961), 195–206.

IGOE, J. T., 'Bachs Bearbeitungen für Cembalo solo—Eine Zusammenfassung', *Bach-Jahrbuch*, lvii (1971), 91–7.

JACOBI, E. R., 'Das Autograph von C. P. E. Bachs Doppelkonzert in Es-dur für Cembalo, Fortepiano und Orchester (W.47, Hamburg 1788)', *Die Musikforschung*, xii (1959), 488–9.

KAHL, WILLI, *Selbstbiographien deutscher Musiker des XVIII. Jahrhunderts* (Cologne, 1948).

KAMIEŃSKI, LUCIAN, 'Mannheim und Italien', *Sammelbände der Internationalen Musik-Gesellschaft*, x (1908–9), 307–17.

KAST, PAUL, *Die Bach-Handschriften der Berliner Staatsbibliothek*, Tübinger Bach-Studien, Heft 2/3 (Trossingen, 1958).

KELLER, HERMANN, 'Die Sequenz bei Bach', *Bach-Jahrbuch*, xxxvi (1939), 33–42.

——, 'Studien zur Harmonik Joh. Seb. Bachs', *Bach-Jahrbuch*, xli (1954), 50–65.

——, *The Organ Works of Bach: a Contribution to their History, Form, Interpretation and Performance*, tr. from the German by H. Hewitt (New York, 1967).

KINSKY, GEORG, *Die Originalausgaben der Werke Johann Sebastian Bachs* (Vienna, 1937).

KIRKPATRICK, RALPH, 'Domenico Scarlatti's Early Keyboard Works', *The Musical Quarterly*, xxxvii (1951), 145–60.

——, *Domenico Scarlatti* (Princeton, 1953).

KLEIN, HANS-GUNTER, *Der Einfluss der vivaldischen Konzertform im Instrumentalwerk Johann Sebastian Bachs*, Collection d'études musicologiques, liv (Strasbourg, 1970).

KNÖDT, HEINRICH, 'Zur Entwicklungsgeschichte der Kadenzen in Instrumentalkonzert', *Sammelbände der Internationalen Musik-Gesellschaft*, xv (1914), 375–419.

KOLNEDER, WALTER, 'Das Frühschaffen Antonio Vivaldis', *Internationale Gesellschaft für Musikwissenschaft, Fünfter Kongress Utrecht 3–7 July 1952, Kongressbericht* (Amsterdam, 1953), 254–62.

——, *Aufführungspraxis bei Vivaldi* (Leipzig, 1955).

——, *Die Solokonzertform bei Vivaldi*, Collection d'études musicologiques, xlii (Strasbourg, 1961).

——, *Antonio Vivaldi: his Life and Work*, tr. Bill Hopkins (London, 1970; first published Wiesbaden, 1965).

——, 'Besetzung und Satzstil zu Johann Sebastian Bachs Violonkonzerte', *Festschrift für Walter Wiora zum 30. Dezember 1966 (Wiora Festschrift)*, ed. Ludwig Finscher and Christoph-Hellmut Mahling (Kassel, 1967), pp. 329–34.

KREY, JOHANNES, 'Zur Entstehungsgeschichte des ersten Brandenburgischen Konzerts', *Festschrift Heinrich Besseler zum sechzigsten*

Geburtstag (Leipzig, 1961), pp. 337–42.

KROSS, SIEGFRIED, *Das Instrumentalkonzert bei Georg Philipp Telemann* (Tutzing, 1969).

KRÜGER, WALTHER, *Das Concerto Grosso in Deutschland* (Reinbek, 1932).

——, 'Das "Concerto grosso" Joh. Seb. Bachs', *Bach-Jahrbuch*, xxix (1932), 1–50.

KÜNTZEL, GOTTFRIED, *Die Instrumentalkonzerte von Johann Friedrich Fasch (1688–1758)* (Frankfurt am Main, 1965).

KURTH, ERNST, *Grundlagen des linearen Kontrapunkts, Bachs melodische Polyphonie* (Bern, 1948).

LANG, PAUL HENRY, *Georg Frideric Handel* (New York, 1966).

DE LA LAURENCIE, LIONEL, 'G. Ph. Telemann à Paris', *Revue de musicologie*, xlii (1932), 75–85.

LEBERMANN, WALTER, 'Zur Frage der Eliminierung des Soloparts aus den Tutti-Abschnitten in der Partitur des Solokonzerts', *Die Musikforschung*, xiv (1961), 200–8.

LEE, DOUGLAS A., 'Christoph Nichelmann and the early clavier concerto in Berlin', *The Musical Quarterly*, lvii (1971), 636–55.

LEICHTENTRITT, HUGO, 'Handel's Harmonic Art', *The Musical Quarterly*, xxi (1935), 208–23.

LEWIS, ANTHONY, 'Handel and the Aria', *Proceedings of the Royal Musical Association*, lxxxv (1958–9), 95–107.

LINCOLN, STODDARD, 'Handel's Music for Queen Anne', *The Musical Quarterly*, xlv (1959), 191–207.

VAN DER LINDEN, ALBERT, 'Zur Frage J. S. Bach-Marcello', *Die Musikforschung*, xi (1958), 82–3.

LOCKSPEISER, E., 'French influences on Bach', *Music and Letters*, xvi (1935), 312–20.

MACKERNESS, E. D., 'Bach's Sinfonie-Satz für Violone Concertirende', *The Music Review*, ix (1948), 161–5.

MAINWARING, JOHN, *Memoirs of the Life of the Late George Frederic Handel* (London, 1760).

MANSFIELD, ORLANDO A., 'The Cuckoo and the Nightingale in Music', *The Musical Quarterly*, vii (1921), 261–77.

MARPURG, FRIEDRICH WILHELM, *Historisch-Kritische Beyträge zur Aufnähme der Musik*, 5 vols. (Berlin, 1754–60; facsimile edn. Hildesheim, 1970).

MATTHESON, JOHANN, *Grundlage einer Ehren-Pforte* (Hamburg, 1740; facsimile ed. Max Schneider, Berlin, 1910, reprinted Kassel, 1969).

VAN DER MEER, J. H., 'The Chalumeau Problem', *The Galpin Society Journal*, xv (1962), 89–91.

MENDEL, ARTHUR, 'On the pitches in use in Bach's time', *The Musical Quarterly*, xli (1955), 332–54, 466–80.

——, 'Recent developments in Bach chronology', *The Musical Quarterly*, xlvi (1960), 283–300.

MENNICKE, KARL HEINRICH, 'Johann Adolph Hasse: eine biographische Skizze', *Sammelbände der Internationalen Musik-Gesellschaft*, v (1903–4), 230–44.

——, 'Zur Biographie Joh. Adolph Hasses', *Sammelbände der Internationalen Musik-Gesellschaft*, v (1903–4), 469–75.

——, *Hasse und die Brüder Graun als Symphoniker* (Leipzig, 1906).

MEYER, ERNST H., 'Händel und Purcell', *Händel-Jahrbuch*, v (1959), 9–26.

MEYLAN, RAYMOND, 'Documents douteux dans le domaine des concertos pour instruments à vent au XVIIIᵉ siècle', *Revue de musicologie*, xlix (1963), 47–60.

MIESNER, HEINRICH, *Philipp Emanuel Bach in Hamburg* (Wiesbaden, 1962; first published Berlin, 1929).

——, 'Philipp Emanuel Bachs musikalischer Nachlass', *Bach-Jahrbuch*, xxxv (1938), 103–36; xxxvi (1939), 81–112; xxxvii (1940–8, 161–81.

MOHR, WILHELM, 'Händels 16. Orgelkonzert', *Händel-Jahrbuch*, xii (1966), 77–91.

——, 'Händel als Bearbeiter eigener Werke: Dargestellt an fünf Orgelkonzerten', *Händel-Jahrbuch*, xiii–xiv (1967–8), 83–112.

——, 'Hat Bach ein Oboe-d'amore-Konzert geschrieben?', *Neue Zeitschrift für Musik*, cxxxiii (1972), 507–8.

MONTAGU, LADY MARY WORTLEY, *The Complete Letters of Lady Mary Wortley Montagu*, ed. R. Halsband, 3 vols. (London, 1965–7).

MÜLLER-BLATTAU, JOSEF M., *Georg Friedrich Händel* (Mainz, 1959).

NEUMANN, WERNER, 'Das „Bachische Collegium Musicum" ', *Bach-Jahrbuch*, xlvii (1960), 5–27.

NEWMAN, WILLIAM S., 'Emanuel Bach's autobiography', *The Musical Quarterly*, li (1965), 363–72.

NEWTON, RICHARD, 'The English Cult of Domenico Scarlatti', *Music and Letters*, xx (1939), 138–56.

NOACK, ELISABETH, 'Georg Philipp Telemanns Beziehungen zu Darmstädter Musikern', *Konferenzbericht der 3. Magdeburger Telemann-Festtage 1967*, ed. G. Fleischhauer and W. Siegmund-Schultze (Magdeburg, 1969), ii. 13–17.

OPPEL, REINHARD, 'Über Beziehungen Beethovens zu Mozart und zu Ph. Em. Bach', *Zeitschrift für Musikwissenschaft*, v (1922–3), 30–9.

PAUL, LESLIE D., 'Bach as Transcriber', *Music and Letters*, xxxiv (1953), 306–13.

PAUMGARTNER, BERNHARD, 'Nochmals "Zur Frage J. S. Bach-Marcello" ', *Die Musikforschung, xi* (1958), 342.

PETZOLDT, R., *Telemann und seine Zeitgenossen*, Magdeburger

Telemann-Studien I, Arbeitskreis 'Georg Philipp Telemann' (Magdeburg, 1966).

——, *Georg Philipp Telemann*, tr. H. Fitzpatrick (London, 1974; first published Leipzig, 1967).

PINCHERLE, MARC, *Antonio Vivaldi et la musique instrumentale*, 2 vols. (Paris, 1948), vol. ii, *Inventaire-Thématique*.

——, *Corelli et son Temps* (Paris, 1954).

——, *Vivaldi Genius of the Baroque*, tr. from the French by Christopher Hatch (London, 1958; first published Paris, 1955).

PIRRO, ANDRÉ, *L'Esthétique de Jean-Sébastien Bach* (Paris, 1907).

PLAMENAC, DRAGAN, 'New light on the last years of Carl Philipp Emanuel Bach', *The Musical Quarterly*, xxxv (1949), 565–87.

PRAETORIUS, E., 'Neues zur Bach-Forschung', *Sammelbände der Internationalen Musik-Gesellschaft*, viii (1906–7), 95–101.

PROD'HOMME, J-G., 'Austro-German Musicians in France in the eighteenth century', *The Musical Quarterly*, xv (1929), 171–95.

PULVER, JEFFREY, 'Music at the Court of Frederick the Great', *The Musical Times*, liii (1912), 599–601.

QUANTZ, JOHANN JOACHIM, *Versuch einer Anweisung die flute traversière zu spielen*, facsimile by Hans-Peter Schmitz (Kassel, 1953) of the 3rd edn. (Breslau, 1789; first published Berlin, 1752). Tr. Edward R. Reilly under the title: *On playing the Flute* (London, 1966).

RATNER, LEONARD G., 'Eighteenth-century theories of Musical Period Structure', *The Musical Quarterly*, xlii (1956), 439–54.

REDLICH, HANS FERDINAND, 'A New "Oboe Concerto" by Handel', *The Musical Times*, xcvii (1956), 409–10.

——, *Zwölf Concerti Grossi Opus 6: Kritischer Bericht*, Hallische Händel-Ausgabe, iv/14 (Kassel, 1964).

——, 'The Oboes in Handel's Opus 6', *The Musical Times*, cix (1968), 530–1.

REILLY, EDWARD R., *Quantz and his 'Versuch': Three Studies*, Studies and Documents, American Musicological Society, no. 5 (New York, 1971).

ROBINSON, M. F., 'The Aria in Opera Seria, 1725–1780', *Proceedings of the Royal Musical Association*, lxxxviii (1961–2), 31–43.

——, *Naples and Neapolitan Opera* (Oxford, 1972).

ROBINSON, PERCY, 'Handel's influence on Bach', *The Musical Times*, xlvii (1906), 468–9.

——, 'Was Handel a Plagiarist?', *The Musical Times*, lxxx (1939), 573–7.

ROLLAND, ROMAIN, *A Musical Tour through the Land of the Past*, tr. Bernard Miall (London, 1922; first published Paris, 1919).

ROUSSEAU, JEAN-JACQUES, *Dictionnaire de Musique*, 2 vols. (Geneva, 1767).

Rühlmann, Julius, 'Antonio Vivaldi und sein Einfluss auf J. S. Bach', *Neue Zeitschrift für Musik*, 1st, 8th, 15th Nov. 1867, lxiii, 393–7, 401–5, 413–16.

Ruhnke, M., 'Telemann als Musik-verleger', *Musik und Verlag: Karl Vötterle zum 65. Geburtstag am 12. April 1968 (Vötterle Festschrift)*, ed. Richard Baum and Wolfgang Rehm (Kassel, 1968), pp. 501–17.

  Proceedings of the Royal Musical Association, lxxxv (1958–9), 17–30.

Ryom, Peter, *Verzeichnis der Werke Antonio Vivaldis* (RV) (Leipzig, 1974).

——, *Handel Concertos*, BBC Music Guides (London, 1972).

Sadie, Stanley, 'Concert Life in Eighteenth Century England', *Proceedings of the Royal Musical Association*, lxxxv (1958–9), 17–30.

——, *Handel Concertos*, BBC Music Guides (London, 1972).

  1962–65 (Leipzig, 1967).

Scheibe, Johann Adolph, *Critischer Musikus*, 2nd edn. (Leipzig, 1745; facsimile edn. Hildesheim, 1970; first published in 2 vols., i (Hamburg, 1738), ii (Hamburg, 1740)).

Schering, Arnold, 'Zur Bach-Forschung', *Sammelbände der Internationalen Musik-Gesellschaft*, iv (1902–3), 234–43; v (1903–4), 565–70.

——, *Geschichte des Instrumentalkonzerts bis auf die Gegenwart* (Leipzig, 1905).

——, 'Zur instrumentalen Verzierungskunst im 18. Jahrhundert', *Sammelbände der Internationalen Musik-Gesellschaft*, vii (1906), 365–85.

——, Foreword to vol. xxix–xxx of *Denkmäler deutscher Tonkunst, Instrumentalkonzerte deutscher Meister* (Leipzig, 1907; rev. edn. H. J. Moser, Wiesbaden, 1958).

——, 'Handels Orgelkonzert in d moll', *Zeitschrift für Musikwissenschaft*, xvii (1935), 457–71.

——, 'Carl Philipp Emanuel Bach und das redende Prinzip in der Musik', *Jahrbuch der Musikbibliothek Peters*, xlv (1938), 13–29.

Schmid, Ernst Fritz, *C. P. E. Bach und seine Kammermusik* (Kassel, 1931).

——, 'Joseph Haydn und Carl Philipp Emanuel Bach', *Zeitschrift für Musikwissenschaft*, xiv (1932), 299–312.

Schmieder, Wolfgang, *Thematisch-systematisches Verzeichnis der musikalischen Werke von Johann Sebastian Bach (Bach–Werke–Verzeichnis)* (Leipzig, 1950).

Schmitz, Hans-Peter, *Die Kunst der Verzierung im 18. Jahrhundert Instrumentale und Vokale Musizierpraxis in Beispielen* (Kassel, 1955).

Schneider, Max, 'Zur Biographie G. Ph. Telemanns', *Sammelbände der Internationalen Musik-Gesellschaft*, vii (1905–6), 414–16.

——, 'Das sogenannte „Orgelkonzert d=moll von Wilhelm Friedemann Bach" ', *Bach-Jahrbuch*, viii (1911), 23–36.

SCHOLES, PERCY ALFRED, *The Puritans and Music in England and New
England* (New York, 1962; first published London, 1934).

SCHULZE, HANS-JOACHIM, 'J. S. Bach's Concerto-arrangements for
organ—studies or commissioned works?', *The Organ Yearbook*, iii
(1972), 4–10.

SCHWEITZER, ALBERT, *J. S. Bach*, tr. Ernest Newman, 2 vols. (London,
1911, first published Leipzig, 1908).

SCOTT, HUGH ARTHUR, 'London's First Concert Room', *Music and
Letters*, xviii (1937), 379–90.

——, 'London Concerts from 1700 to 1750', *The Musical Quarterly*,
xxiv (1938), 194–209.

SEIFFERT, MAX, 'Zur Biographie Johann Adolph Hasse's', *Sammelbände
der Internationalen Musik-Gesellschaft*, vii (1905–6), 129–31.

——, *Georg Philipp Telemann Musique de Table*, Beihefte zu den
Denkmälern deutscher Tonkunst, ii (Wiesbaden, 1960).

SERAUKY, WALTER, 'Bach-Händel-Telemann in ihrem musikalischen
Verhältnis', *Händel-Jahrbuch* [new series] i (1955), 72–101.

——, *Georg Friedrich Händel, sein Leben, sein Werk* (Kassel, 1956).

SHANET, HOWARD, 'Why did J. S. Bach Transpose his Arrangements?',
The Musical Quarterly, xxxvi (1950), 180–203.

SHEDLOCH, J. S., 'Handel's Borrowings', *The Musical Times*, xlii
(1901), 450–2, 526–8, 596–600.

SIEGELE, ULRICH, *Kompositionsweise und Bearbeitungstechnik in der
Instrumentalmusik Joh. Seb. Bachs*, Dissertation (Tübingen, 1957).

SIEGMUND-SCHULTZE, WALTHER, 'Zu Händels Schaffensmethode',
Händel-Jahrbuch, vii–viii (1961–2), 69–136.

SIMON, EDWIN J., 'The Double Exposition in the Classic Concerto',
Journal of the American Musicological Society, x (1957), 111–18.

——, 'A royal Manuscript: Ensemble Concertos by J. C. Bach',
Journal of the American Musicological Society, xii (1959), 161–77.

——, 'Sonata into Concerto: a study of Mozart's first seven concertos', *Acta Musicologica*, xxxi (1959), 170–85.

SMEND, FRIEDRICH, *Bach in Köthen* (Berlin, 1951).

SMITH, WILLIAM C., *A Bibliography of the Musical Works published by the
firm of John Walsh during the years 1695–1720* (London, 1948).

——, *Concerning Handel, His Life and Works* (London, 1948).

——, *Handel: A Descriptive Catalogue of the Early Editions*, 2nd edn.
with supplement (London, 1970; first published 1960).

—— and HUMPHRIES, CHARLES, *A Bibliography of the Musical Works
published by the firm of John Walsh during the years 1721–1766*
(London, 1968).

SPIRO, F., 'Ein verlorenes Werk Johann Sebastian Bachs', *Zeitschrift der Internationalen Musik-Gesellschaft*, vi (1904), 100–4.

SPITTA, PHILIPP, *Johann Sebastian Bach: His Work and Influence on the Music of Germany, 1685–1750*, tr. Clara Bell and J. A. Fuller-Maitland, 3 vols. (London, 1884 and 1899; first published in German, 2 vols. (Leipzig, 1873, 1880)).

——, 'Musikalische Werke Friedrichs des Grossen', *Vierteljahrsschrift für Musikwissenschaft*, v–vi (1889–90), 350–62.

STARCZEWSKI, FELIKS, 'Die polnische Tänze', *Sammelbände der Internationalen Musik-Gesellschaft*, ii (1900–1), 673–718.

STEPHAN, RUDOLF, 'Die Wandlung der Konzertform bei Bach', *Die Musikforschung*, vi (1953), 127–43.

STEVENS, JANE R., 'The Keyboard Concertos of Carl Philipp Emanuel Bach', Doctoral dissertation (Yale, 1965).

——, 'An 18th-Century Description of Concerto First-Movement Form', *Journal of the American Musicological Society*, xxiv (1971), 85–95.

STOCKMANN, BERNHARD, 'Über das Dissonanzverständnis Bachs', *Bach-Jahrbuch*, xlvii (1960), 43–59.

STRUNK, OLIVER, *Source Readings in Music History from Classical Antiquity to the Romantic Era* (London, 1952; first published New York, 1950).

TAGLIAVINI, LUIGI FERDINANDO, 'Johann Gottfried Walther trascrittore', *Analecta Musicologica*, vii (1969), 112–19.

TAYLOR, SEDLEY, *The Indebtedness of Handel to Works by Other Composers* (Cambridge, 1906).

TELEMANN, GEORG PHILIPP, *Georg Philipp Telemann: Briefwechsel*, ed. Hans Grosse and Hans Rudolf Jung (Leipzig, 1972).

TELL, WERNER, 'Die Hemiole bei Bach', *Bach-Jahrbuch*, xxxix (1951–2), 47–53.

TEMPERLEY, NICHOLAS, 'Handel's influence on English music', *The Monthly Musical Record*, xc (1960), 163–74.

TERRY, CHARLES SANFORD, *Bach: a Biography* (London, 1928).

——, *John Christian Bach*, 2nd rev. edn. (London, 1967; first published 1929).

——, 'Bach's Dresden Appointment', *The Musical Times*, lxxiii (1932), 315–16.

——, *Bach's Orchestra* (London, 1932; reprinted 1958).

TERRY, MIRIAM, 'C. Ph. E. Bach and J. J. H. Westphal—a Clarification', *Journal of the American Musicological Society*, xxii (1969), 106–15.

TILMOUTH, MICHAEL, 'A Calendar of References to Music in Newspapers published in London and the Provinces (1660–1719)', *The Royal Musical Association Research Chronicle*, i (Cambridge, 1961;

errata and general index in ii (Cambridge, 1962), 2–15).

TORREFRANCA, F., 'Le Origini della Sinfonia', *Rivista musicale italiana*, xxii (1915), 431–46.

ULDALL, HANS, 'Beiträge zur Frühgeschichte des Klavierkonzerts', *Zeitschrift für Musikwissenschaft*, x (1927–8), 139–52.

——, *Das Klavierkonzert der Berliner Schule und ihres Führers Philipp Emanuel Bach* (Leipzig, 1928).

VALENTIN, CAROLINE, *Geschichte der Musik in Frankfurt am Main* (Frankfurt, 1906; reprint Wiesbaden, 1972).

VALENTIN, ERICH, *Georg Philippe Telemann: eine Biographie* (Burg, 1931).

——, 'Telemanns Magdeburger Zeit', *Zeitschrift für Musikwissenschaft*, xv (1933), 193–208.

——, *Telemann in seiner Zeit*, Veröffentlichungen der Hamburger Telemann-Gesellschaft, i (Hamburg, 1960).

VEINUS, ABRAHAM, *The Concerto* (London, 1948).

VOIGT, WOLDEMAR, 'Über die Originalgestalt von J. S. Bach's Konzert für zwei Klaviere in C moll (Nr. I)', *Vierteljahrsschrift für Musik-wissenschaft*, ii (1886), 482–7.

VRIESLANDER, OTTO, *Carl Philipp Emanuel Bach* (Munich, 1923).

WACKERNAGEL, PETER, 'Beobachtungen am Autograph von Bachs Brandenburgischen Konzerten', *Festschrift Max Schneider zum achtzigsten Geburtstag*, ed. Walther Vetter (Leipzig, 1955), pp. 129–38.

WÄSCHKE, HERMANN, 'Die Hofkapelle in Cöthen unter Joh. Seb. Bach', *Zerbster Jahrbuch*, iii (1907), 31–40.

WALKER, A. D., *Georg Frideric Handel: the Newman Flower Collection in the Henry Watson Music Library* (Manchester, 1972).

WALKER, ERNEST, *A History of Music in England*, 3rd edn. revised and enlarged by J. A. Westrup (Oxford, 1952; first published 1907).

WALKER, FRANK, 'A Little Bach Discovery', *Music and Letters*, xxxi (1950), 184.

WALTHER, JOHANN GOTTFRIED, *Musikalisches Lexikon* (Leipzig, 1932, facsimile edn. by Richard Schaal (Kassel, 1953)).

WARD-JONES, PETER, 'The Concerto at Mannheim c. 1740–1780', *Proceedings of the Royal Musical Association*, xcvi (1969–70), 129–36.

WESTRUP, JACK ALLAN, 'Purcell and Handel', *Music and Letters*, xl (1959), 103–8.

WILLIAMS, PETER F., 'Händel und die Englische Orgelmusik', *Händel-Jahrbuch*, xii (1966), 51–76.

WILSON, MICHAEL, *The English Chamber Organ: History and Development 1650–1850* (London, 1968).

WITTE, MARTIN, 'Die Instrumentalkonzerte von Johann Christoph Graupner 1683–1760', doctoral dissertation (Göttingen, 1963).

WOHLFARTH, HANSDIETER, *Johann Christoph Friedrich Bach: ein Komponist im Vorfeld der Klassik*, Neue Heidelberger Studien zur Musikwissenschaft no. 4 (Bern, 1971).

WOLFF, HELLMUTH CHRISTIAN, 'Der Rhythm bei Johann Sebastian Bach', *Bach-Jahrbuch* xxxvii (1940–48), 83–121.

——, 'Zur Melodiebildung J. S. Bachs', *Festschrift für Erich Schenk* (Graz, 1962), pp. 609–21.

WOLLENBERG, SUSAN, 'Handel and Gottlieb Muffat: a newly discovered borrowing', *The Musical Times*, cxiii (1972), 448–9.

WOTQUENNE, ALFRED, *Thematisches Verzeichnis der Werke von Carl Philipp Emanuel Bach* (Leipzig, 1905).

YORKE–LONG, A., *Music at Court* (London, 1954).

ZIMMERMAN, FRANKLIN B., 'Handel's Purcellian Borrowings in His Later Operas and Oratorios', *Festschrift Otto Erich Deutsch zum 80. Geburtstag*, ed. Walter Gerstenberg, Jan La Rue, and Wolfgang Rehm (Kassel, 1963), pp. 20–30.

——, 'Musical Borrowings in the English Baroque', *The Musical Quarterly*, lii (1966), 483–95.

Index of Works

General Index